The Rose Book

The Rose Book

HOW TO GROW ROSES
ORGANICALLY AND USE THEM
IN OVER 50 BEAUTIFUL CRAFTS

Maggie Oster

Illustrations by Elayne Sears

Rodale Press, Emmaus, Pennsylvania

If you have any questions or comments concerning this book,
please write to:

Rodale Press, Inc.
Book Readers' Service
33 East Minor Street
Emmaus, PA 18098

Library of Congress Cataloging-in-Publication Data

Oster, Maggie.
    The rose book : how to grow roses organically and
use them in over 50 beautiful crafts / Maggie Oster ;
illustrations by Elayne Sears.
        p. cm.
    Includes bibliographical references and index.
    ISBN 0–87596–607–1 hardcover
    1. Roses. 2. Roses—Utilization. 3. Rose culture.
4. Flower arrangement. 5. Organic gardening. I. Title.
SB411.087 1994
635.9'33372—dc20   93–21454
                              CIP

Distributed in the book trade by St. Martin's Press

2 4 6 8 10 9 7 5 3 1 hardcover

Executive Editor: Margaret Lydic Balitas
Managing Editor: Barbara W. Ellis
Editor: Ellen Phillips
Crafts Editor: Cheryl Winters Tetreau
Copy Editors: Laura Stevens and Barbara M. Webb
Senior Research Associate: Heidi A. Stonehill
Indexer: Andrea Chesman
Copy Manager: Dolores Plikaitis
Art Director: Michael Mandarano
Office Manager: Karen Earl-Braymer
Administrative Assistant: Susan L. Nickol
Administrative Assistance: Deborah Weisel
Photographers:
   T. L. Gettings/Rodale Stock Images: pages 55 (top), 60
     (bottom), 65.
   Pamela J. Harper: pages 56 (top and bottom), 60 (top), 67
     (top right), 68 (top left).
   Ed Landrock/Rodale Stock Images: pages 61, 62 (bottom
     left), 63 (top left, and bottom), 66 (bottom).
   Mitch Mandel/Rodale Stock Images: pages 197-212.
   Jerry Pavia: Cover, pages 55 (bottom), 57 (bottom), 58, 59
     (top and bottom), 62 (top), 64, 66 (top), 67 (top left),
     68 (right).
   Rodale Stock Images: page 68 (bottom left).
   Susan A. Roth: pages 53, 54, 57 (top), 62 (bottom right),
     63 (top right).
   judywhite: page 67 (bottom).

Cover and interior design by Darlene Schneck
Illustrations by Elayne Sears
Decorative rose art by Phyllis Stevens

Cover photo: Our cover photo by Jerry Pavia features a
'Dortmund' rose growing in the California garden of
Ruth Bancroft.

      OUR MISSION
We publish books that empower people's lives.
RODALE 🌹 BOOKS

In memory of my father,
E. George Oster,
who always brought love and roses
from the fields and garden

༺❦༻

Contents

Acknowledgments

F EVER THERE WAS A PROJECT THAT exemplified the analogy of book writing to a long-distance race, it is this one. Over the five-plus years since its inception, a panoply of people and experiences have come, gone, twisted, and turned in my life. Many times I have wanted to throw in the towel, but there was always someone at the beginning, middle, and end to encourage me—and a number who survived all three stages.

Among the most significant is my editor, Ellen Phillips. Patient, erudite, selfless, and skilled, she never let me lose sight of my original vision of what this book could offer. She also took the heat for me time and again. Thank you, Ellen, for your sense of humor, insight, and support. To everyone else at Rodale who wanted to give up on me, my deepest appreciation for hanging in there. May your endurance be rewarded.

My parents, George and Lucille Oster, never ceased believing in me and my work and providing every possible kind of sustenance and assistance. Thank you, too, for instilling my love of gardening and roses in the first place.

For the rosarians of the Heritage Roses Group, the Heritage Rose Foundation, and the American Rose Society, I am very grateful. In particular, thank you, Beverly and Stu Dobson, Harm Saville, and Winnie and Fred Edmunds.

Many of the exquisite crafts featured in the photographs and drawings are the work of gifted friends. My deepest appreciation to the wonderfully talented and generous Wendy Cooper, Sybil Kunkel, Peggy Leake, Ione Patton, Bertha Stone, and Mary Jane Taylor.

I am fortunate to have a number of friends around the country who are also garden writers. All are treasured, but I am especially indebted to Susan Roth, Chris Woods, Dick Tracy, and Ann Reilly-Dines. Thanks, also, to my agent, Angela Miller, who has been there through all the ups and downs.

There are so many people who have touched my life and heart, I cannot bear to list names for fear of leaving someone out. To each of you, please know how grateful I am, how much I care in return, and how much the hugs, the phone calls, the many thoughtful things you've done have meant to me.

Introduction

Rethinking Roses

There should be beds of Roses, banks of Roses, bowers of Roses, hedges of Roses, edgings of Roses, pillars of Roses, arches of Roses, fountains of Roses, baskets of Roses, vistas and alleys of the Rose.

—S. Reynolds Hole
A Book About Roses, 1895

No one can precisely define the magical quality of roses, but they have been beloved for many centuries and by many different cultures. Indeed, they continue to fascinate and mean more than any other flower. Suffice it to say that our national flower has many personalities and faces. For each of us, the rose has its own unique meaning.

But roses—for all the love and admiration they receive—are misunderstood and misused in the garden. They have an undeserved reputation for being difficult to grow, which—coupled with the expectations placed on them—keeps entirely too many people from discovering that having roses in their yard not only is highly rewarding, but also requires no more effort than growing healthy, productive tomato plants. By rethinking roses to take advantage of their versatility throughout our yards and homes, we can give ourselves a most satisfying gift.

What *do* you need to grow roses successfully? Basically, no more than the time it takes to find out which rose types and cultivars are the toughest, most disease- and pest-resistant, most low-maintenance, and best adapted to your area. Unfortunately, it's not always easy to find these outstanding roses when local nurseries tend to stock only the finicky varieties. But the good news is that more and more local and mail-order nurseries are carrying these tough "landscape roses." (See "Rose Resources" on page 280 for a source list.)

The best news is that we can look forward to more and more of these easy-care roses from breeders in the future. Many rose breeders are trying to cut down on the environmental impact of traditional high-pesticide, high-fungicide rose care by developing resistant plants. For example, the successful series of Meidiland landscape roses were developed by Meilland in France after the company asked the Green Party for input on the need for environmentally friendly roses.

Once you've decided which roses are tough, resistant, low-maintenance, and suited to your area, you can narrow your choices by considering other characteristics. How do you want to use them in the landscape? If you want a low groundcover rose, don't pick a climber. Are you looking for certain colors, flower shapes, or foliage characteristics? Do you want a repeat-blooming rose for flowers in late spring and again in fall, or a rose that blooms all summer? Do you want fragrant flowers or colorful, showy rose hips? Are you looking for roses with orna-

Right

Wrong

Siting roses right. Don't grow your roses like a row crop or garden center sale display—they'll look leggy and unattractive and be more prone to pest and disease attacks. Instead, make roses part of your landscape—clambering over a fence, grown as a hardy hedge, or mixed with perennials and herbs in a flower bed.

mental thorns, or would you rather have as few thorns as possible? Chapters 1 and 2 provide in-depth guidance on choosing and buying roses.

In addition to rethinking how to choose roses, you should start rethinking how to use them. Traditionally, monocultures of soldier-straight rows of rose bushes marched in geometric beds. Though this approach may be stunning on a grand scale, if you look at a single rose bed, you'll see that it's just the way roses grown for sale would look at the garden center.

Instead, by thinking of roses as garden plants rather than a specialty crop, you'll discover delightful possibilities. You can grow roses as flowering shrubs, in flower beds and borders, in mixed plantings, among herbs, in containers, underplanted with herbs and flowers, surrounding a mailbox, screening a fence, scrambling up trees, posts, or the sides of buildings, trailing over arches or arbors, or cascading down a bank or over a wall. In fact, you can grow roses anywhere in your yard—at least, anywhere it's sunny!

If you think of roses as versatile landscape plants, you'll start looking at them differently. The bare-legged hybrid tea, with just a few stiff stems, suddenly looks a little paltry in the landscape, while a fuller shrub rose with a softer outline seems much more beautiful. This is part of the reason that "old" roses, as well as the newer hybrids with that old-fashioned look, are having a new heyday.

Year-round interest has become a byword of the new style of landscape gardening that includes ornamental grasses and plants like 'Autumn Joy' sedum and black-eyed Susans that bear ornamental seed heads well into winter. While few roses are interesting all year round (except perhaps for *Rosa sericea* var.

pteracantha, with its showy red thorns), many have ornamental buds, foliage, and rose hips that make them showy from before bloom into winter. The shape of a rose bush can also add to its ornamental value. And brightly colored rose hips will add to its value for wildlife—birds love them!

Choosing the right roses is half the battle; the other is caring for them intelligently. Roses—even highly resistant ones—are still sometimes susceptible to a variety of pests and diseases. Your primary line of defense is to make sure your plants are healthy and vigorous by preparing the soil diligently, planting carefully, and feeding and watering as needed. Beyond that, if problems occur, there are safe controls. Chapters 3 and 4 will tell you how to grow great roses without resorting to chemical fertilizers, pesticides, and fungicides.

For some people, just growing roses well is reward enough. But for those of us who want more, bringing roses indoors is essential. Use them to highlight your home in fresh and dried arrangements, in craft projects, pressed on lamp-shades and stationery, or in deliciously scented potpourris and beauty products. You'll find dozens of beautiful projects in Part Two, "Rose Arrangements and Country Crafts."

Roses have always been and still are part and parcel of my life. Every June, my father was sure to bring bouquets of wild roses from the fencerow to my mother as he came in from the fields. "Slips" of old roses are part of the social currency among my gardening friends. Exuberant bouquets and simple bud vases adorn the house all summer, and dried roses, sachets, and other rose crafts brighten my rooms all year. I hope you use this book to make beautiful roses a vital part of your home life, indoors and out.

Part One

Roses
in the
Landscape

Chapter 1

Choosing the Right Rose

THERE'S A RENAISSANCE GOING ON for roses and rose gardening. Now, with so many "old rose" nurseries starting up, and with the remarkable successes of breeding programs that focus on tough, self-reliant landscape roses, you can choose beautiful roses for every part of your garden. Forget the image of roses as fussy hypochondriacs that demand constant intensive care. Today you can combine the best old and new roses—roses that are long-lived and healthy, with luxuriant colors, rich fragrance, and a natural form requiring a minimum of pruning—to create the garden of your dreams.

Whether "old" or "new," roses are incredibly versatile in the garden. What other plant has flowers in so many colors and forms, with blooms from early summer to frost, and has plants growing in all sizes and shapes from climbers to shrubs?

Given the range of forms and thousands of cultivars, it's difficult to imagine where you *couldn't* use roses in the landscape. Other than our imaginations, the only limiting factor is the necessary six hours of sun a day. Given enough sun and a little foresight in choosing cultivars that suit your needs as well as the climate, roses can become the focus of your garden or provide colorful accents for buildings, outdoor furniture, or other plantings.

But how do you choose which roses to plant? When you open a rose catalog, the selection can be overwhelming. I confess, I love them all! But even I can only grow so many. In this chapter, I'll help you narrow your choices by discussing the different kinds of roses and the advantages and disadvantages of each. There's also a very special feature in this chapter. When I began this book, I polled all the consulting rosarians of the American Rose Society and other rose experts across the country. I asked them which roses they would choose as the best in each category. You'll find a list of their top picks following the general description of each type of rose (of course, I added my own favorites, too!).

Chapter 2 will give you more ways to think about which roses you want to grow. It's all about using roses in the landscape. You'll find checklists and other design tools for thinking about your own property, how and where you want to use roses, and what you want your roses to do in your landscape. I've also included six designs of different kinds of rose gardens, from an island bed to a shrub border, to inspire you.

Once you've looked at Chapter 2 and jotted down notes on your own garden plans or even done a design of your own, turn back to this chapter and look at the lists of roses again. Turn to page 29 to find descriptions of the best roses for special landscape uses. And think about the features of roses that are most important to you.

The Rose Plant Revealed

You'll be more comfortable working with, buying, and reading and talking about roses if you take a few minutes to familiarize yourself with the terms for the parts of a rose bush. Then you'll know what to do when someone says to cut flower stems just above a node, and you can check for a bud union on a plant at the garden center to see if the rose has been grafted.

Basic Plant Structure Terms

Anchor root: A thick root that holds the rose bush stable in the soil.

Basal shoot or cane: The thick, strong main cane of a rose bush, arising from the bud union of the plant at its base.

Bud: A growth bud, or eye, found on a cane; a vegetative growing point located in the axil where a leaf joins a stem.

Bud union: The swollen point on the stem where the bud that forms the top of the plant was joined to the rootstock.

Cane: A main stem or basal shoot of a rose, usually arising at or very near the bud union.

Crown: The area of the rose bush where the canes or basal shoots sprout from the bud union.

Feeder roots: Thin, fine-textured roots that absorb nutrients and water from the soil; also called hair roots.

Internode: The section of a stem between one node and another.

Lateral cane (branch): A side branch arising from a main, or basal, cane.

Main shoot: A basal or strong lateral cane.

Rootstock: The host plant or root portion (understock) onto which a scion, or bud, is grafted.

Shoot: A stem or cane.

Stem: A branch of a cane that emerges from a bud and bears leaves and at least one flower.

Sucker: A growing stem that arises from the rootstock below the bud union.

Thorn: The prickle, or sharp spine, found on the stems of roses.

Leaf Terms

Leaf: A rose leaf is attached to a cane just below a bud, or eye, and is usually composed of 3 to 19 leaflets arranged along a leaf stalk in opposite pairs with one leaflet at the tip.

Leaflet: A leaflike segment of a compound leaf.

Leafstalk: The stalk, or petiole, by which a leaf is attached to a stem.

Node: The point on a stem where a leaf and bud arise.

Rachis: The central stem of a compound leaf, to which leaflets are attached.

Flower and Fruit Terms

Calyx: The protective green cover of a flower bud, composed of five sepals.

Corolla: Collectively, the petals of a flower.

Flower bud: A developing, unopened flower.

Peduncle: The flower stalk that supports a single flower.

Petal: In roses, the showy flower part within the sepals and surrounding the stamens and pistils.

Petaloids: Small, sometimes twisted, petals near the center of a flower.

Reverse: The back surface of a fully expanded petal.

Rose hip: The fruit or seedpod of a rose, often scarlet or red when ripe; may be showy.

Sepal: One of the five green divisions of the calyx surrounding the petals.

Do you want cold-hardiness and disease resistance? Or is fragrance the real reason you grow roses? On page 24, you'll find descriptions of the best roses for these and other features. If you need a particular color or want a certain flower shape, you can narrow the list down even more. Now when you pick up the catalog again, you can choose your roses with new—and well-founded—confidence.

OLD ROSES OR NEW?

For much of the twentieth century the high-centered, long-stemmed hybrid tea roses have

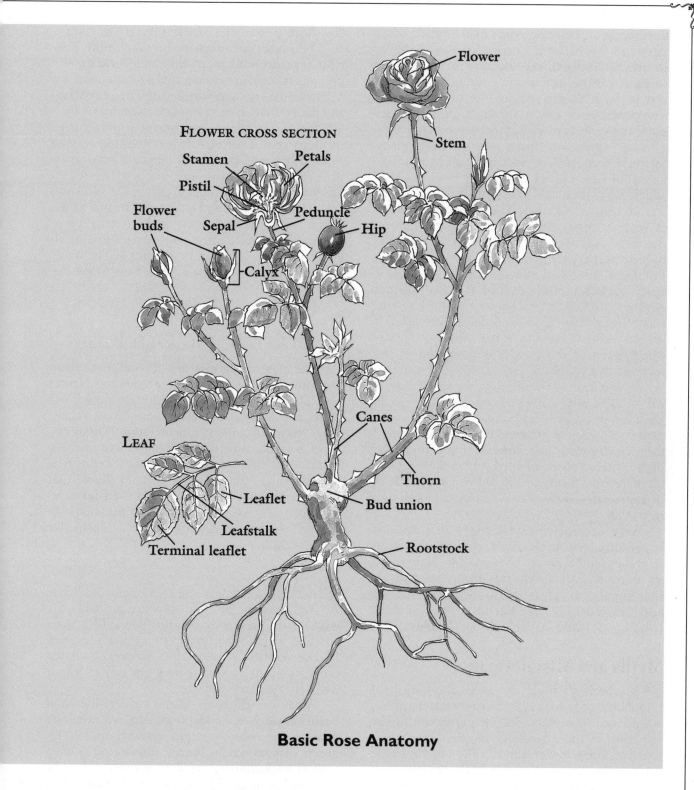

FLOWER CROSS SECTION

Stamen
Petals
Pistil
Flower
buds
Sepal
Peduncle
Hip
Calyx
Flower
Stem
Canes
Thorn
Bud union
LEAF
Leaflet
Leafstalk
Terminal leaflet
Rootstock

Basic Rose Anatomy

held first place in the hearts and gardens of rose lovers everywhere. But there have always been a few gardeners who continued to sing the praises of the older roses, with their vigorous habit and fragrant single flowers or round, full blooms. In the last several decades, these older roses have come back into prominence because of their charm and especially their reputation for fragrance. There has also been much excitement in the rose world over new types like the English roses that combine the look and scent of old roses with the reblooming habit of modern ones, yet also have a more shrublike form.

Between modern roses like hybrid teas and

floribundas, landscape roses like English roses and the Meidiland series, old roses like Bourbons and gallicas, and the many species roses, it can be intimidating trying to sort out and understand the peculiarities of the various rose types. How can you even begin to understand the various roses and make good choices?

One significant distinction has been made by the American Rose Society. They have designated all rose classes developed before 1867, which was when the first hybrid tea rose was introduced, as old roses. These "old rose" classes include alba, Bourbon, centifolia, China, damask, eglanteria, gallica, hybrid foetida, hybrid perpetual, hybrid spinosissima, moss, Portland, tea, and species roses. The "new rose" classes include hybrid tea, floribunda, climber, miniature, polyantha, rambler, and shrub roses. Even if a rose is developed today, if it is an old-rose type, then that is how it is classified. Each of these types is described in the sections that follow.

As you look at the different classes of rose, it will become obvious that no one type does it all. Each has good and bad points. There is also the matter of personal preference as to the style and form of the plant and flowers. If you think the high-centered shape of a hybrid tea flower is the ultimate rose form, you might not recognize—or appreciate—a rounded, quartered bloom as a rose at all.

As a group, the best roses in terms of appearance, hardiness, vigor, disease resistance, fragrance, and a variety of forms are the modern shrub roses. Fortunately, this group has cultivars that are sure to please aficionados of both old and new roses. Some shrub roses resemble hybrid teas, while others look like the old roses.

Myths and Misinformation

Maybe it's a backlash against the long-held popularity of hybrid teas, but nowadays there's a tendency to romanticize the perfection of the old roses at the expense of modern rose types. Old roses are undeniably lovely, but don't be taken in by claims that only old roses have this or that. If an old rose can do it, a new rose can, too; it's just a question of picking a cultivar with the desirable trait. Let's review a few of these myths.

"Only old roses are *really* fragrant." Much has been made of the fragrance of old roses, yet studies have shown that a similar percentage of new roses are just as fragrant. Many of the mod-

ern shrub roses, in particular, are very fragrant.

"Old roses are much hardier and more pest-resistant than modern roses." Older roses aren't necessarily hardier—some are, and some aren't. Many of the modern shrub roses are exceptionally hardy. Pest resistance is about even as well.

"Old rose plants are better-looking than modern rose bushes." It's sad but true that modern roses, especially the hybrid teas, grandifloras, and floribundas, tend to be leggy, awkward-looking plants. Many of the old roses are more shrublike and adaptable to mixed use in the landscape. But some of them have floppy canes and are difficult to use, while some modern roses are handsome bushes with lovely foliage. Again, you just have to choose the right cultivar.

UNDERSTANDING OLD ROSES

The many categories of old roses make them a confusing maze for most gardeners. Names like alba and centifolia conjure up musty old texts, not flowers. But with the old-rose renaissance, more of these plants are appearing in catalogs, so we can finally connect a picture to the name. And the old roses have many qualities, like fragrance, toughness, and plant shape, that make them outstanding shrubs in the landscape. It's worth the few minutes it takes to familiarize yourself with these groups and their distinctive characteristics.

The Albas

Very ancient roses, albas were probably the white roses grown by the Romans 2,000 years ago and brought to Britain by Caesar's legions. In the Middle Ages, albas were grown for medicinal purposes, and they are still excellent roses for the herb garden.

Albas are still some of the most refined and beautiful plants for today's garden, with delicate flowers, vigorous, upright growth, and blue-green or gray-green leaves. Blooming once a year in midsummer, the 3-inch flowers may be semidouble or double and white or pink. Their fragrance has reminded people of hyacinths, spiced apples, and honey. They are tough, healthy, reliable, long-lived plants that will grow under difficult conditions, even surviving in light shade. Most grow 4 to 8 feet tall, with few thorns and large hips, especially on *Rosa alba* 'Semi-Plena'. Albas are hardy to –30°F (USDA

Plant Hardiness Zone 4) but sometimes withstand temperatures as low as –40°F (Zone 3).

Albas grow best on their own roots, in which case they will spread slowly by runners. They bloom best on two-year-old wood, and they don't need much pruning except to shorten any ungainly shoots by one-third, to remove older wood after four to six years, and to trim back the lateral growth (side shoots).

Use albas as hedges, in the back of flower borders, as part of mixed shrub borders, and for naturalizing; use the tall types as climbers.

Best Albas

The rosarians and other rose experts I polled chose these as the best of the albas:

'Belle Amour', a 6' bush with semidouble, pale salmon-pink flowers that have a myrrh fragrance, blue-green disease-resistant leaves, and showy hips; hardy to –30°F (Zone 4).

'Celestial', a 5' bush with double light pink, very fragrant flowers, blue-gray leaves on robust plants, and showy hips; hardy to –30°F (Zone 4).

'Felicité Parmentier', a 3' bush with very double, very fragrant quartered light pink flowers and gray-green, disease-resistant foliage; not tolerant of dry soil; hardy to –30°F (Zone 4).

'Jeanne d'Arc', a 6' bush with very fragrant double white flowers and dark gray-green, disease-resistant foliage; sprawling growth; hardy to –30°F (Zone 4).

'Konigin von Danemark', a 5' bush with very fragrant, very double quartered pink flowers and coarse gray-green, disease-resistant foliage; more thorny and open than most albas; hardy to –30°F (Zone 4).

'Madame Legras de St. Germaine', a 7' bush with very double, very fragrant white flowers and gray-green, disease-resistant leaves; almost thornless; can be used as a climber; hardy to –30°F (Zone 4).

'Madame Plantier', an 8' bush with very double, very fragrant white flowers with a button eye and pale green, disease-resistant leaves; can be used as a climber; hardy to –30°F (Zone 4).

'Semi-Plena', an 8' bush with sweetly fragrant semidouble white flowers and gray-green, disease-resistant leaves on arching canes; good for naturalizing; hardy to –30°F (Zone 4).

The Bourbons

Arising from a natural cross between *Rosa chinensis* 'Old Blush' and *Rosa damascena* var. *bifera* (also called the 'Autumn Damask'), Bourbon roses were found in 1817 on the Île de Bourbon, now Réunion Island, in the Indian Ocean. Many cultivars were developed in the 1800s from this cross, with a wide range of sizes, forms, and colors.

There are Bourbon rose cultivars that grow 10 to 15 feet tall and bloom only once; cultivars that grow 8 to 10 feet tall and are somewhat reblooming; and cultivars that are less than 6 feet tall and rebloom heavily, except in the South. Flowers may be white, pink, maroon, purple, crimson, or striped. The intensely fragrant flowers are spherical, with quartered centers and many silken petals, reaching 3 to 4 inches across. Most cultivars have thick, strong canes bearing large, glossy, bright green leaves sometimes shaded with purple. They are somewhat susceptible to mildew and blackspot. Most withstand winter temperatures ranging from –10° to –20°F (Zone 5).

In the landscape, you can plant Bourbon roses among other shrubs. Use the taller cultivars as climbers, train them on pillars, walls, or tripods, or peg them down as a groundcover.

Prune Bourbon roses in late winter or early spring by removing one-third of the main shoots and two-thirds of the laterals (side shoots). After the flowers bloom, cut the laterals back again by one-third, or to three growth buds. Remove any aging, dead, or diseased wood. Grow Bourbons in rich, moist soil that is mulched well.

Best Bourbons

Here are my experts' picks for best Bourbon cultivars:

'Boule de Neige', a 4' bush with very double, richly fragrant white roses and pink buds and deep green, leathery leaves on arching canes; good for small gardens; flowers may ball with rain; hardy to –10°F (Zone 6).

'Commandant Beaurepaire', a 4' bush with very fragrant, double deep pink flowers with pink, purple, and white stripes and mottling; long, pointed, wavy light green leaves on thorny canes; best in cool weather; hardy to –10°F (Zone 6).

'Honorine de Brabant', a 5' bush with double, quartered blush-pink flowers striped with mauve and purple; large, lush, leathery leaves on vigorous plants with few thorns; good cut flower; can be used as a climber; hardy to –10°F (Zone 6).

'Louise Odier', a 4' bush with very fragrant, very double bright pink flowers and rich green leaves on slender branches with few thorns; good cut flower; hardy to –10°F (Zone 6).

'Madame Isaac Pereire', a 5' bush with raspberry-scented double, globose deep rose-pink flowers with magenta shading; good cut flower; good for moist, cool climates; can be grown on a pillar or pegged as

(continued on page 10)

Talking about Rose Flowers

A rose is *not* a rose is *not* a rose. Rose flowers vary in terms of the number of petals, color combination, and shape. And there's a special terminology to describe the variations. For example, in a rose catalog, you would find 'Rosa Mundi' described as having semidouble striped rosette flowers. Understanding rose terminology will help you know what type of flowers to expect, including the number of petals, color combination, and the shape of the bloom.

Rose flowers are often described by their shape and the way their centers are formed. The combination of centers and shapes differs from cultivar to cultivar and may vary due to the effects of weather and growing conditions. The center and shape also change as the flower opens and matures.

Two important flower terms not listed below involve *how* roses bloom: once-blooming and repeat-blooming. Once-blooming roses, typically the old roses, have one big flush of bloom, like the flowering shrubs they are. Repeat-blooming roses, typically the modern roses, have flushes of bloom all season.

Flower Fullness

Single: 5 to 7 petals in a single row. Examples: 'Ballerina', 'Betty Prior', 'Dainty Bess', 'Dortmund'.

Semidouble: 8 to 20 petals in two or three rows. Examples: 'Celsiana', 'Europeana', 'Rosa Mundi'.

Moderately full double: 21 to 29 petals in three or four rows. Examples: 'Harison's Yellow', 'Olympiad', 'Sea Pearl', 'Tiffany'.

Full double: 30 to 39 petals in four or more rows. Examples: 'Frau Karl Druschki', 'Iceberg', 'Queen Elizabeth'.

Very full double: 40 or more petals in numerous rows. Examples: 'Crested Moss', 'Madame Hardy', 'Pink Peace'.

Flower Color

Single: Petals have similar color throughout. Example: 'Europeana' (red).

Bicolor: The reverse, or back, of each petal is a distinctly different color from the front. Example: 'Love' (red with white reverse).

Blend: Two or more distinct colors on the front of each petal. Examples: 'Double Delight' (white with hot pink edges), 'Paradise' (mauve with red edges).

Striped: Two or more distinct colors on each petal, with at least one in distinct stripes or bands. Example: 'Rosa Mundi' (white flowers striped with red and pink).

Single

Semidouble

Double

Rose Flower Types

Quartered

High-centered

Globular

Open-cupped

Rose Flower Shapes

Flower Center

Button center: A round green center, or eye, in a fully open rose bloom, formed in very double roses. Examples: 'Belle de Crecy', 'Fantin-Latour', 'Madame Hardy'.

High center: The long, inner petals of the bud arranged in a pointed cone. The form most often found in hybrid teas, grandifloras, and floribundas. Example: 'Iceberg'.

Muddled center: Double or semidouble flower with inner petals forming an irregular central area that conceals the stamens when the flower is fully open. Examples: 'Rose de Rescht', 'William Lobb'.

Open center: Stamens are prominent when the flower is fully open; single, semidouble, and double forms may have this characteristic. Example: 'Othello'.

Quartered center: Inner petals folded into three, four, or five distinct sections (or quarters) in a fully open flower. Examples: 'Baronne Prevost', 'Konigin von Danemark', 'Souvenir de la Malmaison'.

Flower Shape

Globular: Very double flower with petals curving inward to form a globelike shape. Example: 'Constance Spry'.

Open-cupped: Double or semidouble flower forming a distinctly rounded, cuplike shape. Examples: 'Duchesse de Brabant', 'Ferdinand Pichard', 'Graham Thomas', 'Heritage'.

Pompon: Very double flower with short petals evenly arranged into a rounded bloom. Examples: 'Alba Meidiland', 'Sea Foam', 'The Fairy'.

Reflexed: Outer petals reflex (curve back and down) as they open. Very double types almost form a ball, while other double and semidouble cultivars form a looser, less pronounced ball shape. Examples: 'Boule de Neige', 'Comte de Chambord', 'Felicité Parmentier'.

Rosette: A double flower with short petals evenly arranged into a flat, low-centered bloom. Example: 'Cornelia'.

Saucer: Single, semidouble, or double flower with outer petals curving slightly upward in a saucerlike shape. Examples: 'Betty Prior', 'Harison's Yellow'.

a groundcover; must have rich, moist soil; hardy to −20°F (Zone 5).

'Souvenir de la Malmaison', a 3' bush with spicily fragrant double, quartered blush to pale pink flowers; flowers do not open well in wet weather; does best grown on own roots; cuttings root readily; climbing form available; hardy to −10°F (Zone 6).

'Zephirine Drouhin', a 10' climber with raspberry-scented semidouble bright pink flowers and semi-glossy, dark green leaves with new growth red; thornless; 'Kathleen Harrop' is a pale pink sport; hardy to −10°F (Zone 6).

The Centifolias

Known as the cabbage rose, Provence rose, and Holland rose, centifolia roses are a complex natural hybrid probably originating in southern Europe before the 1600s. They bear very double, quartered, button-centered flowers in shades of pink, white, crimson, purple, or mauve and bloom once during midsummer. Their scent is rich, intense, and heady. Borne singly or in clusters, the heavy flowers nod from slender stems. Foliage is large, rounded, wrinkled, and gray-green, with yellow fall color. Stems are gaunt and thorny, forming lax, open bushes often needing staked support or close planting. Centifolia cultivars range in size from 3 to 6 feet.

Centifolia roses need full sun with rich, moist soil. Generally withstanding winter temperatures to −30°F, they take several years to become well established. Prune lightly after flowering, cutting back by no more than one-third in order to maintain graceful, arching growth; also remove dead or spindly growth. Centifolia cultivars are somewhat susceptible to blackspot and mildew, and flowers may be damaged by rain.

Best Centifolias

The rose experts and I chose these as the best centifolias:

'Fantin-Latour', a 5' bush with very fragrant, very double, button-centered pale pink flowers; prolific bloom; few thorns; may need support; hardy to −30°F (Zone 4).

'Petite de Hollande', a 3' bush with sweetly fragrant double, quartered rose-pink flowers on bushy, thorny plants; long bloom period; use whole blooms dried in potpourri; good for small gardens or for pegging as a groundcover; hardy to −30°F (Zone 4).

'Robert le Diable', a 3' bush with double crimson-pink flowers with purple and gray shadings; best color in hot, dry weather; blooms late; let plants grow over a low wall; combine with silver-leaved plants; hardy to −30°F (Zone 4).

'Tour de Malakoff', a 6' bush with very fragrant double, loose, papery mauve-pink flowers shaded with purple and gray; profuse bloom; good as a climber or for pegging as a groundcover; combine with purple flowers; hardy to −30°F (Zone 4).

The China Roses

Many roses are native to China, but 'Slater's Crimson China', 'Parson's Pink China' (now called 'Old Blush'), 'Humes's Blush Tea-Scented China', and 'Park's Yellow Tea-Scented China' are the ones that are most important in the history of roses in the West. Brought to Europe and England in the late 1700s, these repeat-blooming roses bear single or loosely double flowers that darken with age. These roses contributed their repeat-blooming characteristics and yellow—a new color for Western roses—to subsequent rose breeding programs, making modern roses possible. The delicate, twiggy growth is hardy to 0°F (USDA Plant Hardiness Zone 7). Stems have few thorns, and the sparse foliage is light green, shiny, and semi-evergreen.

Where they're hardy, China roses are among the best of the old roses because they are disease-resistant, tolerant of alkaline soils, and long-lived. Growing 3 to 6 feet tall, they are useful in hedges, in shrub borders, in containers, or as specimens. The silken flowers are not affected by high humidity, and they are available in many colors, including red, apricot, and yellow as well as pink and white.

Because they bloom almost continuously, Chinas must be fed and watered regularly. Prune lightly, cutting back by one-third in late winter and shortening laterals (side shoots) after flowering to two or three growth buds.

Best Chinas

Here are the rose experts' favorite China roses:

'Archduke Charles', a 3' bush with fragrant double flowers that open rose-red with a pale center and age to crimson; glossy leaves red when young on smooth, reddish canes with few red thorns; showy hips; blends well with perennials; hardy to 0°F (Zone 7).

'Cramoisi Superieur', a 3' bush with double crimson roses with a sweet, fruity fragrance; flowers in drooping clusters create a mass of color; climbing form available; hardy to 0°F (Zone 7).

'Hermosa', a 3' bush with pointed buds opening to fragrant, high-centered, double light pink flowers; glossy, blue-green, disease-resistant leaves, with red new growth; good for mass plantings, containers, and low hedge; plant several bushes together; hardy to −10°F (Zone 6).

'Louis Philippe', a 3' bush with double dark crimson flowers; good soil essential; hardy to 0°F (Zone 7).

'Mutabilis', a 5' bush with pointed copper-red buds opening to single copper-yellow flowers turning pink, then crimson; reddish leaves; graceful, excellent, long-lived plant; slow to establish; hardy to 0°F (Zone 7).

'Old Blush', a 6' bush with double light pink flowers darkening with age and a sweet pea fragrance; profuse bloom; not for cutting; showy orange hips; climbing form available; hardy to −10°F (Zone 6).

The Damask Roses

Considered by many to have the most intoxicating fragrance of all roses, the damasks are the roses used to make attar of roses for perfume. For gardeners, they are among the best roses to dry for potpourri. The earliest records of damasks in Europe date to the 1500s, but their ancient ancestry, probably from Persia, is uncertain. Until the introduction of the China roses, the 'Autumn Damask' (*Rosa damascena* var. *bifera*) was the only repeat-blooming rose in the West; other damasks bloom only once a year. The 'Autumn Damask' has been known since the tenth century B.C. and was an important parent in the development of the Portland roses.

Damask roses bear nodding sprays of semidouble or double pink or white frilly flowers with centers of golden stamens. Ranging in size from 4 to 7 feet, damasks are arching, informal plants with both large and small thorns. Leaves are light green and downy on the underside. Plants have hardiness ranges from −30° to −40°F (USDA Plant Hardiness Zones 4 and 3).

Provide rich, moist soil for damask roses. Little care is needed except to trim laterals by one-third after blooming, remove the oldest canes occasionally to encourage replacement canes, and cut out dead wood. You can also shorten long shoots by one-third in winter.

Best Damasks

These are the experts' and my picks for best damask roses:

'Autumn Damask', a 4' bush with repeat-blooming, very fragrant, double pink flowers with crumpled petals; use in potpourri; downy, gray-green leaves on sprawling canes; 'Perpetual White Moss' is a sport; hardy to −30°F (Zone 4).

'Celsiana', a 4' bush with once-blooming, very fragrant, semidouble light pink flowers with thin, crinkled petals and golden stamens; profuse bloom over long period; use in potpourri; gray-green leaves on branching, graceful shrub; showy hips; good for beginners; plant among blue flowers and gray-foliaged plants; hardy to −40°F (Zone 3).

'Gloire de Guilan', a 4' bush with once-blooming, very fragrant, double light pink flowers with yellow stamens; soft green, disease-resistant leaves on sprawling plant with small thorns; provide support; hardy to −30°F (Zone 4).

'Ispahan', a 5' bush with once-blooming, very fragrant double pink flowers; long bloom season; good cut flower; one of the best roses; hardy to −40°F (Zone 3).

'Leda', a 3' bush with slightly repeat-blooming, fragrant, very double blush flowers with crimson tips and button center; dark green rounded leaves on sprawling canes; provide support; 'Pink Leda' is a pink sport; hardy to −30°F (Zone 4).

'Madame Hardy', a 5' bush with once-blooming, very fragrant, very double white flowers with green eye; large, bright green leaves on strong canes; susceptible to mildew; must have rich, moist soil; one of the most beautiful roses; can be used on a pillar; hardy to −30°F (Zone 4).

'Madame Zoetmans', a 4' bush with once-blooming, very fragrant, very double pale pink flowers with green eye; rich green leaves on graceful, compact plant; hardy to −30°F (Zone 4).

'Marie Louise', a 4' bush with once-blooming, very fragrant, very double deep pink flowers with green eye; rich green leaves on arching stems; use above a low retaining wall; hardy to −30°F (Zone 4).

'Rose de Rescht', a 3' bush with repeat-blooming, very fragrant, double deep crimson-pink flowers with button eye; vigorous plants; prune hard; hardy to −30°F (Zone 4).

The Eglantines

Ancient roses descended from the sweetbriar rose (*Rosa eglanteria*), the eglantines are large plants reaching 6 to 12 feet tall and as wide. The young leaves smell delightfully like apples, especially when wet. Very dense and thorny, eglantines make excellent hedge, border, and screening plants. Mostly once-blooming, the flowers are small, single or semidouble, and pink, yellow, red, or orange. Some cultivars are fragrant, and showy scarlet hips often develop in the fall. Eglantines are reliably hardy to −30°F (USDA Plant Hardiness Zone 4), but sometimes will withstand −40°F (Zone 3).

Eglantine roses are adaptable, but they do best in rich, moist, well-drained soil. Prune them back after flowering to encourage the growth of the fragrant young foliage.

Kordes of Germany has developed cultivars from this species that are fairly pest-resistant. The Penzance hybrids were developed in the late 1800s in England, and they are somewhat susceptible to mildew and blackspot.

Best Eglantines

These two eglantines topped the list in my experts' poll:

'Goldbusch', a 6' bush with once-blooming, lightly fragrant, semidouble yellow flowers; long blooming season; disease-resistant bright green leaves on sprawling canes; needs support; Kordes hybrid; hardy to −30°F (Zone 4).

'Herbstfeuer', a 6' bush with repeat-blooming, double bright red flowers and glossy, light green, disease-resistant leaves on dense, bushy plant; showy pear-shaped orange hips; Kordes hybrid; hardy to −30°F (Zone 4).

The Gallicas

Most likely the oldest cultivated rose in the West, *Rosa gallica* was used medicinally by the ancient Romans, who took plants throughout their empire. Significant in the breeding of many old garden roses, gallicas comprised much of Empress Josephine's collection. Hardy to −30°F (USDA Plant Hardiness Zone 4), gallicas are compact, slender-stemmed, upright to arching plants growing 3 to 5 feet tall and spreading by suckers if on their own roots. Bearing few thorns, they have many tiny bristles to compensate.

The 2- to 3-inch-wide fragrant flowers of the species are single and a deep, bright pink color; cultivars may be mauve, pink, red-purple, maroon, or blush and may be ornamented with stripes, marbling, mottling, or flecks. Double flowers are spherical and quartered. Blooming once a season for about six weeks at the beginning of summer, gallicas flower best when they're older, established plants. Single and semidouble cultivars produce hips in the fall.

Though they're tolerant of heat, cold, and a wide range of soils, gallicas respond well to good conditions. The rough, dark green leaves are round to oval. Foliage is somewhat susceptible to mildew when the weather is hot and dry. Prune out some old wood after flowering to encourage new growth.

Gallicas are good border plants for small gardens, especially when underplanted with old-fashioned flowers or grown with other deciduous shrubs. They also grow well in containers.

Gallica hybrids developed in the twentieth century include 'James Mason' and 'Scarlet Fire'. Two of the most famous early roses, the 'Apothecary's Rose' (*Rosa gallica* var. *officinalis*) and 'Rosa Mundi' (*R. gallica* var. *versicolor*), are hardy garden shrubs and good sources of petals for potpourri.

Best Gallicas

The experts and I chose these favorite gallicas. Unless otherwise noted, all are hardy to −30°F (Zone 4):

'Apothecary's Rose', a 3' bush with very fragrant, semi-double bright magenta-crimson flowers with yellow stamens; dark green, disease-resistant leaves; showy hips; bristly canes; 'Rosa Mundi' is a sport with beautiful red, pink, and white striped flowers.

'Belle de Crecy', a 4' bush with honey-scented, very double mauve-pink flowers with green button eye, turning lavender-gray; long-blooming; free-flowering and reliable; gray-green, disease-resistant leaves; sprawling, bristly canes; needs support and water.

'Cardinal de Richelieu', a 4' bush with very fragrant, double burgundy flowers darkening to purple; good for potpourri; arching mounds of glossy, dark green, disease-resistant leaves; requires good cultivation and annual removal of some older growth.

'Charles de Mills', a 4' bush with very fragrant, very double quartered purple-crimson flowers; dark, disease-resistant leaves on sprawling canes; may need support; blends well with pink flowers.

'Complicata', a 5' bush with fragrant, single deep pink flowers with white eye and yellow stamens; fragrant; large, disease-resistant leaves densely covering strong, arching canes; showy orange hips; tolerates light, sandy soils; use as a climber; good with yellow flowers; hardy to −20°F (Zone 5).

'Empress Josephine', a 4' bush with fragrant, semidouble deep pink flowers flushed with purple and with dark veins; gray-green leaves on dense, sprawling plants; few thorns; showy turban-shaped hips.

'Gloire de France', a 3' bush with fragrant, very double pink flowers; profuse bloom; gray-green leaves on bristly, spreading canes.

'James Mason', a 5' bush with fragrant, semidouble deep red flowers with gold stamens; dark green, disease-resistant leaves; large thorns; urn-shaped orange hips; can be used as spreading shrub or climber.

'President de Seze', a 4' bush with fragrant double magenta-crimson flowers with paler edges; large gray-green, disease-resistant leaves.

'Scarlet Fire', a 6' bush with single scarlet-crimson flowers with yellow stamens; long bloom period; arching stems; large pear-shaped hips; use as a climber.

'Superb Tuscan', a 4' bush with fragrant double deep maroon-crimson to purple flowers with golden stamens; use in potpourri; dark green leaves on bristly canes forming rounded, compact plants.

The Hybrid Perpetuals

The precursors of the hybrid teas, hybrid perpetual roses are complex hybrids popular in the latter half of the 1800s. They have large, mostly double flowers in shades of pink, maroon, or white. Hybrid perpetuals generally bloom profusely in early summer and then again in the fall. This class also has some crimson cultivars, which were rare in the late 1800s. Tall, narrow, and upright, hybrid perpetuals are grown more for their blooms than for their garden appearance. The best ones are very fragrant and free-flowering, with old-rose style.

Hybrid perpetuals need generous amounts of fertilizer and water. Prune back by one-half to maintain size and to encourage the new growth that produces the best (as well as the most) flowers. Hybrid perpetuals are hardy to −30°F (USDA Plant Hardiness Zone 4).

Best Hybrid Perpetuals

These hybrid perpetuals topped the list in my experts' rose popularity poll:

'Baron Girod de l'Ain', a 4' bush with moderately repeat-blooming, very fragrant double red flowers tipped in white; semiglossy, dark green leaves on erect, stiff canes; showy hips.

'Baronne Prevost', a 5' bush with repeat-blooming, very fragrant double rose-pink flowers; blooms over a long period; dark green leaves on upright, vigorous, thorny canes.

'Ferdinand Pichard', a 5' bush with repeat-blooming, fragrant double pink and red striped flowers; leathery leaves on upright, nearly thornless canes.

'Frau Karl Druschki', an 8' bush with repeat-blooming, double high-centered white flowers; light green, disease-resistant leaves; provide rich, moist soil; use as climber or large bush; underplant with perennials.

'General Jacqueminot', a 5' bush with repeat-blooming, very fragrant double bright red flowers on long cutting stems; susceptible to rust.

'Mrs. John Laing', a 4' bush with repeat-blooming, very fragrant double pink flowers and large gray-green, disease-resistant leaves.

'Reine des Violettes', a 5' bush with moderately repeat-blooming, very fragrant, very double mauve-violet flowers; gray-green leaves on strong, erect, nearly thornless canes.

The Moss Roses

Natural sports, mainly from centifolias but also a few from 'Autumn Damask', moss roses are named for the mossy, resinous growth covering the outside of the flower buds. The moss on centifolia sports is soft and green, while that of damasks is stiff and brown. Found in the late 1600s, moss roses were very popular in the mid-1800s. Some cultivars are crosses with Chinas,

so they have repeat bloom, while others bloom only once a year.

Flowers of moss roses are usually very fragrant, fully double, and pink, white, or red. Borne in clusters, individual flowers vary from 1 to 3 inches across. The plants range in size from miniatures less than a foot tall to 10-foot climbers, with most in the 4- to 6-foot range. Most are hardy to −30°F (USDA Plant Hardiness Zone 4).

Prune repeat-flowering cultivars heavily in late winter, cutting new growth back by one-half and later, just before leaf bud break, to about three growth buds. Prune once-blooming cultivars more lightly. Grow moss roses in humus-enriched soil that is kept moist. Plants may mildew after flowering, especially if the soil is dry.

Best Moss Roses

You'll enjoy trying the experts' and my favorite moss roses:

'Communis', a 4' bush with once-blooming, very fragrant, very double quartered, button-centered pink flowers; thick reddish moss on buds and stems; dark green, disease-resistant leaves on arching, open growth; canes bristly and thorny; one of the best moss roses.

'Comtesse de Murinais', a 6' bush with once-blooming, very fragrant, double quartered, button-centered blush to white flowers; blooms for a long period; green, balsam-scented moss; light green leaves; provide support or peg as a groundcover.

'Crested Moss', a 5' bush with once-blooming, very fragrant, very double pink flowers; moss only on bud tips; disease-resistant leaves on arching, open growth; very bristly and thorny; may need support; susceptible to mildew and blackspot.

'Dresden Doll', a 12" bush with repeat-blooming, fragrant semidouble pale pink flowers with golden stamens; thickly mossed buds; glossy, leathery leaves; modern moss miniature bred by Ralph Moore; also consider miniatures 'Scarlet Moss' and 'Little Gem', growing 2–3' tall.

'General Kleber', a 5' bush with once-blooming, very fragrant double lilac-pink flowers with button eye; bright green moss; lush leaves on arching canes; may need support.

'Henri Martin', a 5' bush with once-blooming, fragrant double crimson flowers fading to deep rose; bright green moss; dark green, disease-resistant leaves on graceful, arching canes.

'Nuits de Young', a 4' bush with once-blooming, fragrant double dark red-purple flowers fading to violet-maroon, with golden stamens; dark moss; small leaves tinged purple; arching, open growth; susceptible to mildew; grown for distinctive color; looks good with yellow flowers.

'Salet', a 4' bush with repeat-blooming, double rose-pink flowers with a sweet musk fragrance; crimson-mossed buds; bristly, arching canes; sturdy, reliable, good for small gardens.

'White Bath', a 4' bush with once-blooming, very fragrant, very double quartered, button-centered white flowers; heavily mossed; dark green leaves on loose, open growth; one of the best moss roses.

'William Lobb', a 6' bush with once-blooming, fragrant, double dark crimson-purple flowers with white centers; pine-scented thick moss; small leaves on arching, bristly, thorny canes; needs support; use on a pillar or wall.

The Noisettes

The first class of rose to originate in the United States, noisettes were a cross between the musk rose (*Rosa moschata*) and the China rose (*R. chinensis*). Created by John Champneys, of Charleston, South Carolina, in the early 1800s, they were further developed by Louis Noisette in Paris, who crossed them with Bourbon, China, and tea roses. One of the best of the old roses for the South, noisettes are tall, graceful, everblooming shrubs and climbers. They bear clusters of fragrant, double flowers in shades of pink, cream, or yellow and are repeat-blooming.

Hardy to 0°F (USDA Plant Hardiness Zone 7), noisettes are excellent plants for training on walls, on fences, on arbors, and into trees. They're also attractive when allowed to form loose, arching shrubs. They need very little pruning except to shape, remove faded flowers, shorten laterals (side shoots) by two-thirds, and, in the winter, remove some of the oldest canes. They are somewhat susceptible to blackspot and mildew.

Best Noisettes

If you live in the South, try these top-rated noisettes:

'Alister Stella Gray', a 10' climber with double pale yellow flowers with a tea fragrance; flowers in clusters; dark green leaves on flexible, nearly thornless canes.

'Blush Noisette', an 8' bush with very fragrant double pale pink flowers; glossy light green leaves may be red when young; smooth, nearly thornless stems; use on a pillar or as a loose shrub.

'Jaune Desprez', a 15–20' climber with double, quartered yellow flowers shaded with apricot and a green eye; fruity fragrance; flowers in clusters; light green leaves and dark mottled stems.

'Mary Washington', an 8' bush with fragrant semidouble white flowers tinted with pink; flowers in clusters; use on a pillar or as a hedge or specimen.

'Reve d'Or', a 12' climber with fragrant double buff yellow flowers with some peach; flowers in clusters; glossy, disease-resistant leaves are bronze when young.

The Portlands

Descendants of the 'Autumn Damask', gallica, and China roses, Portland roses were prized for their brilliant scarlet flowers. Developed in the late 1700s, they were especially popular in the mid- to late 1800s, before hybrid perpetuals and Bourbons supplanted them.

Neat, compact, rounded plants growing to about 4 feet tall, with smooth canes and shiny, light green leaves, Portland roses are ideally suited for the small garden. They are reliably repeat-blooming, with spherical, very double flowers with a strong damask fragrance.

Hardy to –10°F (USDA Plant Hardiness Zone 6), Portlands need humus-enriched soil and plenty of fertilizer and water. Prune Portlands like hybrid teas—cut back canes in late winter by one-third to one-half, and remove all dead or thin growth.

Best Portlands

Here are my experts' top picks for Portland roses:

'Comte de Chambord', a 4' bush with very double, quartered deep pink flowers with pale edges and a strong damask fragrance; large, gray-green leaves on sturdy, upright canes with dense prickles; somewhat susceptible to blackspot and mildew.

'Jacques Cartier' (more correctly known as 'Marquise Boccella'), a 3' bush with fragrant, double pale pink flowers with darker centers and a button eye; leathery, dark green leaves.

'Rose du Roi', a 3' bush with very fragrant, double bright red flowers shaded with violet; pointed, dark green leaves; straggly growth.

Tea Roses

Developed in the nineteenth century from crosses of different China roses with Bourbons and noisettes, tea roses are generally slender plants with high-centered flowers. Hardy only to 0°F (USDA Plant Hardiness Zone 7), they thrive in the summer heat of the South and the West Coast. With smooth, glossy leaves that are often red when young and few thorns, tea roses form twiggy, upright plants usually 4 to 6 feet tall and 3 to 4 feet wide. They bloom for a long period in early summer, then repeat-bloom somewhat later in the season. Flowers may be single, semidouble, or double, and cultivars are available in most rose colors except deep yellow and dark red. Their cool, smoky fragrance is described as that of tea, hence the name.

Best Tea Roses

Southern and West Coast gardeners can choose from this list of top tea roses, all from my experts' poll. Unless noted otherwise, plants are hardy to 0°F (Zone 7):

'Bon Silene', a 5' bush with fragrant, double deep pink flowers; disease-resistant and easily grown.

'Catherine Mermet', a 4' bush with fragrant double, high-centered pale pink flowers; good cut flower; leaves tinged with copper; withstands hot weather; hardy to 15°F (Zone 8).

'Duchesse de Brabant', a 5' bush with very fragrant, double pink flowers and wavy, disease-resistant leaves; best of tea class; use as a specimen; hardy to −10°F (Zone 6).

'Maman Cochet', a 3' bush with violet-scented, double, high-centered pink flowers; flowers do not open well in high humidity; leathery, dark green leaves on smooth, nearly thornless canes; climbing, white, and red forms available.

'Marie van Houtte', a 6' bush with fragrant double yellow flowers aging to pale pink; dark, disease-resistant leaves; 'Mrs. Dudley Cross' is similar but smaller.

'Perle des Jardins', a 4' bush with fragrant double yellow flowers; good for cutting; dark, disease-resistant leaves are purple when young; climbing form available.

'Safrano', a 5' bush with fragrant double, high-centered buff-apricot flowers; flowers are best in spring and fall; dark green, disease-resistant leaves are purple when young; 'Isabella Sprunt' is a yellow sport; hardy to −10°F (Zone 6).

'Sombreuil', a 10' climber with very fragrant, double creamy white flowers; good cut flower; dark green, disease-resistant leaves; large thorns; use on a pillar, fence, or wall.

SPECIES ROSES

Species roses, as their name implies, were the first roses, from which all the old roses and, ultimately, the modern roses were bred. Depending on the authority, there are some two hundred or so rose species. Basically a species rose is defined as one that bears single, five-petaled flowers and will self-pollinate and produce offspring identical to the parent. Species roses are often classed with old roses.

There are species roses native to all parts of the Northern Hemisphere, ranging widely in size, form, and hardiness. For the most part, they bloom only once a season, usually early in the summer. The flowers are followed by seed-bearing rose hips, which are usually red.

Don't overlook the species roses when you're choosing roses for your garden. As a group, they're tough and disease-resistant. Species roses are excellent for naturalizing and as part of the shrub border. Many offer several seasons of landscape interest, due to their showy hips, bark, or growth habit, as well as their bloom.

Best Species Roses for Gardens

In our gardens, the species roses listed here offer the most interest and are easiest to grow and keep in bounds. You'll recognize the names of some famous roses here, like the Lady Banks rose and Father Hugo's rose, as well as Shakespeare's eglantine. Some other species roses, such as the rugosa rose (*Rosa rugosa*), the Scotch rose (*Rosa spinosissima*), and the Memorial rose (*Rosa wichuraiana*), are discussed with their hybrids in the shrub roses section on page 20.

Cherokee rose (*Rosa laevigata*), a 10–15' climber with once-blooming, fragrant single white flowers; thorny canes with bright, glossy green leaves; semi-evergreen; bristly red hips; hardy to 0°F (Zone 7).

Chestnut or burr rose (*Rosa roxburghii*), a 6' bush with repeat-blooming, double bright pink flowers and very evenly spaced leaves on gray canes with peeling bark; hardy to −10°F (Zone 6).

Eglantine or sweetbriar (*Rosa eglanteria*), a 10' bush with once-blooming, very fragrant single pink flowers; small, glossy, disease-resistant leaves; wet foliage smells of apples; showy scarlet hips; hardy to −30°F (Zone 4).

Father Hugo's rose (*Rosa hugonis*), a 6' bush with once-blooming, single pale yellow flowers and small light green leaves; hardy to −10°F (Zone 6).

Lady Banks rose (*Rosa banksiae* var. *alba-plena*, also called *R. banksiae* var. *banksiae*), a 20' climber with once-blooming, fragrant double white flowers; small light green leaves; almost thornless; yellow form (Yellow Lady Banks rose, *R. banksiae* var. *lutea*) available; hardy to 10°F (Zone 8).

Prairie rose (*Rosa setigera*), a 6' bush with once-blooming, single pink flowers with yellow stamens; use as a sprawling shrub or climber; hardy to −40°F (Zone 3).

Rosa glauca (formerly *R. rubrifolia*), a 6' bush with once-blooming, starlike single bright pink flowers; leaves are gray-green with a reddish iridescent cast; foliage prized for flower arranging; dark purple canes; long purple-red hips; good fall color; hardy to −50°F (Zone 2).

MODERN ROSES DEMYSTIFIED

Most of us are more familiar with the modern roses, but it's still easy to become confused. What's the difference between a grandiflora and a hybrid tea? What's a polyantha? Are English roses shrub roses? Where do the Meidiland roses fit in? You'll find the answers to these questions and more on the pages that follow. Just turn to the category you want to know more about, and read on!

Don't scorn modern roses because of the old roses' newfound chic. I think a hybrid tea is as beautiful as any other rose, and the shrub roses are hard to beat by any standard. Just be a discriminating buyer when choosing the roses for your garden: Make sure the modern rose cultivars you choose have the characteristics you want, such as fragrance, cold-hardiness, or disease resistance. I've listed my picks for the best modern roses to help you make good choices.

New cultivars come out every year and are fun to try, but those listed have a proven track record.

The Floribundas

Developed by crossing hybrid tea and polyantha roses, floribunda roses are bushy plants that grow 2 to 4 feet tall. They are excellent for low hedges and mass plantings, and as specimens in flower borders. Borne in sprays throughout the growing season, floribunda flowers may be single, semidouble, or double, and they come in the entire color range for roses. Some are fragrant. Most are hardy to −10°F (USDA Plant Hardiness Zone 6); they'll withstand colder temperatures with winter protection. Prune floribundas to maintain their shape and to remove weak, dead, or old wood as well as faded flowers. (For more on winter protection and pruning, see Chapter 4, which discusses the care and feeding of roses.)

Types of modern roses. Modern roses bloom all summer, so you get nonstop color and landscape impact. **Miniatures** are great for edgings, at the front of the border, and in containers. Free-flowering **floribundas** are showy in mass plantings and make colorful hedges. **Hybrid teas** and **grandifloras** are lovely in a perennial bed or mixed border. **Shrub roses** are handsome, versatile plants you can use anywhere you'd plant a shrub—in hedges, as specimens, in a foundation planting or mixed border, in an old-fashioned herb or cottage garden, or pegged as groundcovers. **Standard (tree) roses** are eye-catching accent plants, whether used in a formal garden, grown in containers on the patio, or set in handsome pots along the front walk or beside the front door. **Climbers** are beautiful vertical accents for a trellis, arbor, or post; you can also train them to bloom along a fence or wall.

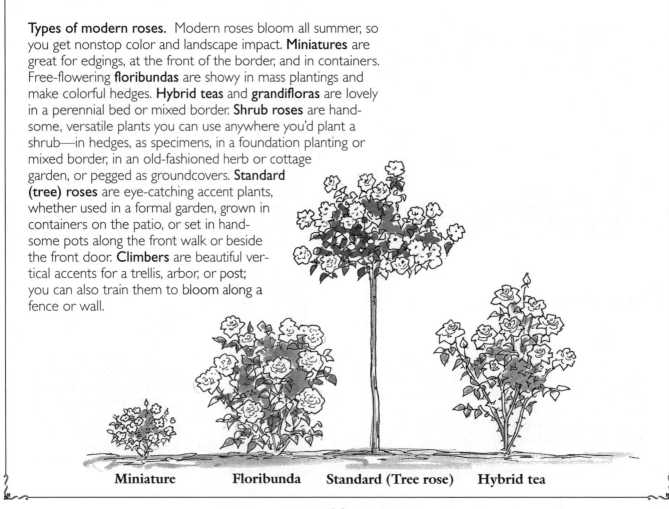

Miniature   Floribunda   Standard (Tree rose)   Hybrid tea

Best Floribundas

When it came to the best floribundas, the rose experts I polled chose these:

'Anabell', a 3' bush with large sprays of double, high-centered, fragrant orange-red flowers and good disease resistance, hardy to −20°F (Zone 5).

'Betty Prior', a 5' bush with prolific single hot pink flowers, hardy to −20°F (Zone 5).

'Cherish', a 3' bush with double, high-centered, coral-pink blooms with a spicy fragrance and glossy, disease-resistant leaves, hardy to 10°F (Zone 7).

'Class Act', a 4' bush with long, pointed buds opening to double white flowers with a fruity fragrance, borne singly or in sprays, and disease-resistant leaves, hardy to −10°F (Zone 6).

'Escapade', a 3' bush with semidouble flowers that are a pink blend with white centers, disease-resistant, hardy to −10°F (Zone 6).

'Europeana', a 3' bush with huge sprays of double velvety red flowers and bronzy–dark green, disease-resistant leaves, hardy to −10°F (Zone 6).

'Gene Boerner', a 4' bush with double, high-centered pink flowers, hardy to −20°F (Zone 5).

'Iceberg', a 4' bush with double white fragrant flowers, hardy to −20°F (Zone 5).

'Lilac Charm', a 2½' bush with very fragrant single mauve blooms with showy golden stamens, compact plants, hardy to −10°F (Zone 6).

'Little Darling', a 3' bush with double, high-centered flowers that are a yellow and pink blend and glossy, disease-resistant leaves, hardy to −20°F (Zone 5).

'Margaret Merril', a 2½' bush with fragrant double white flowers with showy golden stamens, borne in clusters, hardy to −10°F (Zone 6).

'Nearly Wild', a 3' bush with single pink flowers, nonstop bloom, disease-resistant, hardy to −30°F (Zone 4).

'Pleasure', a 3' bush with double, ruffled coral-pink flowers, good cut flower, disease-resistant, hardy to −10°F (Zone 6).

'Sea Pearl', a 5' bush with double pink flowers suffused with yellow, flowers borne singly, disease-resistant leaves, hardy to −10°F (Zone 6).

'Sunsprite', a 2' bush with fragrant double golden yellow flowers, disease-resistant, hardy to −20°F (Zone 5).

The Grandifloras

A result of crossing hybrid tea and floribunda roses, grandifloras combine the classic hybrid tea rose flower form with the floriferous bloom habit of the floribundas. Grandifloras generally grow 4 to 6 feet or taller, with high-centered

Shrub　　　　　**Grandiflora**　　　　　**Climber**

flowers borne singly or in clusters on long stems. Grandifloras bloom continuously throughout the growing season. Their flowers may or may not be fragrant, depending on the cultivar. Most are semidouble or double, and there are cultivars in all rose colors. Because grandifloras become tall plants, use them at the back of flower beds or in shrub borders. Most are hardy to at least 0°F (USDA Plant Hardiness Zone 7) without winter protection.

Best Grandifloras

The rose experts voted in favor of these grandifloras:

'Aquarius', a 5' bush with double, high-centered pink and cream flowers and leathery, somewhat disease-resistant leaves, flowers good for cutting, hardy to –20°F (Zone 5).

'Camelot', a 5' bush with double coral-pink flowers with a spicy fragrance that are borne in sprays and good for cutting, and glossy, disease-resistant leaves, hardy to –10°F (Zone 6).

'Love', a 4' bush with double, high-centered flowers that are bright red with white reverse, borne singly or in sprays, and sparse, dark green, disease-resistant leaves on thorny canes, hardy to –10°F (Zone 6).

'Pink Parfait', a 4' bush with prolific double high-centered pink flowers with darker edges, borne singly or in sprays on long, slender stems, and leathery, disease-resistant leaves, hardy to –20°F (Zone 5).

'Queen Elizabeth', a 6' bush with prolific sprays of double high-centered pink fragrant flowers that are good for cutting and glossy, disease-resistant leaves on nearly thornless canes, hardy to –10°F (Zone 6).

'Shreveport', a 5' bush with double high-centered orange blend flowers that are good for cutting and shiny, disease-resistant leaves on thorny canes, hardy to –10°F (Zone 6).

'Tournament of Roses', a 5' shrub with double high-centered pink-orange blend flowers and dark green, disease-resistant leaves, hardy to –10°F (Zone 6).

The Hybrid Teas

For most of us, "rose" means hybrid tea. Long, narrow, high-center buds borne singly on long stems characterize the modern notion of rose beauty that's epitomized by hybrid tea roses. Hybrid teas essentially evolved from hybrid perpetuals and tea roses in the latter part of the nineteenth century. They produce flowers continually throughout the growing season, are available in all rose colors, and are usually double or semidouble. Hardiness, disease resistance, and fragrance vary greatly from cultivar to cultivar.

Hybrid teas' blooms may be flawless, but their plant form is another matter. Basically, these are narrow, upright bushes growing 3 to 5 feet tall and are often bare at the base—not particularly attractive. This makes them best suited to mixed borders, herb gardens, and perennial beds, where lower-growing plants can hide their gawky legs.

Hybrid teas also require a lot of maintenance, especially when compared with self-reliant roses like the shrubs and polyanthas. Winter protection is a fact of life for hybrid teas in most of the country, since most hybrid teas can survive without winter protection only where temperatures do not fall below 10°F (USDA Plant Hardiness Zone 8). Because of hybrid teas' heavy bloom, rich soil, plenty of fertilizer, and ample water are necessities. Prune these plants hard to encourage new growth and abundant flowering.

Best Hybrid Teas

Of all the hybrid teas, these are the ones the rose experts chose as their top picks:

'Broadway', a 5' bush with double high-centered yellow fragrant flowers with pink edges and dark green, leathery, disease-resistant leaves, hardy to –10°F (Zone 6).

'Dainty Bess', a 4' bush with fragrant single pink flowers with showy maroon stamens and disease-resistant leaves on thorny canes, hardy to –10°F (Zone 6).

'Electron', a 3' bush with very fragrant double high-centered deep pink flowers and leathery leaves on thorny canes, hardy to –10°F (Zone 6).

'Fragrant Memory', a 5' bush with double high-centered lavender-pink flowers that are good for cutting, flowers have damask fragrance, light green, disease-resistant leaves, hardy to –10°F (Zone 6).

'Gina Lollobrigida', a 4–5' upright bush with double high-centered very fragrant yellow flowers and bright green leaves, hardy to –10°F (Zone 6).

'Ingrid Bergman', a 3' bush with double high-centered dark red flowers and dark green, disease-resistant leaves, hardy to –20°F (Zone 5).

'Just Joey', a 3' bush with very fragrant double ruffled buff-apricot flowers that are good for cutting and dark green, leathery leaves, hardy to –10°F (Zone 6).

'Keepsake', a 5' bush with very fragrant double high-centered multi-shaded pink flowers, borne singly and in clusters, and glossy leaves on dense, sturdy, thorny canes, hardy to –20°F (Zone 5).

'Mister Lincoln', a 5' bush with very fragrant double high-centered dark red blooms that are good for cutting and dark green, leathery leaves, hardy to –10°F (Zone 6).

'Mon Cheri', a 3' bush with double high-centered pink-edged red flowers with a light spicy fragrance and glossy, dark green, disease-resistant leaves, hardy to –20°F (Zone 5).

'Olympiad', a 5' bush with double high-centered bright red flowers and semiglossy leaves on thorny canes, hardy to –10°F (Zone 6).

'Pascali', a 4' bush with double high-centered creamy white flowers that are good for cutting and sparse, dark green, disease-resistant leaves, hardy to –10°F (Zone 6).

'Perfect Moment', a 4' bush with double high-centered yellow flowers with red edges that are good for cutting and dark green, very disease-resistant leaves, hardy to –10°F (Zone 6).

'Pink Peace', a 5' bush with very fragrant, very double high-centered deep pink flowers and disease-resistant, leathery leaves, hardy to –10°F (Zone 6).

'Polarstern' also called 'Polarstar', a 5' bush with creamy white flowers and very disease-resistant leaves, hard to –20°F (Zone 6).

'Precious Platinum', a 4' bush with double high-centered red flowers that are good for cutting and leathery, glossy, disease-resistant leaves, hardy to –20°F (Zone 5).

'Uncle Joe', a 5' bush with double high-centered dark red flowers that are good for cutting and leathery, dark green leaves, best in hot weather, hardy to –10°F (Zone 6).

'Yves Piaget', a 2½–3' bush with peony-like very double pink flowers that are highly fragrant and deep green, disease-resistant leaves, hardy to –10°F (Zone 6).

The Miniatures

Every aspect of miniature roses is reduced in size, including the stems, leaves, and flowers. No one is sure of the origin of miniatures, although it was probably China. Miniatures were popular in the early 1800s, lost ground in favor of the opulent roses sweeping the rose world, then reappeared in the 1920s, with hundreds of cultivars on the market today.

Minis bear single, semidouble, or double flowers in every rose color, and roses may or may not be fragrant, depending on the cultivar. Plant height varies from less than 6 inches to over 2 feet. Plant habit includes climbing and groundcover forms.

You can grow miniatures indoors as houseplants if you give them bright light, cool temperatures, and high humidity. But they grow and look best outdoors, where they are excellent in raised beds as well as low borders, in massed plantings, as specimens, or in containers. Most minis, including the ones in the list below, are hardy without protection to –20°F (USDA Plant Hardiness Zone 5). Prune miniature roses to remove dead wood, to thin, or to improve shape.

Best Miniatures

Here are my experts' top picks for mighty minis:

'Avandel', a 12" bush with double pink-yellow blend flowers and a fruity fragrance, and leathery, dark green, disease-resistant leaves.

'Black Jade', an 18–24" bush with double, velvety, high-centered dark red flowers that are good for cutting and glossy, dark green, disease-resistant leaves.

'Cinderella', an 8–10" bush with very double white blooms, a spicy fragrance, and no thorns.

'Debut', a 12–18" bush with double high-centered pale yellow flowers with red edges and dark green, disease-resistant leaves.

'Dee Bennett', a 14–18" bush with double bright apricot blooms that make long-lasting cut flowers.

'Jean Kenneally', a 10–16" bush with double high-centered pale apricot flowers and semiglossy leaves.

'Jeanne Lajoie', a 4–8' climber with double pink flowers with darker reverse and glossy, dark green leaves; use as climber or hanging over walls.

'Magic Carrousel', a 30" bush with double white flowers with red edges and shiny green to bronze, very disease-resistant leaves.

'Mary Marshall', a 14" bush with double high-centered deep coral flowers with yellow and pink overtones that make good cut flowers and semiglossy, disease-resistant leaves; climbing form grows to 5'.

'New Beginning', a 14–20" bush with very double orange flowers with yellow reverse and dark green, disease-resistant leaves.

'Old Glory', a 16–20" bush with double red flowers and dark green, vigorous foliage.

'Pacesetter', an 18–24" bush with very double high-centered white fragrant flowers and abundant dark green, disease-resistant leaves.

'Peach Fuzz', a 14–20" bush with fragrant double apricot-pink flowers, mossed buds and stems, and glossy, disease-resistant leaves.

'Popcorn', a 10–14" bush with semidouble white flowers with showy yellow stamens and a honey fragrance and glossy leaves.

'Single's Better', a 15–18" bush with single bright red fragrant flowers with showy yellow stamens, mossed buds, and glossy leaves.

'Snow Bride', a 15–18" bush with double white flowers and dark green foliage.

'Winsome', a 16–20" bush with double high-centered deep magenta flowers and semiglossy, dark green, disease-resistant leaves.

The Polyanthas

Polyanthas are bushy, 2-foot plants that were developed in the late nineteenth century with crosses of the multiflora rose with Chinas or hybrid teas. They have narrow, finely textured leaves and great quantities of continuously produced clusters of 1-inch single, semidouble, or double flowers. Hardy to –30°F (USDA Plant Hardiness Zone 5), polyanthas bloom in shades of pink, white, red, orange, or yellow. Their popularity was surpassed in the twentieth century by floribundas, but polyanthas are being appreciated again as sturdy, trouble-free plants for massing, edgings, and hedges as well as foreground plantings.

Polyanthas withstand a wide range of soils, but do best in humus-rich, moist but well-drained soil. Little pruning is needed except to remove dead or diseased wood and to shape the plants. For winter protection, remove about one-third of the growth to prevent wind-whipping and winter injury.

Best Polyanthas

Rose experts across the country voted for these polyanthas:

'Cecile Brunner', a 3' bush with fragrant double high-centered pale pink flowers and small, dark green, disease-resistant leaves on slender stems; climbing cultivar, 'Climbing Cecile Brunner', available; also consider the taller 'Bloomfield Abundance' and the buff-apricot 'Perle d'Or'.

'China Doll', a 2' bush with double pink flowers and bright green, disease-resistant leaves.

'Margo Koster', a 12–18" bush with large sprays of semi-double, cupped salmon-pink flowers and semiglossy, gray-green leaves on smooth, nearly thornless canes.

'Nathalie Nypels', a 2' bush with fragrant semidouble rose-pink flowers with coral shading that are good for cutting and dark green, disease-resistant leaves; heat-tolerant.

'The Fairy', a 2' bush with great quantities of double pink flowers and abundant tiny, glossy, disease-resistant leaves; late-bloomer.

The Shrub Roses

"Shrub rose" is a catch-all designation created by the American Rose Society that includes a wide variety of hardy, easily grown shrubby plants. Plants range in size from groundcovers to giants over 12 feet tall. Some are once-blooming, while others repeat. Shrub roses are available in single, semidouble, or double blooms in all rose colors. Depending on the cultivar, flowers may or may not be fragrant.

Because of their handsome shape—think of roses that are attractive even out of bloom!—and low-maintenance toughness, shrub roses in general are among the most important roses for the landscape. Some of the best for garden use include the hybrid rugosas, hybrid moyesiis, hybrid musks, hybrid Scotch roses, and kordesii roses, as well as shrub roses such as David Austin's English roses, Meidiland landscape roses from the House of Meilland, Griffith Buck roses, and Explorer Series and Parkland roses from Canada. I'll discuss each of these types of shrub roses, with the best cultivars of each, on the pages that follow.

The Rugosas

Rosa rugosa, a native of Asia, has given us a treasure trove of cultivars that are exceptionally disease-resistant. Tolerant of salt, they survive in the poor, dry soil near seashores and roadsides and will thrive in any garden setting. Some are hardy to –50°F (USDA Plant Hardiness Zone 2), and most survive –30°F (Zone 4).

Rugosas grow 3 to 6 feet tall and 4 feet wide. Most cultivars have exceptionally fragrant clove-scented flowers and bear large, showy hips that are high in vitamin C (the source of rose-hip tea). You can often recognize a rugosa rose by its strikingly handsome rough, wrinkled leaves. Repeat-blooming, the single, semidouble, or double flowers are white, purple, pale to bright pink, or yellow. Prune to shape or limit plant size, and remove the oldest canes at ground level in the winter.

The finest rugosa cultivars include:

'Blanc Double de Coubert', with very fragrant semidouble white flowers, showy hips, and yellow fall color.

'David Thompson', with fragrant double deep pink flowers.

'Delicata', with fragrant semidouble mauve-pink flowers and large hips.

'Frau Dagmar Hastrup' ('Frau Dagmar Hartopp'), with single light pink flowers and a strong clove fragrance.

'Hansa', with fragrant double dark mauve flowers.

'Monte Cassino', with semidouble deep pink flowers on compact plants.

'Scabrosa', with single mauve flowers and showy yellow stamens.

'Schneezwerg', a semidouble white with showy yellow stamens.

'Therese Bugnet', with double dark rose-pink flowers, exceptionally hardy.

Hybrid Musks

Hybrid musk roses evolved at the beginning of the twentieth century from the multiflora rose, ramblers, polyanthas, noisettes, teas, and hybrid teas. Growing 5 to 6 feet tall, the hybrid musks repeatedly bear sprays of small, fragrant flowers in soft, delicate colors.

These graceful plants look their best in borders, as hedges, and as specimen plants. They need rich soil and good care to grow well; they are hardy to −10°F (USDA Plant Hardiness Zone 6). Shape them as needed, shorten the canes by one-third in late winter, and remove the oldest growth at the base.

The best hybrid musks include:

'Ballerina', with single pink flowers with a white center and showy yellow stamens, and disease-resistant leaves borne on graceful, arching canes.

'Buff Beauty', with double pale apricot-yellow flowers and disease-resistant leaves on arching canes.

'Cornelia', with double pink flowers with mauve and yellow shading.

'Erfurt', with very fragrant semidouble pink flowers with yellow centers.

'Kathleen', with large clusters of single pale pink flowers with golden stamens and disease-resistant, dark green leaves on vigorous, upright canes.

'Nymphenberg', with semidouble salmon-pink flowers with a fruity fragrance and orange hips.

'Penelope', with semidouble pale pink flowers and coral-pink hips.

'Vanity', with very fragrant single deep pink flowers and dark green, leathery leaves on vigorous, arching canes.

Hybrid Moyesiis

Hybrid moyesii roses were developed from the Chinese species brought to the West in 1903. Cultivars have single or semidouble pink, red, orange, or white 2-inch flowers followed by flagon-shaped hips. Some cultivars are repeat-blooming, while others bloom only once. None are fragrant. Stiff, open plants grow 8 to 10 feet tall and as wide, making them good for the back of borders. These disease-resistant plants are hardy from −20° to −30°F (USDA Plant Hardiness Zones 5 to 4).

The showiest hybrid moyesiis are 'Geranium', a once-blooming rose with single bright orange-scarlet flowers with showy golden stamens, gray-green leaves, large thorns on upright canes, and orange-red, flagon-shaped hips; also consider the single red 'Highdownensis'. 'Nevada' is repeat-blooming, with single white flowers and small, semiglossy, gray-green leaves on red canes. Also consider the single pink sport 'Marguerite Hilling', which needs heavy pruning.

Hybrid Scotch Roses

Rosa spinosissima (formerly *R. pimpinellifolia*) is commonly known as the Burnet or Scotch rose. Native to the British Isles, it naturally grows in poor, sandy soil. Because of its hardy, tough reliability, the Scotch rose has yielded a group of adaptable plants. The many slender stems are covered with small bristles and delicate, fernlike leaves. The uniquely scented flowers are followed by maroon-black hips. To keep plants from suckering and spreading widely, plant grafted plants with the bud union aboveground. Where you need a groundcover, however, grow these roses on their own roots or bury the bud union.

Best Scotch roses include 'Fruhlingsmorgen', a once-blooming rose with very fragrant single cherry pink flowers that have yellow centers and showy maroon stamens, dark green leaves, and large red hips, hardy to −20°F (Zone 5); 'Harison's Yellow', once-blooming, with semi-double yellow blooms borne along arching canes and small green leaves, hardy to −40°F (Zone 3); and 'Stanwell Perpetual', repeat-blooming, with fragrant double pale pink flowers fading to white and borne along the canes, and ferny dull green, disease-resistant leaves, hardy to −40°F (Zone 3).

Kordesii Hybrids

Kordesii hybrids were developed in Germany by Reimer Kordes in the twentieth century from *Rosa rugosa* and *R. wichuraiana*. They are generally hardy to −30°F (USDA Plant Hardiness Zone 4) and are disease-resistant. They withstand rigorous growing conditions. Kordesii roses are available in a range of plant sizes and flower colors. Many can be grown as shrubs or trained as climbers. They also make attractive pillar roses.

The best kordesiis include:

'Alchymist', a once-blooming rose with fragrant double apricot blend flowers and glossy, dark green, disease-resistant leaves on very thorny, stiff canes.

'Cerise Bouquet', repeat-blooming, with semidouble cerise-crimson flowers with a raspberry fragrance and small, gray-green, disease-resistant leaves on upright to arching canes.

'Dortmund', repeat-blooming, with single bright red fragrant flowers with a white eye, orange hips, and glossy, dark green, disease-resistant leaves on upright canes.

'Leverkusen', repeat-blooming, with double, high-centered light yellow flowers and glossy, light green, disease-resistant leaves; hardy to −20°F (Zone 5).

'Parkdirector Riggers', repeat-blooming, with semidouble deep red flowers and glossy, dark green, leathery, disease-resistant leaves on upright canes.

'Sparrieshoop', repeat-blooming, with single light pink fragrant flowers with showy golden stamens and abundant, leathery, disease-resistant leaves on upright canes.

English Roses

English roses are the late-twentieth century developments of English breeder David Austin. His goal has been to create plants with old-rose characteristics, including soft colors and intense fragrance, on shrubby plants that repeat-bloom. The success of his breeding program has been phenomenal, combining the best of the old and modern roses into fine landscape plants.

English roses are hardy to −20°F (USDA Plant Hardiness Zone 5) and require the same good growing conditions you'd give a hybrid tea—rich soil, lots of fertilizer, and ample water. Dozens of cultivars have been introduced, and because they're so new, it will take some time for the most adaptable ones to emerge.

Some of the best English roses include:

'Bredon', with large sprays of double buff-yellow flowers with a strong fruit fragrance and small, leathery, disease-resistant leaves.

'Constance Spry', a once-blooming double pink rose with a myrrh fragrance and leathery, disease-resistant leaves on arching canes.

'Fair Bianca', with double white flowers with a green eye and myrrh fragrance on strong, compact growth.

'Graham Thomas', with double yellow flowers with a tea rose fragrance and light green, disease-resistant leaves on slender canes.

'Heritage', with very fragrant double blush pink flowers, disease-resistant leaves, and few thorns on smooth stems.

'Mary Rose', with double pink flowers with a damask fragrance and disease-resistant leaves on compact, robust canes.

'The Dark Lady', with very fragrant deep red flowers.

'The Prince', with very fragrant double crimson to dark purple flowers and dark, dense foliage.

'Windrush', with fragrant semidouble pale yellow flowers and disease-resistant foliage.

'Yellow Button', with double yellow flowers with a button eye and fruity fragrance.

Buck Hybrids

Dr. Griffith J. Buck was a professor of horticulture at Iowa State University in Ames, Iowa. There he developed a group of roses that were hardy, robust, and disease-resistant. Some resemble modern roses such as floribundas and polyanthas, while other are more shrublike.

They range in height from 3 to 5 feet and are equally wide. Flowers may be single, semidouble, or double, and cultivars are available in most rose colors. Plants are generally hardy to −30°F (USDA Plant Hardiness Zone 5).

Some of the best Buck hybrids include:

'Apple Jack', with semidouble pink flowers and showy orange hips.

'Carefree Beauty', with fragrant semidouble coral-pink flowers, olive green disease-resistant leaves, and orange-red hips.

'Folksinger', with fragrant double yellow-peach flowers and glossy, leathery leaves.

'Prairie Harvest', with pink buds that open to double yellow fragrant flowers.

'Prairie Princess', with semidouble coral-pink flowers.

All of these roses are repeat-bloomers.

Canadian Hybrids

Canadian rose breeders have developed disease-resistant rose cultivars that are hardy to −30° or −40°F (USDA Plant Hardiness Zones 4 and 3), including the Explorer Series and the Parkland roses. With an appearance between that of shrub and floribunda roses, these cultivars bloom profusely throughout the growing season. Their heritage is varied, but many are derived from Kordesii and rugosa roses.

Try these hardy cultivars if you want foolproof roses in the North:

'Champlain', with profuse double velvety deep red flowers and disease-resistant sparse foliage.

'John Cabot', a double deep pink-red with disease-resistant leaves, good used as a shrub or climber.

'John Davis', with large clusters of spice-scented double pink flowers and glossy, leathery, disease-resistant leaves on arching canes, best as a trailing shrub or small climber.

'Morden Centennial', with large clusters of fragrant double pink flowers borne on new wood and disease-resistant leaves.

'Prairie Dawn', with double bright pink flowers and disease-resistant leaves on upright canes.

'William Baffin', with semidouble deep pink flowers and disease-resistant leaves, good used as a shrub or climber.

Meidiland Roses

France's House of Meilland has recently introduced shrub and groundcover roses that are generally hardy to −30°F (USDA Plant Hardiness Zone 4), pest-resistant, and adaptable to rigorous growing conditions. These landscape roses are showy and tough, ideal for a low-maintenance landscape where you want a cheerful splash of color. Meidiland roses may not be the best choice for Deep South gardens, where humidity encourages blackspot.

The best Meidiland roses include:

'Alba Meidiland', a double white that makes a great groundcover; also consider 'White Meidiland'.

'Bonica '82' ('Bonica'), a semidouble pink with small leaves and showy hips.

'Pink Meidiland', with single bright pink flowers and orange-red hips.

'Scarlet Meidiland', a double scarlet that makes a good groundcover and tolerates some shade.

'Sevillana', a double red with showy scarlet hips that's good as a hedge or for mass plantings.

Other Outstanding Shrub Roses

There are plenty of other great shrub roses to beautify your garden. Here are some classics, all repeat-bloomers:

'All That Jazz', a semidouble coral-salmon with light damask fragrance and glossy, dark green, disease-resistant leaves.

'Bloomin' Easy', with double bright red flowers and dark green, disease-resistant leaves on dense growth.

'Carefree Wonder', with semidouble bright pink flowers with cream reverse and white eye as well as disease-resistant leaves on rounded plants.

'Golden Wings', a fragrant semidouble yellow with showy orange stamens.

'Lavender Dream', with semidouble lavender-pink flowers in clusters on arching canes.

'Little White Pet' ('White Pet'), with double white flowers borne in large clusters, forming a symmetrical mound of disease-resistant foliage.

'Maybelle Stearns', with fragrant double peach-pink flowers that are good for cutting and disease-resistant leaves.

'Maytime', with fragrant single coral flowers and bronze-green, leathery leaves.

'Sally Holmes', with apricot buds that open to single cream flowers borne in large clusters and dark glossy leaves on vigorous plants.

'Sea Foam', a double creamy white.

ASSESSING YOUR LANDSCAPE NEEDS

With over 30,000 species and cultivars available, choosing the right rose isn't always easy. Roses vary in height from less than 6 inches tall to well over 20 feet and may be climbing, rambling, trailing, or shrubby. Flowers are borne in many shapes and sizes and come in every color but blue and black. They also come in combinations, like yellow with pink edges, or red-, white-, and pink-striped petals. And there are roses that will thrive in every USDA Plant Hardiness Zone.

Given this diversity, you could find any number of roses to suit virtually every site in your landscape. Other than your imagination, the only limiting factor is sunlight: Roses demand no less than six hours a day. So let's begin your quest to choose the right roses for your needs by asking yourself a question: "What do I want my roses to do?" And let's turn the sunlight factor into a starting point.

The first step is to go into your yard. Look at it from every angle—from the porch, from the street, from the driveway, from the big maple in the backyard. Don't forget to look outside from inside the house, too! You'll want to see plenty of beautiful roses from your windows. As you wander through the yard, run through this checklist:

- Which areas get at least six hours of sun?
- Of these areas, which would look more beautiful and inviting if I added roses?
- Could I add color to a shrub border with roses?
- Could I add structure to a perennial border with roses?
- Do I have a bare wall, fence, or pillar that would look better if roses were growing on it?
- Would my porch look more inviting with a rose trellis on one or both sides?
- Do I have a bare spot for a rose arbor?
- Is there a sunny slope where I could plant a colorful groundcover rose?
- Would container roses brighten my patio or deck?
- Do I have an eyesore—an old toolshed, ugly garage, or tree stump—that I could blend into the landscape with a climbing rose?
- Is there room in my yard for a specimen rose?
- Could I increase privacy with a rose hedge?
- Do I want to plant a wildlife garden and include roses with showy, edible hips?

If you've answered "yes" to one or more of these questions, here's what to do: Read the sections on landscape options and special uses. Scan "Roses for Special Situations" on page 24 and "Best Roses for Landscape Use" on page 29. Then turn to Chapter 2, "Using Roses in Your Landscape," for more on how to evaluate

(continued on page 26)

Roses for Special Situations

Sometimes you need roses that fill a very particular need. If you live where winters are very cold, for example, the average rose wouldn't make it through to spring. But, luckily for far-north rose-lovers, some roses are real Vikings when it comes to cold. Dixie gardeners don't have it any better than their Yankee counterparts if their summers are extremely hot and humid. Lots of roses stop blooming and start mildewing during long bouts of moist heat. But some roses can take the heat—they'll keep blooming and looking good all through the long, hot summer. In the lists below, I've chosen the most cold- and heat-tolerant roses for your gardens.

If you want to grow roses without a lot of fuss, choose cultivars that are especially pest- and disease-resistant. Then you can enjoy your roses without battling Japanese beetles and blackspot all season. Organic pest and disease controls are safe and effective, but they do take time to apply—time you'll save with these super-tough plants. I've listed the most resistant roses here.

For some of us, roses aren't roses unless they *smell* like roses—one reason florist's roses are often such a disappointment. Fragrance can be the best reason to grow a certain rose. And if your roses are close to the house, along a walk, or in pots on a patio, fragrance can provide enormous pleasure as you pass nearby or lean out the window. Some roses are unusually fragrant. These are the roses that tend to haunt our memories and create lasting impressions on visitors. I've listed my favorite fragrant roses below.

Many of the roses I've listed will fall into more than one category—a cultivar may be cold-hardy, disease-resistant, and fragrant, for example. I've listed all the desirable traits for each rose, so when you're making your choices, you can weigh their advantages. I say, "The more, the merrier!"

Most Cold-Hardy Roses

'John Cabot': repeat-blooming; 3" double deep pink-red blooms; plant 8' × 6'; disease-resistant leaves; use as a shrub or climber; hardy to −40°F (Zone 3).

'John Davis': repeat-blooming; 3" double pink blooms; spicy fragrance; flowers in large clusters; plant 6' × 4'; glossy, leathery disease-resistant leaves on arching canes; use as trailing shrub or small climber; hardy to −40°F (Zone 3).

'Marie Bugnet': repeat-blooming; 3" double white blooms; fragrant; plant 3' × 3'; light green, textured leaves; hardy to −40°F (Zone 3).

'Mrs. John McNab': once-blooming; 3" semidouble pale pink-white blooms; fragrant; plant 5' × 5'; large, dark, leathery leaves; hardy to −40°F (Zone 3).

'Morden Centennial': repeat-blooming; 3" double pink blooms; fragrant; flowers in large clusters; plant 5' × 4'; blooms on new wood; disease-resistant leaves; hardy to −40°F (Zone 3).

'Prairie Dawn': repeat-blooming; 2" double bright pink blooms; plant 5' × 4'; disease-resistant leaves on upright canes; hardy to −40°F (Zone 3).

Rosa alba cultivars: once-blooming; 3" semidouble to double white or pink blooms; very fragrant; plant 4–8' × 4–8'; disease-resistant blue-green leaves; reliably hardy to −30°F (Zone 4) but will often withstand −40°F (Zone 3).

Rosa glauca (formerly *R. rubrifolia*): once-blooming; 1" single bright pink blooms; plant 6' × 5'; gray-green leaves with reddish iridescence; long purple-red hips; good fall color; hardy to −50°F (Zone 2).

Rosa rugosa cultivars: repeat-blooming; 3" single, semidouble, or double pink, purple, white, or yellow blooms; strong clove fragrance; plants 3–6' × 3–6'; large red hips; species is hardy to −50°F (Zone 2); most cultivars range from −20° (Zone 5) to −40°F (Zone 3), but 'Blanc Double de Coubert', 'Charles Albanel', 'Dart's Dash', 'Frau Dagmar Hastrup', 'George Will', 'Henry Hudson', 'Jens Munk', 'Scabrosa', 'Schneezwerg', 'Souvenir de Philemon Cochet', 'Wasagaming', and 'Will Alderman' are all able to withstand −50°F (Zone 2) if well grown.

Rosa setigera var. *serena*: once-blooming; 3" single pink blooms with showy yellow stamens; plant 8' or taller; use as a sprawling shrub or climber; hardy to −40°F (Zone 3).

Rosa spinosissima cultivars: species is once-blooming, but most cultivars are repeat-blooming; 1–2" single, semidouble, or double white, pink, or yellow blooms; fragrant; plants 3–4' × 3–4'; species and most cultivars are hardy to −40°F (Zone 3), but some are hardy only to −20°F (Zone 5); best known and hardiest cultivar is 'Stanwell Perpetual'.

'William Baffin': repeat-blooming; 3" semidouble deep pink blooms; plant 8' × 6'; disease-resistant leaves; use as a shrub or climber; hardy to −40°F (Zone 3).

Most Heat-Tolerant Roses

Cherokee rose (*Rosa laevigata*): once-blooming; 3" single white blooms; fragrant; plant 5' × 10–15'; thorny canes with bright, glossy green leaves; semi-evergreen; bristly red hips; use as a climber; hardy to 0°F (Zone 7).

China roses: repeat-blooming; 1–4" semidouble to double white, pink, red, yellow, or green blooms; fragrant; plants 1–8' × 1–6'; sometimes susceptible to mildew; hardiness varies from 0° (Zone 7) to −10°F (Zone 6).

Hybrid multiflora roses: once-blooming; 1–2" semidouble to double pink, mauve, or white blooms; fragrant; plants 5–15' × 8'; most cultivars are best used as climbers; disease-resistant; 'Trier' is repeat-blooming; hardiness varies from 0° (Zone 7) to −20°F (Zone 5).

'Iceberg': repeat-blooming; 3" double white blooms; fragrant; plant 4' × 4'; susceptible to blackspot, but resistant to mildew; floribunda; hardy to −20°F (Zone 5).

Lady Banks rose (*Rosa banksiae* var. *albo-plena*): once-blooming; 1" double white blooms; fragrant; plant 20' tall; use as climber; yellow variety (*R. banksiae* var. *lutea*) available; hardy to 10°F (Zone 8).

'Nathalie Nypels': repeat-blooming; 2" semidouble rose-pink blooms with coral shading; fragrant; plant 2' × 2'; dark green, disease-resistant leaves; hardy to −30°F (Zone 4).

Noisette roses: repeat-blooming; 1–3" semidouble to double white, yellow, or pink blooms; fragrant; plants 3–15' × 2–5'; most cultivars are best as climbers; disease-resistant; hardy to 0°F (Zone 7).

'Queen Elizabeth': repeat-blooming; 4" double pink blooms; fragrant; plant 5–7' × 4'; glossy, leathery, disease-resistant leaves; grandiflora; hardy to −10°F (Zone 6).

Tea roses: repeat-blooming; 3" single, semidouble, or double white, pink, or bright red blooms; smoky fragrance; plants 3–6' × 3–5'; disease-resistant when given plenty of sun and good air circulation; hardy to 10°F (Zone 8).

Most Insect- and Disease-Resistant Roses

'Avandel': repeat-blooming; 1" double pink-yellow blend blooms; fruity fragrance; plant 12"; glossy, dark green leaves; miniature; hardy to −20°F (Zone 5).

'Black Jade': repeat-blooming; 1" double dark red blooms; plant 18–24"; glossy, dark green leaves; miniature; hardy to −20°F (Zone 5).

'Blanc Double de Coubert': repeat-blooming; 3" semidouble white blooms; very fragrant; plant 5' × 4'; leathery, wrinkled leaves with yellow fall color; hips; rugosa; other rugosas are also good; hardy to −40°F (Zone 3).

'Bonica '82' ('Bonica'): repeat-blooming; 2" semi-double pink blooms; 5' × 5'; small leaves; showy hips; hardy to −30°F (Zone 4).

'Bredon': repeat-blooming; 3" double buff yellow blooms; strong fruit fragrance; flowers borne in large sprays; plant 4' × 3'; small, leathery leaves; English rose; hardy to −20°F (Zone 5).

'Carefree Wonder': repeat-blooming; 4" semidouble pink blooms; plant 4' × 4'; glossy leaves; showy hips; hardy to −30°F (Zone 4).

'Celestial': once-blooming; 3" double light pink blooms; very fragrant; plant 5' × 4'; blue-gray leaves on robust plants; showy hips; alba; hardy to −30°F (Zone 4).

'Champlain': repeat-blooming; 2" double deep red blooms; plant 3' × 3'; hardy to −30°F (Zone 4).

'Constance Spry': once-blooming; 3" double pink blooms; myrrh fragrance; plant 10' × 6'; leathery leaves on arching canes; use as shrub or climber; hardy to −30°F (Zone 4).

'David Thompson': repeat-blooming; 3" double deep pink blooms; fragrant; plant 3' × 3'; leathery, wrinkled leaves; rugosa; hardy to −40°F (Zone 3).

'Dortmund': repeat-blooming; 3" single bright red blooms with white eye; fragrant; plant 10' × 6'; glossy, dark green leaves on upright canes; use as shrub or climber; hardy to −20°F (Zone 5).

'Frau Dagmar Hastrup' ('Frau Dagmar Hartopp'): repeat-blooming; 3" single light pink blooms; strong clove fragrance; plant 4' × 3'; wrinkled leaves; showy hips; rugosa; hardy to −40°F (Zone 3).

(continued)

Roses for Special Situations—*Continued*

'Geranium': once-blooming; 2" single bright orange-scarlet blooms with showy golden stamens; plant 8' × 6'; gray-green leaves and large thorns on upright canes; orange-red, flagon-shaped hips; also consider the similar single red 'Highdownensis'; hardy to −30°F (Zone 4).

'Graham Thomas': repeat-blooming; 3" double yellow blooms; tea fragrance; plant 8' × 5'; light green leaves on slender canes; English rose; hardy to −20°F (Zone 5).

'John Cabot': repeat-blooming; 3" double deep pink-red blooms; plant 8' × 6'; use as shrub or climber; hardy to −40°F (Zone 3).

'John Davis': repeat-blooming; 3" double pink blooms; spicy fragrance; flowers in large clusters; plant 6' × 4'; glossy, leathery leaves on arching canes; use as trailing shrub or small climber; hardy to −40°F (Zone 3).

'Konigin von Danemark': once-blooming; 3" very double quartered pink blooms; very fragrant; plant 5' × 4'; coarse gray-green leaves; thorny plant with open habit; alba; hardy to −30°F (Zone 4).

'Magic Carrousel': repeat-blooming; 2" double white blooms with red edges; plant 30"; shiny green to bronze leaves; miniature; hardy to −20°F (Zone 5).

'Mary Rose': repeat-blooming; 4" double pink blooms; damask fragrance; plant 4' × 4'; compact, robust stems; English rose; hardy to −30°F (Zone 4).

'Pacesetter': repeat-blooming; 1" double white blooms; fragrant; plant 18–24"; dark green leaves; miniature; hardy to −20°F (Zone 5).

Rosa glauca (formerly *R. rubrifolia*): once-blooming; 1" single bright pink blooms; plant 6' × 5'; gray-green leaves with reddish iridescence; long purple-red hips; good fall color; hardy to −50°F (Zone 2).

'Stanwell Perpetual': repeat-blooming; 3" double pale pink blooms fading to white; fragrant; blooms are borne along canes; plant 4' × 4'; ferny, dull green leaves; hardy to −40°F (Zone 3).

'The Fairy': repeat-blooming; 1" double pink blooms; great quantities of flowers; plant 2' × 3'; abundant tiny, glossy leaves; polyantha; hardy to −30°F (Zone 4).

'William Baffin': repeat-blooming; 3" semidouble deep pink blooms; plant 8' × 6'; disease-resistant leaves; use as a shrub or climber; hardy to −40°F (Zone 3).

Most Fragrant Roses

Bourbon roses: somewhat repeat-blooming; 3–4" very double white, pink, purple, crimson, or striped blooms; plants 3–5' × 3–5'; susceptible to mildew and blackspot; hardiness varies from −10° (Zone 6) to −20°F (Zone 5).

Cabbage roses (*Rosa centifolia* cultivars): once-blooming; 3" very double pink white, crimson, or mauve blooms; sweetly fragrant; plants 3–6' × 3–5'; hardy to −30°F (Zone 4).

'Chrysler Imperial': repeat-blooming; 5" double deep red blooms; damask fragrance; plant 5' × 3'; susceptible to mildew in cool, wet weather; hybrid tea; hardy to −10°F (Zone 6).

Damask roses: somewhat repeat-blooming; 3" semidouble to double pink or white blooms; attar of roses fragrance; plants 4–7' × 3–6'; arching canes; hardiness varies from −30° (Zone 4) to −40°F (Zone 3).

your site and start "seeing" roses in it. You'll find six exciting garden designs featuring roses for every landscape use—a perennial garden, shrub border, herb garden, island bed, entrance garden, and even a patio or deck design—beginning on page 39. These doable designs should provide plenty of food for thought, especially about new ways to use roses and exciting ways to combine roses with other plants in your landscape.

USING ROSES IN THE LANDSCAPE

Once you've summed up all the ways you can use roses in your landscape, it's time to review the possibilities in more detail. If you find yourself getting a little fuzzy about rose classifications as you look at these landscape suggestions, refer back to "Understanding Old

'Double Delight': repeat-blooming; 5" double creamy white blooms with red edge; spicy fragrance; plant 4' × 3'; susceptible to mildew in cool, wet weather; hybrid tea; hardy to −10°F (Zone 6).

English roses: once-blooming or repeat-blooming; 1–4" single, semidouble, or double white, pink, red, yellow, or apricot blooms; fragrance varies, but most cultivars selected for "old rose" fragrance; plants 2–8' × 2–8'; hardiness varies from −10° (Zone 6) to −30°F (Zone 4).

'Fragrant Cloud': repeat-blooming; 5" double coral-red blooms; damask fragrance; highly fragrant; plant 5' × 3'; dark green, glossy foliage; hybrid tea; hardy to −10°F (Zone 6).

'Fragrant Memory': repeat-blooming; 5" double lavender-pink blooms; damask fragance; extremely fragrant; plant 5' × 3'; light green leaves; hybrid tea; hardy to −10°F (Zone 6).

Hybrid perpetual roses: repeat-blooming; 3–4" semidouble to double white, pink, or maroon blooms; plants 4–5' × 3–4'; 'Frau Karl Druschki' is not fragrant; hardy to −30°F (Zone 4).

'Mister Lincoln': repeat-blooming; 5" double dark red blooms; very fragrant; plant 5' × 3'; very glossy leaves on thorny canes; hybrid tea; hardy to −20°F (Zone 5).

Moss roses: once-blooming or repeat-blooming; 3" double white, pink, or red blooms; highly fragrant; plants 4–6' × 4'; mossy buds are also fragrant; hardy to −30°F (Zone 4).

Noisette roses: repeat-blooming; 1–3" semidouble to double white, yellow, or pink blooms; fragrant; plants 3–15' × 2–5'; most cultivars are best as climbers; disease-resistant; hardy to 0°F (Zone 7).

'Paradise': repeat-blooming; 4" double mauve blooms with red edges; delightfully fragrant; plant 4' × 2½'; dark green, glossy leaves; susceptible to mildew in cool, wet weather; hybrid tea; hardy to −10°F (Zone 6).

Portland roses: repeat-blooming; 3" double pink or red blooms; plants 3–4' × 2–3'; compact, rounded plants with smooth canes; hardy to −10°F (Zone 6).

Rosa alba cultivars: once-blooming; 3" semidouble to double white or pink blooms; very fragrant; plants 4–8' × 4–8'; disease-resistant blue-green leaves; reliably hardy to −30°F (Zone 4) but will often withstand to −40°F (Zone 3).

Rosa gallica cultivars: once-blooming; 2–4" single or double pink, mauve, maroon, or striped blooms; plants 3–5' × 3–4'; bristly, suckering canes; hardy to −30°F (Zone 4).

Rosa rugosa cultivars: repeat-blooming; 3" single, semidouble, or double pink, purple, white, or yellow blooms; strong clove fragrance; plants 3–6' × 3–6'; large red hips; species is hardy to −50°F (Zone 2); most cultivars range from −20° (Zone 5) to −40°F (Zone 3).

Rosa spinosissima cultivars: species is once-blooming, but most cultivars are repeat-blooming; 1–2" single, semidouble, or double white, pink, or yellow blooms; fragrant; plants 3–4' × 3–4'; species and most cultivars are hardy to −40°F (Zone 3), but some are hardy only to −20°F (Zone 5); best known and hardiest cultivar is 'Stanwell Perpetual'.

'Tiffany': repeat-blooming; 4" double pink blooms; highly fragrant; plant 4' × 2'; dark green, glossy leaves; hybrid tea; hardy to −10°F (Zone 6).

Roses" on page 6, "Best Species Roses for Gardens" on page 15, and "Modern Roses Demystified" on page 16.

The Rose Garden. The time-honored way to use roses in the landscape is as a bedding plant in a rose garden. If your heart is set on one, don't grow the roses all by themselves like a crop. A bed with nothing in it but roses will attract pests and diseases, and it will look dull when the roses have finished blooming. Instead, underplant your roses with herbs like lavender and catmint (*Nepeta × faassenii*) for a lovely contrast. For a formal rose garden or border that will look best for the longest time, choose a mixture of repeat-blooming roses, including hybrid teas, floribundas, grandifloras, miniatures, shrubs, rugosas, polyanthas, hybrid perpetuals, and repeat-blooming old garden roses.

Perennial and Shrub Borders. In mixed borders, where roses share the billing with other plants, multi-seasonal interest is not critical for each rose—other plants can easily take over when rose bloom is past. In a perennial or shrub border, you can base your choice of roses on color, plant and flower form, and personal preference. The shrub, old garden, species, and grandiflora roses are all excellent choices.

Structures. You may want to enhance or obscure a fence, arbor, trellis, pergola, wall, building, or other structure with roses. In either case, the tall climbers, ramblers, and more aggressive shrub and old roses are ideal. Use the shorter climbers for low fences or train them on pillars. Miniature climbers have a powerful impact for their diminutive size, especially if you use them where you'll appreciate their delicate blooms at close range, such as on a mailbox or lamppost. Think about combining roses with other climbers like clematis for even more beauty and bloom, and underplant them with cheerful annuals in complementary colors or with cool, handsome foliage plants like hostas to create ground-level interest.

Groundcovers. Although not as impenetrable as more traditional groundcovers, sprawling roses like *Rosa wichuraiana*, climbing roses like 'New Dawn', and some of the Meidiland landscape rose cultivars like 'Alba Meidiland' make colorful, effective groundcovers. They're most effective if you install them with a combination of plastic mulch and an organic mulch like bark chips, or with a thick organic mulch like shredded leaves.

Edgings. Rose edgings or low borders are useful along walks and paths, around terraces, and for outlining beds. The best roses for edging are miniatures and small cultivars of shrub roses, especially polyanthas.

Containers. Roses look lovely in containers. The miniature roses and shorter sprawling cultivars are graceful in hanging baskets. You can also grow roses in containers on decks, terraces, porches, and patios, and throughout the yard. The smaller-growing types such as miniatures are particularly effective, as are the floribundas and polyanthas. I like to combine roses with attractive annuals like ivy geraniums, annual candytuft, sweet alyssum, and petunias for two-story color, or create a more subtle look with herbs like prostrate rosemary or creeping thyme. Overwintering of potted roses in colder climates requires some effort, though, so be prepared to bring them indoors or provide protection if you live where temperatures dip below 20°F. (For winter protection techniques, see Chapter 4.)

Hedges. The shrub, old garden, and taller grandiflora roses are perfect for creating hedges as a background, screen, or barrier. Although the plants will lose their leaves in winter, the thorny branches will still create a physical barrier and shelter for wildlife. In addition, many of these roses have beautiful hips in fall and winter, enhancing the winter landscape and attracting birds to your yard.

Choosing Roses for Low Maintenance

Bear in mind low maintenance when you choose your roses. Look to the shrub roses first for trouble-free growing, especially the rugosas, polyanthas, and Meidiland roses. Then consider the hardy, pest-resistant cultivars of the old garden roses, the species roses, and the most pest- and disease-resistant of the modern hybrid teas, floribundas, grandifloras, and miniatures. You'll find some of the best in "Roses for Special Situations" on page 24 and in "Best Roses for Landscape Use" on page 29.

Choosing Roses for Color, Form, and Fragrance

When you've decided where you want to put roses—and therefore what shape or type of plant you want—you can narrow your selection further by focusing on the flowers. Do you have favorites? Is a rose only a rose for you if it's a double red? Or do you want a particular color to go with other flowers or features? A yellow, white, or peach rose might look a lot better in front of an orange brick wall than a red or pink rose.

The species and older roses tend more toward shades of pink, white, and mauve, with a few yellows, an orange here and there, and some very deep purple and striped flowers. Species and old rose flowers may be flat single or semi-double flowers, or many-petaled doubles that are cupped, globular, or quartered. More recent hybrids include many more reds, oranges, and yellows, as well as pinks, whites, and bicolors. The form of many of these modern rose flowers is high-centered, with long inner petals forming a prominent central cone that rises from a flatter cup of outer petals—the classic hybrid tea shape.

Fragrance is also an important aspect, whether you're enjoying your roses in the garden or indoors. Although it's generally true that the older types seem more fragrant than new roses,

(continued on page 35)

Best Roses for Landscape Use

When you want a rose for a specific land-scape use, like a climber for a trellis or a shrub for a rose hedge, the choices can seem endless and con-fusing. How can you tell which roses make good hedges? I've demystified the selection process by providing lists of the best roses for groundcovers, borders and low hedges, hedges, walls, fences, and pillars, massing, special landscape effects, and mixed flower borders. Just find the heading you're looking for and you'll have your roses at a glance!

Recommended Roses for Groundcovers

Groundcover roses aren't really short. Instead, they're flat—the long canes lie on the ground, rather than forming an upright or fountaining bush. The best groundcover roses cover the ground thick-ly to help choke out weeds. These roses all make lovely groundcovers.

'Charles Albanel': repeat-blooming; flowers semi-double mauve-red; plant 2' x 5'; disease-resistant; showy hips; rugosa; hardy to –50°F (Zone 2).

'Max Graf': once-blooming; flowers single pink, fra-grant; plant 2' x 8'; disease-resistant; hardy to –30°F (Zone 4).

Meidiland Series: repeat-blooming; flowers single or double white, red, pink, or scarlet, 2–4" wide; plants 2–4' x 6'; disease-resistant; showy hips; hardy to –30°F (Zone 4).

'Red Cascade': repeat-blooming; flowers double dark red, 1" wide; plant 1' x 3'; small leaves; miniature; hardy to –20°F (Zone 5).

Rosa x *paulii*: once-blooming; flowers single white, fragrant; plant 3' x 10'; disease-resistant; good fall color; best on own roots; pink-flowered variety (*R.* x *paulii* var. *rosea*) available; hardy to –50°F (Zone 2).

'Sea Foam': repeat-blooming; flowers double creamy white, 2" wide; plant 2' x 8'; small, leath-ery leaves; disease-resistant; hardy to –30°F (Zone 4).

'Snow Carpet': repeat-blooming; flowers double white, 1" wide; plant 1' x 3'; miniature; hardy to –20°F (Zone 5).

'The Fairy': repeat-blooming; flowers double pink, 1" wide; plant 2' x 4'; tiny leaves; disease-resistant; polyantha; hardy to –30°F (Zone 4).

Recommended Roses for Low Hedges

These roses are more upright than ground-cover roses but still reach mature heights of only 1 to 4 feet. Most floribundas, polyanthas, low shrubs, and miniatures grow beautifully as low hedges. They make a boundary that is well delin-eated but still keeps the view. Here are some of my favorites.

'Anabell': repeat-blooming; flowers double orange-silver blend, 4" wide; fragrant; plant 3' x 2'; dis-ease-resistant; hardy to –20°F (Zone 5).

'Avandel': repeat-blooming; flowers double yellow with pink, 1" wide; very fragrant; plant 1' x 1'; disease-resistant; miniature; hardy to –20°F (Zone 5).

'Bredon': repeat-blooming; flowers double apricot, 2½" wide; fruity fragrance; plant 3' x 3'; rough, leathery leaves; disease-resistant; English rose; hardy to –20°F (Zone 5).

'Escapade': repeat-blooming; flowers semidouble magenta-rose and white, 3" wide; plant 3' x 2'; light green leaves; disease-resistant; hardy to –20°F (Zone 5).

'Magic Carrousel': repeat-blooming; flowers semi-double white with red edges, 2" wide; plant 18" x 2'; disease-resistant; miniature; hardy to –20°F (Zone 5).

'Mary Marshall': repeat-blooming; flowers double deep coral, 1½" wide; plant 1' x 1'; disease-resistant; miniature; hardy to –20°F (Zone 5).

'Peaches'n'Cream': repeat-blooming; flowers dou-ble pink and cream blend, 1½" wide; plant 18" x 18"; dark green leaves; disease-resistant; minia-ture; hardy to –20°F (Zone 5).

'Popcorn': repeat-blooming; flowers single white, ¾" wide; honey fragrance; plant 1' x 1'; glossy leaves; disease-resistant; miniature; hardy to –20°F (Zone 5).

'Regensberg': repeat-blooming; flowers double white mottled and edged with pink, 3" wide; apple fragrance; plant 2' x 2'; McGredy Hand-Painted Series; hardy to –10°F (Zone 6).

'Sunsprite': repeat-blooming; flowers double yellow, 3" wide; plant 2' x 2'; disease-resistant; hardy to –30°F (Zone 4).

(continued)

Best Roses for Landscape Use—Continued

'The Fairy': repeat-blooming; flowers double pink, 1" wide; plant 2' × 4'; tiny leaves; disease-resistant; polyantha; hardy to −30°F (Zone 4).

'Wife of Bath': repeat-blooming; flowers double pink, 3" wide; myrrh fragrance; plant 3' × 3'; disease-resistant; English rose; hardy to −20°F (Zone 5).

Recommended Roses for Tall Hedges

Roses can make a thick, beautiful blooming tall hedge—far more attractive than privet or forsythia. You simply have to choose the right rose—one that's upright, densely bushy, and disease-resistant, so it that doesn't need coddling. These roses all grow 4 to 8 feet tall (perfect hedge size). You can also mix roses of similar size and compatible flower colors (if you choose roses that bloom at the same time), or mix roses with other shrubs, for a more informal, colorful hedge.

'Bloomin' Easy': repeat-blooming; flowers double bright red, 3" wide; plant 5' × 4'; dense, dark green leaves; disease-resistant; hardy to −20°F (Zone 5).

'Bonica '82' ('Bonica'): repeat-blooming; flowers double pink, 2" wide; plant 4–6' × 4'; small, glossy leaves; disease-resistant; hardy to −20°F (Zone 5).

'Carefree Beauty': repeat-blooming; flowers semidouble coral-pink, 4" wide; plant 6' × 5'; olive green leaves; disease-resistant; showy hips; hardy to −30°F (Zone 4).

'Carefree Wonder': repeat-blooming; flowers semidouble pink with white reverse, 4" wide; plant 5' × 4'; disease-resistant; hardy to −30°F (Zone 4).

Eglantine or sweetbriar roses (*Rosa eglanteria* and cultivars): once-blooming; flowers single, semidouble, or double pink, red, white, or yellow, 1" wide; very fragrant; plants 8–10' × 8'; showy hips; wet leaves smell of apples; hardy to −30°F (Zone 4).

'John Davis': repeat-blooming; flowers double pink; plant 5' × 5'; disease-resistant; hardy to −40°F (Zone 3).

'Mary Rose': repeat-blooming; flowers very double pink, 4" wide; very fragrant; plant 4' × 4'; English

rose; hardy to −20°F (Zone 5).

***Rosa alba* cultivars:** once-blooming; flowers semidouble or double white or pink; very fragrant; plant 4–6' × 4–8'; blue-green leaves; disease-resistant; hardy to −40°F (Zone 3).

***Rosa rugosa* and cultivars:** repeat-blooming; flowers single, semidouble, or double white, pink, red, or yellow, 3–4" wide; very fragrant; plant 3–6' × 3–6'; disease-resistant; very showy hips; hardiness varies from −30° (Zone 4) to −50°F (Zone 2), depending on the cultivar.

***Rosa sericea* var. *pteracantha*:** once-blooming; flowers single white; plant 8' × 8'; fernlike leaves; large, winged prickles, red and translucent when young; cut back to encourage new growth; hardy to −10°F (Zone 6).

***Rosa spinosissima* and cultivars:** most once-blooming but a few repeat-blooming; flowers single, semidouble, or double white, yellow, pink; fragrant; plant 3–4' × 3–4'; disease-resistant; hardiness varies from −20° (Zone 5) to −40°F (Zone 3), depending on the cultivar.

'William Baffin': repeat-blooming; flowers semidouble bright pink, 4" wide; plant 8' × 8'; disease-resistant; hardy to −30°F (Zone 4).

Recommended Roses for Walls, Fences, and Pillars

One of the most spectacular ways to showcase roses is to grow them spilling over a fence or trained up a wall or pillar. The roses I've chosen will give you a rainbow of colors to choose from. Just be sure to pick a rose that won't clash with the material of your house or fence! (Red roses might be lost against a dark brick wall, and pink roses might clash with orange or yellow brick, for example.) I've given only the heights of these roses, since it's really how "long" they are, not how wide, that matters when you're training them to a fence, pillar, or trellis.

'Alberic Barbier': once-blooming; flowers double cream, 3" wide; green apple fragrance; plant 20' tall; blackspot-resistant; rambler; hardy to −20°F (Zone 5).

'Alchymist': once-blooming; flowers very double apricot, 3–4" wide; fragrant; plant 8–12' tall; disease-resistant; stiff, use as pillar; Kordes rose from Canada; hardy to −20°F (Zone 5).

'**Blaze**': repeat-blooming; flowers semidouble scarlet, 2–3" wide; plant 10–15' tall; hardy to −30°F (Zone 4).

'**Climbing Cecile Brunner**': some repeat-blooming; flowers double pale pink, 1½" wide; plant 10–15' tall; disease-resistant; hardy to −20°F (Zone 5).

'**Compassion**': repeat-blooming; flowers double salmon pink to apricot; plant 10–15' tall; good basal growth; hardy to −20°F (Zone 5).

'**Constance Spry**': once-blooming; flowers double pink, 4–5" wide; myrrh fragrance; plant 6–10' tall; blackspot-resistant; hardy to −30°F (Zone 4).

'**Dortmund**': repeat-blooming if deadheaded; flowers single red with white eye, 3" wide; fragrant; plant 10–12' tall; disease-resistant; showy hips; hardy to −30°F (Zone 4).

'**Dublin Bay**': repeat-blooming; flowers double red, 4" wide; light fragrance; plant 8–12' tall; very disease-resistant; hardy to −20°F (Zone 5).

'**Eden**': repeat-blooming; flowers double pink and yellow, 3" wide; fragrant; plant 6–8' tall; disease-resistant; hardy to −20°F (Zone 5).

'**Henry Kelsey**': repeat-blooming; flowers double deep red; spicy fragrance; plant 6–10' tall; disease-resistant; hardy to −30°F (Zone 4).

'**John Cabot**': repeat-blooming; flowers double reddish-pink, 2–3" wide; fragrant; plant 6–10' tall; disease-resistant; hardy to −30°F (Zone 4).

'**New Dawn**': repeat-blooming; flowers semidouble pale pink; plant 12–15' tall; very disease-resistant; hardy to −20°F (Zone 5).

'**Parade**': repeat-blooming; flowers double deep pink, 4" wide; fragrant; plant 8–12' tall; disease-resistant; hardy to −20°F (Zone 5).

'**Sanders White Rambler**': once-blooming; flowers double white, 1" wide; fragrant; plant 10–15' tall; also consider single white 'Seagull' and semidouble white 'The Garland'; hardy to −20°F (Zone 5).

'**Veilchenblau**': once-blooming; flowers semidouble purplish mauve and white, 1" wide; fragrant; color best in light shade; plant 6–10' tall; hardy to −20°F (Zone 5).

'**White Dawn**': repeat-blooming; flowers double white, 3" wide; fragrant; plant 15' tall; hardy to −20°F (Zone 5).

'**William Baffin**': repeat-blooming; flowers semidouble deep pink, 3" wide; plant 6–9' tall; disease-resistant; Kordes hybrid from Canada; hardy to −30°F (Zone 4).

'**Zephirine Drouhin**': repeat-blooming; flowers semidouble bright pink; fragrant; plant 8' tall; few thorns; hardy to −10°F (Zone 6).

Recommended Roses for Massing

If you want a splash of summer color, grow a group of roses together in a mass. Use all one cultivar rather than mixing them, so you don't dilute the effect. Three to five bushes is usually enough to create quite an impact. Shrub roses, floribundas, polyanthas, miniatures, and bushy, low-growing hybrid teas and grandifloras are usually best for massing, since they are repeat-bloomers and will give a long season of color.

'**Celestial**': once-blooming; flowers double light pink, 3" wide; very fragrant; plant 5' × 4'; blue-gray leaves on robust plants; showy hips; disease-resistant; alba; hardy to −30°F (Zone 4).

'**Champlain**': repeat-blooming; flowers double deep red, 2" wide; light fragrance; plant 3' × 3'; disease-resistant; hardy to −30°F (Zone 4).

'**Frau Dagmar Hastrup**' ('**Frau Dagmar Hartopp**'): repeat-blooming; flowers single light pink, 3" wide; strong clove fragrance; plant 4' × 3'; wrinkled leaves; showy hips; disease-resistant; rugosa; hardy to −40°F (Zone 3).

'**Fruhlingsmorgen**': once-blooming; flowers single pink with yellow base, 3" wide; fragrant; plant 6' × 5'; Kordes hybrid; also consider related 'Fruhlingsgold'; hardy to −30°F (Zone 4).

'**Henry Hudson**': repeat-blooming; flowers double white, 3" wide; very fragrant; plant 3' × 3'; rugosa; suckers readily; needs deadheading; disease-resistant; hardy to −50°F (Zone 2).

Hybrid musks: repeat-blooming; flowers single or double white, pink, or yellow, 2–4" wide; fragrant; plants 2–8' × 2–8'; can be pruned hard; hardy to −10°F (Zone 6).

(continued)

Best Roses for Landscape Use—Continued

'Konigin von Danemark': once-blooming; flowers very double quartered pink, 3" wide; very fragrant; plant 5' × 4'; coarse gray-green leaves; thorny plant with open habit; disease-resistant; alba; hardy to −30°F (Zone 4).

'Morden Centennial': repeat-blooming; flowers double pink, 3" wide; fragrant; flowers in large clusters; blooms on new wood; plant 5' × 4'; disease-resistant leaves; can be pruned hard; hardy to −40°F (Zone 3).

'Nearly Wild': repeat-blooming; flowers single pink, 2" wide; fragrant; plant 3' × 3'; disease-resistant; floribunda; hardy to −40°F (Zone 3).

'Nevada': repeat-blooming; flowers single white with some pink tinges, 4" wide; plant 8' × 7'; dense growth; disease-resistant; also consider 'Marguerite Hilling'; hardy to −20°F (Zone 5).

'Stanwell Perpetual': repeat-blooming; flowers double pale pink fading to white, 3" wide; fragrant; blooms are borne along canes; plant 4' × 4'; ferny, dull green leaves; hardy to −40°F (Zone 3).

'The Fairy': repeat-blooming; flowers double pink, 1" wide; plant 2' × 4'; tiny leaves; disease-resistant; polyantha; hardy to −30°F (Zone 4).

Recommended Roses for Mixed Flower Borders

Roses are natural partners in the perennial or herb garden, adding height, texture, fragrance, and (depending on the cultivars you choose) season-long bloom. Consider shrub roses, old garden roses, floribundas, polyanthas, and miniatures when you plan your next flower bed. Plant tall roses in the back of the bed, shorter ones in the middle, and minis in the front, the same way you'd use perennials. In an island bed designed to be seen from all sides, put the tallest plants in the center and work down from there.

'All That Jazz': repeat-blooming; flowers semidouble coral-salmon, 5" wide; fragrant; plant 5' × 4'; glossy, dark green, disease-resistant leaves; floribunda; hardy to −10°F (Zone 6).

'American Rose Centennial': repeat-blooming; flowers double white edged in pink, 1" wide; long-lasting flowers; plant 15–18"; dark green leaves; miniature; hardy to −20°F (Zone 5).

'Ballerina': repeat-blooming; flowers single pink with white center, 2" wide; plant 4' × 4'; disease-resistant; hybrid musk; hardy to −10°F (Zone 6).

'Blanc Double de Coubert': repeat-blooming; flowers semidouble white, 3" wide; very fragrant; plant 5' × 4'; leathery, wrinkled leaves with yellow fall color; hips; rugosa; disease-resistant; hardy to −40°F (Zone 3).

'Cecile Brunner': repeat-blooming; flowers double high-centered pale pink, 1" wide; fragrant; plant 3' × 2'; small, dark green, disease-resistant leaves on slender stems; polyantha; hardy to −30°F (Zone 4).

'Celsiana': once-blooming; flowers semidouble pale pink, 4" wide; very fragrant; plant 4' × 4'; downy gray-green, disease-resistant leaves; damask; hardy to −40°F (Zone 3).

'Champlain': repeat-blooming; flowers double velvety deep red, 2" wide; light fragrance; very floriferous; plant 3' × 3'; disease-resistant sparse foliage; Explorer series; hardy to −30°F (Zone 4).

'Dainty Bess': repeat-blooming; flowers single pink with showy maroon stamens, 4" wide; fragrant; plant 4' × 3'; leathery, disease-resistant leaves; hybrid tea; hardy to −20°F (Zone 5).

'David Thompson': repeat-blooming; flowers double deep pink, 3" wide; fragrant; plant 3' × 3'; leathery, wrinkled leaves; disease-resistant; rugosa; hardy to −40°F (Zone 3).

'Dresden Doll': repeat-blooming; flowers semidouble pale pink with showy golden stamens, 1½" wide; plant 18–24"; heavily mossed buds; miniature moss; hardy to −30°F (Zone 4).

'Duchesse de Brabant': repeat-blooming; flowers double rosy pink, 3" wide; very fragrant; plant 4' × 3'; disease-resistant; tea rose; hardy to −10°F (Zone 6).

'Escapade': repeat-blooming; flowers semidouble magenta-rose with white center, 3" wide; light fragrance; plant 3' × 2'; light green leaves; disease-resistant; floribunda; hardy to −20°F (Zone 5).

'Frau Dagmar Hastrup' ('Frau Dagmar Hartopp'): repeat-blooming; flowers single light pink, 3" wide; strong clove fragrance; plant 4' × 3'; wrinkled leaves; showy hips; disease-resistant; rugosa; hardy to −40°F (Zone 3).

'**Golden Wings**': repeat-blooming; flowers single yellow, 4" wide; light fragrance; plant 5' × 4'; disease-resistant; also consider 'Windrush'; shrub; hardy to −20°F (Zone 5).

'**Graham Thomas**': repeat-blooming; flowers double yellow, 3" wide; tea fragrance; plant 8' × 5'; light green leaves on slender canes; disease-resistant; English rose; hardy to −20°F (Zone 5).

'**Gruss an Aachen**': repeat-blooming; flowers double pale pink, 3" wide; fragrant; plant 3' × 3'; very tough; old-rose appearance; few thorns; floribunda; hardy to −20°F (Zone 5).

'**Iceberg**': repeat-blooming; flowers double white, 3" wide; fragrant; plant 4' × 4'; susceptible to blackspot, but very resistant to mildew; floribunda; hardy to −20°F (Zone 5).

'**Ispahan**': once-blooming; flowers double pink, 3" wide; very fragrant; plant 4' × 3'; arching; disease-resistant; damask; hardy to −40°F (Zone 3).

'**Lilian Austin**': repeat-blooming; flowers salmon-pink with showy gold stamens, 3" wide; fragrant; plant 4' × 4'; disease-resistant leaves; English rose; hardy to −20°F (Zone 5).

'**Little White Pet**' ('White Pet'): repeat-blooming; flowers double white, 1" wide; flowers borne in large clusters; plant 2' × 2½'; symmetrical mound of disease-resistant foliage; hardy to −10°F (Zone 6).

'**Margaret Merril**': repeat-blooming; flowers double white with showy golden stamens, 3" wide; fragrant; flowers borne in clusters; plant 2½' × 2'; dark green leaves; floribunda; hardy to −10°F (Zone 6).

'**Mrs. John Laing**': repeat-blooming; flowers double pink, 4" wide; fragrant; plant 4' × 3'; large gray-green, disease-resistant leaves; hybrid perpetual; hardy to −30°F (Zone 4).

'**Monte Cassino**': repeat-blooming; flowers semidouble deep pink, 3" wide; clove fragrance; plant 3' × 3'; compact plants with dark green, wrinkled, disease-resistant leaves; showy hips; hardy to −40°F (Zone 3).

'**Nathalie Nypels**': repeat-blooming; flowers semidouble rose-pink with coral shading, 2" wide; fragrant; plant 2' × 2'; dark green, disease-resistant leaves; polyantha; hardy to −30°F (Zone 4).

'**Nearly Wild**': repeat-blooming; flowers single pink, 2" wide; fragrant; nonstop bloom; plant 3' × 3'; disease-resistant; floribunda; hardy to −40°F (Zone 3).

'**Old Glory**': repeat-blooming; flowers double red, 1" wide; plant 16–20"; dark green, vigorous foliage; miniature; hardy to −20°F (Zone 5).

'**Pacesetter**': repeat-blooming; flowers very double high-centered white, 1" wide; fragrant; plant 18–24"; abundant dark green leaves; disease-resistant; miniature; hardy to −20°F (Zone 5).

'**Pink Meidiland**': repeat-blooming; flowers single dark pink, 2" wide; nonstop flowers; plant 4' × 3½'; disease-resistant leaves; showy orange-red hips; shrub rose; hardy to −30°F (Zone 4).

'**Red Coat**': repeat-blooming; flowers semidouble red, 4" wide; plant 5' × 4'; disease-resistant; floribunda; hardy to −20°F (Zone 5).

'**Salet**': repeat-blooming; flowers double rose-pink, 3" wide; sweet musk fragrance; plant 4' × 3'; sparse, soft leaves on bristly, arching canes; crimson-mossed buds; moss rose; hardy to −30°F (Zone 4).

'**Single's Better**': repeat-blooming; flowers single bright red with showy yellow stamens, 1" wide; fragrant; plant 15–18"; mossed buds; glossy leaves; miniature; hardy to −20°F (Zone 5).

'**Snow Bride**': repeat-blooming; flowers double white, 1" wide; plant 15–18"; dark green foliage; miniature; hardy to −20°F (Zone 5).

'**Sparrieshoop**': repeat-blooming; flowers single pink, 4" wide; plant 5' × 4'; upright, bushy; disease-resistant; Kordes hybrid; hardy to −30°F (Zone 4).

'**Stanwell Perpetual**': repeat-blooming; flowers double pale pink fading to white, 3" wide; fragrant; blooms are borne along canes; plant 4' × 4'; ferny, dull green leaves; disease-resistant; hardy to −40°F (Zone 3).

'**The Fairy**': repeat-blooming; flowers double pink, 1" wide; plant 2' × 4'; abundant tiny, glossy leaves; disease-resistant; polyantha; hardy to −30°F (Zone 4).

'**The Prince**': repeat-blooming; flowers double crimson to dark purple, 3" wide; very fragrant; plant 2½' × 2½'; dark, dense foliage; English rose; hardy to −20°F (Zone 5).

'**Valerie Jeanne**': repeat-blooming; flowers double magenta-pink, 1" wide; plant 15–18"; vigorous, easy to grow; miniature; hardy to −20°F (Zone 5).

(continued)

Best Roses for Landscape Use—Continued

'Wild Flower': repeat-blooming; flowers single yellow with touch of pink, 1" wide; Scotch briar fragrance; plant 2' × 2½'; small, disease-resistant leaves on thin, arching canes; English rose; hardy to −20°F (Zone 5).

'Winsome': repeat-blooming; flowers double high-centered deep magenta, 2" wide; plant 16–22"; semiglossy, dark green, disease-resistant leaves; miniature; hardy to −20°F (Zone 5).

'Yellow Button': repeat-blooming; flowers double yellow, 1" wide; fragrant; plant 2½' × 2½'; spreading growth; English rose; hardy to −20°F (Zone 5).

Recommended Roses with Special Landscape Qualities

Sometimes you need a special feature for your landscape—showy berries or bark, glossy or purple foliage, weeping or columnar form. Like trees, shrubs, and ornamental grasses, roses can provide many special effects in the landscape—if you pick the right rose. These roses have showy hips or thorns, colorful canes, interesting shapes, outstanding foliage, or other special features. They're the kind of plant you want to spotlight or use for a particular need in the garden. Plant them as specimens where you'll be able to appreciate them. Species, old garden, and shrub roses often make the best specimen plants.

'Apple Jack': some repeat-blooming; flowers semi-double pink, 3" wide; fragrant; flowers in clusters; plant 5' × 5'; vigorous, rounded shrub; showy orange hips; hardy to −30°F (Zone 4).

'Carefree Beauty': repeat-blooming; flowers semi-double coral-pink, 4" wide; fragrant; plant 6' × 5'; olive green leaves; disease-resistant; showy orange-red hips; hardy to −30°F (Zone 4).

'Cerise Bouquet': repeat-blooming; flowers semi-double cerise-crimson, 3" wide; raspberry fragrance; plant 8' × 8'; arching; gray-green, disease-resistant foliage; use as shrub or climber; Kordes hybrid; hardy to −30°F (Zone 4).

Chestnut rose (*Rosa roxburghii*): some repeat-blooming; flowers double bright pink, 2" wide; plant 6' × 5'; very evenly spaced leaves on gray canes with peeling bark; prickly flower buds; showy hips; hardy to −10°F (Zone 6).

'Dunwich Rose': once-blooming; flowers single pale yellow, 2" wide; fragrant; blooms produced along canes; plant 2' × 4'; small, gracefully arching mounds of ferny foliage; hardy to −30°F (Zone 4).

Eglantine or sweetbriar roses (*Rosa eglanteria* and cultivars): once-blooming; flowers single, semidouble, or double pink, red, white, or yellow, 1" wide; very fragrant; plant 8–10' × 8'; small, glossy, disease-resistant leaves; showy hips; wet leaves smell of apples; hardy to −30°F (Zone 4).

Father Hugo's rose (*Rosa hugonis*): once-blooming; flowers single pale yellow, 2" wide; plant 6' × 6'; small light green leaves; hardy to −10°F (Zone 6).

'Harison's Yellow': once-blooming; flowers semidouble yellow, 2" wide; blooms produced along arching canes; plant 6' × 5'; small green leaves; showy hips; hardy to −40°F (Zone 3).

Meidiland Series: repeat-blooming; flowers single or double white, red, pink, or scarlet, 2–4" wide; flowers borne in clusters; plants 2–4' × 6'; disease-resistant; showy hips; hardy to −30°F (Zone 4).

'Prairie Harvest': repeat-blooming; pink buds open to double yellow flowers, 3" wide; fragrant; plant 4' × 3'; dark, leathery, glossy leaves; hardy to −30°F (Zone 4).

***Rosa alba* cultivars:** once-blooming; flowers semidouble or double white or pink, 3" wide; very fragrant; plant 4–6' × 4–8'; blue-green leaves; disease-resistant; graceful plants; hardy to −40°F (Zone 3).

***Rosa glauca* (formerly *R. rubrifolia*):** once-blooming; flowers single, bright pink, starlike, 1" wide; plant 6' × 5'; gray-green leaves with reddish iridescence; long purple-red hips; dark purple canes; good fall color; hardy to −50°F (Zone 2).

Rosa macrantha: once-blooming; flowers single pale pink, 2" wide; flowers born in clusters; plant 5' × 10';

dull, rough leaves on thin, arching canes; showy hips; use as groundcover on banks or for covering stumps; hardy to −20°F (Zone 5).

Rosa macrophylla: once-blooming; flowers single deep pink, 3" wide; plant 12' × 12'; very large leaves on red-brown stems; bristly red flagon-shaped hips; hardy to −20°F (Zone 5).

Rosa moyesii cultivars: once-blooming or repeat-blooming; flowers single or semidouble, pink, red, orange, or white, 2" wide; plant 8' × 7'; large flagon-shaped hips; hardy from −20° (Zone 5) to −30°F (Zone 4).

Rosa × paulii: once-blooming; flowers single white with golden stamens, 3" wide; clove fragrance; plant 3' × 10'; disease-resistant; good fall color; thorny; best on own roots; pink-flowered variety (*R. × paulii* var. *rosea*) available; hardy to −50°F (Zone 2).

Rosa rugosa and cultivars: repeat-blooming; flowers single, semidouble, or double white, pink, red, or yellow, 3–4" wide; most have strong clove fragrance; plant 3–6' × 3–6'; leathery, wrinkled leaves; disease-resistant; very showy large red hips; good fall color; hardiness varies from −30° (Zone 4) to −50°F (Zone 2), depending on the cultivar.

Rosa sericea var. *pteracantha:* once-blooming; flowers single white, 2" wide; plant 8' × 8'; fernlike leaves on arching stems; showy hips; large, winged prickles, red and translucent when young; cut back to encourage new growth; hardy to −10°F (Zone 6).

Rosa spinosissima and cultivars: most once-blooming but a few repeat-blooming; flowers single, semidouble, or double white, yellow, pink, or apricot, 2–4" wide; fragrant; plant 3–4' × 3–4'; blooms are borne along graceful, arching canes; small, fernlike, disease-resistant foliage; showy hips; hardiness varies from −20° (Zone 5) to −40°F (Zone 3), depending on the cultivar.

many newer cultivars have delightful fragrance, and there are old roses without a trace of fragrance. Fortunately, fragrance seems to be back on the rose-breeder's agenda, so we can look forward to more new roses that "smell like a rose."

Extending the Pleasure

Finally, you might be influenced in your choices by how you plan to use your roses. Most of us think of roses as the ultimate cut flowers. And there's hardly a rose that doesn't look lovely in a vase or more humble container. Hybrid tea roses, with their long stems, are ideal cut flowers, but you can use all types of roses as fresh flowers. However, some roses have a longer vase-life than others. For a list of the best roses for cutting, see Chapter 5, "Designing Fresh Rose Arrangements."

If you want to make potpourri or beauty products with your roses, remember that fragrance isn't as straightforward as it seems. The fragrance doesn't always last once the petals are preserved. For more on roses that hold their perfume, see Chapter 9, "Rose Crafts for Scent and Beauty."

If your goal is dried roses for crafts projects, give the miniatures, small-flowered hybrid teas, polyanthas, and shrub roses first priority. Note that roses will change color as they dry, and choose accordingly. Oranges like 'Tropicana' are actually great for drying, since they dry to red. Red roses turn black when they're air-dried, while whites and yellows turn tan to brown. You can hold the color better with silica gel. Turn to Chapter 6, "How to Dry Roses," for detailed drying instructions, and to Chapters 7, "Using Dried Roses," and 8, "Rose Wreaths and Garlands," for a wealth of step-by-step projects.

Chapter 2

Using Roses in Your Landscape

EOPLE AREN'T VERY IMAGINATIVE when it comes to growing roses. We tend to plant our roses all together like a crop. It would be easy to blame Napoleon's Josephine for setting the landscaping style of rose beds that make the typical rose garden look more like a nursery. But the real culprit may be the collector instinct— there are so many rose cultivars available, it's tempting to acquire as many as possible. Or it may be the rose-growing mystique that makes us think roses need so much coddling that they just won't grow with anything else.

Lucky for us, there are lots of great ways to use roses in the landscape. In fact, roses are perfect landscape plants: Think of them as part shrub, part perennial, and part vine. You can grow them with your herbs, in a cottage garden, or in a perennial border or flower bed just like a perennial. You can grow them as a hedge, in a shrub border, or as a specimen, like other shrubs. Or you can train them up a lamppost, trellis, or arbor like a vine. Whether you want to add a dozen or so roses to your yard or you want to make roses be the cornerstone of your landscaping, your imagination is the only limit to creating a garden that's both interesting and beautiful.

When you stop to think about it, roses are really quite adaptable, since they're available in so many shapes, sizes, and colors. Take advan-

tage of roses to solve a wide variety of landscaping dilemmas and needs. There are cultivars that make excellent tall formal hedges, others for loose, open, informal hedges, and still more for low divider plantings. Some roses look splendid when massed, while others make good groundcovers because of their long, sprawling branches. Pillars of roses create a strong vertical element in a new garden with no mature trees or shrubs. Climbing roses can cover a wall or fence, or you can train them to cascade out of a tree. You can plant roses with both deciduous and evergreen shrubs in borders or foundation plantings.

Roses are especially spectacular in a mixed flower border or formal herb garden. And although the most ardent rose enthusiasts may disagree, roses planted in beds showcasing them look even better when combined with low plantings of perennials, herbs, or other plants.

Where do you start the process of designing a yard that includes roses? I'll begin this chapter with some basic, easy-to-use design principles so you can think about the ways roses can fit into your yard, your garden's color scheme, or your other plantings. Then I'll present a gallery of exciting garden designs that feature roses in different ways and settings. You can use my designs as a springboard to think about ways to use roses throughout your yard.

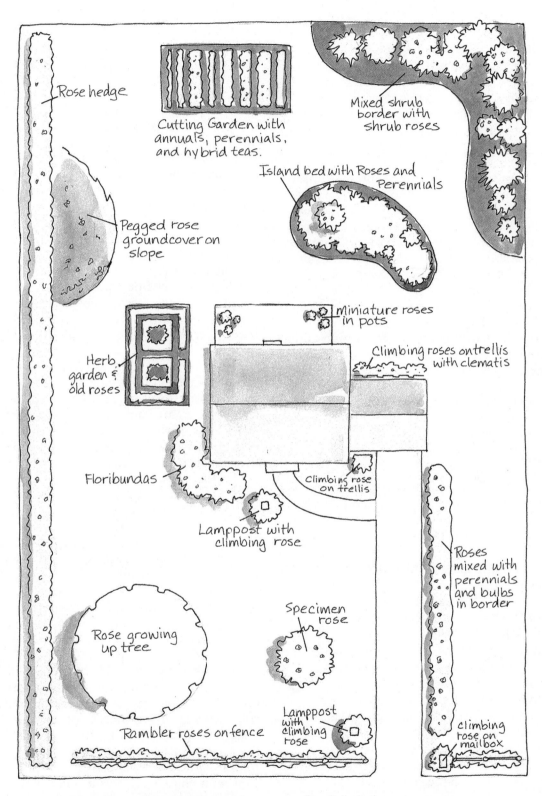

Rose hedge

Cutting Garden with annuals, perennials, and hybrid teas.

Mixed shrub border with shrub roses

Pegged rose groundcover on slope

Island bed with Roses and Perennials

miniature roses in pots

Herb garden & old roses

Climbing roses on trellis with clematis

Floribundas

Climbing rose on trellis

Lamppost with climbing rose

Roses mixed with perennials and bulbs in border

Specimen rose

Rose growing up tree

Lamppost with climbing rose

Rambler roses on fence

climbing rose on mailbox

A whole-yard approach to using roses. Don't limit the way you use roses in your landscape to a bed of hybrid teas. Here are a few of the many ways you can use roses in a typical suburban yard. You might not want to use all these ideas in the same yard, but you can choose the ones that work best with the other landscape features in your own yard.

PLANTING FOR COLOR

Whether you grow roses that bloom once a year or the repeat-blooming types, the main reason for growing roses is their flowers. When you plant roses, you're using color in the landscape. And while it's easier to get away with less-than-ideal color combinations outdoors than in the interiors of our homes, you'll be more satisfied and your garden will look more beautiful if you choose rose colors carefully.

A color wheel, available from art supply stores, will help you understand how to mix colors to create harmonious color combinations. On a color wheel, the three primary colors—yellow, blue, and red—are spaced at equal intervals. The colors on the wheel between the primaries are created when two primary colors are mixed. For example, yellow and blue make green, red and blue become violet, and yellow and red become orange. You can combine the colors on the wheel many different ways, but some combinations are more effective than others. The goal is to use colors that harmonize together rather than clashing with each other.

Choose one of these basic color combinations to give your garden a beautiful, harmonious color scheme:

- Grow roses and other flowers in variations of a single color. For example, you could use the shades (darker tones) and tints (lighter tones) of red—pink and burgundy, for example—as well as true red roses. This color scheme is the most soothing and easiest to use.

- For a slightly more dramatic look, use flowers with colors that are side by side on the color wheel, like red, violet, and blue.

- Colors directly opposite each other on the color wheel, like yellow and violet or blue and orange, are considered complementary. These combinations are very powerful and must be used judiciously—a large mass of complementary flowers can quickly overwhelm a garden, but a small group can add needed punch to a drab area.

- Another effective way to use color is to combine a color with the color that is next to its opposite on the color wheel—for example, blue with yellow-orange or red-orange instead of orange flowers. These color combinations create excitement but aren't as overwhelming as complementary combinations.

Hot Tips and Cool Colors

Pink, the color so often seen in roses, is a tint of red. It is especially attractive in combination with blues and purples. White flowers take on a variety of roles in the garden. White can serve to buffer or unify, but use it in a large enough quantity so that it makes a strong statement rather than a creating a distraction by looking spotty. White and pale pinks are especially good for gardens that are viewed in the evening, as these colors stand out in low light. Don't forget neutral colors—grays, greens, and buffs (very pale yellow can also act as a neutral)—your garden's peacekeepers. You can connect areas with different and potentially clashing color schemes by using large drifts of soothing neutrals.

The color schemes you choose should reflect your personality as well as complement the exterior colors and materials of your home and other plantings. Your color schemes should also be in keeping with the effect you want to convey in your garden. Bright yellows, reds, and oranges—hot colors—draw attention and communicate enthusiasm and cheerfulness. They also make an area appear hotter. Use them as a focal point, perhaps in conjunction with a piece of sculpture or other outdoor art, beside a garden bench or seating area, or at the end of a vista. Don't use these hot colors around a patio where you like to entertain on scorching summer days—your guests will be hot enough without the visual reminder!

Soft pinks, blues, and purples—cool colors—are better for creating a garden of relaxation and contentment. They are ideal for blending with other garden flowers or concealing an unsightly object. In a small garden, these cool colors create an illusion of distance, since they retreat from the eye rather than advancing like hot colors.

Probably the most difficult aspect of incorporating roses into your yard is resisting the one-of-each-color temptation and keeping to a color scheme. If you must have that one orange rose, don't plant it with pink roses just because it's a rose. Instead, place it in another part of the yard where it won't clash—perhaps in company with blues, scarlets, and soft yellows.

You can learn a lot about color and how to use it just by looking around. For ideas and inspiration, study pictures in garden books and magazines, visit other gardens, and note down combinations found in nature.

OTHER DESIGN FACTORS

There's more to designing a rose garden than creating good color combinations. You also need to consider the shape, size, texture, and form of the flowers, the leaves, and the plant as a whole. The high-centered hybrid tea rose with glossy leaves and several tall, stiff stems has a much more formal appearance than a blowsy old-fashioned rose with rough, matte leaves, supple stems, and rounded growth. There are many variations within these two extremes. Once more, rather than lumping all your roses together in one area, use the different types in various parts of your yard where their particular characteristics blend best with other plantings.

One good reason not to grow a bed that's all roses is that the eye quickly tires of repetition—it just gets boring. Rose foliage is medium-textured, not bold like rhododendron leaves and hosta foliage or fine-textured like ferns and feathery artemisias. Mixing these textures, as well as surface textures like glossy and dull, papery and leathery, smooth and ribbed, will hold your eye (and your interest) a lot longer than using a single texture.

Seeing roses growing firsthand is the best way to make sound design choices. Visit public rose gardens, visit and talk with other people in your area who grow roses, and read books, magazines, and catalogs to glean all the information you can before choosing and buying your roses.

A ROSE GARDEN GALLERY

These six garden designs should inspire you to think about ways to use roses in your own landscape. Each is shown as a plot plan and in an illustration that will let you see how the mature garden will look. You'll find a perennial garden with roses mixed in among the perennials; a shrub border featuring shrub roses; an herbal rose garden that features plants for drying (a great help if you enjoy making the flower crafts in Part Two); an island bed; an entrance garden with roses; and a container garden design for a deck or terrace. You can use all these designs in your yard, mix and match to suit your site, or choose one and adapt it for your dream garden.

Perennial Garden with Roses

For those who love flowers, nothing compares to a perennial garden, with its visual feast of colors, textures, and forms. Roses can play an integral part, especially if you choose cultivars that bloom repeatedly through the summer and fall and have a shrubby growth habit. By carefully choosing perennials and roses, you can have flowers for many months of the year in your favorite colors.

This garden design features my own favorite colors and plants. Pinks, blues, and white—with a dash of red for accent—are the colors. The perennials are mainly traditional favorites, but I've added some newer ones for ease of maintenance. Most of the plants have a long bloom season. To extend bloom even more, you can add spring- and fall-blooming bulbs and perennials as well as annuals.

The design itself is small and simple. It could fit into the corner of the house or yard, perhaps surrounded on two sides by a fence or an evergreen hedge. Choose a site with full sun and compost-enriched, well-drained soil. If desired, you could plant it as a straight border rather than with the right angle. The paved flagstone area in front could be constructed with other materials or kept as grass, although I think the paving particularly sets off the plants. The backless bench allows you to enjoy the garden from several perspectives.

The trellis with the climbing bourbon rose 'Zephirine Drouhin' frames the setting. This rose, grown as early as 1868, has bright pink-red flowers, which are produced especially freely once it's well established. For colder areas, substitute 'Chloris', a hardier rose that's also less susceptible to mildew. A tall-growing alba rose, 'Chloris' has fragrant, pale pink flowers and thornless stems like 'Zephirine Drouhin', but it blooms only once a year.

Plants for a Perennial Garden

Among the other roses I've chosen, 'The Fairy' is unsurpassed for its abundance of small pink double flowers, its stamina, and its hardiness. A polyantha rose, it grows 2 to 3 feet tall and as wide. The affable English rose 'Mary Rose' grows 4 feet tall and as wide and bears 3- to 4-inch double pink flowers with the fragrance of damask roses. It, too, is a bushy, branching plant. The only thing wild about 'Nearly Wild' is its name. A well-behaved floribunda with single pink flowers, it is very hardy and forms a neat mound 3 feet tall and wide. Repeating the simplicity of the single or almost-single flowers is 'Lilac Charm', another floribunda, with pastel

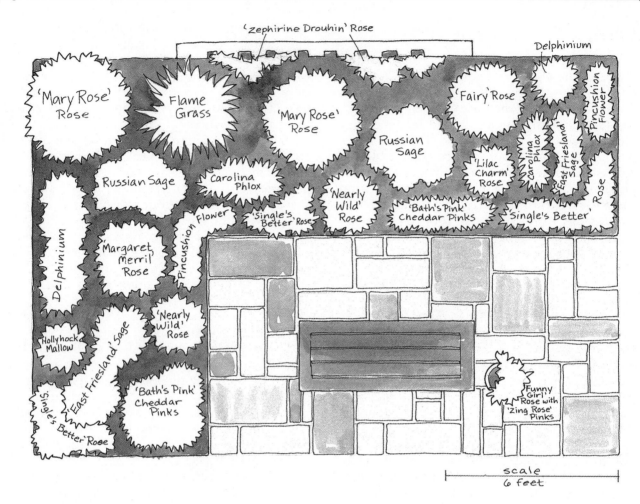

Perennial garden with roses. Numbers in brackets refer to the number of each plant you'll need for the design. **1.** *Rosa* 'Zephirine Drouhin' [2]. **2.** *Rosa* 'Funny Girl' grown as 18" standard [1], underplanted with 'Zing Rose' maiden pinks (*Dianthus deltoides* 'Zing Rose') [5]. **3.** *Rosa* 'The Fairy' [1]. **4.** *Rosa* 'Mary Rose' [2]. **5.** flame grass (*Miscanthus sinensis* 'Purpurascens') [2]. **6.** Russian sage (*Perovskia atriplicifolia*) [5]. **7.** 'Peace' belladonna delphinium (*Delphinium* x *belladonna* 'Peace') [8].

8. 'Fastigiata' hollyhock mallow (*Malva alcea* 'Fastigiata') [1]. **9.** *Rosa* 'Single's Better' [15]. **10.** 'Bath's Pink' cheddar pinks (*Dianthus gratianopolitanus* 'Bath's Pink') [13]. **11.** *Rosa* 'Margaret Merril' [1]. **12.** 'East Friesland' or 'Lubecca' violet sage (*Salvia* x *superba* 'East Friesland' or 'Lubecca') [7]. **13.** *Rosa* 'Nearly Wild' [2]. **14.** 'Butterfly Blue' pincushion flower (*Scabiosa caucasica* 'Butterfly Blue') [7]. **15.** 'Miss Lingard' Carolina phlox (*Phlox carolina* 'Miss Lingard') [7]. **16.** *Rosa* 'Lilac Charm' [2].

mauve coloring. 'Single's Better' is an unusual miniature with single flowers. Bright red and fragrant with mossy buds, the roses are borne on 18-inch plants.

White flowers open up a planting and are particularly beautiful when you're enjoying the garden in the evening. 'Margaret Merril' rose has lovely high-pointed buds and a lush fragrance. The dark green leaves of this 3-foot floribunda rose are disease-resistant. Phloxes are classic perennials. 'Miss Lingard'

Carolina phlox (*Phlox carolina* 'Miss Lingard') blooms in late spring and early summer with lush 2-foot spires of fragrant white flowers borne on compact plants. Unlike most garden phloxes, 'Miss Lingard' is also resistant to mildew.

Rounding out the roses in this garden is a standard or "tree rose" grown in a container. 'Funny Girl' is a pink double miniature. (Another good choice would be the pink-and-white 'Child's Play'.) Grown on an 18-inch

A look at the perennial garden with roses. Picture this lovely perennial garden in your own yard. It's late spring or early summer as you walk across the lawn toward the flagstone patio and the inviting bench that beckons you to stop and smell the roses. In this view, 'Mary Rose', 'Margaret Merril', 'Zephirine Drouhin', and 'Nearly Wild' roses are all in bloom, with 'Peace' delphinium, 'East Friesland' violet sage, 'Miss Lingard' Carolina phlox, 'Butterfly Blue' pincushion flower, and 'Fastigiata' hollyhock mallow adding blue, white, and pink perennial flower color. Supporting the blooming plants is the strong upright accent of flame grass and the shrubby blue-green Russian sage; both will bloom later in the summer.

trunk, 'Funny Girl' provides just the right accent for this garden. Except in warm climates, overwinter potted standards in an unheated garage or basement that stays above freezing. The strawberry-pink-flowered perennial 'Zing Rose' maiden pinks (*Dianthus deltoides* 'Zing Rose') soften the base of the standard.

Ornamental grasses add a graceful linear quality to this garden. The grass I've chosen, flame grass (*Miscanthus sinensis* 'Purpurascens'),

forms handsome clumps that grow only to 3 or 4 feet tall. Its leaves turn purple-red in the fall when the plumy flowers appear.

Four blue-flowered perennials contribute the contrasting color in this border. Russian sage (*Perovskia atriplicifolia*) is a stunning background plant with silvery leaves and airy 3-foot spikes of violet-blue flowers borne from mid- to late summer. Classic in the perennial garden, delphiniums are usually high-maintenance plants, but 'Peace' (*Delphinium × belladonna*

'Peace') is a German hybrid with sturdy branching stems of deep blue flowers. Cut back faded flowers for repeat bloom. More reliable and longer-lived than other hybrids, 'Peace' grows 4 feet tall. 'East Friesland' violet sage (*Salvia × superba* 'East Friesland') has narrow spikes of dark violet-blue flowers borne on 18-inch plants. Providing a low, rounded effect, the dwarf-growing pincushion flower (*Scabiosa caucasica* 'Butterfly Blue') reaches only 12 inches. Lacy, 2-inch pale blue flowers adorn these plants.

I've repeated the pink of the roses in two perennials. Blooming in late spring, the spicy scent of 'Bath's Pink' cheddar pinks (*Dianthus gratianopolitanus* 'Bath's Pink') graces an entire planting. Its low mounds of gray-green leaves are a perfect groundcover at the front of the border. Later in the season, from mid- to late summer, the spires of 'Fastigiata' hollyhock mallow (*Malva alcea* 'Fastigiata') punctuate the garden with their 2-inch flowers borne on bushy 3-foot plants.

Other Plant Options

It's fun and rewarding to take the framework of a garden design, then customize it by substituting some of your own favorite plants for the ones the designer chose. You'll get the best effect if you choose plants that bloom in the same colors and at the same times as the ones you're replacing; the plant habit should be similar, too. That way, you won't disrupt the garden's color scheme or overall look, but you *will* make it distinctively your own. I've listed some other perennials here that work well in this design; if you'd like, choose some of them instead of my own favorites, or use them as a springboard to start thinking about other options.

White perennial flowers for a sunny border include Shasta daisy (*Chrysanthemum × superbum*), white coneflower (*Echinacea purpurea* 'Alba'), white cultivars and varieties of gayfeather (*Liatris* spp.), and 'Summer Snow' false dragonhead (*Physostegia virginiana* 'Summer Snow'). Besides white flowers, remember to use silver-leaved foliage plants in your garden. Silver-foliaged plants to consider are 'Lambrook Silver' or 'Powis Castle' wormwood (*Artemisia absinthium* 'Lambrook Silver' or 'Powis Castle') and silvermound artemisia (*A. schmidtiana* 'Nana', often sold as 'Silver Mound').

Good blue-flowered perennials you could plant in this garden include ladybells (*Adenophora liliifolia*), willow amsonia (*Amsonia tabernaemontana*), 'Monch' Frikart's aster (*Aster × frikartii* 'Monch'), baptisia (*Baptisia australis*), cultivars of Siberian iris (*Iris sibirica*), lavender (*Lavandula angustifolia*), 'Dropmore' Persian catmint (*Nepeta × faassenii* 'Dropmore'), other violet sage cultivars like 'Lubecca' (*Salvia × superba* 'Lubecca'), Stokes' aster (*Stokesia laevis*), and the speedwells (*Veronica* spp.).

When designing your own perennial border, consider these other excellent pink flowers: purple coneflower (*Echinacea purpurea*), hardy geraniums (*Geranium* spp.), gayfeathers (*Liatris* spp.), bee balm (*Monarda didyma*), 'Vivid' false dragonhead (*Physostegia virginiana* 'Vivid'), stonecrops (*Sedum spectabile* and *S. spurium* cultivars), and prairie mallows (*Sidalcea* spp.).

For a Different Look

For a garden with a golden to orange palette, think about replacing the pink and white perennials with 'Coronation Gold' yarrow (*Achillea* 'Coronation Gold'), chartreuse-flowered lady's-mantle (*Alchemilla mollis*), golden marguerite (*Anthemis tinctoria*), butterfly weed (*Asclepias tuberosa*), coreopsis (*Coreopsis* spp.), fiery scarlet 'Lucifer' crocosmia (*Crocosmia × crocosmiiflora* 'Lucifer'), 'Dazzler' blanketflower (*Gaillardia × grandiflora* 'Dazzler'), daylilies (*Hemerocallis* cultivars), St.-John's-wort (*Hypericum calycinum*), swordleaf inula (*Inula ensifolia*), torch lily (*Kniphofia uvaria*), 'Goldsturm' rudbeckia (*Rudbeckia fulgida* 'Goldsturm'), gray- and chartreuse-leaved lavender cottons (*Santolina chamaecyparissus* and *S. virens*), orange stonecrop (*Sedum kamschaticum*), and hybrid goldenrod (× *Solidaster*).

Combine these with yellow roses like 'Abraham Darby', 'Allgold', 'Fruhlingsgold', 'Goldbusch', 'Golden Wings', 'Graham Thomas', 'Harison's Yellow', 'Leverkusen', 'Perdita', 'Sunsprite', 'The Pilgrim', and 'Windrush'.

Shrub Border

Long before roses were pampered garden pets, they thrived in fields and fencerows as the graceful shrubs they are. Today, among the many stiff-stemmed hybrids, there are still roses that grow with graceful shrubby shapes and forms. Many of these are species roses or older cultivars, but there are also a number of new roses that make ideal shrubs for the landscape. I've chosen the best of old and new roses to feature with other shrubs in this attractive border—a perfect frame for the backyard.

A border of shrubs surrounding an expanse of lawn creates a private island, shutting out the sights and sounds of a less-than-ideal world. A shrub border will attract songbirds to your yard, giving them nesting sites, shelter, and even food from berries and rose hips. An attractive shrub border like this one will also increase your property value. By using a mixture of deciduous and evergreen trees and shrubs, you can create a little park that is enchanting year-round. Adding a gazebo allows you to retreat to that woodland atmosphere, whether you want to have a picnic or a cup of tea, to read a book, or simply to sit and relax.

For many years, people complained about the once-blooming shrub roses, even though our other most-loved shrubs, like lilacs and forsythia, bloom only once a year. Now, even those people can't complain, because there are a number of very hardy, disease-resistant shrub roses that bloom repeatedly throughout the summer. Couple this with a strong framework of evergreen and flowering trees and other shrubs, and you have a garden that needs little maintenance, especially if the area is mulched well with shredded bark.

If you want to add a little extra color, underplant your shrub border with plants that tolerate light shade. For spring bloom, these include daffodils and the small spring bulbs such as winter aconite, crocus, and scilla, as well as the hellebores. Shade-tolerant annuals for summer include impatiens and begonias. For fall, add chrysanthemums.

Anchoring this plan is a 6-foot privacy fence. Lumberyards and fencing companies offer a wide range of styles. Make your selection based on the maintenance that the fence requires (do you mind fence-painting, or do you want a rot-resistant fence?), how well the fence suits the style of your home, and the cost of the fence.

Plants for a Shrub Border

I think one of the most lovely sounds is the whisper of the pines in the wind. I've included two types of pine trees in this plan, eastern white pine (*Pinus strobus*) and Austrian pine (*P. nigra*). Both are long-lived.

On the left side of the border are two beautybushes (*Kolkwitzia amabilis*). A dense shrub growing to 12 feet tall, beautybush is covered with small pink flowers in early summer. Flaking brown bark provides visual interest in the winter. 'Bonica' roses also have small pink flowers. They bloom all summer on very hardy plants growing to 5 feet, with red hips in the winter. Daphnes have among the most fragrant of flowers. Whether you choose the rare 'Carol Mackie' Burkwood daphne (*Daphne × burkwoodii* 'Carol Mackie') or the more available February daphne (*D. mezereum*), the deciduous 3- to 4-foot plants are attractive for their rounded form, pink flowers, and red berries. I've finished the left side of the border with 'Shirobana' Japanese spireas (*Spiraea japonica* 'Shirobana'). Growing 2 to 3 feet tall with pendulous branches, 'Shirobana' bears white, red, and pink flowers.

On the left of the gazebo are plants of the 'White Rose of York' (*Rosa alba* 'White Rose of York', also called 'Semi-Plena'). These magnificent shrubs bear their semidouble fragrant white flowers on arching branches in early summer. Extemely tough, hardy plants, they have lovely blue-green leaves that blend well with the white pine trees. 'White Rose of York' also bears loads of showy bright red rose hips. Directly beside the path, where you can enjoy its flowers and fragrance up close, is a 'Miss Kim' Manchurian lilac (*Syringa patula* 'Miss Kim'). 'Miss Kim' grows only 5 feet tall and blooms in early summer, with fragrant blue flowers that are pink in bud. Showcased in front of the pines are three plants of 'Heritage', a continual-blooming English rose with 4-inch pink flowers on 4-foot plants. At the entrance to the path is another 'Shirobana' spirea.

Sheltering the gazebo in front and on the side are two 'Toba' hawthorns (*Crataegus × mordenensis* 'Toba'), with large, fragrant clusters of double white flowers that mature to pink. Glossy leaves, red berries, and attractively twisted trunks enhance their landscape appeal. If you don't like hawthorns, can't find 'Toba', or have fireblight in your area, you can substitute other small-growing flowering trees like crape myrtles (*Lagerstroemia indica*) or dogwoods (*Cornus florida*).

Several interesting shrubs surround the hawthorn in front of the gazebo. Summersweet (*Clethra alnifolia*) is unusual for a shrub, in that it blooms in late summer. The spikes of pink flowers are wonderfully fragrant and are followed by showy black seeds. The deciduous

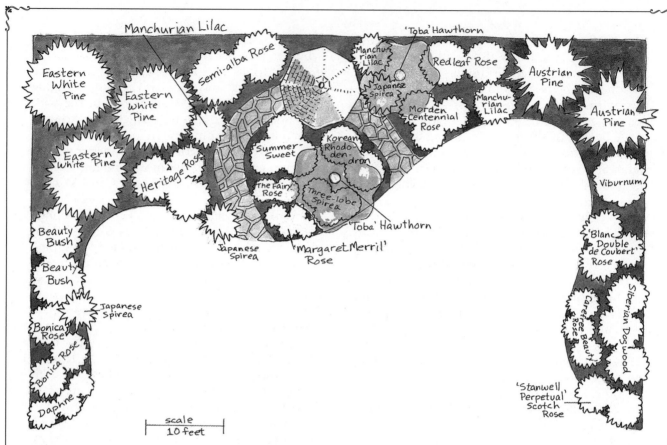

Manchurian Lilac · Eastern White Pine · Eastern White Pine · Semi-alba Rose · 'Toba' Hawthorn · Manchurian Lilac · Japanese Spirea · Redleaf Rose · Austrian Pine · Eastern White Pine · Morden Centennial Rose · Manchurian Lilac · Austrian Pine · Heritage Rose · Summer-Sweet · Korean Rhodo-den-dron · The Fairy Rose · Three-lobe Spirea · Viburnum · Beauty Bush · Japanese Spirea · 'Toba' Hawthorn · 'Margaret Merril' Rose · 'Blanc Double de Coubert' Rose · Beauty Bush · Japanese Spirea · Bonica Rose · Bonica Rose · Daphne · Carefree Beauty Rose · Siberian Dogwood · 'Stanwell Perpetual' Scotch Rose

scale
10 feet

Shrub border. Numbers in brackets refer to the number of each plant you'll need for the design. 1. Eastern white pine (*Pinus strobus*) [3]. 2. Austrian pine (*Pinus nigra*) [2]. 3. *Rosa alba* 'White Rose of York' [2]. 4. redleaf rose (*Rosa glauca*, syn. *R. rubrifolia*) [2]. 5. *Rosa* 'Heritage' [3]. 6. 'Shirobana' Japanese spirea (*Spiraea japonica* 'Shirobana') [3]. 7. *Rosa* 'Blanc Double de Coubert' [3]. 8. *Rosa* 'Margaret Merril' [4]. 9. *Rosa* 'Carefree Beauty' [3]. 10. *Rosa* 'Bonica' [3]. 11. summersweet (*Clethra alnifolia*) [3]. 12. Siberian dogwood (*Cornus alba* 'Sibirica') [3]. 13. 'Miss Kim' Manchurian lilac (*Syringa patula* 'Miss Kim') [2]. 14. Koreanspice viburnum (*Viburnum carlesii*) [1]. 15. 'Carol Mackie' burkwood daphne (*Daphne* × *burkwoodii* 'Carol Mackie') or February daphne (*Daphne mezereum*) [3]. 16. beautybush (*Kolkwitzia amabilis*) [2]. 17. *Rosa* 'Morden Centennial' [3]. 18. 'Stanwell Perpetual' Scotch rose (*Rosa spinosissima* 'Stanwell Perpetual') [2]. 19. *Rosa* 'The Fairy' [2]. 20. 'Swan Lake' three-lobe spirea (*Spiraea trilobata* 'Swan Lake') [3]. 21. 'Cornell Pink' Korean rhododendron (*Rhododendron mucronulatum* 'Cornell Pink') [2]. 22. 'Toba' hawthorn (*Crataegus* × *mordenensis* 'Toba') [2].

leaves of the 4- to 6-foot plants turn yellow and orange in the fall. 'Swan Lake' three-lobed spirea (*Spiraea trilobata* 'Swan Lake') has gracefully arching branches covered with clusters of white flowers in late spring and early summer on plants growing 3 to 4 feet tall. The 'Cornell Pink' Korean rhododendron (*Rhododendron mucronulatum* 'Cornell Pink') is a deciduous cultivar with soft pink flowers borne in early spring on 4-foot plants. 'Margaret Merril', a floribunda rose, is a splendid low-growing shrub. From Harkness Roses in England, it has continuous clusters of fragrant double white flowers flushed with pink.

The tough, compact polyantha rose 'The Fairy' bears hundreds of small pink flowers during the growing season.

To the back and right of the gazebo are two more plants of 'Miss Kim' lilac, so that the fragrance can be enjoyed from within the enclosure, as well as another 'Shirobana' spirea. The rose that is the delight of flower arrangers for its foliage, redleaf rose (*Rosa glauca*, formerly *R. rubrifolia*), is also here. A dusty red-green, the leaves and stems are accented in early summer by small single pink flowers that are followed by reddish-purple hips. Plants of redleaf rose can reach 6 feet tall. In front and beside the path are

A look at the shrub border. The heart of this beautiful shrub border is the gazebo pictured here. The flagstone walk invites you to approach, while encouraging you to pause and enjoy the fragrant plantings along the way. In this view, a 'Toba' hawthorn creates a canopy of white over a cluster of fountaining 'Swan Lake' white-flowered spireas. 'Morden Centennial' roses add their pink blooms to the front planting, while groups of summersweet and 'Cornell Pink' rhododendron provide foliage accents. To the right of the path, a showy 'Shirobana' Japanese spirea displays white, red, and pink flower clusters in back of the 'Morden Centennial' roses, while a dwarf 'Miss Kim' lilac and the redleaf rose lure you deeper into the border.

one of the hardy Canadian roses, 'Morden Centennial'. Fragrant 3-inch double pink flowers in clusters on 4- to 5-foot plants invite close inspection.

In front of the pines on the right arm of the border is the highly fragrant Koreanspice viburnum (*Viburnum carlesii*). Its pinkish white flower clusters in spring are followed by blue-black fruit on the 5-foot plants. You can use similar viburnums like Burkwood viburnum (*V. × burkwoodii*), fragrant viburnum (*V. × carlcephalum*), and Judd viburnum (*V. × juddii*) instead, if you prefer them. For fragrance in summer and fall, I've used the rugosa rose 'Blanc Double de Coubert'. Pure white, double 3-inch flowers followed by showy red hips adorn the 5-foot plants with roughly textured leaves.

For winter color, the red-twigged Siberian dogwood (*Cornus alba* 'Sibirica') is one of my favorites, so I've added it to the right of the border, too. Its blue berries add to the effect. Siberian dogwood can grow 7 feet tall. It needs to be pruned hard in spring to encourage production of the more brightly colored young growth. 'Carefree Beauty' is a shrub rose bred by noted Iowa rosarian Griffith Buck. The semidouble, repeat-blooming pink flowers on

5-foot plants are followed by red hips. Rounding out the planting is one of the best and easiest shrub roses to grow, the Scotch rose hybrid 'Stanwell Perpetual'. A repeat-bloomer, its arching canes form a 3-foot-tall mound with fragrant, double, 3-inch blush-pink blooms borne along the stems.

Herbal Rose Garden

No type of garden is more romantic or is of so much historical significance as the herb garden. Herbs have been used through the ages as medicines and cosmetics as well as for seasoning food and as decorations. For many centuries, roses were an integral part of herb gardens and stillrooms (where herbs were dried and herbal preparations were made). This garden reflects that heritage by combining a selection of classic old roses with herbs that offer the full spectrum of herbal uses. I have chosen my favorites, but consider others of similar size that may appeal more to you.

One of the pleasures of growing herbs is that not much space is needed to grow a large number of different types. This relatively small garden includes 8 roses and 29 herbs. At the the height of summer, it will be a tumult of color and fragrance, combining the cottage garden look with the formal, symmetrical tradition of herb gardens. If you're willing to take on the extra maintenance, a closely clipped border of germander or boxwood would emphasize the formality.

I can picture this garden placed against either a wall or a fence, tucked away in a hedge-enclosed garden room, sited as the focal point at the end of a vista of lawn, or placed in a corner of the house near a terrace or kitchen door. The 5- to 6-foot trellis provides a striking background combined with the tall plants surrounding the central bench. Including a bench in an herb garden seems almost essential—you just *have* to have a place to sit and enjoy the delightful scents and tranquil feeling you get among all those herbs and roses.

If you vary the materials used in the low trellis, bench, and paving, this garden will blend with a range of styles. Use a twig-and-vine trellis with a twig bench, a length of log for the sundial pedestal, and pea gravel or shredded bark for the circular path to create a rustic image. Try white-painted treillage and a wooden or metal bench, with a column of marble or granite for the sundial and gray cobblestones, for a sophis-

ticated urban or French feel. For that traditional English look, use redwood or teak for the trellis and bench, brick paving, and a simple traditional sundial pedestal.

Roses for the Herb Garden

Because one of the most important aspects of herbs and herb gardens is their fragrance, I chose each rose for this garden because of its scent, which is retained well when dried. Use these roses in potpourris, beauty preparations, bouquets, and other garden crafts. For those who like to cook with roses and use rose hips, these rose cultivars will provide flavorful fare.

All these roses are classics. The 'Apothecary's Rose' (*Rosa gallica* var. *officinalis*) is the rose probably grown in Western gardens the longest and most used for its efficacious properties. Blooming in early summer, the vivid magenta, semidouble flowers are borne on plants growing 3 to 4 feet tall and wide with rough green leaves. It may tend to sucker unless it's grafted, so keep a watchful eye and a ready pair of shears out if you're growing an own-root rose. Probably brought to Europe by the Crusaders from Damascus, it is thought to be the "Red Rose of Lancaster" from the English War of the Roses.

'Celestial' is an alba rose, a group of such ancient origins that they were probably brought to England by the Romans. The charming pale pink, semidouble flowers have a heavenly scent. Plants are hardy and survive negligence. The foliage is bluish-green on robust 4-foot bushes. Plants bloom once a year.

The damask roses, also brought to Europe from Persia by the Crusaders, are represented by 'Celsiana', grown for almost 250 years, and 'Ispahan', grown since before 1832. Both have the strong damask scent of citrus and spice and are a source of commerical rose oil. Blooming once a year, 'Celsiana' has delicate sprays of large, translucent pink semidouble flowers rising above gray-green leaves. The 4- foot plants are quite graceful and add to the beauty of this rose. 'Ispahan' flowers once a year as well, but it blooms for up to seven weeks. The double, warm pink flowers are good for cutting. With canes to 7 feet tall, it can be grown as a sprawling specimen shrub or trained to a trellis, as it is in this garden.

The musk-scented glands on the stems and buds of the moss rose 'Salet' add to its appeal. 'Salet' bears very double, pink flowers in early summer and again in the fall, with a few blooms scattered throughout summer. Plants reach about 3 feet tall and wide. The foliage may look a bit weary in the heat of summer, but the rest of the season more than makes up for it.

Although the bourbon roses are more susceptible to fungal diseases than some of the other old roses, the luxuriant growth and repeat flowering once they're established make them stellar garden additions. Developed in the later half of the 1800s, 'Zephirine Drouhin' and 'Madame Isaac Pereire' both have semidouble to double bright pink flowers. 'Zephirine' is a stronger grower, with thornless 8-foot canes and purplish new growth, while 'Madame Isaac' reaches 5 to 7 feet tall.

I give rugosa roses star billing for their sturdy, rough-textured, disease-resistant leaves, repeat bloom, and large red hips. The silken pink petals of the single-flowered 'Frau Dagmar Hastrup' form chalices of fragrant, translucent beauty. In the fall, the leaves of the 3-foot plants turn first purple, then gold—an unexpected bonus in a rose.

Herbs for the Garden

The herbs I've chosen to plant with this group of roses include both standard and unusual culinary herbs, edible flowers, and herbs for crafts. With the pun fully intended, the sundial is surrounded with thyme (*Thymus vulgaris*), in this case the full-flavored 'Narrowleaf English'. Scattered about on the circular path are pots of herbs that are less hardy and should be overwintered indoors. These include sweet bay (*Laurus nobilis*), rosemary (*Rosmarinus officinalis*), and rose geranium (*Pelargonium graveolens*), which is scrumptious when used to flavor cakes, cookies, and other desserts and is also great dried to scent potpourris. Because of mint's tendency to spread, I like growing it in a pot as well. The curly-leaved cultivar I've chosen is a pungent peppermint (*Mentha × piperita* 'Crispa').

The feathery purple-brown leaves of bronze fennel (*Foeniculum vulgare* var. *purpureum*) make it an outstanding addition to both herb and perennial gardens for its striking textural and color contrast. Angelica (*Angelica archangelica*) is a statuesque plant that deserves wider use, both in the landscape and in cooking—it's especially good with fruits. Both are perennials.

'Marshall's Delight' bee balm (*Monarda didyma* 'Marshall's Delight') is an unusual pink-flowered cultivar of this perennial; if you don't enjoy its intense hot-pink color or if you can't find it, you can substitute the softer 'Croftway Pink'. 'Marshall's Delight' is mildew-resistant, but to be on the safe side, cut down the plants after blooming. Anise hyssop (*Agastache foeniculum*) is a native American perennial with late-blooming purple flowers. Use both anise hyssop's flowers and its foliage in cooking. Cut off the faded flowers before they can set seed, unless you want lots of volunteer seedlings next spring.

I've included both curly parsley (*Petroselinum crispum* var. *crispum*) and Italian parsley (*P. crispum* var. *neapolitanum*), so you can enjoy both the mild-mannered version and its strong-flavored Italian cousin. Both are biennial. 'Genova' annual sweet basil (*Ocimum basilicum* 'Genova') is considered one of the best-flavored, while 'Minimum' (*O. basilicum* 'Minimum') has both good flavor and fine-textured leaves.

For drying to use in crafts projects, as well as for the lovely silver foliage color they add to the landscape, the southernwood (*Artemisia abrotanum*), lamb's-ears (*Stachys byzantina*), and 'Silver King' artemisia (*A. ludoviciana* 'Silver King') I've included can't be beat. You might also want to try one of the excellent cultivars of wormwood (*A. absinthium* 'Lambrook Silver' or 'Powis Castle'). Garden sage (*Salvia officinalis*) and 'Munstead' lavender (*Lavandula angustifolia* 'Munstead') also add gray leaves to the design, as well as material for cooking and crafts. All are perennials.

Some of the other traditional culinary herbs I've chosen are true French tarragon (*Artemisia dracunculus* var. *sativa*), which should be purchased only from cutting-grown plants, chives (*Allium schoenoprasum*), sweet marjoram (*Origanum majorana*), wild marjoram (*O. vulgare*), the celery taste-alike lovage (*Levistichum officinale*), and 'Fernleaf' dill (*Anethum graveolens* 'Fernleaf'), a new cultivar noted for its compact growth. The cucumber-flavored foliage of burnet (*Poterium sanguisorba*) is great in salads and vinegars. Dill is an annual, but the other herbs are perennials. If your marjoram, which is not very hardy, doesn't overwinter, treat it as an annual and buy new plants every year.

Garlic chives (*Allium tuberosum*) is among my favorite herbs for its pungent flavor, long season of ornamental effect, and lovely white flowers that are edible and good for cutting

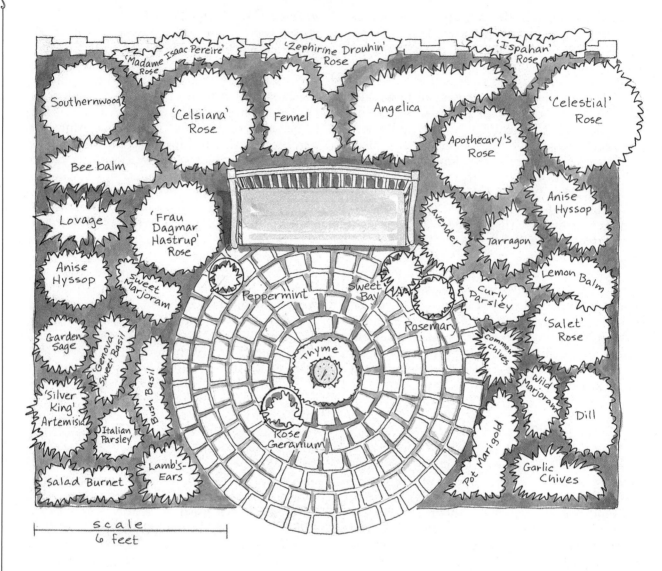

Within the garden diagram, the following labels appear:

'Madame Isaac Pereire' Rose
'Zephirine Drouhin' Rose
'Ispahan' Rose
Southernwood
'Celsiana' Rose
Fennel
Angelica
'Celestial' Rose
Apothecary's Rose
Bee balm
Anise Hyssop
Lovage
'Frau Dagmar Hastrup' Rose
Lavender
Tarragon
Anise Hyssop
Sweet Marjoram
Peppermint
Sweet Bay
Curly Parsley
Lemon Balm
Garden Sage
Rosemary
'Salet' Rose
'Genova' Sweet Basil
Thyme
Common Chives
Bush Basil
'Silver King' Artemisia
Wild Marjoram
Italian Parsley
Rose Geranium
Dill
Salad Burnet
Lamb's-Ears
Pot Marigold
Garlic Chives

scale
6 feet

Herbal rose garden. Numbers in brackets refer to the number of each plant you'll need for the design. **1.** 'Apothecary's Rose' (*Rosa gallica* var. *officinalis*) [1]. **2.** *Rosa* 'Celsiana' [1]. **3.** *Rosa* 'Celestial' [1]. **4.** *Rosa* 'Salet' [1]. **5.** *Rosa* 'Madame Isaac Pereire' [1]. **6.** *Rosa* 'Zephirine Drouhin' [1]. **7.** *Rosa* 'Ispahan' [1]. **8.** *Rosa* 'Frau Dagmar Hastrup' [1]. **9.** sweet bay (*Laurus nobilis*) [1]. **10.** rosemary (*Rosmarinus officinalis*) [1]. **11.** 'Narrowleaf English' thyme (*Thymus vulgaris* 'Narrowleaf English') [8]. **12.** curly parsley (*Petroselinum crispum* var. *crispum*) [2]. **13.** 'Genova' sweet basil (*Ocimum basilicum* 'Genova') [3]. **14.** anise hyssop (*Agastache foeniculum*) [4]. **15.** southernwood (*Artemisia abrotanum*) [1]. **16.** French tarragon (*Artemisia dracunculus* var. *sativa*) [1]. **17.** 'Marshall's Delight' bee balm (*Monarda didyma* 'Marshall's Delight') [3]. **18.** lamb's-ears (*Stachys byzantina*) [3]. **19.** borage (*Borago officinalis*) [2]. **20.** common chives (*Allium schoenoprasum*) [3]. **21.** 'Fernleaf' dill (*Anethum graveolens* 'Fernleaf') [2]. **22.** 'Munstead' lavender (*Lavandula angustifolia* 'Munstead') [2]. **23.** lemon balm (*Melissa officinalis*) [2]. **24.** lovage (*Levistichum officinale*) [2]. **25.** 'Bon Bon Yellow' pot marigold (*Calendula officinalis* 'Bon Bon Yellow') [5]. **26.** 'Crispa' peppermint (*Mentha* x *piperita* 'Crispa') [1]. **27.** sweet marjoram (*Origanum majorana*) [4]. **28.** wild marjoram (*Origanum vulgare*) [2]. **29.** garden sage (*Salvia officinalis*) [1]. **30.** rose geranium (*Pelargonium graveolens*) [1]. **31.** bronze fennel (*Foeniculum vulgare* var. *purpureum*) [3]. **32.** angelica (*Angelica archangelica*) [4]. **33.** bush basil (*Ocimum basilicum* 'Minimum') [5]. **34.** Italian parsley (*Petroselinum crispum* var. *neapolitanum*) [2]. **35.** 'Silver King' artemisia (*Artemisia ludoviciana* 'Silver King') [2]. **36.** salad burnet (*Poterium sanguisorba*) [3]. **37.** garlic chives (*Allium tuberosum*) [4].

both fresh and dried. This plant is handsome enough for any perennial garden. The flowers also produce very ornamental black seeds. Keep in mind that these readily self-sow; cut off flower heads if you don't want lots of seedlings.

Lemon balm (*Melissa officinalis*) is a luxuriant perennial herb with highly fragrant foliage that's good for teas and other beverages, desserts, and potpourri. You'll find you can tolerate the coarse, floppy foliage of annual borage (*Borago officinalis*) once you see its exquisite

blue, star-shaped edible flowers. Annual 'Bon Bon Yellow' pot marigold (*Calendula officinalis* 'Bon Bon Yellow') continues blooming all summer, providing plenty of showy, edible flowers.

You can substitute your own favorite herbs for mine, as long as you keep their mature size in mind. Whatever you choose, an herb garden that includes roses, as the gardens of old did, offers a tranquil retreat for world-weary souls. It will also be a succoring source of color, fragrance, flavor, and delight.

A look at the herbal rose garden. The sundial provides a focus for this traditional herb garden while reminding us that time is fleeting, so we should take the poet's advice and "gather ye rosebuds while ye may." Looking across the cobblestone circle, you can see trellised roses trained to allow their heavenly fragrance to cascade down toward the teak bench. Beside the bench, 'Frau Dagmar Hastrup' bears a wealth of fragrant pink roses over handsome crinkled foliage; later, she'll produce showy red rose hips full of vitamin C. Behind her, 'Celsiana' features fragrant foliage as well as intensely fragrant pale pink roses. A wealth of culinary and craft herbs, including sweet marjoram, 'Marshall's Delight' bee balm, and lovage, attract bees and butterflies, with the promise of a hummingbird visit inviting you to linger.

Island Bed

If you'd like to add more roses and don't have room in your flower beds or borders, consider adding an island bed to your yard. Island beds offer many possibilities in the landscape. In a flat yard, either just one or several interlocking beds can add the dimension of height. They also break up an expanse of lawn, creating vistas and garden rooms. To be most effective, they should relate to the rest of the garden's color, texture, and form, with the lines of the island bed reflecting those of your borders. Undulating curves especially soften the landscape, creating a relaxed, informal atmosphere.

Island beds are designed to look attractive from all sides. To make this possible, the taller plants are usually placed in the center, with progressively shorter plants placed toward the edges of the bed. Since this is a relatively small island, some of the taller plants extend to the edges. By choosing roses that produce branches near the ground as well as having arching branches, nothing needs to be planted in front of them to conceal an ungainly base.

To maintain the shape and make the islands low-maintenance, use an edging. This can be either the flexible black plastic type or a more elaborate edging of brick or stone. Beds can also be edged by hand or with a mechanical edger—but when your bed is an island in the lawn, you'll find that an edging is best for keeping the lawn grass where it belongs.

This design features flowers in shades of yellow. Associated with sunshine and cheerfulness, yellow is not always an easy color to incorporate into the garden, especially since the majority of flowers are in shades of pink. When you're combining yellow with other flower colors, you'll find that it goes particularly well with blue, white, red, or orange flowers. Brown- or purple-leaved plants also complement yellow.

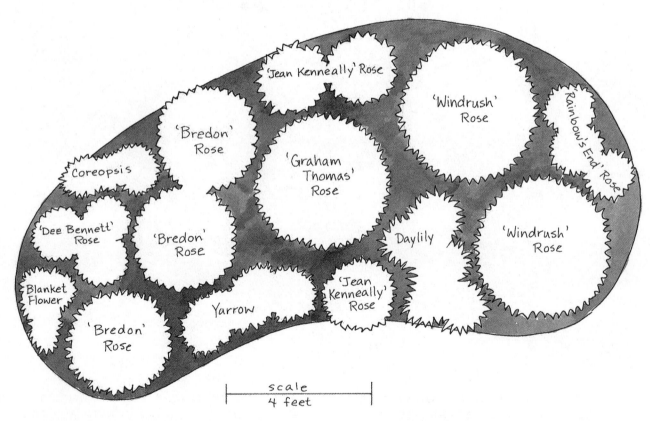

scale
4 feet

Island bed. Numbers in brackets refer to the number of each plant you'll need for the design. 1. *Rosa* 'Windrush' [2]. 2. *Rosa* 'Graham Thomas' [1]. 3. 'Happy Returns' daylily (*Hemerocallis* 'Happy Returns') [5]. 4. *Rosa* 'Jean Kenneally' [3]. 5. *Rosa* 'Bredon' [3]. 6. *Rosa* 'Dee Bennett' [3].

7. 'Moonbeam' threadleaf coreopsis (*Coreopsis verticillata* 'Moonbeam') [3]. 8. 'Baby Cole' blanketflower (*Gaillardia* x grandiflora 'Baby Cole') [6]. 9. *Rosa* 'Rainbow's End' [3]. 10. 'Moonshine' yarrow (*Achillea* 'Moonshine') [3].

Roses for an Island Bed

Three outstanding David Austin English roses anchor this design. 'Windrush' is a second-generation descendent of the excellent single-flowered, large-growing shrub rose 'Golden Wings'. 'Windrush' is also related to the hardy, pest-resistant, fragrant Scotch roses. A strong-growing, twiggy plant, 'Windrush' freely repeat-blooms with 5-inch pale lemon flowers that have a few more petals than a single rose. Yellow stamens center the flowers. Plants grow about 4 feet tall and wide.

'Graham Thomas' is one of David Austin's favorite English roses. Apricot-pink buds open to fully double, intensely colored golden yellow cupped flowers. Produced in clusters throughout summer, blooms are 3 to 4 inches across. The strong fragrance brings tea roses to mind. Although the plants are slightly vase-shaped, growth is vigorous and plants branch freely from top to bottom. The shrubby plants grow 4 to 6 feet tall and 5 feet across, with smooth leaves similar to those of 'Iceberg', part of its ancestry. Plants withstand heat well.

Resembling a floribunda rose in many aspects, 'Bredon' is another David Austin English shrub rose. Growing only 3 feet tall, it will spread 4 feet or more. The 2½-inch buff-yellow flowers are borne all summer in sprays over the entire plant. Perfectly formed rosettes with many small petals, the blooms have a fruity fragrance much like rambler roses. The disease-resistant leaves are small with a rough texture. Besides its use in this island bed, 'Bredon' works well in mass plantings or as a low hedge. The name is derived from Bredon Hill, immortalized in Alfred Edward Housman's poems.

Besides 'Golden Wings', some other repeat-blooming yellow roses you could substitute include 'The Pilgrim', another English rose, and (where hardy) the hybrid musk roses 'Buff Beauty' and 'Penelope', all of which grow 5 or 6 feet tall and as wide. 'J.P. Connell' is a hardy yellow shrub rose bred in Canada, while 'Zitronenfalter' is a slightly less hardy shrub rose from Germany. Floribundas to consider include 'Allgold', 'Gold Badge', 'Sun Flare', and 'Sunsprite'.

The diminutive nature of miniature roses belies their adaptability in the garden. Here they are planted in clusters to maximize their landscape impact. The colors were chosen to carry on the scheme of yellow with accents of apricot to red-orange. 'Rainbow's End', bred by Harm Saville, has high-centered, hybrid tea–like flowers

A look at the island bed. In summer, this sunny island bed is glowing with bright flowers. The roses 'Graham Thomas', 'Windrush', 'Bredon', and miniatures 'Jean Kenneally', 'Dee Bennett', and 'Rainbow's End' cover the yellow spectrum, from red to warm apricot through pale lemon.

A supporting cast of 'Moonshine' yarrow, 'Happy Returns' daylilies, 'Sunray' coreopsis, and 'Baby Cole' blanketflower provides its own perennial chorus of yellows and reds. Like all island beds, this one is designed to be appealing from every angle.

of bright yellow with scarlet edges. The rounded, compact plants are vigorous and easy to grow. Plants reach 14 to 18 inches tall.

The two apricot-colored miniature roses also have beautifully formed flowers of hybrid-tea shape. 'Dee Bennett' is another miniature from Harm Saville. Blooming constantly from spring through fall, the symmetrical plants grow 14 to 18 inches tall. 'Dee Bennett' has slightly more yellow in the flowers than its counterpart, 'Jean Kenneally', which was bred by amateur hybridizer Dee Bennett. 'Jean Kenneally' is one of the taller-growing miniatures, reaching 22 to 30 inches. There are also a number of other excellent yellow, yellow-and-red-blend, and apricot miniature rose cultivars you can substitute for the three I've suggested.

Perennials for an Island Bed

To complement the sunny roses in this island bed, I've chosen a group of easily grown, long-blooming perennials. The surging popularity of daylilies (*Hemerocallis* spp. and cultivars) is based on their adaptability to various sites and their ability to thrive on neglect. The grasslike leaves provide excellent contrast in texture to the divided rose foliage and the feathery leaves of the yarrow. 'Happy Returns' is a hybrid of the well-known 'Stella d'Oro'. Bred by Dr. Darrell Apps, it has 3½-inch lemon yellow flowers with ruffled petals. The flowers open at dusk and stay open until the following evening, a boon for those whose work keeps them from getting home until many cultivars' flowers have closed. The major flowering period of 'Happy Returns' is in midsummer, with repeat bloom after a short rest. Of course, you could substitute 'Stella d'Oro' or a short- to medium-height yellow or apricot daylily with a long bloom season.

Available in single and double forms and with medium- or fine-textured leaves, coreopsis forms neat, compact mounds with yellow flowers and blooms for much of the summer. It thrives in a wide range of soils, is tolerant of heat, and has no pests. 'Sunray' lance-leaved coreopsis (*Coreopsis lanceolata* 'Sunray') is an award-winning cultivar with 2-inch semidouble to double golden flowers that are good for cutting. Plants grow 20 inches tall. 'Moonbeam' threadleaf coreopsis (*C. verticillata* 'Moonbeam') is a good alternative; it has single, pale yellow flowers and fine, needlelike leaves.

Massed at the front edge of this island bed

is the brightly colored dwarf blanketflower 'Baby Cole' (*Gaillardia × grandiflora* 'Baby Cole'). The 8-inch mounds are covered with red-and-yellow daisy-like flowers with bristly centers. Well-drained soil is essential for its survival overwinter. 'Goblin' is similar but grows taller, to 1 foot.

Yarrows (*Achillea* spp.) are soft-textured plants with large flat heads of tiny flowers that are excellent as fresh and dried cut flowers. They are tolerant of hot, dry weather and grow easily in any well-drained soil. 'Moonshine' has bright yellow flowers on 18- to 24-inch stems rising above gray foliage. Plants bloom off and on through summer.

For a Different Look

Other perennials you could use in a planting of roses with a yellow color scheme include cushion spurge (*Eurphorbia polychroma*), 'The Rocket' ligularia (*Ligularia stenocephala* 'The Rocket'), butterfly weed (*Asclepias tuberosa*), gold-and-silver chrysanthemum (*Chrysanthemum pacificum*), St.-John's-wort (*Hypericum calycinum*), torch lilies (*Kniphofia* spp.), and orange coneflower (*Rudbeckia fulgida*). Ornamental grasses, especially variegated cultivars of sedge (*Carex* spp.) or 'Morning Light' Japanese silver grass (*Miscanthus sinensis* 'Morning Light'), would also make striking additions to the island bed.

Annuals are also a colorful and long-blooming alternative to the perennials I've chosen for this island bed. Pale lemon-colored 'Signet' marigolds, calendulas, yellow-plumed celosia, dwarf cosmos, and nasturtiums are the best ones to consider.

Another idea is to create mirror-image islands in the lawn on either side of the house by flipping one "kidney" so that the wide ends face each other. Because of the rounded sides of the island bed, two of them would look lovely on facing sides of a round or oval swimming pool or large water garden.

If you like my planting scheme but don't have a large enough lawn to set off an island bed, never fear. You can transform an island bed into a border or corner bed by removing the shorter plants on one side and placing the taller plants at the back. Or use the appealing curves of the island planting to soften the straight lines of a fence or wall. If you choose this option, move the taller plants to the back of the bed, where the wall or fence will act as a backdrop for them.

Roses in Your Landscape

The finishing touch. Roses can be the perfect low-maintenance plants for adding color to your yard. Imagine this landscape without roses on the fence! If you want to grow roses on a fence, choose climbers or ramblers. You'll find descriptions of the best cultivars in "Best Roses for Landscape Use" beginning on page 29.

▲ **A stunning composition.** 'Dortmund', our cover rose, blooms in sparkling profusion on a rustic arbor above the fragrant pink rugosa rose 'Therese Bugnet'. You'll find 'Dortmund' listed with other top-ranked roses in "Most Insect- and Disease-Resistant Roses" on page 25; look for 'Therese Bugnet' with other fine rugosa cultivars on page 20.

◀ **Making a match.** Your landscape will look better if you match the type of rose you plant to the style of fence it's on. A heavy, double-flowered rose might overwhelm this simple fence, but a single-flowered species rose like the Cherokee rose (*Rosa laevigata*) adds just the right feeling. You'll find "Best Species Roses for Gardens" on page 15.

▲ **Capture the cottage look.** Bouquets of pink roses spill over a classic picket fence, creating a look even Tom Sawyer would love. Old-fashioned rambler roses are ideal for a Victorian or cottage-style garden. You'll find some of the best roses for fences in "Best Roses for Landscape Use" beginning on page 29.

▶ **Fall color from roses.**
Extend your roses' landscape impact by choosing roses that produce colorful fruits (called rose hips) after their flowers fade. *Rosa rugosa,* shown here, and rugosa rose cultivars like 'Blanc Double de Coubert' and 'Delicata', are renowned for their showy hips. For more on rugosa roses, see page 20.

▲ **Dressed-up steps.** 'Blaze' roses add color to these stairs while softening the impact of the massive stone steps. 'Blaze' is a short climbing rose with season-long bloom—an important feature when the rose is used alone. Using rose bushes of the same cultivar creates a formal look, which fits perfectly in this landscape.

▲ **Roses and lavender.** Roses always look better when they're planted with herbs or perennials to hide their bare "legs." A planting of lavender adds a fragrant counterpoint to the roses in this garden. It also unifies the border, adding a sense of continuity to the many sizes and colors of the roses. The showy red climbing rose in the foreground is 'Dortmund'.

◄ **A backyard rose garden.** Roses, roses, and more roses add color to this Oregon yard. These gardeners have trained climbing roses on wooden trellises, planted beds of roses, and even have roses in containers, including a standard or "tree" rose. The result is a blaze of color. For ideas on using roses to set off your home, see the "Entrance Garden" design on page 70.

▲ **A fairy-tale setting.** The lush flowers and bushy habit of 'Betty Prior' create a magical entry for the fairy-tale turret of this house. 'Betty Prior' is one of the best floribunda roses, with showy clusters of hot pink flowers that bloom until frost. It is also disease-resistant, and it's handsome enough to showcase as a specimen plant.

▲ **Roses for rock gardens.** Roses add color and softness spilling over the rocks in this informal garden. The best roses for this situation are low-growing groundcover roses like the Meidiland Series, 'Sea Foam', and 'The Fairy'. You'll find these and other excellent groundcover roses in "Best Roses for Landscape Use" beginning on page 29.

▲ **Up against the wall.** You'll get more blooms on your climbing roses if you train the canes horizontally, as these gardeners have done. The horizontal branches also create a graceful living sculpture on the wall. Color counts, too: Note how the choice of a pink-flowered rose really brightens the gray wall.

▲ **The classic cottage garden.** Roses are the star attraction in this beautiful garden. 'Iceberg', 'Liverpool Echo', 'Europeana', 'Royal Dane', and 'French Lace' roses bloom among annual candytuft (*Iberis umbellata*), 'East Friesland' violet sage (*Salvia × superba* 'East Friesland'), common sundrops (*Oenothera tetragona*), and other cottage flowers. For more on creating your own classic cottage look, see the "Herbal Rose Garden" on page 48.

▶ **The well-trained rose.** To stay on a fence, roses need a helping hand. Tie your climbing rose's canes to the fence with green plastic stretch-ties, heavy cord, or string. The best way to avoid damaging the canes is to tie them to the fence using a figure-eight, which puts pressure on the tie, not the cane. For more how-to on rose training techniques, see "Training Climbing Roses" on page 104.

▲ **A new breed of hybrid tea.** 'Yves Piaget' not only looks different from the typical hybrid tea, it acts different, too! This exquisite, disease-resistant rose bears 5- to 6-inch, highly fragrant peony-shaped blooms on a 2½- to 3-foot-tall bush.

▲ **A bright combination.** The hot tones of 'Betty Prior' floribunda roses look great with cool white perennial feverfew (*Chrysanthemum parthenium*). Both are floriferous, easy-care plants with a long bloom season. The feverfew adds foliage and color around the rose's "legs," too, providing welcome concealment of the bare lower canes.

▲ **A perfect hybrid tea.** 'Gina Lollobrigida' is a lovely hybrid tea in a hard-to-find shade—clear yellow. 'Gina' bears fragrant 5- to 6-inch flowers on upright 4- to 5-foot bushes. You'll find more choice cultivars in "Best Hybrid Teas" on page 18.

▼ **Roses in the perennial garden.** The pastel pink of 'Bonica' shrub roses blends beautifully with the purples and yellows of this perennial garden. For ideas on combining roses with perennials, see the "Perennial Garden with Roses" design on page 40.

▲ **A miniature delight.** Miniature roses can be every bit as attractive as their full-sized cousins, as 'Popcorn' shows. You'll find 'Popcorn' with the "Best Miniatures" on page 19. Miniatures are perfect for containers and for the front of the perennial or mixed border.

▲ **Brightening a shrub border.** One of the favorite roses of all time is 'The Fairy', shown here spilling out of a shrub border. This compact, disease-resistant polyantha rose bears hundreds of small pink roses during the growing season. 'The Fairy' is featured in the "Shrub Border" design on page 44 and in "Best Polyanthas" on page 20.

◀ **Tops for fragrance.** It's a myth that modern hybrid teas don't smell as good as their forebears. You just have to choose cultivars that have been bred for fragrance, like 'Electron', which bears its rose-pink flowers on tidy 3-foot bushes. You'll find 'Electron' in "Best Hybrid Teas" on page 18; for other fragrant roses, see "Most Fragrant Roses" on page 26.

▲ **An inviting arbor.** Some garden structures beg you to come closer, like this beautiful archway into an enclosed garden. Its simple wooden framework makes an effective wall when filled with the fragrant old gallica rose, 'Apothecary's Rose'. The 'Apothecary's Rose' is one of the most famous and historic of all roses, and its petals are excellent for potpourri. Find out more about this special rose in "The Gallicas" on page 12.

▶ **Simple but effective.** In contrast to the elaborate arching arbor above, this rustic structure is plain and angular. But it's a perfect frame for an exuberant climbing rose, giving full play to the color and form of the flowers. It's also easy to build. For directions on simple arbor construction, see "Make Your Own Rose Arbor" on page 108. Let the roses do the talking!

▲ **Colorful and care-free.** For eye-popping color, hardiness, and low-maintenance gardening, it's hard to beat this border of mixed daylily cultivars and rugosa roses (*Rosa rugosa*). The large, scarlet rose hips of the rugosa roses will keep the show going well into fall. For another simple and colorful way to mix roses and perennials, see the "Island Bed" design on page 50.

▶ **What's a grandiflora?** This rose category is confusing to gardeners, since grandiflora roses like 'Camelot' often look a lot like hybrid teas. They're the result of crosses between hybrid teas and floribundas, and they combine the best of both: the classic hybrid tea flower and the floribunda's floriferous habit. Grandifloras bloom on tall bushes, so use them at the back of the border or the shrub border. For more on 'Camelot', see "Best Grandifloras" on page 18.

◀ **A southern belle.** The yellow Lady Banks rose (*Rosa banksiae* var. *lutea*) provides a cream-yellow shower over a bed of blue-flowered ajuga (*Ajuga reptans*). Lady Banks reaches a height of 20 feet, and both the yellow- and white-flowered varieties rate a place in "Most Heat-Tolerant Roses" on page 25, making them ideal for southern gardens.

▲ **A new class of roses.** Apricot-yellow 'Graham Thomas' exemplifies the English roses developed by British rose breeder David Austin. He has combined the fragrance and form of old roses with the shrubby habit and repeat-bloom of the modern roses. See page 22 for more English roses.

◀ **Rosy arches.** A simple structure has a big impact in this garden, where rose arches lure strollers along a curving walk. A seating area nearby lets visitors enjoy the roses' fragrance and color, while evergreens form a restful backdrop. This rose is the classic 'American Pillar'.

◀ **Make the most of container roses.** You'll get twice the color if you underplant potted roses with colorful annuals. Annuals will bloom nonstop all summer, along with the roses. Here, 'Pillow Talk' is growing in a vibrant carpet of annual lobelia. For more unbeatable container combinations, see the "Container Garden for a Terrace or Deck" design on page 74.

▲ **A cool combination.** Sometimes the simplest combinations are the loveliest, as in the case of this pastel-flowered rose and French lavender (*Lavandula stoechas*). It's the showy bracts at the top of the lavender that give them their appeal.

◀ **The ultimate easy-care rose.** Rugosa roses are pest- and disease-resistant, exceptionally hardy, and salt- and drought-tolerant. And rugosas have something to offer a landscape from spring, when their beautiful corduroy-like foliage emerges, through summer bloom to fall, when their showy scarlet hips stand out against the foliage.

Entrance Garden

The entrance to our homes not only extends a welcome but also tells people who see it something about us. I often wonder what the marching soldiers of evergreen shrubs lined up across the front of many houses must be guarding within. Think how much more appealing and pleasurable to make at least a part of your front yard into an inviting landscape of trees, shrubs, and flowers. It also provides a beautiful picture for viewing from your front windows.

I created this design for the traditional suburban home, with a driveway to the garage along one side and a short curving walk to the front door. The area is enclosed with a low, open fence, which could be split-rail, picket, or whatever material and style is in keeping with the house design.

The 5-foot-wide flagstone walk is wide enough for two people to walk side by side. You could use other paving materials, such as brick, slate, or concrete. A narrower path branches off to a small backless bench beneath the purple-leaved cultivar of redbud (*Cercis canadensis* 'Forest Pansy'). If purple foliage isn't your favorite, grow the green-leaved species or consider other small-growing, spring-flowering trees like dogwoods (*Cornus* spp.), hawthorns (*Crataegus* spp.), and crab apples (*Malus* spp.).

A small pre-formed, black plastic pool reflects the sky and adds the pleasure of water to this small garden. It is easy to install and maintain. If you have an outdoor electrical outlet, you could add a small fountain to the pool.

The colors I chose feature shades of pink, red, blue, and white. The perennials are all known for their long bloom period and ease of maintenance. I've selected shrubs that are sturdy plants with good track records. The roses are a mixture of the latest shrub cultivars from England, France, and Canada, plus a miniature. All are repeat-blooming, giving you a wealth of stunning flowers all summer long.

If you want more of a good thing, you could easily enlarge the garden area, perhaps curving the large bed along the driveway out to the street and stretching it along the entire front of the house. Or you could repeat the plantings at the other corner of the house and in the outside corner of the front yard. Many other plants could be substituted for the ones I've chosen. Select plants that grow well in your area, using a mix of evergreens, flowering shrubs, and perennials. For still more bloom power, supplement the planting with annuals, spring-blooming bulbs, and chrysanthemums bought and planted in bloom in the fall.

Plants for an Entrance Garden

For training along the fence, 'William Baffin' is an extremely hardy and disease-resistant climbing rose. Bred from *Rosa × kordesii* in Canada, it has 3-inch deep pink double flowers in large clusters. Interplanted with it along the fence is a rugosa hybrid from Canada, 'David Thompson'. The rounded 3-foot plants are also hardy and disease-resistant, with 3-inch deep pink double flowers that are very fragrant. From the House of Meilland in France comes the low, spreading 'Alba Meidiland', growing 30 inches tall and 4 or more feet wide with masses of small white double flowers. If you can't find 'Alba Meidiland', substitute the similar 'White Meidiland', which has larger flowers and foliage.

To anchor the bench beneath the 'Forest Pansy' redbud and to accent the front steps I've used the English rose 'Mary Rose'. Rich pink flowers with a damask fragrance adorn the 4-foot plants. 'The Prince' is another English rose, this one with dark red flowers. On each side of the walk are plants of 'Champlain' roses, with dazzling 2-inch dark red flowers borne in clusters on 3-foot plants. Completing the rose selection in this entrance garden is the miniature 'Old Glory'. A hybrid from Frank Benardella, the fragrant red flowers are borne on 18-inch plants.

The rhododendron I've selected, 'P.J.M.', is among the hardiest of these broadleaved evergreen shrubs. Able to withstand winter minimum temperatures as low as −10°F, 'P.J.M.' hybrid rhododendron (*Rhododendron* 'P.J.M.') has masses of vivid lavender-pink flowers in midspring. In fall, its foliage turns purple. Plants reach 5 feet tall. If you live in a colder area, use a deciduous azalea instead of 'P.J.M.'; if you're in a warmer area, you have a wide range of rhododendron cultivars to choose from.

The compact form of the European cranberrybush viburnum (*Viburnum opulus* 'Compactum') is an outstanding deciduous shrub with three-season interest. It has white flowers in spring, showy clusters of bright red fruit that last into winter, and red fall foliage. I've sited a group of these viburnums in front of the house, where the 4- to 6-foot plants will have a lot of impact. Because they're deciduous, they'll shade

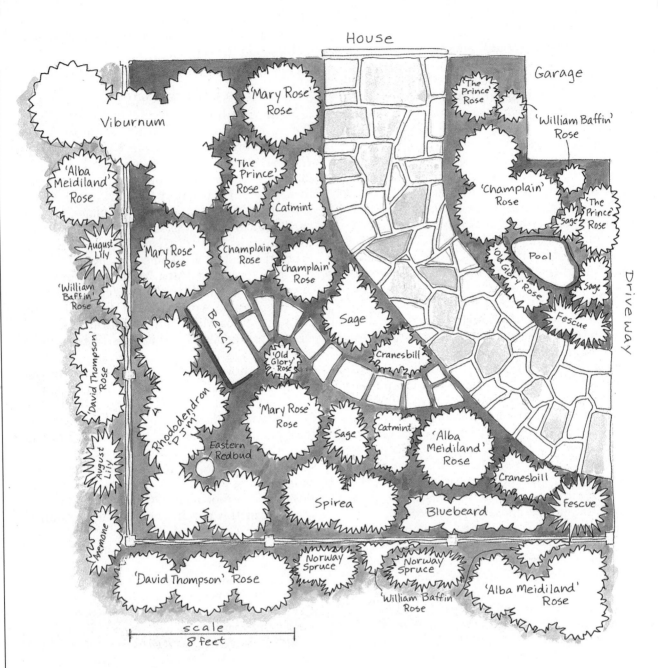

Entrance garden. Numbers in brackets refer to the number of each plant you'll need for the design. **1.** *Rosa* 'William Baffin' [5]. **2.** 'Forest Pansy' eastern redbud (*Cercis canadensis* 'Forest Pansy') [1]. **3.** *Rhododendron* 'P.J.M.' [5]. **4.** *Rosa* 'Mary Rose' [3]. **5.** *Rosa* 'Champlain' [5]. **6.** *Rosa* 'Alba Meidiland' or 'White Meidiland' [4]. **7.** 'Compactum' European cranberrybush viburnum (*Viburnum opulus* 'Compactum') [4]. **8.** *Rosa* 'David Thompson' [5]. **9.** 'Grandiflora' August lily (*Hosta plantaginea* 'Grandiflora') [4]. **10.** Japanese anemone (*Anemone tomentosa* 'Robustissima'), or 'Honorine Jobert' Japanese anemone (*Anemone* x *hybrida* 'Honorine Jobert') [5]. **11.** bird's-nest Norway spruce (*Picea abies* 'Nidiformis') [6]. **12.** 'Shirobana' Japanese spirea (*Spiraea japonica* 'Shirobana') [3]. **13.** 'Longwood Blue' bluebeard (*Caryopteris* x *clandonensis* 'Longwood Blue') [3]. **14.** Lancaster cranesbill (*Geranium sanguineum* var. *striatum*) [9]. **15.** 'Elijah Blue' fescue (*Festuca cinerea* 'Elijah Blue') [18]. **16.** 'East Friesland' or 'Lubecca' violet sage (*Salvia* x *superba* 'East Friesland' or 'Lubecca') [18]. **17.** *Rosa* 'Old Glory' [4]. **18.** *Rosa* 'The Prince' [6]. **19.** 'Dropmore' catmint (*Nepeta* x *faassenii* 'Dropmore') [16].

A look at the entrance garden. You'll get a warm welcome from this inviting entrance garden! In the view shown here, you can see the tranquil pool luring you along the stone entry walk, promising visual relief from the searing summer heat. 'Elijah Blue' fescue adds its blue blades to the cooling theme, as does 'East Friesland' violet sage with its deep purple flower spikes. Count on the roses to heat things up again, though—the glowing reds of 'Champlain', 'William Baffin', and the miniature 'Old Glory' provide a counterpoint to the extraordinary rich crimson and royal purple blooms of 'The Prince', a delightfully fragrant Austin English rose.

the front windows during the growing season and let in more light through their bare branches during winter. If you'd prefer, you can substitute the compact American cranberrybush viburnum (*Viburnum trilobum* 'Compactum'). These 6-foot shrubs have a more upright habit and finer branch structure than their European counterparts, but the tradeoff is fair to middling yellow fall foliage color.

Japanese spireas (*Spiraea japonica*) are rounded, deciduous shrubs growing to 4 feet tall, but the cultivar 'Shirobana' grows only 2 to 3 feet tall. Its arching branches bear clusters of white, red, and pink flowers from summer into fall. It is easily grown and has no pests. I've grouped three 'Shirobana' Japanese spireas near

the front of the entrance garden to bid visitors a cheery hello as they arrive.

The bird's-nest Norway spruce (*Picea abies* 'Nidiformis') has evergreen needles on dwarf, dense growth that eventually reaches 2 feet tall and slightly wider. I've used these dwarf conifers in groups of three to frame the 'William Baffin' rose in front of the fence. If you'd like a dwarf conifer for a slightly larger area, try a mugo pine (*Pinus mugo* var. *mugo* or *P. mugo* 'Compacta').

A selection from Longwood Gardens outside of Philadelphia, the 'Longwood Blue' bluebeard (*Caryopteris* × *clandonensis* 'Longwood Blue') is a 4-foot shrub with silvery leaves. Its spires of blue flowers in late summer and fall attract butterflies and are good for cutting. If growth dies back during winter, it will often sprout from the base if you prune back dead wood in the spring.

I chose only a few different perennials for this garden but have used them in repeating clusters throughout. By planting in masses, you get a stunning effect from the impact of the solid bloom color as well as a sense of continuity from the repetition of plants. If you're a plant collector at heart, feel free to subsitute a wider selection of flowers.

For the lightly shaded areas near the redbud tree, the spectacular large-leaved August lily (*Hosta plantaginea* 'Grandiflora'), which bears spires of fragrant white flowers in August, complements the fall-blooming white flowers of 'Honorine Jobert' Japanese anemone (*Anemone × hybrida* 'Honorine Jobert'). There are many other excellent hostas on the market, especially the variegated 'Francee', 'Francis Williams', and 'Gold Standard', and the blue-leaved *Hosta sieboldiana* 'Elegans'. Go with my choice or use your favorite. Another good fall-blooming Japanese anemone is grape-leaved anemone (*A. tomentosa* 'Robustissima'), which bears metallic-pink flowers instead of the crisp white of 'Honorine Jobert'.

If you'd like to expand the selection of plants under the tree, other fine perennials for shade include goatsbeard (*Aruncus dioicus*), astilbe (*Astilbe × arendsii*), evergreen European wild ginger (*Asarum europaeum*), ferns, American bugbane (*Cimicifuga americana*), fringed bleeding heart (*Dicentra eximia*), red-leaved 'Palace Purple' heuchera and its cousin coralbells (*Heuchera micrantha* 'Palace Purple' and *H. sanguinea*), Solomon's-seals (*Polygonatum* spp.), and spiderwort (*Tradescantia virginiana*).

In the sunnier areas along the main walkway and around the pool, I've spotlighted four perennials. A superb, low-growing edging, Lancaster cranesbill (*Geranium sanguineum* var. *striatum*) bears soft pink, 1-inch flowers above divided, dark green leaves on 8-inch mounds. Other low-growing geraniums could also be used. Ornamental 'Elijah Blue' fescue (*Festuca cinerea* 'Elijah Blue') is a spiky, fine-leaved grass that grows 10 inches tall. This cultivar holds its blue leaf color especially well, but many other cultivars are available.

Repeating the blue color of the fescue, I've used Persian catmint (*Nepeta × faassenii*), with gray-green leaves and pale blue flowers borne in early summer. Trim off the faded flowers to encourage a second blooming. Among the cultivars of Persian catmint, look for 'Dropmore', which has the best foliage. 'East Friesland' violet sage (*Salvia × superba* 'East Friesland') intensifies the color scheme with deep violet-blue spikes of flowers growing 18 inches tall. Blooming throughout the summer, its flowers are good for cutting. 'Lubecca' is another excellent violet sage cultivar for a sunny site.

Container Terrace or Deck Garden

Whether you have a large deck, a townhouse patio, or high-rise balcony, gardening in containers offers flexibility and an opportunity to enjoy your plants at close range. Colors and fragrance bring an immediate pleasure while you're dining or relaxing in an outdoor living area graced with container plantings. Having plants literally right under your nose means that you'll want to keep them in top form, but this is easy to do simply because they are so accessible.

One of the greatest pleasures of container gardening is that it's like having furniture. You can move the garden around to suit your mood or the occasion. (At least you can if large containers have rollers attached or are placed on plant dollies!) The best arrangements of containers are in informally arranged, odd-numbered groups of different-sized pots, but it's always fun to experiment with different looks and groupings.

Just about any plant can be grown in a container. The container size should be in proportion to the plant's natural garden size, although particularly large plants will never attain the same size they would in the ground. For most full-sized roses, the minimum pot size is 14 inches deep and 18 inches wide. Miniatures need pots 6 to 10 inches in diameter. You can use any substantial vessel that can hold potting soil. A wide range of attractive plastic pots are available at garden centers. Or you can hide an ugly plastic pot in an attractive cachepot or plastic-lined basket.

Clay pots range from ornate, imported terracotta to the familiar plain, standard-issue garden variety. Half whiskey barrels are inexpensive choices for casual settings, while the wooden "Versailles" planters give a more formal appearance. Wooden planters can be specially made to match the deck or house. Whatever you choose, be sure there are drainage holes in the bottom. Before you add potting soil, place a layer of screening in the bottom to keep soil from escaping.

I've made this container garden design more understated than usual because my goal was a simple, elegant planting. Rather than using many different plants, I've designed each container to feature a rose with an underplanting of a trailing or creeping annual or perennial. I chose some of the plants for their fragrance; others, for their color or form. And I added excitement with herbs, fruit, and flowers for cutting. There are both antique and modern roses, and all are repeat-bloomers. The three container groupings are monochromatic, one each in shades of red, white, or pink. If you prefer, a single color could be featured throughout.

Care for Container Gardens

Gardeners have been growing in containers long before the advent of "soilless potting mix," but the admonition to use such a mixture rather than garden soil is valid. Soil straight from the garden is too dense for adequate drainage in pots. The soilless potting mixes developed by universities have greatly expanded the ease of container gardening. Generally, these mixtures are composed of equal parts sphagnum peat moss and perlite or vermiculite. With the environmental concerns over the mining of sphagnum bogs, alternatives must now be considered. Try mixing equal parts of compost, pulverized pine or fir bark, and perlite or vermiculite. For every cubic foot of mix, add 4 ounces dolomitic limestone, 1 pound rock phosphate or colloidal phosphate, 4 ounces greensand, 1 pound granite dust, and 2 ounces blood meal to create a balanced organic fertilizer.

The rich, exuberant look that sets the best container plantings apart is the result of overplanting, then watering and feeding well. Never consider a large-scale container planting unless you have a faucet and hose nearby. A watering can is fine for a few pots, but not much more, unless you really enjoy running back and forth to the house. At the height of summer, pots may need to be watered at least once a day, or whatever it takes to keep the soil evenly moist. To conserve water and time, you may want to appraise the merits of a drip-watering system. Because the amount of soil is limited and the frequent watering washes out nutrients, plenty of fertilizer is needed for lush growth. Seaweed, fish emulsion, compost or manure tea, and other water-soluble organic plant foods can be applied as part of the weekly or biweekly watering program. Besides incorporating into the original potting soil a commercially available complete organic fertilizer or different organic fertilizers as listed above, you can lightly dig more into the soil surface during the growing season.

Unlike growing annuals, which die and are composted at season's end, roses present the dilemma of overwintering in all but the mildest climates. Although it is possible to keep roses alive outdoors in containers when the temperature falls below 28°F, it is safest to move them to an unheated garage, basement, or other shelter at that point.

Plants for a Container Garden

Because of their tenderness, standard or "tree" roses are difficult to maintain in colder climates. By growing them in containers, which have to be moved indoors in winter anyway, you can have the pleasure of their stately appearance. I've chosen to feature 'Europeana', a floribunda rose with rich red flowers, as a standard. A lavish bloomer, the flowers are long-lasting and withstand heat well. Young leaves are mahogany red, turning deep green with age. The formality of the standard rose and square pot is softened with the creeping stems of the edible prostrate rosemary (*Rosmarinus officinalis* 'Prostratus'). The soft blue of the flowers provides contrasting color to the red of the rose. As an alternative to rosemary, you could choose some type of prostrate annual, such as verbena, alyssum, or petunias.

The next grouping of four pots features red roses with various underplantings. 'The Dark Lady' is a David Austin English rose with deep red, 5-inch flowers. Loosely double, the blooms have a heady old-rose scent. 'The Dark Lady' grows 4 to 5 feet tall and 3 to 4 feet wide. 'Summer Showers' is a hybrid ivy-leaved geranium you can start from seed. Bushy, gracefully trailing stems bear 5-inch flower heads in a mixture of burgundy, red, pink, lavender, and white. You could substitute another ivy-leaved geranium.

'Champlain' is one of the best of the Canadian-bred roses in the Explorer Series. Dark-red, 2-inch flowers are borne in clusters on hardy, mildew-resistant plants that grow 3 feet tall and as wide. The scarlet flowers of the perennial creeping thyme (*Thymus praecox* subsp. *arcticus* 'Coccineus') smother the tiny dark green leaves of the cascading stems. Even though the foliage is highly fragrant, if you prefer a

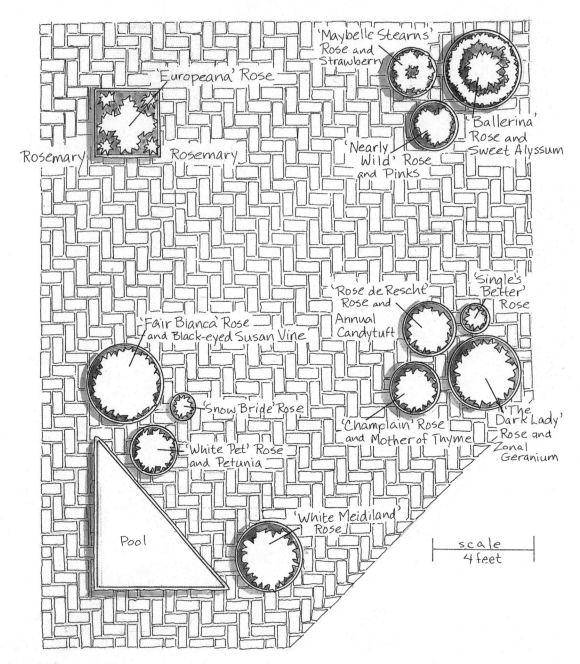

'Maybelle Stearns' Rose and Strawberry

'Europeana' Rose

Rosemary   Rosemary

'Ballerina' Rose and Sweet Alyssum

'Nearly Wild' Rose and Pinks

'Rose de Rescht' Rose and Annual Candytuft

'Single's Better' Rose

'Fair Bianca' Rose and Black-eyed Susan Vine

'Snow Bride' Rose

'White Pet' Rose and Petunia

'Champlain' Rose and Mother of Thyme

'The Dark Lady' Rose and Zonal Geranium

Pool

'White Meidiland' Rose

scale
4 feet

Container garden for a terrace or deck.
Numbers in brackets refer to the number of each plant you'll need for the design. 1. *Rosa* 'Europeana' grown as a standard [1] and underplanted with prostrate rosemary (*Rosmarinus officinalis* 'Prostratus') [4]. 2. *Rosa* 'The Dark Lady' [1] underplanted with 'Summer Showers' ivy-leaved geranium (*Pelargonium peltatum* 'Summer Showers') [7]. 3. *Rosa* 'Champlain' [1] underplanted with 'Coccineus' creeping thyme (*Thymus praecox* subsp. *arcticus* 'Coccineus') [6]. 4. *Rosa* 'Rose de Rescht' [1] underplanted with 'Brilliant Mixture' annual candytuft (*Iberis umbellata* 'Brilliant Mixture') [6]. 5. *Rosa* 'Single's Better' [1]. 6. *Rosa*

'Ballerina' [1] underplanted with 'Wonderland Rose' sweet alyssum (*Lobularia maritima* 'Wonderland Rose') [10]. 7. *Rosa* 'Maybelle Stearns' [1] underplanted with 'Pink Panda' strawberry (*Fragaria* 'Pink Panda') [6]. 8. *Rosa* 'Nearly Wild' [1] underplanted with 'Zing Rose' maiden pinks (*Dianthus deltoides* 'Zing Rose') [6]. 9. *Rosa* 'Fair Bianca' [1] underplanted with 'Susie White' black-eyed Susan vine (*Thunbergia alata* 'Susie White') [7]. 10. *Rosa* 'Little White Pet' [1] underplanted with 'White Madness' petunia (*Petunia* x *hybrida* 'White Madness') [5]. 11. *Rosa* 'Snow Bride' [1]. 12. *Rosa* 'Alba Meidiland' or 'White Meidiland' [1].

A look at the container garden. If you enjoy sunning, entertaining, or just plain sitting on your terrace, patio, or deck, you can enhance the pleasure with clever container plantings. A triangular pool forms an interesting contrast to the circular pots grouped in front of it. By underplanting roses with long-blooming annuals and perennials, you can extend container color and add extra appeal—as well as create living mulch! In a container planting like this, fragrance is key, since you'll be very close to the plants. Containers are also perfect to showcase standard (tree) roses like this 'Europeana', since it's easy to provide the necessary indoor protection over winter.

thyme for culinary use, grow common thyme (*Thymus vulgaris*).

With a haunting, intense fragrance, the 2½-inch flowers of 'Rose de Rescht' are a fuchsia-red with purple undertones. The bushy, compact plants grow 3 feet tall and 2½ feet wide. Classed as a Portland, the foliage resembles that of gallica roses, and its heritage is really a mystery. The small clusters of flowers are borne most heavily on younger growth, so prune this rose hard. 'Brilliant Mixture' annual candytuft (*Iberis umbellata* 'Brilliant Mixture') is a fine-textured annual with globes of pink, red, purple, and white flowers. Cut off spent flowers to keep plants blooming all summer.

'Single's Better' is unusual for a miniature rose, with its single, five-petalled flowers. Bright red with a yellow eye, the flowers are fragrant, as is the "moss" on the sepals. Bred by Harm Saville, plants are vigorous, symmetrical, and grow 15 to 18 inches tall.

In another corner of the deck or terrace, a cluster of three pots provides a pink theme. Among the best of shrubs, 'Ballerina' is an outstanding hybrid musk rose with great clusters of small, single, pale pink flowers with a white center. It grows 4 feet tall and wide, with lush, abundant foliage. 'Wonderland Rose' sweet alyssum (*Lobularia maritima* 'Wonderland Rose') is a low, spreading annual with tiny fragrant flowers of bright pink.

'Maybelle Stearns' is an unusual shrub rose

from the 1930s. Composed of many petals, the clusters of fragrant pink flowers are excellent for cutting, lasting up to 10 days in water. Disease-resistant and cold-hardy, plants grow only 2 feet tall but spread to 3 or 4 feet. To go with a unique rose, I thought it only fitting to choose a curious companion. The 'Pink Panda' perennial strawberry (*Fragaria vesca* 'Pink Panda') is an everbearing edible strawberry with showy deep pink flowers. Introduced by Englishman Adrian Bloom, it grows 6 to 8 inches tall and spreads by runners.

Echoing the simplicity of 'Ballerina' is another single-flowered rose, 'Nearly Wild'. An extremely hardy floribunda rose, it forms a neat, tidy mound 3 feet tall and wide. The large, non-stop pink flowers are reminiscent of wild roses. The spicy fragrance of carnations highlights the edible flowers of 'Zing Rose' maiden pinks (*Dianthus deltoides* 'Zing Rose'). Forming a dense groundcover of grassy leaves 6 inches tall, the single bright rose-pink blooms of 'Zing Rose' appear all summer.

White is an especially good color for patios or decks that are used a lot at night, since white shows up particularly well then. I've designed a group of white-flowering container plantings to cluster beside a small triangular water garden. I think the contrast of the triangle shape with the circular containers makes a very effective design, though you could substitute a circular pool to echo the containers' shapes. The pool's sides are 12 inches high, so if you wished, you could surround them with low, 8- to 12-inch decking for a poolside seat. It would be lovely to have a white-flowered, night-blooming waterlily in the water garden near this group of containers featuring white roses.

With the fragrance of myrrh, the pure white flowers of 'Fair Bianca' have classic old-rose form, with their cupped shape and green button eye. This English rose grows 4 feet tall and 3 feet wide. Cascading, twining stems of the white-flowered 'Susie White' black-eyed Susan vine (*Thunbergia alata* 'Susie White') set off its 1-inch blooms.

A sport of the climbing hybrid sempervirens 'Felicite et Perpetue', 'Little White Pet' (also known as 'White Pet') is a rose that belies its delicate appearance. The small, very double white flowers are borne in open clusters among dark green leaves. An excellent rose for any garden, the 'Pet' grows 2 feet tall and wide. The Madness series of petunias are among the most free-flowering of this annual staple of the garden. In this combination, of course, I chose 'White Madness'. For a finer-textured effect, try a white-flowered sweet alyssum instead.

'Snow Bride' is a miniature rose with perfectly formed, hybrid tea–like flowers on plants growing to 18 inches tall. 'Pacesetter' is another excellent white miniature you could use instead; it grows 18 to 24 inches tall. Both have dark green foliage.

Few roses have had such impact on landscaping as the Meidiland Series from the House of Meilland in France. Exceptionally hardy and disease-resistant, they are vigorous, versatile plants. 'Alba' has very double 2-inch flowers in clusters. Growing 24 to 30 inches tall with a 5- to 6-foot spread, it is used as a groundcover in the landscape, but here in a container it provides a soft, cascading effect. If you can't find a source for 'Alba Meidiland', substitute the similar 'White Meidiland', with 4-inch flowers and larger foliage.

Chapter 3

Buying and Planting Roses

*D*O YOU ENJOY PLANT SHOPPING, OR is it just another time-consuming chore? For me, shopping is an adventure. I think it's thrilling to find the rare or especially lovely rose among the commonplace. Although I occasionally allow myself the indulgence of casual rose-shopping, more often time constraints make me opt for a more efficient method. But whether I'm casually browsing or purposefully plant-hunting, I want the best possible plants. A cheap plant that's weak or sickly is no bargain.

In order to get top value when buying roses, it's important to first know what you want. (If you're not sure, review Chapter 1, "Choosing the Right Rose," to help you decide.) Next, you need to know how to recognize quality in roses and, finally, to know the differences among the sources.

Buying the best quality roses possible gives the greatest value for the money over the years. This doesn't necessarily mean buying the most expensive roses. The pricing of roses is determined by a variety of factors, including the degree of difficulty in propagating the rose, the length of time the rose has been available, the royalty payment that is due to the patent holder if the rose is patented, and the rarity of the cultivar. But as far as we gardeners are concerned, buying the best quality means buying the strongest, healthiest plants

available. In this chapter, you'll learn how to recognize these top-notch rose plants.

As important as picking the right plants is, there's more to getting the most from your roses—and that's getting them off to a good start. When you consider using roses in your landscape, it's important to keep in mind the basic cultural requirements roses need to grow well with the fewest problems. To make sure you site them where their needs are met, I'll review roses' simple requirements in "Siting Roses in the Landscape" on page 82. When you match your landscape needs with what your site and climate have to offer, and then choose appropriate roses from the many cultivars available, you'll be able to create a beautiful yard without a lot of extra effort.

There's one more thing you need to get your roses started off right, and that's proper planting technique. Planting roses right gives them a real head start in the garden. So I'll end this chapter with a clear, step-by-step review of planting techniques for both bareroot and container-grown roses, plus some aftercare tips to help them through their most vulnerable weeks.

Keep in mind as you read this chapter that the key to successful rose planting is to prepare the planting site before the plant arrives. If you're mail-ordering, you can order your plants, note down the projected arrival date, and make sure you've done your homework before the big day arrives. If you plan to buy roses from a garden center or nursery, try to prepare the site before you head for the store.

HOW ROSES ARE PROPAGATED

When you're buying roses, it helps to know how the plants were propagated, since each method has advantages and disadvantages. Budding—a form of grafting—is the most common method of commercial rose propagation. It involves removing a growth bud from a stem of the rose cultivar you want to grow and implanting it into the stem of another rose (called the understock) that will provide the root system for the new plant. The plants most often used for the understock are the tough, readily available multiflora rose (*Rosa multiflora*) and another cultivar, 'Dr. Huey'. Selling roses as grafted plants became popular because a great many more plants can be propagated from stock plants by using buds rather than stem cuttings.

It's easy to propagate roses from cuttings, but a 6-inch hardwood cutting will produce only one plant, while that same cutting may have three to six buds. However, miniatures are almost all produced from cuttings, and cuttings are a good way for people to share non-patented cultivars or grow more of these cultivars for their own use. Although there is not conclusive evidence, the general opinion among rose breeders is that own-root roses are usually hardier than budded plants. Own-root roses may be smaller than budded plants at the time you buy them, but don't let that discourage you.

Some rose growers specialize in own-root roses and sell only cutting-propagated plants. If you live in a cold-climate area like New England, the Great Lakes region, or much of Canada, you may want to buy own-root roses from some of the mail-order nurseries that feature them. Look for these nurseries in "Rose Resources," beginning on page 280. For more on the techniques of grafting and raising your own roses from cuttings, see Chapter 4.

Occasionally, you can find roses for sale that were grown by tissue culture. Tissue culture, or micropropagation, is a laboratory technique of propagation that involves taking either a single cell or a small number of cells from a plant and growing them on a sterile medium. In time, tiny, fully formed plants develop from this microscopic beginning, because each cell has the necessary genetic information to create a new plant.

The advantages of tissue culture are that many plants can be produced from a mother plant in a relatively short period of time and that these plants can be guaranteed disease-free if certified virus-free stock is used. But not all roses take to this method, plants may be expensive, and they are usually sold when small, so extra care and time must be given for them to develop in the garden.

HOW ROSES ARE SOLD

The vast majority of commercially available roses are sold as grafted plants. They are grown for two years in fields, mostly in California, Arizona, and Texas, then dug in the fall and placed in cold storage. From there, they may be shipped as bareroot plants from mail-order suppliers; packaged as bareroot plants for sale in nurseries, garden centers, or other stores; or sold to nurseries and garden centers to be potted into containers for sale.

Most roses are shipped bareroot to save shipping costs; pots and soil are bulky and heavy. The roots should be packed in moist sphagnum and plastic-wrapped to prevent dehydration. Some nurseries still sell bareroot roses stored in bins or boxes of sawdust, but this practice is not as common as it once was. See "Buying Roses Locally" and "Successful Mail-Ordering," both on the opposite page, for more on the advantages and disadvantages of container-grown and bareroot roses.

Going By the Numbers

Roses grown and sold as two-year-old, grafted, field-grown plants are graded No. 1, No. 1½, or No. 2, in compliance with industry standards first established in 1923 and revised periodically since then by the American Association of Nurserymen. Number 1 plants are the best quality and will provide you the strongest growth and most bloom, both the first year and in succeeding years.

You can recognize a No. 1 plant because it will have three or more healthy canes that are at least 6 inches long and ½ inch wide. Number 1½ plants have fewer and smaller canes, but with a little extra effort they'll produce good growth. Number 2 plants are even smaller—avoid these, since they require a great deal of tender loving

Buying Container-Grown Roses

Most nurseries and garden centers grow some or all of their rose stock in containers. Usually they buy the plants bareroot in midwinter, plant them in 5-gallon pots, and grow them in greenhouses. By the time the last frost is over, these plants are vigorously growing and often blooming.

Although they are more expensive than bareroot plants, container-grown roses offer several advantages: You know that the plants are growing well, you can see first-hand what the plants and flowers look like, and you'll get that "instant landscape" effect. The best time to buy and plant container-grown stock is from spring to midsummer.

The drawbacks of container-grown roses are the extra cost and the limited number of cultivars available (think of the difference between the 10 to 20 roses most garden centers offer and the many hundreds available bareroot from catalogs). You also have to be careful when you're planting container-grown roses, especially if the weather is sunny and hot. If you can, plant them on a cool, cloudy day when rain is predicted. Be especially careful to keep the soil watered well throughout the first growing season.

You can sometimes get bargains on container-grown plants in the fall. But by then, the plants will probably be potbound. When planting, be sure to loosen the roots so that they can grow outward. Provide plenty of winter protection as well.

care and still may never measure up.

The mail-order catalog description or the copy on the packaging of a bareroot plant may indicate the grade. If not, use the descriptions I've given to determine the grade when buying locally. If the mail-order catalog does not give the grade, call the company to see if they know what they ship. If not, you may want to consider other sources. Many companies that normally ship No. 1s may substitute No. 1½ stock when the stock of 1s is depleted, unless you tell them on the order form not to.

BUYING ROSES LOCALLY

Buying rose plants locally, either at a nursery or garden center, gives you the advantage of seeing first-hand the quality of the plant. First, you'll be able to check the number and size of the canes. A container-grown plant should have at least three or four young shoots growing near the base. Choose a plant that is well shaped, without branches that are crossed or growing inward.

Next, check to be sure the stems are hard, green (not brown), plump, and unwrinkled. There should be no sign of disease, no abnormal swellings, and no discolored stems or roots. The stems and roots should not be dried out or mushy. Withered stems will have wrinkles running lengthwise along them. If it's possible to see the roots, choose a plant with numerous, well-branched, stout roots that are long but not potbound.

Notice how and when the plants are stored or displayed. Discount department, drug, and grocery stores often bring in packaged, bareroot roses early in spring, keeping them inside where it's warm. In the warm stores, the roses begin to sprout. If bought and planted too early, this tender growth will never withstand the rigors of frost; if the shoots are long and white, they'll probably die no matter what.

Most of the roses offered at places like those are of lower grades and are cultivars 30 or 40 years old. I'll admit that I can't resist looking through these assortments, sometimes finding that older cultivar that still has merit. With extra care and patience, in several years the plant can be flourishing. But for well-grown, high-quality roses, buy from a nursery, garden center, or mail-order catalog.

As advantageous as it is to see first-hand what you're buying, most local nurseries and garden centers can offer only a limited number of roses. Considering that there are thousands of cultivars in cultivation, it seems a pity to confine yourself when there over 60 mail-order sources in the United States and Canada offering roses of one type or another, in one form or another. For addresses and more information, see "Rose Resources" on page 280.

SUCCESSFUL MAIL-ORDERING

Mail-ordering is not without it perils and pitfalls, but with a little judicious catalog reading (including between the lines), it's quite easy

Smart Garden-Center Shopping

Buying roses at garden centers, nurseries, and other local outlets gives you the advantages of getting the plants exactly when you want them and of seeing exactly what you're getting. Although the selection of roses will be much smaller than when buying by mail, many people prefer buying at least some of their roses this way. Both dormant plants and container-grown plants that have leafed out (and are often flowering) will be available. In order to get the most for your money, follow these tips:

• Buy plants as early as possible to get the best selection, but be sure to wait until it's time for you to plant in your area. (See "Regional Rose-Planting Guide" on page 82 if you're not sure.)

• If possible, shop during the middle of the week to avoid weekend crowds.

• Make a list of what you want, to avoid impulse purchasing. If a cultivar is unfamiliar, write it down, then go home and read about it rather than buying it on the spot; or take a rose reference along when you shop.

• Dormant plants should be labeled as to grade and be completely dormant, with no leaf buds beginning to open. Avoid plants with diseased or shriveled stems. Don't buy dormant plants that have been kept indoors.

• Buy healthy container-grown roses that are clearly labeled. A healthy plant will have sturdy stems with rich green disease- and insect-free leaves. The soil in the container should be moist.

• Signs of trouble in a container-grown plant include wilted leaves, weeds growing in the pot, dry soil, signs of insects or disease, a split pot, a thick root or roots growing through the base of the pot, and lopsided growth.

• Ask about replacement guarantees, and always keep your receipt.

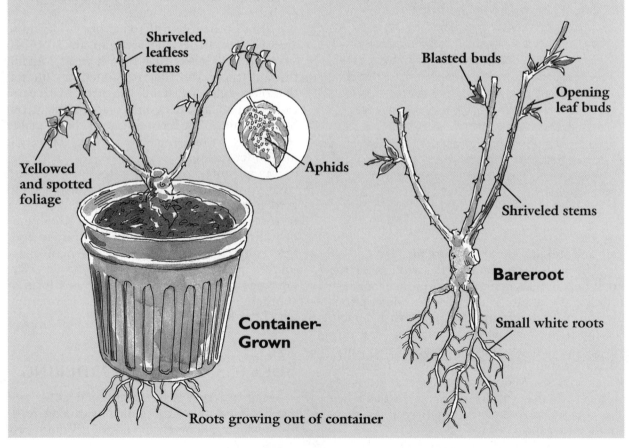

Shriveled, leafless stems

Aphids

Yellowed and spotted foliage

Container-Grown

Roots growing out of container

Blasted buds

Opening leaf buds

Shriveled stems

Bareroot

Small white roots

to buy successfully by mail. It also pays to take the time to talk with other people who grow roses; find out who they buy from and why. One of the side benefits of mail-ordering roses is the wealth of information about roses and rose growing in many of the catalogs.

There are several types of mail-order suppliers, including companies that offer a variety of plants besides roses, and companies that specialize in modern-day roses, old garden and shrub roses, or miniature roses. Most of the companies that specialize in roses are relatively small and are owned and operated by people who are very devoted to gardening and to roses. One of the benefits of getting involved with roses and joining a rose society is the opportunity to get to know or at least correspond with many of these fine rosarians and rose growers.

Buying Something Special

An exploration of the "Rose Resources" on page 280 will show you one of the most exciting aspects of rose gardening in recent years. There are a number of new, small nurseries offering older or less well known roses. Many of these companies are labors of love by people who hold down other jobs. Usually they don't produce great quantities of plants, so it's best to order early.

Some of these small nurseries provide the service of custom grafting or propagating, so that you can ask for a specific cultivar and they'll grow it for you. This means you may have to wait two years for your plant or else buy it as a recently budded or one-year-old plant, but it's worth it if you can't find the rose elsewhere.

Smart Mail-Order Shopping

With thousands of rose cultivars available, not even the best local garden centers and nurseries can begin to carry more than a comparative handful. Mail-order nurseries fill a critical need, since they can maintain a much larger range of stock for sale. If you buy from mail-order companies, you'll have access to every rose in commerce. Most mail-order companies are very reliable, but even with the best, it's important to know exactly what they're offering. Here are some tips for getting the most from mail-order shopping:

• Whenever possible, use companies that have been recommended by other gardeners. Talk to as many people as possible, especially neighbors with gardens you admire and members of the American Rose Society, to get as much input as possible.

• Be wary of companies that make outrageous claims or have prices that are far below the other catalogs'.

• Compare descriptions of rose cultivars in different catalogs and rose books. If possible, visit gardens where you can see the roses you're interested in for yourself. Remember that catalog shopping offers you the luxury of time to make calculated choices. Make sure you take advantage of this opportunity.

• Read the introduction to the catalog and the order blank. The best suppliers give specifics on the size, age, and grade of the roses, shipping information, whether the plants are own-root or grafted, replacement guarantees, substitution policies, and the involvement and knowledge of the owners (many of whom are first-class rose enthusiasts whose interest grew into a business).

• Learn to read between the lines of rose descriptions. Catalog writers are trying to sell their product. Terms like "light scent" can be misleading—it usually means the rose has hardly any fragrance. And "exhibition-quality" flowers may be great for rose shows, but the plants may not look good in the landscape. Seldom are plants quite as glorious, hardy, or disease-resistant as described. If some of the descriptions are honest about the pitfalls of given cultivars, then you'll know that the more extravagant claims are probably fairly accurate as well.

• Don't be so overcome by what's in the catalog description that you don't see what's missing. If you don't see "fragrant," "disease-resistant," "attractive foliage," "reblooms," and other desirable qualities, it may be because the rose doesn't have them.

• For the best selection, order as early as possible. Many of the smaller growers have limited quantities, especially of unusual or popular cultivars.

WHEN TO BUY AND PLANT ROSES

In order to have the rose cultivars you want, it's best to mail-order or purchase them locally as early as possible. When buying locally, wait to buy dormant plants until the proper planting time in your area. Buying bareroot roses late in the spring means the top growth has started without a well-established root system; plants are likely to succumb to hot, dry weather unless you give them proper care. Container-grown roses are often put on sale in summer and early fall, but by that time they will be potbound, again needing special care to survive. (See "Buying Container-Grown Roses" on page 79 for suggestions.)

In temperate climates, dormant bareroot plants are usually planted a month or so before the last spring frost. For warmer regions, fall and winter planting is best. Fall planting used to be more widely practiced because it gives plants an opportunity to become established during the fall and winter months. With attentive care, it is still a viable option. See "Planting Your Roses Right" on page 86 and "Aftercare for Newly Planted Roses" on page 88 for more information.

Regional Rose-Planting Guide

Use these guidelines, based on where you live, to determine when you should buy and plant roses.

Pacific and Gulf Coast: December–January

Inland Pacific Coast, Southwest, and Mid-South: January–February

Upper South and Mid-Atlantic Coast: March–April

Lower Mountain Elevations and Lower Midwest: April

Mid-Mountain Elevations, Plains, Upper Midwest, and Lower Northeast: April–May

Higher Mountain Elevations, Northern Plains, and Upper Northeast: May

HANDLING YOUR PURCHASES

Mail-order suppliers ship dormant bareroot roses to arrive at the best planting time for your area, or whenever you request them to ship your order. Try to plant the roses as soon as possible after they are delivered or after you buy them locally. If you can't plant your new roses right away, keep them cool and the sphagnum or other packing material around their roots moist until you're able to plant them.

If you must wait more than several days and the ground is not frozen, heel the plants in. "Heeling in" means digging a sloping trench, preferably in a shaded spot, and laying the plants on the slope with the roots at the bottom, then covering both roots and stems with soil that is kept moist.

If your bareroot roses are sent in shredded bark (excelsior) or a thin layer of sphagnum and you can't plant them right away, an alternative is to pack the roots with a thick layer of a material such as moistened sand, sawdust, long-fibered sphagnum peat moss, vermiculite, or perlite. Store the roses in a cool place that is kept above freezing. Keep the material moist, and cover the canes with dampened newspaper or burlap.

Container-grown roses are a lot easier to handle. Keep them watered and in the same amount of sunlight they were displayed in at the nursery or garden center (partial shade if you can't remember). It's still best to plant them as soon as you can so their roots can spread out and you won't have to water them as often. Plan to buy them on a day when you know you'll have time to put them in the ground.

SITING ROSES IN THE LANDSCAPE

Now that you feel confident about ordering roses for your landscape, let's consider the next step: planting. Although roses are highly adaptable plants—think how many of the older types you see surviving at abandoned homesteads and old cemeteries—they grow and bloom best if you give them the best conditions possible. When you're deciding where to plant roses, the factors to consider include soil, light, water, humidity, wind, extreme temperatures, and accessibility.

Soil and light are the two primary considerations. The ideal soil is rich in organic matter and nutrients and is moist but well drained—in other words, good garden soil. If the soil in your chosen site does not meet these criteria and you absolutely *must* grow your roses there, correct any drainage problems and work in lots of compost and other organic matter prior to planting, as described in "Planting Your Roses Right" on page 86.

Let There Be Light

Almost all roses need a site that gets direct sun at least six hours a day in order to grow and bloom well. An area with morning sun is better than one that gets afternoon sun, because the dew will dry more quickly, reducing the incidence of disease. In very hot climates, morning sun is less intense, so it's less likely that foliage, flowers, and new growth will get burned.

You'll know if your roses are not getting enough light by their lanky growth. Spindly canes with leaves spaced far apart and few flowers also tell the tale. Either move the plants to a sunnier site or create more light by removing limbs or objects in the way. A white wall or fence reflects light, brightening up a dark area. Water in a pool or water garden and a light-colored mulch (like white pebbles) work the same way.

Still another option is a temporary reflecting screen made from white-painted plywood or sheeting stapled to a wooden frame. Set this screen up behind the roses to reflect more light on them; but be sure the screen is well anchored so it won't topple, or you could do more harm than good. An advantage of the screen is that you can take it down and store it when you're expecting visitors!

If your whole property is shady or you must plant roses in a site with less than optimal light, all is not lost. You just need to focus on those roses that can make do with less. Roses that thrive with only four hours of direct sun include the hybrid musks, miniatures, and most climbers.

Watering Right

Like most other garden plants, roses grow best with an even supply of moisture—the equivalent of about 1 inch each week. The repeat-blooming hybrid teas, grandifloras, and floribundas are more dependent on steady, even moisture than species and cultivars that bloom only once a year. Rugosas, albas, and many

shrub roses are relatively drought-tolerant. If you're unable or unwilling to water your roses and must rely exclusively on rainfall, choose one of these tough shrubs.

No matter which roses you plant, mulch them well. Mulch not only conserves soil moisture, it also keeps disease-bearing spores and nematodes from splashing up off wet soil onto your plants. The rules for watering roses are simple: Water deeply (for good root growth and maximum drought tolerance), don't water in the evening (you'll encourage disease), and don't water overhead or splash water on the foliage (another invitation to disease). One good way to satisfy these watering rules is to use drip irrigation. I'll discuss both mulching and watering in greater detail in Chapter 4, "Rose Care and Feeding."

Too much water, especially if it's standing water caused by soil that doesn't drain well, is as much a problem as too little. If the site you're considering has poor drainage, then consider growing roses in another part of the yard, installing a drainage system, or growing your roses in raised beds or containers.

Airing Out

The moisture in the air also has an effect on the health of roses. Fungal diseases are usually most prevalent in moist, stagnant conditions. If your region naturally has high humidity, grow only the most disease-resistant cultivars (you'll find these listed in "Roses for Special Situations" on page 24), or else you'll find yourself applying frequent remedies and your plants will suffer.

Siting your roses in an area of the yard with gently moving air will lessen the ill effects of high humidity. In humid areas, don't plant roses near walls, fences, hedges, or other structures that restrict air movement. The moist, salty air of the seaside can be especially damaging; if you live near the shore, plant salt-tolerant rugosa roses.

Even though balmy breezes may help your roses through a hot, wet summer, strong winds can hurt your plants. Winds dry out rose leaves and canes and can loosen the plants in the soil, damaging their roots and making frost heaving more likely in winter. If your yard is whipped by strong winds, protect your roses by planting a windbreak of evergreens or setting up a fence. Make sure you put the windbreak far enough away from your roses to prevent shading, competition, and air turbulence. To be on the safe side, plant the roses at least four to six times their mature height from the windbreak.

Heat and Cold

Your area's humidity isn't the only climatic factor that can affect your roses. Extremes of both heat and cold can slow down the growth of your roses. Choose cultivars that are recommended for your area, since they'll be most tolerant of your conditions. Most roses can grow without winter protection in areas with minimum winter temperatures of 0°F. Roses that are hardy in colder conditions include the hybrid perpetuals, eglantine rose, swamp rose, 'Stanwell Perpetual', prairie rose, and most of the gallica, alba, damask, rugosa, shrub, and moss roses. If you're a cold-climate gardener, don't plant roses in parts of your yard that naturally accumulate cold air, such as low spots.

Roses don't enjoy extreme heat, either; but while cold threatens their survival, heat hampers their bloom. If you think about it, you'll remember that most roses' best blooms come in early summer and in fall, when temperatures are more moderate. If you're a Deep South or Southwest gardener, you'll find that planting in areas with only morning sun gives the best results.

The Gardener's Footsteps

The final key in successfully siting your roses is to choose locations in your yard that are readily accessible. Having roses growing where you see them regularly means that you will notice the first signs of a problem—often the difference between a quick solution and an endless battle. You'll also be able to feed and care for your plants efficiently.

PREPARING THE SOIL

Some people enjoy planting and replanting in the garden, much like moving furniture. For most of us, however, the planting process isn't our favorite aspect of gardening. If planted in the proper location from the beginning and adequately maintained, a rose will live for many years. It makes sense, then, to have prepared the soil the best way possible when you plant. All the care in the world later will not make up for inadequate soil preparation.

Soil Type and pH

Soil is basically composed of sand, silt, and clay particles plus decayed organic matter, called humus. The relative proportions of these components determine the soil type. Unless there is an impervious layer beneath the topsoil, a sandy soil drains quickly. This means that plants need frequent watering and feeding. A clay soil may have drainage problems if the proportion of clay is too high. The goal is to have a soil that does not drain too quickly yet has enough pore space so there's plenty of air for plant roots.

A fast, easy way to determine your soil type is to pick up a handful of soil several days after a rain or watering. Squeeze the soil and open your hand. If the soil ball retains its shape, you have a clay soil. If it falls apart and is gritty, your soil is sandy. A ball that partially crumbles apart is referred to as loam. Loam has a mixture of 30 to 50 percent sand, 30 to 40 percent silt, and 10 to 20 percent clay particles. Roses do best in a loam that's close to 20 percent clay.

The pH, or acidity or alkalinity, of your soil determines how well nutrients are absorbed from the water in the soil. It also affects soil microbial growth. A scale of 0 to 14 is used to measure pH, with 7 being neutral, the lower numbers being acid, and the higher numbers alkaline. Roses grow best with a pH of 6.0 to 6.5 (slightly acid to near-neutral), but they will tolerate a range from 5.5 to 7.8.

Soil testing, done with home-test kits, or by a private soil-testing laboratory or your county agricultural extension service, will tell you the nutrient levels and pH. Test your soil before preparing the soil for planting and again every one or two years.

Getting Soil in Shape

For roses, as well as most other plants, preparing the soil at least several months before planting is ideal. This allows the soil to settle and the organic soil amendments to blend with the soil and develop the active microbial growth so essential to plant health.

First, remove the grass, weeds, or other plants growing on the site, along with any large stones. Whether you're planting one rose or many, dig into the soil one spade's depth, then loosen the soil below with a spading fork. Mix in the equivalent of one-third by volume of organic material (like rotted leaves or manure, or compost) with two-thirds of soil. Use the extra third of soil in other parts of the garden, unless you are making raised beds. The only other additional "magic" element to add at this time is a cupful of alfalfa meal per plant, which can be purchased from garden supply companies and farm supply stores. Alfalfa meal is high in nitrogen, and it adds trace elements and a natural plant growth stimulant to the soil.

What organic material you incorporate into your soil depends on availability. There is no one "right" material. The most readily available options include homemade or purchased compost, well-rotted manures, and finely ground composted leaves or bark. The important factor is that the organic matter be well decomposed, to the extent that most of the material is not recognizable. If the material is not thoroughly decomposed, then decomposition will have to take place in the soil. This can generate heat that damages roots as well as using up nitrogen in the soil. No matter what you use or what type of soil you have, organic matter holds the water and nutrients necessary for plant growth like a sponge, creates air spaces for roots, and provides food for beneficial soil microorganisms and earthworms.

Balancing pH

Most garden soil will have a pH within the acceptable range for roses, but now is the time to correct it if it is not right. Remember that organic matter will slightly raise or lower pH; a steady diet of compost or other organic matter will gradually bring and keep your garden soil in balance. If you need a quicker fix, however, read on.

Adding limestone in the form of ground calcitic limestone (calcium carbonate) or ground dolomitic limestone (calcium-magnesium carbonate) raises the soil pH. Use this rule of thumb to raise the pH of slightly acid soils: Apply 5 pounds of lime per 100 square feet to raise the pH one point. Never use hydrated lime (calcium hydroxide), as it can damage plant roots.

Agricultural sulfur is used to lower the pH. Your soil test kit or laboratory report will tell you the amount to add in relationship to the type of soil you have. Spread the material evenly over the soil and dig it several inches deep into the soil.

Lightening Up

Gypsum (calcium sulfate), sand, perlite, vermiculite, and pumice are sometimes recommended for improving heavy clay soils. These are necessary only in highly localized conditions, which will be identified by soil test or the advice of local rosarians. Gypsum can also make a soil more acid, so you shouldn't apply it unless directed to by soil test results. In most cases, adding lots of organic matter is all that is necessary; even in extreme cases, creating raised beds will usually take care of the problem.

Dealing with Drainage

The other key test before planting roses (or any other garden plant, for that matter) is checking drainage. To test, dig a hole 6 inches wide and 12 inches deep. Fill the hole with water, allow it to drain, and fill it again immediately. Note how long this second filling takes to drain. If it takes 6 to 8 hours, adding organic matter will be enough to improve soil drainage. If longer than 8 hours, consider having drainage tiles installed or growing your roses in raised beds or containers. If the hole takes less than 6 hours to drain, add organic matter to help hold the water in your soil.

Creating raised beds 6 to 12 inches high is possible simply by not removing any soil and by mixing in one-half as much organic matter. To keep the soil from washing away, slope the sides slightly, or edge the beds with timbers, stone, or brick. Do not use wood that's been pressure-treated or treated with preservatives like creosote, which can harm plants and leach chemicals into the soil.

Preparing Containers

Whether you have all your roses in containers because of necessity, or have only a few containers for decoration, growing roses in pots or tubs is easy and satisfying. Bushy, repeat-flowering roses perform best in containers, especially the miniatures, polyanthas, floribundas, many shrub types, and any of the short older cultivars. See my container planting design, "Container Terrace or Deck Garden," on page 72 for specific cultivars for containers.

Miniatures need a container at least 8 inches wide and deep. Full-sized roses must have one 18 inches wide and deep. Choose from containers of wood, clay, plastic, or concrete. There must be at least one drainage hole in the bottom or on the sides near the bottom. If you have a decorative container with no holes and holes can't be drilled into it, double-pot by planting the rose in a slightly smaller pot and setting it on several inches of pebbles inside the larger one.

Whatever container you use, scrub it thoroughly if it has been used before. Put screening in the bottom over the drainage hole to keep soil from escaping. Use a soilless potting mix bought from a garden supply store, or mix one at home following the directions in "Care for Container Gardens" on page 73, making sure to include the organic fertilizer.

PLANTING YOUR ROSES RIGHT

Once the soil is prepared, the key factors in planting roses are timing, spacing, and depth. Whether you buy your roses locally or by mail order, they may be bareroot or in containers and may be grafted or on their own roots. (See page 79 for the advantages and disadvantages of shopping locally versus mail-ordering.)

Timing Is Everything

Bareroot roses are usually dormant and should be planted either in late fall or in early spring. If mail-ordered, they are sent as close as possible to the best planting time for your area.

Container-grown roses are actively growing and can be planted anytime during the growing season. However, my motto is "The earlier, the better." If possible, plant in the spring once frosts are over, since the roses will have more time to grow in the ground—a big advantage over being held in their containers, where they risk drying out and nutrient deficiency as well as root constriction.

Spacing Out

The spacing for roses depends on their ultimate size and use. Most important to consider is having enough space around the rose for

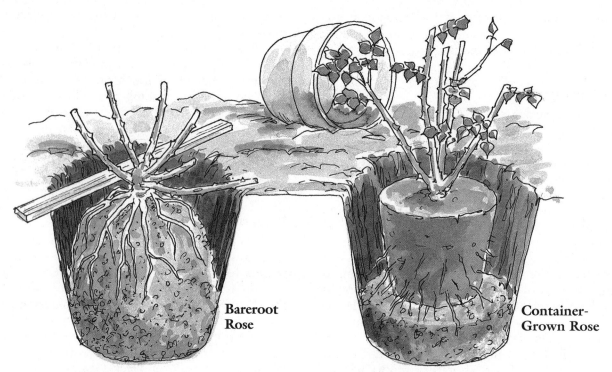

Bareroot Rose

Container-Grown Rose

How to plant roses. To plant a bareroot rose (*left*), mound soil in the bottom of the planting hole and set the plant on top of the mound, spreading its roots down the sides. Adjust the height of the soil mound so that the bud union (the knobby point where the top of the bush was grafted to the rootstock) is just above soil level, at soil level, or 1 to 2 inches below soil level, depending on your climate. Fill in around the plant with soil, and water it in, adding more soil as need-

ed. To keep the canes from drying out, mound soil over the lower 6 inches of the plant until new growth starts elongating, then gently hose the mound away. Planting container-grown roses (*right*) is easy. Put enough soil in the hole so the bud union is at the correct depth. Carefully remove the plant from the container, loosening the root ball if it is rootbound. Fill in around the root ball with soil. Water and add more soil, if necessary.

adequate air circulation. Second, if you're planting more than one rose together in an area, you want them close enough to one another to create a mass and make a visual impact. Climate also plays a part, since in colder areas roses never achieve the size they would in milder regions.

In areas with extended periods of freezing weather, set hybrid teas, floribundas, and grandifloras 24 to 30 inches apart. Space polyanthas 18 to 24 inches apart. Set miniature, shrub, and old garden roses about as far apart as their mature height. For a hedge, space roses 3 to 4 feet apart. If you're planting full-sized standard or tree roses in the ground, space them about 4 feet apart. Set climbers planted along fences 8 to 10 feet apart, but if you're training them up a wall, plant them 3 feet apart. In climates with no frost or only short periods of frost, add 6 inches to the spacing.

Planting Bareroot Roses

To plant bareroot roses, choose a day when the soil is relatively dry, since digging in wet soil can destroy soil structure and create compaction. If your bareroot roses arrive or you buy them when planting conditions are not right, either plant them into containers or dig a trench, lay the plants in at a 45-degree angle, and completely cover them with soil (a process called heeling in).

When you're ready to plant bareroot roses, set the plants in a bucket of water so that the roots don't dry out during the planting process. Prune off any damaged or dead roots. Then prune off any dead or damaged canes, cutting back to a healthy bud. Dig a hole large enough for the roots to spread out naturally.

If the plants are grafted, set the graft at the depth suggested in the table "How Deep to Plant Roses" below. (In the summer, pull the soil away from the bud union to give it exposure to the sun.) Set own-root roses at the same depth as they were growing previously. Make a mound of soil in the bottom of the planting hole. Set the rose on this mound, spreading out its roots. Completely cover the roots with soil, tamp gently, and water well (the soil will settle). Then finish filling the hole with soil.

Container and Standard Roses

Compared to planting bareroot roses, planting container-grown roses is easy. Dig a hole large enough to hold the pot, making sure the top of the soil in the container is just below ground level. Then tip the container and tap it to release the soil ball, or cut the container away from the root ball. Set the rose into the hole, holding on to the top of the soil/root ball

How Deep to Plant Roses

Unless you order own-root roses, most of the roses you buy will be grafted. You can recognize a grafted rose by looking for a swelling or knobby area on the trunk, called the bud union, where the cultivar you've bought was grafted onto a tough understock that provides the root system. When you plant roses, you can decide how deep to set them in the soil based on where you live. The colder your climate, the deeper you should set your plants, so they'll get the maximum winter protection from the soil's natural insulation. In the following table, look in the left-hand column for your area's average winter minimum temperatures. Then, depending on whether you're planting hybrid teas, grandifloras, or other roses, look in the center or right-hand column to see how deep to set your plants. The number of inches refers to how deep to set the bud union below the soil surface.

Winter Minimum	Hybrid Teas and Grandifloras	All Others
32°F	1–2" above soil surface	2" deep
20°F	Just above soil surface	2" deep
Less than 20°F	1–2" deep	2" deep

rather than grasping the rose by its stem (a painful prospect at best, and a broken stem at worst). If your rose is rootbound, loosen the root ball before planting. Once the rose is in the ground, water it in.

When you're planting a standard (tree) rose in the ground, drive a support stake into the hole before setting in the rose. The stake should be long enough to reach the bud union at the top. This will keep the rose from snapping off at the graft in a storm or high wind. Otherwise, proceed as you would for any container rose.

TRANSPLANTING ROSES

No matter how carefully you plan a garden, there are times when it's obvious that a plant is in the wrong place. It may not have turned out to be the right color, it may have overgrown its site or not ever gotten as big as you thought it would, or you may have decided to redo the garden with a different design. Other reasons for relocating roses are that you're moving to a new home or that you want to save roses that are destined to be destroyed (on an abandoned property that's about to be bulldozed, for example).

The best time to transplant roses is when they're dormant. Water the soil well a day or so before digging. Try to remove a soil ball at least 18 inches across, disturbing roots as little as possible. Cut the top growth back by one-half.

For a particularly cherished plant that is long-established, you'll be able to transplant with the least setback if you use a two-step process. A month before transplanting, root-prune your rose. With a spade, cut a circle 18 inches in diameter around the circumference of the plant. This causes small new roots to develop at the outside of the root ball. Then when you dig, make a 24-inch circle so you won't cut off all the new roots. This way, you'll get a mass of actively growing roots to nourish your plant rather than shell-shocked, severed roots.

For plants that must be moved when they're

actively growing, use the two-step process outlined above if you can. Then, when it's time to transplant, remove all flowers and buds as well as half the top growth. Water transplants well and supply shade with snow fencing, or the white row-cover fabric sold for frost protection of vegetables, until the plants have recovered and resumed growth.

AFTERCARE FOR NEWLY PLANTED ROSES

To prevent the canes of your newly planted or transplanted rose from drying out in warm, windy weather, mound 6 to 8 inches of soil around the base of the plant. Bring the soil in from another part of the garden. If you're planting in the fall and you live where the soil freezes, provide winter protection as well. (See Chapter 4 for more on winter protection.) For late-spring planting, shade the plants with row covers or snow fencing until they're established.

When new growth is 1 to 2 inches long, wash the soil mound away with gently flowing water (don't blast it off with the hose; you could break some of the canes or new growth). Check plants once or twice a week to make sure they're growing well and don't need any special care; watch for aphids and other pests. Water regularly, as necessary, to keep the soil from drying out. Remove the shading over spring plantings gradually until the plants are fully exposed to the sun. Do not fertilize your new roses until after the first bloom period is finished.

Once your design is complete and your lovely new roses are up and growing, you'll need to help them through their first season. Loving care during the first year can make or break a new planting. Turn to Chapter 4, "Rose Care and Feeding," to find all the growing basics, from feeding and watering through pest, disease, and weed control to deadheading, pruning, and winter protection.

Chapter 4

Rose Care and Feeding

"I LOVE ROSES, BUT . . ."

I've heard this sentence with any number of endings, ranging from " . . . they need too much water" to " . . . they can only be grown with pesticides," " . . . pruning is too complicated," "they always die in the winter," or the ultimate, all-inclusive " . . . they're just too hard to grow."

Quite honestly, roses can be a lot of work if you're growing disease-susceptible, thirsty, fertilizer-hungry cultivars in a cold climate. But it doesn't have to be that way. With the right system, it's no harder to grow roses than any other shrub or perennial. As I've discussed in Chapter 1, the first step is selecting cultivars that are hardy for your climate, pest-resistant, and able to naturally withstand harsher conditions. By joining those traits with careful soil preparation and planting, covered in Chapter 3, you've already made growing roses infinitely easier.

If you bring careful plant selection, good soil preparation, and proper planting together with the basic organic gardening techniques that I'll go over in this chapter, you'll be rewarded with gorgeous flowers and attractive landscape plants. It will only require a few hours per season—and you won't have to resort to harmful chemicals. You'll also find that with this basic system, even the more tem-

peramental cultivars like hybrid teas do much better than you'd expect.

How much time and effort you want to put into your roses is up to you. Some people who grow roses love to experiment with different fertilizer mixes and schedules, different pruning or training techniques, or even propagating their own roses. Others just want nice, healthy plants with a minimum of bother. In this chapter, my goal has been to present various options, from the most basic methods of rose care to some of the more detailed techniques available for those who enjoy spending a lot of time in the garden. Don't be overwhelmed by these suggestions if you're only interested in simple growing techniques—you'll still get great roses by following my basic plan.

Since the worst rose bug is the one that bites you, you may find yourself wanting to grow more roses or to experiment with more advanced growing techniques. Once you get bitten really badly, pick up one of the various rose society publications and more specialized rose books, many of which are listed in "Recommended Reading" on page 293. Don't forget to share your experiences with other organic rose gardeners in your area—you'll learn a lot from their first-hand experience about what works well in your area.

MAKING YOUR SYSTEM WORK

One of the most important lessons I've learned as a gardener is that not only is there no one "right" way, but also that you have to develop a sense of the factors involved in healthy plant growth. This is true for two fundamental reasons. First, there are so many variables of climate, soil, and growing conditions that there can't possibly be just one solution for all situations. (For example, saying that plants need about an inch of water a week doesn't take into account soil quality, wind, amount of sun or shade the plant gets, air temperature, or root growth.) Second, plants are incredibly adaptable; they can survive, and even thrive, under a lot of different growing regimes.

Try the suggestions I've made in this chapter for the environmentally sensitive care and feeding of roses. Observe what works for you and what doesn't. Make sure you give these techniques time to work. It can take two or three years for a garden's ecological balance to shift from a chemical system into a fully functioning organic system. The first year, there may be more problems than you'd like. Don't despair or use synthetic chemicals—try to use a preventive approach, and where that doesn't stem the tide, use some of the organic controls listed later in this chapter. Keep working toward the goal of beautiful, flourishing roses with techniques that ensure healthy gardens and gardeners for generations to come.

Let's review the basics of good rose growing: mulch, watering, feeding, pest and disease control, weeding, pruning, training, and winter care. I'll also discuss rose propagation, so that if you'd like, you can get more plants of your favorite roses for free!

MULCHING FOR MORE ROSES

Looking for a simple, inexpensive way to have healthier rose bushes and fewer gardening chores? One of the best ways is using a layer of organic material, called mulch, to cover the soil surface around your plants. Mulching with plant residues like chopped leaves or compost is one of the most important organic gardening techniques. Most gardeners know that mulching helps reduce water use, minimize weeding, moderate soil temperature fluctuations, and improve soil quality. Mulch also increases plant vigor and improves garden appearance. Here's why mulching works:

It reduces watering. A mulch slows down the evaporation of moisture from the soil, even during hot, dry weather. This either eliminates the need for anything other than natural rainfall or else reduces the amount of water—and watering time—you have to use. It also helps rainfall penetrate the soil by preventing a hard crust from forming and by slowing down water runoff.

It controls weeds. An organic mulch won't prevent weed growth as well as a plastic or fabric mulch, but it will inhibit the germination and growth of many weeds. (In fact, placing several layers of newspaper under an organic mulch works very well to control weeds. Replace the paper and mulch each season.) The weeds that do grow are easier to pull because a mulched soil is looser than an unmulched one. When weeding, scrape the mulch away from the weed, bring up as little soil as possible with the weed, then replace the mulch.

It moderates the soil temperature. Temperature extremes in the soil can be harmful to plant health, and a mulch keeps soil cooler in summer and warmer longer in winter. Cool soil in summer encourages earthworm activity, which adds nutrients and aeration to the soil. Warmer soil in winter means less root damage from frost heaving, a result of the effects of soil freezing and thawing in winter.

Keep the mulch lighter in spring with newly planted roses, since you want the soil to warm up quickly for fast root development. In cold-climate areas, a heavier spring mulch on established plantings will maintain cool soil longer as the weather warms up. This will slow down early spring growth, possibly saving tender shoots from late frost damage.

It reduces soil erosion. A mulch protects the soil from washing away from rainfall or overhead watering. This is especially important when planting beds are on even a slight slope.

It enriches the soil. Plant residues and manures contain nutrients necessary for plant growth. These become available to plants as the mulch decomposes. (For more about plant nutrients, see "Feeding Roses Naturally" on page 93.)

It improves soil structure. As mulch decomposes, it gradually adds humus to the soil. This addition of organic matter enhances your soil's ability to retain moisture while at the same time improving soil aeration.

Best Materials for Mulching Roses

When picking a mulch for your roses, choose one that looks clean and attractive—after all, the mulch should enhance your garden's appeal. It should be heavy enough not to wash or blow away from your plants. And, of course, it should be inexpensive and readily available. Some mulch materials, like mushroom soil, spent hops, apple pomace, ground tobacco stems, sugar-cane residue, and peanut hulls, are regional specialties. Look for good local materials and see what your area has to offer. Other mulches are available nationwide. Here are my top picks:

• **Cocoa shells:** The dark brown shells of cocoa beans absorb $2\frac{1}{2}$ times their weight in water, so they're fairly stable. Their appealing chocolate scent disappears quickly but makes cocoa shells fun to apply. Attractive. Easy to apply. Sold in bags.

• **Compost:** Finished compost is not only the best soil amendment but also an attractive mulch, especially if the composted materials have been shredded for an even texture. Homemade or sold in bags.

• **Corncobs:** Corncobs ground into 1-inch pieces have a high sugar content, so they nourish soil microorganisms. They also improve soil texture. Because they need nitrogen to decompose, apply a high-nitrogen fertilizer such as blood meal, bonemeal, or compost to the soil before putting down the mulch. Sold in bulk.

• **Grass clippings:** One of the most accessible and inexpensive mulches and a quick source of nitrogen. But there are some drawbacks: Clippings can form a thick mat that water can't get through. They can also rot quickly, building up a great deal of damaging heat and making them a short-lived mulch. If you want to use clippings as a mulch, try composting them first. Be sure the clippings are not from a lawn treated with broadleaf weed killers. Apply no more than 2 inches thick.

• **Leaves:** For roses, leaves are best used shredded or composted into leafmold, since unshredded tree leaves tend to become a sodden mess if not mixed with a lighter material such as straw. Attractive.

• **Manure:** To use for mulch, manure must be aged for six months so it doesn't burn plants. Manure and compost are my top two mulch choices. A manure mulch will prevent or cure "soil sickness," a condition in which rose growth declines after several years in the same location. Don't let manure come into direct contact with rose stems. Sold in bags or bulk.

• **Wood bark, chips, and shavings:** Commercially available wood bark may be from fir, pine, cedar, or redwood trees. Wood chips and shavings are usually available in bulk from tree-trimming companies free or for a nominal cost. All wood mulches need nitrogen to break down, so they can tie up nitrogen normally available to plants. To avoid this, spread an inch of compost or aged manure on the soil before adding the bark, chips, or shavings, or apply a high-nitrogen fertilizer such as blood meal, bonemeal, or compost. Attractive and long-lasting. Use medium or coarse grades. Sold in bags or bulk.

It keeps plants clean and healthy. Water splashing onto soil will splatter the soil onto the plants. This not only is unattractive, it can also spread soilborne pests and diseases, especially blackspot and nematodes. Studies have shown that organic mulches can suppress harmful soil fungi and nematodes. And mulch will keep the soil from splashing onto your plants.

It improves your garden's appearance. Mulching gives a uniform look to beds and borders throughout your yard. It provides a finished look to plantings: Instead of bare soil, you'll have a smooth mulch blanket around your plants.

Using Mulch

You can apply mulch at any time during the year, but usually it's best to apply a fresh layer in spring after the winter protection has been removed and the soil has warmed. Before mulching, remove weeds and work the soil lightly so that a hard, impenetrable layer does not form between the soil and the mulch.

Depending on the material used, the mulch layer should usually be about 3 inches thick, but many gardeners use 4 to 6 inches without harming their plants. If you live in a wet climate or have a heavy clay soil that doesn't dry out quickly, you might want to use less than 3 inches of mulch so your soil can dry out faster.

As your mulch decomposes during the growing season or from year to year, add more to bring the level up to 3 inches. Before adding fresh mulch, work the remaining mulch into the top layer of the soil or remove and compost it.

WATERING WISELY

More than any other aspect of gardening, determining the water needs of plants requires sensitivity, not only to the plants themselves but to their environment, including soil, nutrient levels, wind, humidity, temperature, and sun. Today, concern about dwindling water supplies has caused water conservation to become law in many areas and habit in many more. As we become more aware of the limited amount of water at our disposal, we as gardeners have the added responsibility of using water wisely.

At one time, rose gardeners were encouraged to feed and water roses as much as possible so that hybrid teas and other modern roses could live up to their billing. Gardeners can no longer lavish precious resources on their plants in good conscience. We must look for ways to use less water. Fortunately, that doesn't mean we have to sacrifice having healthy, beautiful free-flowering roses.

Can you have roses with just normal rainfall and no extra watering? The answer is a qualified yes, depending on what the normal rainfall is in your area. Most garden plants require the equivalent of 1 inch of water per week during the growing season. In most areas of the United States, with a thick mulch and normal rainfall you'll get average growth, flowers, and fruit, with some plants growing better than others.

Roses are no exception. Certain species and cultivars, especially the rugosas, are very tolerant of dry conditions. Many other cultivars will grow adequately with normal rainfall but will really show off with just a bit of additional watering. In this era of water conservation, then, our goals are to select those roses that will grow best with the least additional watering and to maximize the effectiveness of the water that we do provide.

Tips for Using Less Water

There are a number of ways you can help your roses thrive with less water, as well as ways to conserve water. Reading through these will also help you develop a feel for when, how, and how much to water. Here are the factors to take into account:

Choose your site carefully. Don't grow roses in windy locations that cause both plants and soil to lose water quickly. Also avoid sites that tend to be dry, such as under eaves and next to south-facing walls, as well as areas with very sandy soil. (If all the soil in your garden is very sandy, as in a seaside garden, plant rugosa roses or grow your roses in raised beds with amended soil.)

Prepare the soil well. Organic matter helps soil retain moisture for a longer period, while at the same time increasing aeration around the roots so they don't get waterlogged. When planting roses, enrich the soil with plenty of organic matter, such as compost, shredded leaves, peat moss, well-rotted manure, or mushroom soil. Work the soil as deeply as possible to encourage deep rooting.

Mulch. Apply a 3-inch-deep layer of organic mulch during the growing season to slow down soil moisture evaporation and lessen water losses from runoff. (For more on mulch, see "Mulching for More Roses" on page 90.)

Use drip irrigation. Drip irrigation systems conserve water by delivering moisture directly to the soil with no runoff, a drawback of hose watering. Drip irrigation is also preferable to overhead sprinklers, which waste a lot of water because of runoff and evaporation. Sprinklers also wet plants' foliage, encouraging foliar diseases like mildew and blackspot. (One benefit of overhead watering is that it reduces spider mite populations. If your plants have spider mites, turn the sprinkler on them for 15 minutes on dry mornings once a week until the mites are gone.)

A drip irrigation system can be as simple as an inexpensive soaker hose, which is usually made from recycled tires and oozes water droplets all along its length. It's easy to install: Just lay it down beside your plants before you put down mulch, and put the mulch on top. You won't even know it's there—but your plants will! Make sure you site your planting near an outside faucet, so you can connect a standard hose to the faucet and attach the soaker hose to it.

You can also create your own more elaborate drip system with hose lines, spaghetti tubes, and emitters that allow water to emerge drop by drop at the base of each plant. These systems, like soaker hoses, are available from garden supply stores and catalogs. If you want a large, elaborate multi-line system, you can have it custom-designed for your property and professionally installed.

Another benefit of drip systems is that you can apply liquid fertilizers, like liquid seaweed, fish emulsion, and compost or manure tea, through the system when you water. If you do fertilize through your drip system, check the emitters regularly to make sure they don't get blocked.

Reduce fertilization. Plants need to have soil moisture not only to absorb nutrients from the soil but also to use them within the plant. Fast-acting chemical fertilizers especially require large amounts of water to be effective, and the resulting lush, succulent growth is a water-hog. Using slower-acting organic fertilizers at a moderate rate produces "leaner, meaner" roses that have lower water needs.

Try basins and soaker nozzles. If you have just a few roses or roses growing among other plants that need less water, or if you prefer to hand-water your plants, here's a clever and effective technique. Create a basin about 12 to 18 inches in diameter around the plant and about 2 to 3 inches tall to act as a dam to hold in the water. Fill the basin and let it drain two to four times. When you're watering, use a soaker, or bubbler, nozzle on the end of the hose so that the water comes slowly out of the hose, preventing runoff and waste.

Water deeply. Deep-rooted plants have the greatest chance of surviving droughts because, even at the height of summer, the soil 8 to 18 inches deep will remain moist for a week or more. Besides deep soil preparation, another way to encourage deep rooting is by soaking the soil thoroughly at long intervals. Light, frequent sprinklings promote root growth in the top few inches of soil. This upper layer of soil dries out quickly in hot, dry weather, causing plant death or requiring more frequent watering to keep plants alive.

Due to variables such as soil type, watering method, and water pressure, there is no blanket recommendation for length of watering time. Once you determine what method you're going to use for watering, start applying water and use a soil moisture gauge or a narrow-bladed trowel to check the depth of soil moisture every 5 or 10 minutes. When the water has reached 12 inches deep in the soil at a point 18 inches from the plant (assuming you're applying water at the base of the plant), use the time it took as a guideline for future waterings.

Consider the weather and season. During hot, dry, windy weather, the soil dries out more quickly and plants transpire more moisture, combining to mean more frequent watering. Plants need less water during cool, humid weather. Warm spring and summer days when growth is most active is when moisture needs are highest. During the end of summer and through the fall, give your roses less water, not only because they are growing less but also to harden off their growth for a better chance at winter survival.

Water only when necessary. Don't just water every week whether your plants need it or not. Instead, get in the habit of digging into the soil before watering to determine if the top 3 to 4 inches of the soil is dry. If it is, turn on the tap; if not, just stop and smell the roses!

FEEDING ROSES NATURALLY

Ask a hundred rose gardeners what, when, and how they fertilize their roses and you'll get a hundred different answers. Obviously, there are many paths to the same destination. Choosing the one that's right for you involves some understanding and knowledge of plants, soil, and growing conditions, as well as plant nutrition and fertilizers. Read this section, and try out the fertilizer mixes I've listed in "Organic Feeding Formulas" on page 95 to see which works best for you. If you'd like to make your own mix, study the table "Organic Fertilizer Overview" on page 96, and try to concoct a formula that meets your roses' nutritional needs.

Although plants get a few of their nutrients from the air and can absorb nutrients applied in a water solution on the leaves, the main supply of nutrients is absorbed by the plant roots from water in the soil. Because the nutrients can be depleted by the plants, or lost from the soil by leaching or erosion, a steady supply of nutrients is necessary for plants to survive. In the wild, this is supplied by the natural accumulation and decomposition of leaves, stems, and other plant and animal matter, along with the breakdown of rocks in the soil. For the gardener who wants to have maximum growth and flowering in the shortest period of time as well as to have healthy plants that flourish year after year, an additional source of nutrients is imperative.

What are these essential nutrients? There are 16 essential nutrients, or elements. Of these, carbon, oxygen, and hydrogen are absorbed from air and water. The remaining major elements, or macronutrients, are nitrogen, phosphorus, potassium, sulfur, calcium, and magnesium. The other seven elements are called trace elements, or micronutrients, because plants need them in much smaller quantities. These include iron, manganese, boron, copper, zinc, molybdenum, and chlorine. If any of these elements is missing or in short supply, a plant will not grow or bloom normally.

The Big Three: NPK

Of all the plant nutrients, nitrogen (N), phosphorus (P), and potassium (K) are needed in the greatest quantities. These elements are represented, always in the above order, in the three numbers listed on fertilizer bags and boxes.

Nitrogen

Plants need more nitrogen than any other nutrient. Nitrogen is essential to the formation of the amino acids that make up plant proteins and is also a component of chlorophyll. With adequate nitrogen, plants have strong, sturdy growth with lots of leaves and flowers. A deficiency of nitrogen results in stunted growth, small pale green or yellow leaves (especially the older leaves), weak stems, and few flowers. With too much nitrogen, growth is soft and weak, making it susceptible to cold, drought, diseases, and pests. Roses that are overdosed on nitrogen also tend to produce leaves instead of flowers and roots.

Nitrogen leaches rapidly from the soil and is used quickly by plants, so gardeners have to supply it throughout the growing season. Organic sources of nitrogen remain in the soil longer than most inorganic forms but require soil microorganisms to make it available. A soil rich with organic matter, especially compost or leafmold, will naturally have these bacteria available.

Phosphorus

Even though phosphorus is found in much smaller amounts than nitrogen in plants, it still plays a very important part in photosynthesis, respiration, energy transfer within the plant, and disease resistance. Another key role is in the development and production of roots. Phosphorus also helps plant tissues to mature, which is necessary for winter hardiness. You can recognize a phosphate deficiency if your plant's leaves turn dark green on the upper sides and red to purple on the undersides.

Soil microorganisms release phosphorus from organic matter. Phosphorus availability is influenced by the soil pH, but the more organic matter in the soil, the less the effect of the pH. Phosphorus readily forms insoluble compounds in the soil and doesn't move far from the site where it is worked into the soil. That's why it's important when applying phosphorus fertilizers to get them down to the root depth so they'll be available to your plants.

Potassium

Potassium is involved in cell metabolism, protein synthesis, water use and retention, and the movement of plant foods throughout the plant. You can recognize a potassium deficiency from weak stems, low disease resistance, wilting, and poor flower production.

Potassium is relatively mobile in the soil but is usually retained longer than nitrogen. Leaching is worst in light, sandy soils. If your soil is sandy, you'll need to apply potassium fertilizers more often.

Know Your Soil

Determine the type of soil you have, as described in Chapter 3. Sandy soils lose nutrients faster than other soils, so you need to apply fertilizer more often. Clay-rich soils can hold water too long, promoting root rot. A soil rich in organic matter, with a balance of clay and sand, supplies nutrients best. Organic matter can also help sandy soils hold water and clay soils drain faster, correcting both problems. Test your soil once a year, either sending it to a soil testing laboratory or doing it yourself with a soil-testing kit.

Check your soil's pH about three times a year to be sure it stays in the ideal range for roses, 6.0 to 6.5 (slightly acidic). Most of the essential elements are available in this pH range, and microbial activity is also greatest at this level. You'll find more about pH in Chapter 3.

Organic Fertilizers

Developing an organic garden is a gradual process that involves many factors that affect one another. One of the key factors to healthy, blooming plants is biologically active soil. The organic matter in the soil, consisting of partially or wholly decayed vegetative matter (humus), is the cornerstone of an ideal soil. It provides nutrients for the plants and increases the ability of the soil to retain water, while at the same time improving drainage and aeration. A soil high in organic matter also provides a rich environment for the earthworms that aerate the soil and leave behind rich castings and for a host of beneficial soil microorganisms.

Providing as many nutrients as possible from organic sources is obviously one of the goals of organic gardening. Certain nutrients are also supplied from naturally occurring mineral sources.

The most frequently used of these include rock, or colloidal, phosphate for supplying phosphorus; greensand for potassium plus micronutrients; and calcitic or dolomitic limestone to add calcium (and magnesium, in the case of dolomite) and to raise the pH of acidic soils to maintain the ideal pH range. These mineral sources are sold ground or powdered. They become slowly available to plants through biological processes in the soil at the rate plants need.

Why not just reach for a bag of chemical fertilizer? Organic gardeners avoid synthetically manufactured chemical fertilizers because they are highly energy-consuming to produce and use up precious finite resources, they pollute ground water, they destroy soil structure and microbial life, they increase pest and disease susceptibility, and they impair nutrient uptake.

Developing an organic feeding program takes more time and effort than simply dumping

(continued on page 98)

Organic Feeding Formulas

Give your roses a nutrient boost to keep them looking and blooming their best. These formulas are all excellent for roses. Try them all and pick your favorite, or rotate them to give your roses a range of nutrient pick-me-ups.

Spring and fall tonic. This one's simple: Just add ½ cup of alfalfa pellets or meal per rose bush, plus an ounce of Epsom salts. Apply in early spring just after pruning, sprinkling them in a circle beneath each rose bush. Scratch the alfalfa and Epsom salts lightly into the soil. Add Epsom salts to your regular spray mix to get beautiful green foliage and to promote new basal breaks. Follow with a readily available source of nitrogen like blood meal or guano. Some growers follow the first bloom with Epsom salts and nitrogen again, with another application in August where the growing season is long. A 2-pound box of Epsom salts from the drugstore will treat 32 rose bushes.

Alfalfa tea. To make this nutritious "tea," you'll need alfalfa meal, several 4-gallon buckets, a rake or hoe handle, water, and a 16-ounce plastic cup. Add 32 ounces of dry alfalfa meal to each 4-gallon bucket; fill the bucket with water, stirring constantly with a rake or hoe handle to wet the meal.

Set aside for two to five days, depending on when you need the tea; stir the buckets daily for about 30 seconds. This mixture will give you a concentrate.

For alfalfa tea, put about ¾ gallon of concentrate into an empty 4-gallon bucket and fill it with water; stir and apply to your roses. Each bucket of concentrate will make 16 to 20 gallons of pure alfalfa tea. Feed 1 gallon per plant no more than four times a year. Another way to make alfalfa tea is to add about 12 cups of alfalfa pellets to a barrel of water and let it steep for a few days, stirring once a day. Bail out a gallon or so per rose bush.

Fish emulsion–alfalfa mix. Add a cup of fish emulsion to 5 gallons of water with a handful or two of alfalfa pellets. You can make manure-alfalfa tea the same way: Suspend a sackful of manure in a barrel of water and throw in a pound of alfalfa pellets.

Howard Walters' special. Developed by a longtime rosarian and member of the American Rose Society. Combine ⅓ cubic yard of coarse compost or leaves, 10 pounds of coarse-ground bark or mulch, 10 pounds of composted poultry manure, 10 pounds of alfalfa meal or pellets, 5 pounds of bonemeal, and 5 pounds of fishmeal. Use as a soil amendment, top-dressing, or basic feeding formula.

Organic Fertilizer Overview

Here are the best organic sources of nutrients for roses, with the nutrients they supply, the recommended application rate, and additional information about how and when to use them.

Fertilizer	Nutrients Supplied
Alfalfa meal	5% nitrogen (N), 1% phosphorus (P), 2% potassium (K)
Blood meal, dried blood	10–15% N, 0–3% P, 0% K
Bonemeal, steamed	0.7–4% N, 11–34% P, 0% K; 20–30% calcium
Colloidal phosphate, soft phosphate	0% N, 14–20% P, 0% K; 16–20% calcium; 2–3% iron; 20% silica; trace minerals
Compost	0.5–4% N, 0.5–4% P, 0.5–4% K
Fish meal, fish emulsion	Fish meal: 5–12% N, 1–6% P, 1–2% K; Fish emulsion: 4–5% N, 1–4% P, 1–2% K; 5% sulfur
Granite dust	0% N, 0% P, 3–5% K; 67% silica; 19 trace minerals
Greensand, glauconite	0% N, 1% P, 6–7% K; 50% silica; 18–23% iron oxide; 32 trace minerals
Guano, bird or bat	Variable; can be 1–14% N, 4–15% P, 0–3% K; plus trace minerals
Gypsum, calcium sulfate	23–57% calcium; 17.7% sulfur
Hoof and horn meal	10–14% N, 2% P, 0% K
Kelp meal, kelp extract, seaweed extract, liquid seaweed	1–3% N, 0% P, 1–3% K; contains many trace minerals, micronutrients, amino acids, and vitamins
Langbeinite, Sul-Po-Mag, K-Mag	0% N, 0% P, 22% K; 22% sulfur; 10–18% magnesium
Lime, limestone, dolomite	51–96% calcium carbonate
Magnesium sulfate, Epsom salts	9.8% magnesium; 6% sulfur
Manure, cattle	Variable, but usually about 2% N, 1% P, 1% K
Manure, chicken, cricket, horse, rabbit, or sheep	Variable, but usually about 4% N, 2% P, 2% K
Rock phosphate	0% N, 33% P, 0% K; 30% calcium; 2.8% iron; 10% silica; trace minerals
Soybean meal	7% N, 0.5% P, 2.3% K
Sulfur	100% sulfur

Application Rate	Comments
3–5 lb. per 100 sq. ft. or 3–6 oz. per sq. yd.	One of the most recommended fertilizers for roses; contains a natural fatty acid growth stimulant called triaconatol, plus trace minerals.
No more than 3 lb. per 100 sq. ft. or 3 oz. per sq. yd.	Apply as powder or diluted liquid; fast-acting source of nitrogen; applying too much can burn plants; slightly acidic; lasts 3–4 months; repels deer and rabbits.
Up to 5 lb. per 100 sq. ft. or 6 oz. per sq. yd.	Very good source of phosphorus; raises pH; lasts 6 months.
Up to 5 lb. per 100 sq. ft. or 6 oz. per sq. yd.	Contains both short- and long-term source of phosphorus; lasts 2–5 years; half the pH-raising value of ground limestone; best on neutral soils; apply when preparing soil for planting or in fall.
100 lb. per 100 sq. ft. or 10 lb. per sq. yd.	Slow-acting fertilizer and excellent soil amendment; slightly acidic; usually home-made but becoming more commercially available.
Fish meal: 5–10 lb. per 100 sq. ft. or ½–1 lb. per sq. yd.; Fish emulsion: Mix 1 part emulsion with 20 parts water, or 2–10 T. per gallon of water.	Fish meal: Apply in early spring or when transplanting; slow-acting; lasts 6–8 months; acidic. Fish emulsion: Apply to roots or as a foliar spray for an extra boost.
Up to 10 lb. per 100 sq. ft. or 1 lb. per sq. yd.	Very slow release of nutrients; lasts up to 10 years; use mica-rich type; good source of potassium.
5–10 lb. per 100 sq. ft. or ½–1 lb. per sq. yd.	Very slow release of nutrients; lasts up to 10 years; apply in fall; loosens clay soils; slightly acid.
3–5 lb. per 100 sq. ft. or ½ lb. per sq. yd.; use 2–4 T. per gallon of water for manure tea, steep 1–2 days, strain, and dilute.	Good phosphorus source; provides both fast and slow release of nutrients; very good soil amendment; expensive.
Up to 4 lb. per 100 sq. ft. or 6 oz. per sq. yd.	Use only from mined sources; improves soil permeability, enhances root growth, improves drainage, leaches salts; has a neutral pH.
4 lb. per 100 sq. ft. or 6 oz. per sq. yd.	Very slowly available; lasts 1 year; alkaline; mix with shredded leaves, sawdust, or other nitrogen-binding soil amendments.
Rate varies from brand to brand; follow manufacturer's directions.	Use as supplement to regular fertilizer program; excellent source of trace minerals, growth hormones, and other factors; stimulates microbial activity in soil; work kelp meal into the soil; dilute liquid kelp with water and apply as a soil soak or foliar spray; diluted liquid kelp also good as a root dip for reducing transplant shock; don't overuse—too much can be damaging; application lasts 6–12 months; increases flowering, drought resistance, stress recovery, and frost survival.
1 lb. per 100 sq. ft. or 1½ oz. per sq. yd.	Rich source of potassium and secondary nutrients; won't alter pH.
2–10 lb. per 100 sq. ft. or ¼–1 lb. per sq. yd.	Main purpose is to raise soil pH; also supplies calcium; dolomite also supplies magnesium.
1–3 heaping T. per rose plant in spring, and again in the fall one month before first fall frost.	Highly soluble and readily available; stimulates leaf and root growth, basal stem development, well-formed flowers, and strong, healthy canes that overwinter well; add to foliar feeding mix in summer.
40 lb. per 50–100 sq. ft. or 7–10 lb. per sq. yd.	Slow release of nutrients; very effective soil amendment; usually alkaline; composted manure is aged with compost; dehydrated, or dried, manure has been pasteurized, reduced to 17–30% moisture, and ground finely.
20 lb. per 50–100 sq. ft. or 3–5 lb. per sq. yd.	Slow release of nutrients; very effective soil amendment; use aged, composted, or dehydrated manure rather than fresh to prevent burning plants and tying up nutrients.
Up to 10 lb. per 100 sq. ft. or 1 lb. per sq. yd.	Very slow release source of phosphorus; lasts about 3 years; works best in acid soils below pH 6.2; natural mineral source of pure mined phosphate rock; must be ground very fine; a non-renewable resource.
4–5 lb. per 100 sq. ft. or 6–7 oz. per sq. yd.	Byproduct of soybean oil production; good source of nitrogen; stimulates soil microbial activity; usually sold as animal food.
1 lb. per 100 sq. ft. will lower pH 1 point.	Used to lower pH of alkaline soils; increases plant proteins; binds excess magnesium; naturally mined mineral; also useful as a fungicide.

on some 10-10-10, but the results will be striking and rewarding. For many years, organic gardeners relied mainly on compost and animal manures, with the natural mineral sources listed above, to achieve their remarkable results. If they wanted fast-acting results, they used fish emulsion or manure tea.

In recent years, more options have become available to those of us who want to garden organically. Many of these are products that otherwise would become refuse, such as feather meal, cricket manure, or blood meal. Most of these are not complete sources of nutrients, so organic gardeners have to use several different products. If you enjoy creating your own organic fertilizer combinations, the table "Organic Fertilizer Overview" on page 96 provides information about materials that are accepted as organic by organic certification groups.

To make it easier on busy gardeners who don't have the time or energy to mix their own fertilizers, companies are beginning to produce what are called complete organic fertilizers. These balanced fertilizers supply significant amounts of nitrogen, phosphorus, potassium, and often trace elements as well. They are as easy to use as synthetics, while providing the benefits of organic fertilizers. Not all of these are truly organic or are from environmentally sensitive sources. The companies listed in "Rose Resources" have been accepted by organic certification groups.

Unfortunately, there is no one magic fertilizing formula for all climates, all soils, all conditions, and all roses. Through the years, however, gardeners have evolved some organic fertilizer combinations that can be used in a wide variety of situations. You'll find the best of these in "Organic Feeding Formulas" on page 95. By testing your soil periodically, continually adding organic matter to your garden, and using balanced organic fertilizers according to the schedule I've provided in "Year-Round Rose-Feeding Schedule" on this page, you'll develop a great soil and a feeding regime that's right for your roses. And you'll have scads of gorgeous flowers on vigorous, healthy plants—better than you ever imagined!

PRUNING ROSES RIGHT

No aspect of gardening is as intimidating as pruning. It's so, well, final. But even though it's almost impossible to grow roses without doing

Year-Round Rose-Feeding Schedule

When's the best time to feed roses? Make the first application about two weeks after spring pruning. Make additional applications at four- to six-week intervals, timing each feeding to fall at the end of a bloom cycle. The last application of fertilizer containing nitrogen should be four to six weeks before the first fall frost.

Base the number of times you feed on where you live and whether you're growing roses for show or just for pleasure. In areas where temperatures fall below freezing (USDA Plant Hardiness Zones 2 to 8), make two applications for a basic fertilizing program; for exhibition roses, use three or more. In frost-free areas or areas where freezing temperatures are late and light (Zones 9 and 10), such as southern Texas and southern California, fertilize a third time after the second bloom cycle.

Always water the day before feeding and again after applying fertilizer. This helps prevent fertilizer burn. Don't feed newly planted roses until they have completed their first bloom cycle. Reduce the amount of fertilizer if you grow miniatures. And remember: Do not overfertilize! You'll get tender, overgrown plants that are susceptible to diseases, pests, and winterkill.

at least a little bit of pruning, the bottom line is that roses are very, very forgiving. Naturally self-renewing, roses produce strong new shoots from the base of the plant each year. In the worst-case scenario, you'll lose a year's bloom if you inadvertently cut back too much growth on roses that bloom on the previous year's growth. Even then, the plant will be unharmed, and you'll have a chance to prune it right the following season.

With only a bit of common sense, some good tools, and a few basic guidelines, rose pruning can become second nature to you. You'll feel confident, no matter whether you're facing a 10-inch miniature or a vigorous 20-foot climber, a hybrid tea or a gallica. In the pages that follow, I'll tell you what to do, when to do it, and what tools you need to do the job right. Then it's up to you to make the first cut. When you do, you'll create the shape you want, improve flowering, and remove old, ugly, thorny growth. Your roses will look better than ever!

Rose Pruning Basics

Follow these simple guidelines to make your rose-pruning chores safe and effective:

- Wear a long-sleeve shirt or jacket, pants, and leather, plastic-coated, or rubber-coated gloves for protection. Roses are thorny!

- Keep pruning shears, lopping shears, and the saw well sharpened so that cuts are clean and stems are not crushed.

- Make cuts ¼ inch above an outward-facing bud—the point where a leaf is or was attached to the stem—with the cut at a 45-degree angle away from the bud. Growth from an outward-facing bud will promote open growth in the center of the bush, allowing good air circulation and less disease, as well as allowing light to reach into the plant for better leaf growth and photosynthesis. Having the cut slope away from

the bud prevents moisture from gathering in the bud and rotting it.

- Remove any dead, diseased, weak, or spindly canes, as well as any canes that crisscross and rub against each other. For hybrid teas, remove any canes that are smaller in diameter than a pencil. But what is considered a thin cane on a modern rose is often quite acceptable on an old garden rose—before you prune, look at the average cane width on your rose bushes and use it as a guideline.

- If the inside, or pith, of the cane is discolored, then cut the shoot back until the pith is white and healthy.

- If your roses are budded onto rootstock, suckers may emerge from the stem just below the ground. You must remove these shoots or they may crowd out the grafted cultivar. Sucker growth is usually long, thin, and arching, with smaller leaves usually composed of seven leaflets. To remove, use a hand trowel and follow the sucker back to the point where it joins the understock, then snap it off with the trowel edge. Do not cut the sucker off at ground level, as

Rose Pruning Terms

You'll find it easier to follow pruning instructions if you review these terms first.

Axil: The angle between the cane and the upper surface of the leafstalk.

Blind shoot: A mature stem that does not produce flowers.

Breaking bud (break): A growth bud, or eye, that has just started to grow.

Bud: A growth bud, or eye, found on a cane; a vegetative growing point located in the axil where a leaf joins the stem.

Cane: A main stem, or basal shoot, of a rose, usually arising at or very near the bud union.

Eye (bud eye): A vegetative bud, or growing point, on a stem in the axil of a leafstalk.

Internode: The section of a stem between one node and another.

Lateral cane (branch): A side branch arising

from a main, or basal, cane.

Main shoot: A basal or strong lateral cane.

New wood: A cane of the current year's growth.

Node: The point on a stem where a leaf and bud arise.

Old wood: A cane of the previous year's growth or older.

Reversion: Suckers from the rootstock choking out or taking over from the growth of the bud graft.

Shoot: A stem or cane.

Stem: A branch of a cane, which emerges from a bud eye and bears leaves and at least one flower.

Sublateral: A stem originating from a lateral.

Sucker: A growing stem that arises from a rootstock below the bud union.

this only causes it to send up more growth. If standard (tree) roses send out shoots along the stem, carefully cut these off.

- If, after pruning, two or three shoots emerge from one eye, pinch out all but one.
- Although there is some disagreement as to the benefit of sealing cut ends, most people agree that putting a bit of clear shellac or wood glue on the fresh cuts protects them from moisture loss and cane borers.
- Burn or otherwise dispose of rose clippings, since they can be a breeding ground for insects and diseases. Don't compost them.

When to Prune

For most roses, the time to do major pruning each year is in late winter or early spring, or about four to six weeks before the last killing frost. That's when most winterkill will already have occurred, but before growth starts. A sign

that the time is right is when about half of the growth buds on the most vigorous canes are beginning to swell. You'll find directions for pruning each type of rose in the sections that follow. Just look for the name of the rose type you want to prune, then read the instructions in that section.

Summer pruning is really just a matter of removing the faded flowers throughout the growing season. Since this promotes new growth, stop pruning in late summer, so that there won't be soft new growth that is easily winter-damaged.

When removing faded flowers, the general rule is to cut back at an outward-facing bud at a first five-leaflet leaf below the flower or flower cluster. When the cut is made too high on the stem, the new growth will be thin and weak.

If roses are grown for their hips as well as flowers, then no summer pruning is needed. Some repeat-blooming roses also bear hips, so prune for the first or second bloom cycle, and

Best Pruning Tools

❧❀❧

Any task is always much easier when it's done with the right tools. Pruning may never be your favorite part of growing roses, but it can certainly go quickly and smoothly if you're using good equipment that's comfortable for you. There are dozens and dozens of different brands and models of pruning tools and equipment available. If you buy yours from a local garden center or hardware store, compare workmanship and how each tool feels in your hand. Avoid lightweight, cheaply made tools. There are also mail-order sources for high-quality pruning equipment, much of it heavy-duty and designed for specific tasks.

Once you invest in good tools and equipment, the second important aspect is keeping them in good shape. Sharpen them periodically—either do it yourself or have someone do it who's specially trained. Wipe metal surfaces after each use with a soft, lightly oiled rag to prevent rust. Store tools in a dry area. Hanging them on hooks keeps you organized and lets you know if you've accidentally forgotten to bring one in.

Here are the pruning tools and accessories I consider essential to get the job done right.

Gloves: Leather, such as cowhide or goatskin, or rubber- or plastic-coated.

Pruning shears: Use scissor-action pruning shears with blades that cross, rather than anvil pruners (unless they are the kind with the pivot bolt off-center) for canes up to about ½ inch in diameter. Select pruners that feel comfortable in your hand. Better-quality pruners may have all replaceable parts. Ratchet action makes it possible to cut thicker canes.

Lopping shears: Essentially, long-handled pruning shears. The increased handle length gives you more leverage for cutting stems 1 to 2 inches in diameter. Ratchet action increases the cutting ability.

Pruning saw: A small handsaw specifically designed for pruning is useful for cutting canes over 2 inches in diameter. Use one with a replaceable blade. Pruning saws are designed to cut as you pull rather than as you push, unlike a carpenter's saw. The blade is not as apt to bind or bend when you pull it, and it can be made of harder steel. These saws cut quickly with very little effort and stay sharp for a long time.

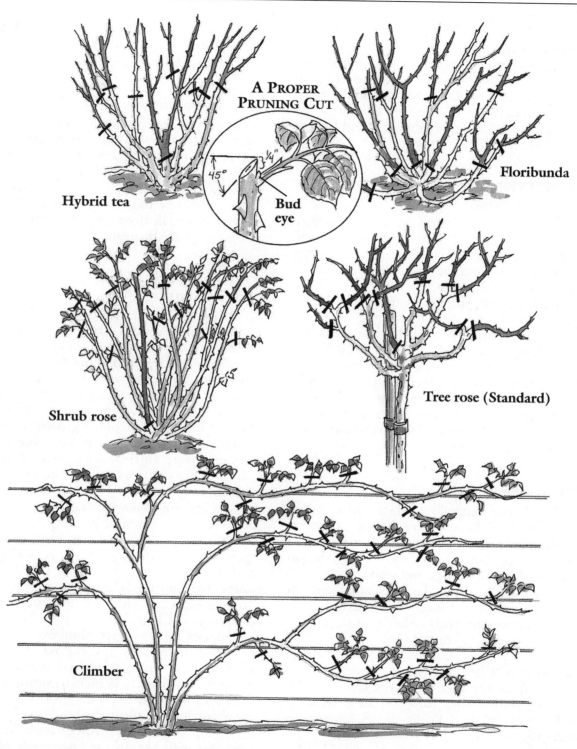

A PROPER
PRUNING CUT

45°   ¼"

Bud
eye

Hybrid tea

Floribunda

Shrub rose

Tree rose (Standard)

Climber

The right way to prune. Make pruning cuts at a 45-degree angle about ¼ inch above an outward-facing leaf bud. Follow these commonsense pruning rules for all roses: Remove suckers, dead and diseased canes, canes that don't flower well, canes that are crossing and rubbing others, and canes that are growing inward. For hybrid teas, cut the oldest stems off at the base, leaving three to six healthy canes, and prune remaining canes to shape the plant. For floribundas, remove the oldest stems at the base, leaving six to eight healthy canes; prune off the top third of each remaining cane. Prune climbers to train and shape them, cutting back side branches to about 6 inches. For tree (standard) roses, cut new shoots and side shoots back to about 6 inches. For shrub roses, prune off the top third of new canes, and cut side shoots on older growth to 4 to 6 inches.

then with the last flowering allow the hips to develop for fall and winter color.

Fall pruning depends greatly on climate and rose type, but in areas with severe winter temperatures, many modern roses should be shortened by one-third to one-half to reduce the chances of wind whipping the plant and loosening the roots.

Pruning Hybrid Teas, Hybrid Perpetuals, and Grandifloras

With hybrid tea, hybrid perpetual, and grandiflora roses, the goal is much the same: a symmetrical, open-centered, bowl-shaped plant with strong growth from the base. Blooming on the current season's growth, most cultivars do best with a moderate to heavy annual pruning to ensure vigorous new growth.

Cut back newly planted hybrid teas, hybrid perpetuals, and grandifloras to about 10 inches, with four to eight growth buds remaining on the plant. In succeeding years, you can cut them back about one-third to one-half. After several years, remove one or two of the oldest canes from the base. Prune faded flowers to encourage the best repeat bloom.

Pruning Floribundas

Floribundas naturally produce bushier plants with abundant clusters of medium-sized flowers produced on new growth. If pruning is too extreme, growth will decline, but if it's too light, bushes will be large and weak.

Prune back floribundas at planting time to about 10 inches, with four to eight growth buds remaining on the plant. After that, a general rule of thumb is to remove about one-fourth of the newer growth each year. Harder pruning each year of a few older canes encourages new growth from the base. Keep the center of the bush somewhat open for good air circulation and light penetration. Prune off faded flowers to encourage the best repeat bloom.

Pruning Miniatures

Miniature roses bloom on the current season's growth. Prune them much the same way you would other modern roses. Maintain a symmetrical plant with an open center and bowl shape. Trim newly planted miniatures back to 4 to 6 inches. In the following years, prune plants back one-quarter to one-third,

removing a few of the older canes back to the base. Prune off faded flowers to encourage the best repeat bloom.

Pruning Polyanthas

Low, shrubby plants, polyantha roses have many slender stems. When first planted, remove any of this twiggy growth and cut main stems back by a third. In succeeding years, light pruning is the rule: Remove no more than one-fourth to (at most) one-third of the growth. Although it's not essential, if you remove faded flowers, you'll encourage the plant to bloom more.

Pruning Species, Shrub, and Old Garden Roses

Although sometimes billed as needing no pruning, most species, shrub, and old garden roses benefit from light pruning to encourage new, vigorous, free-blooming growth from the base. One of the biggest differences between some of these and roses like hybrid teas and floribundas is that some species, shrub, and old roses bloom on older growth from past years, not just on growth from the current season. Some cultivars are once-blooming, while others flower again; some produce attractive hips as well.

General guidelines include doing little or no pruning when planting; pruning to develop a symmetrical plant with strong canes; removing spindly growth after flowering; removing dead and diseased canes; removing faded flowers unless the cultivar is grown for its hips; and pruning off a few inches of all strong canes to encourage side branches.

Species roses (except climbers, the Scotch rose and its hybrids, the rugosa rose and its hybrids, gallica roses, and hybrid musk roses) are generally densely branched, shrubby plants that bloom on short side shoots emerging from year-old or older canes. These roses are slow to produce new growth from the base, especially with age. In the first couple of years, follow the general guidelines listed above. As the plants become established, remove one or two of the main canes that are no longer producing many flowers.

The old garden roses that are not reblooming—including the albas, centifolias, moss roses, most damask roses, and modern shrub roses that bloom just once a year—also flower on the short side shoots emerging from year-old or older canes. These, too, should be pruned along the general guidelines listed above for the first year. They differ in that they naturally produce numerous robust canes from the base of the plant, canes that may grow 4 to 8 feet in a season. The following year, these canes bear the blooming side shoots, or laterals.

To prevent these old roses from becoming top-heavy, but still maintain their lovely arching habit, your early spring pruning should consist of pruning back long new canes by up to one-third. Prune the side shoots from last year to 6 inches. Also remove any old canes that are not blooming well or that are ruining the shape of the plant.

In the summer, remove faded flowers. In late fall, lightly prune the extra-long canes to reduce winter wind damage.

The remaining roses in this category include most of the Chinas, many of the Bourbons, repeat-blooming modern shrub roses, and the most vigorous hybrid teas and hybrid perpetuals. Each year, these roses generally produce a number of long, arching canes from either the base or other strong canes. They bloom repeatedly throughout the growing season on both the current year's canes and the side shoots of last year's canes. For best flowering, light pruning is necessary.

For the first year, follow the general guidelines for this group listed above. In the ensuing years, prune the long canes by no more than a third, maintaining the arching growth. Cut the side shoots to 6 inches and remove any weak or poorly placed canes. During the summer, remove faded flowers and thin the canes lightly. In late fall, cut off the tips of extra-long canes to reduce damage from wind-whipping during the winter.

Pruning Climbers and Ramblers

The many roses that can be grown as climbers or ramblers have a variety of growth habits. How to prune and train these wonderful and useful roses is covered in "Training Climbing Roses" on page 104.

Pruning Standard (Tree) Roses

Because a standard or tree rose can easily become top-heavy, it's important to give these plants a moderate to heavy pruning. The first year, prune the strongest canes back to 6 to 8 inches after planting. During the summer,

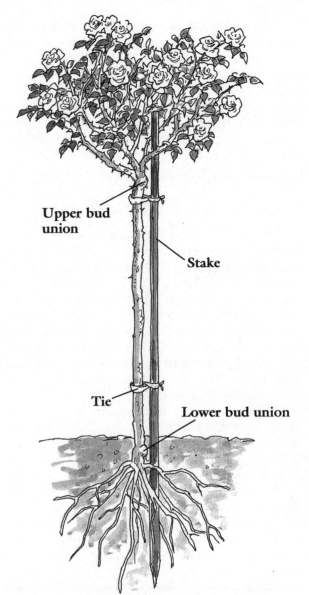

Planting a standard rose. A tree or standard rose often has been budded twice — a hardy rootstock is budded to a tall, straight trunk, which is budded to the choice flowering cultivar that forms the bushy top of the "tree." When you plant a tree rose, dig the hole, then insert the stake before setting in the plant. Make sure your stake is at least a foot taller than the trunk of the tree rose, then set it in the ground a foot deep for support. Tie the trunk to the stake with tree-ties or sturdy rubber-coated wire.

remove faded flowers as described in the appropriate section for the type of rose your standard is (most standards are either hybrid teas, floribundas, or miniatures). In early fall, remove several inches of growth, including any soft, new growth.

When spring-pruning in the following years,

cut all of the previous year's growth back to 6 to 10 inches long. Also remove any dead, diseased, spindly, or criss-crossing growth. Summer- and fall-prune as you did the first year.

To prune weeping standards, remove all two-year-old flowering shoots in late summer or early fall if there is plenty of new growth. If new growth is sparse, leave a few two-year-old shoots, cutting them back to 6 to 10 inches.

TRAINING CLIMBING ROSES

If you're asked to imagine a romantic setting for roses, you'll probably come up with one of two scenarios: a beautiful bouquet of long-stemmed roses, or a garden with roses climbing lushly over some type of structure. Whether you picture a rose-covered fence, trellis, arbor, or gazebo, the image of being completely surrounded by roses is indeed a powerful one. Unfortunately, in real life, gardeners don't use climbing roses as often as they do their shrubby relatives.

That's a shame, since climbing roses have something different to offer than bush roses do. What climbing roses bring to a garden is the vertical dimension—they create green walls. When you add the element of height to a garden, your eye is carried upward, creating the feeling that the garden is bigger than it really is. When you train roses to overhead structures, such as arbors and pergolas, you form a ceiling, creating an intimate space that gives a feeling of safety and comfort.

One reason people are intimidated by climbing roses is their confusion over the different types and how to train them to various supports. In the following pages, I'll discuss all the basic training techniques, as well as how to carefully select climbing roses that fit your garden space and your climate.

Although there is officially a class of roses called climbers, nearly every category has some cultivars with long, flexible canes that can be trained upward. Many modern climbing roses are sports of hybrid tea, floribunda, or grandiflora roses. Remember that no rose truly climbs in the sense of ivy, with its "holdfast" roots, or sweet peas, with their winding tendrils. Instead, in nature, the rose's thorns hook onto tree limbs or shrub branches. In the garden, we help out by tying the canes to whatever support we choose.

Perhaps the biggest mistake gardeners make

is choosing climbing roses that are only marginally hardy for their winters. The most readily available climbers are not necessarily the hardiest. Climbing sports of hybrid teas, floribundas, and grandifloras are not reliably hardy without a great deal of protection where winters drop to single digits and colder (Zones 6 to 2). Fortunately, there are a number of both old and new climbing roses that have been specifically bred to be climbers. These are quite hardy, especially the hybrids from Germany and Canada. You'll find a list of the best climbing roses, with descriptions and hardiness zones, in "Recommended Roses for Walls, Fences, and Pillars" on page 30.

Another important point to remember is that it takes climbing roses several years to become fully established. Be patient. Because climbing roses have so much top growth, it is vital to prepare the soil particularly well and to provide plenty of nutrients and moisture on a regular basis.

When you're planting a climbing rose next to a wall or building, place the plant 24 inches away from the structure, with the roots spread out in a fan shape away from the building. If you're planting a rose against the wall of a building, make sure the plant's roots aren't under or behind the drip line of the roof. If they are, it will get either too much or not enough water.

Pruning Climbing Roses

Knowing the growth and blooming habit of the many roses used as climbers is the key to where and how you place them in the garden and how and when you prune and train them. Read the catalog descriptions carefully, study this and other rose books, and try to see the roses actually growing before you buy them.

The most important aspect of climbing roses, whatever their type, is that most of them produce blooms on side branches called laterals. These laterals are produced in greater abundance when the main stem is more or less horizontal. Growing roses along fences, fan-shaped trellises, and arches naturally provides this, but even wrapping canes around pillars helps to encourage this type of growth.

In his book *Climbing Roses Old and New*, eminent rosarian Graham Stuart Thomas emphasizes that pruning climbing roses is not as complicated as it has been made out to be. His cardinal rule for any climbing rose is to prune immediately after flowering. Beyond that, the major distinction in pruning techniques depends on whether the rose flowers only once during the growing season or whether it blooms repeatedly through the season.

Pruning Once-Blooming Climbers

For once-blooming roses, which usually bloom on wood from the previous season, remove the oldest and weakest canes. If plants produce lots of shoots from the base, cut off several of these almost to ground level. If only a few new canes are produced, cut them back to several feet above the ground. For cultivars grown for their decorative hips as well as their flowers, leave some extra canes for this display, cutting these back in late winter. You can often tell if a rose blooms only once because many of the once-blooming roses have flexible canes and small flowers borne in clusters.

Pruning Repeat-Blooming Climbers

With climbing roses that bloom more than once during the growing season, shorten the side shoots or laterals by two-thirds, or to about 6 inches long, with at least two growth buds left, after flowering. (For cultivars with 'New Dawn' in their heritage, remove only the faded flowers and the first set of leaves.) Make these cuts at a 45-degree angle, ¼ inch above a growth bud. Every couple of years, cut the oldest canes at the ground during the dormant season. You can recognize repeat-bloomers because most of these roses have stiff canes and larger flowers.

Special Pruning Tactics

One way to gain more height or fill additional space with climbers is to use the two largest, strongest laterals on the main canes. Rather than pruning them back, allow them to grow as secondary main canes for thicker overall growth.

After a period of years, a climbing rose may not be producing much new growth from the base. If removing some of the oldest canes does not bring results, try a method called nicking, developed in England by Richard Balfour. Just above a bud near the base of the plant, cut one-third of the way through a stem. This tends to force new growth.

Over a period of time, roses trained to arbors, pillars, and other structures may put on a great deal of growth. Poor light and air circulation in the interior of these plants may lead to disease. This is especially a problem in warmer climates, where there is not much winter dieback. To keep this from happening to your roses, take the entire plant down from its supports every second or third year, and remove the oldest wood as well as any diseased, damaged, or unproductive wood.

Vigorous roses with pliant canes that grow 15 feet or taller often look their best when allowed to grow up into trees or over small buildings like toolsheds. If you've grown a climbing rose this way, remove only dead, damaged, or diseased canes.

Training Your Climbers

The easiest way to grow climbing roses is to let them develop naturally, with no training. The best types of climbers for this use are cultivars with very flexible canes. Let them scramble into trees or shrubs, roam over small structures, or hang over retaining walls.

If you'd like a more classical look, you can train your climbing roses on fences, walls, trellises, arbors, pergolas, posts, or pillars. All of these techniques are based on tying the plants to their supports. Commercially available materials to use for tying plants to supports include green plastic stretch-ties, paper- or foam-covered twist ties, and various kinds of heavy cord or string. You can even make homemade ties from strips of fabric, hosiery, or whatever is available. (Think before you start cutting about how they'll look, though!)

The best way to attach any tie is in a figure-eight, with the middle portion between the cane and the support. (For an illustration of this technique, see the inset in "Tying Canes to a Trellis" on page 107.) Be sure that the tie is loose enough so it won't damage the expanding cane. Contiunue to tie the canes regularly throughout the growing season while the wood is young and pliable. You may have to replace the ties every couple of years.

Training to Walls and Fences

Walls and fences are the first choices for climbing roses. Masonry walls—brick or stone— are best because they never need painting. (A surface that requires you to remove the climbing rose canes to repaint it is a prickly proposition!) Ideally, you should insert eyehooks that

Training roses to a fence. Tie rose canes to a fence using the figure-eight technique shown in the inset in "Tying Canes to a Trellis" on the opposite page. Train the roses to grow horizontally on the fence for best bloom. As canes die or stop flowering well, untie them and cut them off at the base.

extend 4 inches from the masonry wall as it is being built. But you can insert masonry nails into a pre-built wall. You can also buy British-style wall hooks to train roses up walls. If you don't want to put nails or hooks in your masonry, put a trellis in front of the wall and train the rose on it.

For wooden structures, consider attaching a wire trellis to the eave so that the rose can be easily laid down when painting is necessary. If you're training a rose directly on the wooden surface, use U-shaped fencing staples, eyehooks, or hardware specifically designed for this purpose. Then attach the rose canes to the hardware with ties.

Wire fences are the easiest to plant with climbing roses, since they function as trellises for the plants. Both chain-link and woven-wire fences work wonderfully. Rail or picket fences are also quite attractive when planted with climbing roses, which are easily trained along them. Don't try to weave the canes in and out along a fence. Instead, tie the canes horizontally and let the laterals grow naturally through the openings.

Training to a Trellis

Use trellises along walls, beneath pergolas, and as freestanding units. They can add interest to a blank wall, soften a stone or brick wall, and provide privacy or shade. The most important aspects of trellis construction are that they're sturdy and that adequate air circulation can reach the trained roses.

Wire trellises are the easiest to make. Here's how Michael Shoup, owner of The Antique Rose Emporium, prefers to construct a wire trellis under an overhead piece of wood, be it an eave or the wooden beam of an arbor or pergola. Michael recommends driving two pieces of ¼-inch concrete reinforcement bar into the ground in an X shape, with 3 inches extending above the ground, 12 to 15 inches below ground, and the crossing point just at the soil surface. Insert eyehooks into the wood above, and run lengths of wire from the X to the hooks. Run as many lengths of wire as look appropriate where you've set the trellis; six to ten is the usual number.

Lightweight wooden trellises may be fine for annual vines, but they are not sturdy enough for

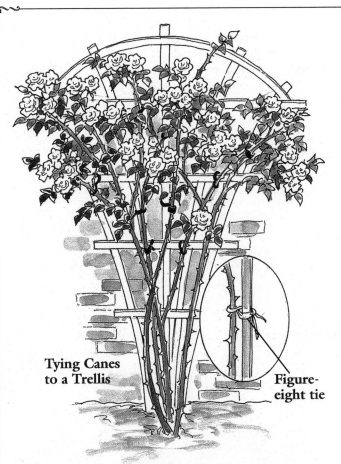

Tying Canes to a Trellis

Figure-eight tie

Training roses to a trellis. Train climbing roses to a trellis by starting on the outside of the plant and working across, spacing the canes evenly against the trellis as you tie them to it. The more horizontally you bend and tie the canes, the more flowers you'll have. Use raffia or rubber- or plastic-coated wire for the ties, making a figure-eight between the cane and the trellis so the tie won't put pressure on the cane (*inset*).

the heavy canes and foliage of roses. Wood should be no smaller than 1 inch by ½ inch, and 2-inch-square lumber is preferable. The wood should be rot-resistant, like recycled redwood or red cedar, or be treated with a borax-based wood preservative that's safe for plants and the environment. (You'll find a formula for an environmentally friendly wood preservative in "Make Your Own Rose Arbor" on page 108.)

Metal trellises, of pipe or other material, are sturdy and long-lasting. The material and style of any support should be in keeping with the rest of the garden and other structures. Choose colors that are subdued and natural, with dark green, black, gray, and brown being the best. A classic white wooden trellis will also show rose foliage and flowers off to advantage.

Training to a Tepee

One of the simplest structures to make is a tepee constructed from wooden posts at least 2 inches in diameter. Place each post at least 2 feet underground and 8 to 10 feet above ground. Tie the tops securely together with wire. Train climbing roses up the sides of the tepee with ties placed strategically up the poles.

Training to a Pillar

Wooden posts at least 4 inches thick and sunk 2 feet in the ground are all you need to grow pillar roses. Round posts make it easier to wrap canes around the pillar. Again, use rot-resistant or treated wood. Train the rose canes up the posts in a spiral, either with all canes going in the same direction or with half the canes going in the opposite direction.

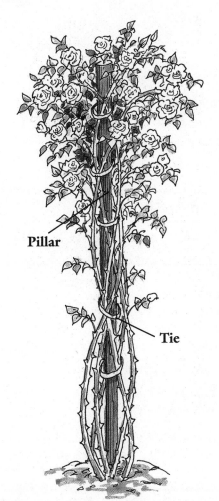

Pillar

Tie

Training roses to a pillar. To cover a pillar or post with roses, train the canes around both sides of the post in a spiral pattern, tying them in place with plastic- or rubber-coated wire, raffia, or thin nylon cord.

Besides posts specifically chosen for this use, don't forget lampposts, clothesline posts, porch columns, or any other vertical element in the landscape. Use both pillar-type roses and tall, more flexible climbers, letting the top cascade outward. A row of rose-covered wooden posts lining a walk is stunning. Linking the posts with chain or heavy rope is a Victorian method for training flexible-stemmed climbing roses. Wrap the roses around the chain or rope to induce the most laterals—and thus the most flowers.

Training on an Arbor, Arch, or Pergola

Arbors and arches are at their best when placed logically in the landscape, such as at a gate, where two paths cross, or at the focal point at the end of a vista. An arbor has straight sides, while an arch curves gracefully at the top. Arbors have an advantage over arches if you like sheltered seating, though—you can put a bench or benches under an arbor, or even build them into the arbor's sides. Whichever you choose, use sturdy wooden or metal structures that are tall and wide enough to allow plenty of head and side room. I've included a design for a simple arbor you can make yourself below.

Pergolas are long arbors, usually covering a path rather than serving as a focal point. You'd walk along a pergola, while you could walk through or to an arbor. Pergolas look best in

Make Your Own Rose Arbor

You can make a simple but effective rose arbor to show off your climbing roses. It's easy! Here's what you'll need:

MATERIALS

4 posts, 4" x 4" x 8', made from cedar, redwood, cypress, or preservative-treated wood

2 cedar, redwood, cypress, or preservative-treated 2 x 4s, 4' long

2 cedar, redwood, cypress, or preservative-treated 2 x 4s, 2' long

48 cedar, redwood, cypress, or preservative-treated 1" lath straps or 1 x 1s, 2' long

Nails

Hammer

Concrete mix

Water

Shovel or post-hole digger

Level

Square

1. Dig four holes 18 inches deep, spacing them in a 2- by 4-foot rectangle and using the square to make the 90-degree angles.

2. Prepare the concrete mix according to package instructions and pour into each hole, filling 6 inches. When this has set, place the four posts 1 foot deep and pour concrete around them to fill the holes. Use the level to make sure the posts are straight.

3. When the posts are set and the concrete has hardened, nail the 2 x 4s to the posts so they are flush with the top of the posts.

4. Nail the lath strips or 1 x 1s to the sides and top of the arbor, spacing them 3 inches apart and starting 3 inches from the 2 x 4s.

Safe Wood Preservatives

Don't use commercially pressure-treated wood, which contains arsenic-based compounds. If you can't find wood that's been treated with safe borax-based preservatives, make your own wood treatment. Try this recipe developed by the USDA's Forest Products Laboratory:

MATERIALS

3 cups exterior varnish or 1½ cups boiled linseed oil

1 ounce paraffin wax

Enough solvent (mineral spirits, paint thinner, or turpentine, at room temperature) to make 1 gallon of mixture

1. Melt the paraffin over water in a double boiler (not over a direct flame).

2. In another container, vigorously stir the solvent, then slowly pour in the melted paraffin.

3. Add the varnish or linseed oil and stir thoroughly.

4. Dip untreated wood into the mixture for 3 minutes, or brush on a heavy application. If you wish, you can paint the wood when it is completely dry.

large, fairly formal gardens and work best where they provide shade for an otherwise sunny path. Like arches and arbors, they need to be large enough to allow plenty of standing room.

Choose climbing roses for your arbor, arch, or pergola that have long, flexible canes, and train them up both sides of the structure. Keep growth neat and trim so as not to snag people who walk through or sit in the rose bower you've created.

Pegging Climbers for Groundcovers

There's one more great technique you can try with climbers if you'd like a beautiful rose groundcover for a sunny slope. Choose a flexible-caned rose like 'Madame Plantier' that will fill out to cover a 6- to 8-foot area. As the rose's branches lengthen, peg them to the ground with wire pins or wooden stakes.

If you use wire pins, make wire U-shaped staples that look like giant hairpins, and pin the rose canes to the ground. If you use wooden pegs, here's the best technique: Use 1½-foot lengths of broom handles or tomato stakes that have a ¾-inch diameter to make the pegs. Drill a hole near the top of each peg. When you need to peg a rose cane down, hammer the peg into the ground where you want the cane to lie, thread a tie through the hole in the peg, and tie

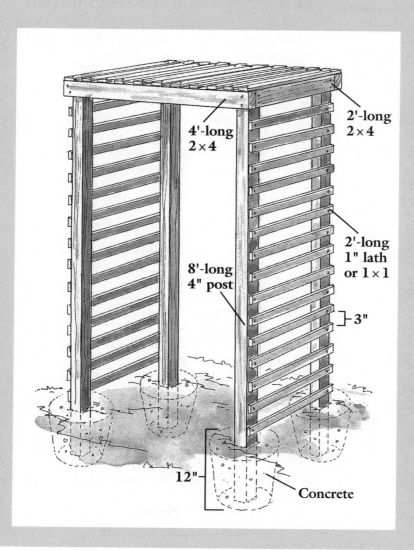

4'-long 2 × 4

2'-long 2 × 4

2'-long 1" lath or 1 × 1

8'-long 4" post

3"

12"

Concrete

An easy rose arbor. There's no need to spend a fortune on an elaborate teak or redwood arbor. Even a simple homemade arbor like this one will look gorgeous when it's covered with blooming roses.

the cane to the peg in a figure-eight.

Don't prune these pegged roses unless canes stop flowering freely or become diseased. In those cases, prune the cane back to its base or to a healthy sideshoot. To keep weeds from taking over, clear the area where you plan to put the roses, work the soil, then put down several layers of newspaper and cover the paper with an organic mulch like shredded leaves. Peg the roses through the mulch. Pegged climbers will create a lush green carpet that will bloom all season.

INSECT AND DISEASE CONTROL

Controlling pests and diseases in an organic garden means looking in a new way at how we consider these problems. Think about it from the beginning: The reason we want to control pests and diseases is that they damage our plants. When you garden organically, you look at your plants to see if there's any damage, rather than just blasting away at the first bug that presents itself. You learn to tell the difference between insects that are harmful to your roses and those that are harmless or even allies. You learn to recognize disease symptoms. You decide when to use controls, and which controls to use.

An organic approach emphasizes keeping pests and diseases at an acceptable level rather than eradicating them. By combining cultural, biological, and physical controls with judicious use of organic pesticides and fungicides, you can minimize pest and disease damage to your roses without damaging your health or the environment.

Here's my three-step program for mastering organic pest and disease control on roses: First, familiarize yourself with the types of controls. I'll tell you what they are and what they work on in the next few pages. Second, turn to "Rose Pests and Diseases" on page 114 to see what insects, fungi, bacteria, and viruses attack roses, what sort of damage they do, and how to control them. Third, collect some basic pest- and disease-control supplies (like baking soda, liquid soap, an antitranspirant, a wide-mouthed jar for Japanese beetles, ryania, and horticultural oil), and keep them in one place so they're at hand when you need them.

Inspect your roses every day or two for signs of trouble. When you see a potential problem, turn to "Rose Pests and Diseases," identify the problem, then check the possible controls in this section. Find the most appropriate control in your arsenal, and you're ready to go!

Cultural Methods for Controlling Pests and Diseases

The easiest and most efficient way to beat rose problems is to keep them from happening. A preventive approach is the key: Choose resistant cultivars, keep your plants healthy and thriving by giving them the right growing conditions, and practice strategic pruning and good garden hygiene. Your plants will stand a better chance against pests and diseases if they're growing well when the problems arrive.

Choose Pest- and Disease-Resistant Plants

Certain rose cultivars are genetically more resistant to or tolerant of pest or disease attacks than others. (There is a difference between these terms: Resistant plants tend not to get a disease or be attacked by a pest, while tolerant plants carry on with business as usual even if they do get the disease or are attacked by the pest. It's useful to keep this distinction in mind when browsing through rose catalogs, especially if you have an aversion to disfigured foliage.)

Resistance to diseases can be due to waxy leaves or a toxin that repels fungal spores. Likewise, insects seem to be attracted to some cultivars, while they will feed lightly on other cultivars or not bother them at all. Pest resistance—even among resistant cultivars—often varies from garden to garden due to differences in soils, climate, and care, as well as the development of new races of pests.

I've recommended some excellent pest- and disease-resistant cultivars in "Roses for Special Situations" on page 24; use those lists as a starting point for choosing your roses. Talk to other gardeners and rose society members in your area to find out which cultivars display the best pest and disease resistance where you live. Remember that trying to grow cultivars that are known to be highly susceptible is only inviting trouble.

Maintain Healthy Plants

Vigorously growing plants are better able to withstand mild attacks by pests and diseases.

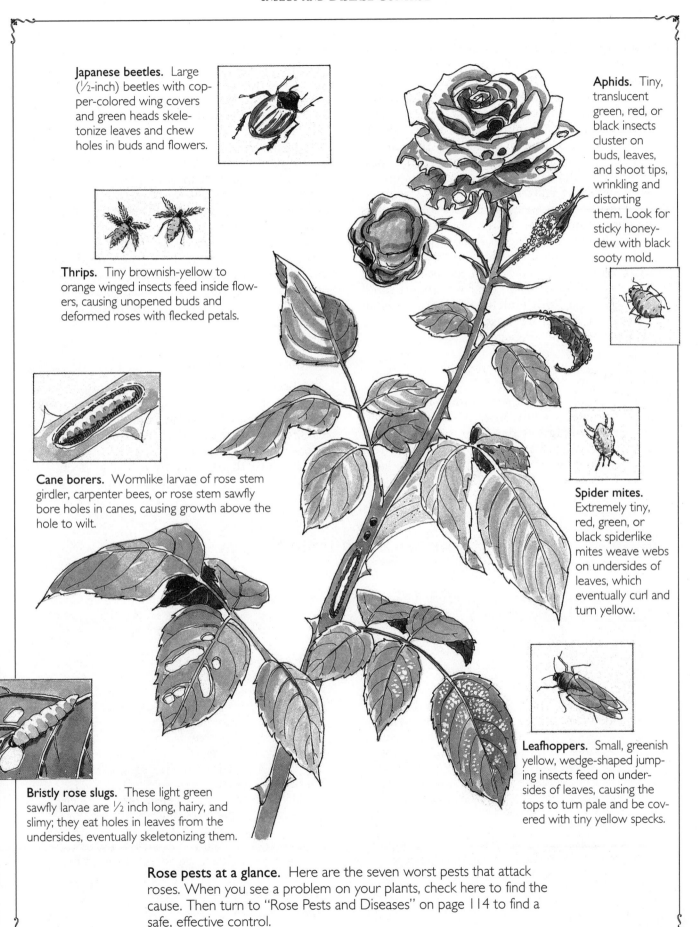

Japanese beetles. Large (½-inch) beetles with copper-colored wing covers and green heads skeletonize leaves and chew holes in buds and flowers.

Thrips. Tiny brownish-yellow to orange winged insects feed inside flowers, causing unopened buds and deformed roses with flecked petals.

Cane borers. Wormlike larvae of rose stem girdler, carpenter bees, or rose stem sawfly bore holes in canes, causing growth above the hole to wilt.

Bristly rose slugs. These light green sawfly larvae are ½ inch long, hairy, and slimy; they eat holes in leaves from the undersides, eventually skeletonizing them.

Aphids. Tiny, translucent green, red, or black insects cluster on buds, leaves, and shoot tips, wrinkling and distorting them. Look for sticky honeydew with black sooty mold.

Spider mites. Extremely tiny, red, green, or black spiderlike mites weave webs on undersides of leaves, which eventually curl and turn yellow.

Leafhoppers. Small, greenish yellow, wedge-shaped jumping insects feed on undersides of leaves, causing the tops to turn pale and be covered with tiny yellow specks.

Rose pests at a glance. Here are the seven worst pests that attack roses. When you see a problem on your plants, check here to find the cause. Then turn to "Rose Pests and Diseases" on page 114 to find a safe, effective control.

They also recover faster from these attacks. Healthy plants are well fed but not overfed. Too much nitrogen makes for lush, succulent foliage that is especially appealing to sucking insects and powdery mildew. An advantage of organic fertilizers is that the nitrogen is released slowly and steadily. Studies have shown that plants grown with organic fertilizers have smaller pest populations than the same type of plants grown with chemical fertilizers.

Maintaining healthy plants also means avoiding water stress. In dry conditions, plants are especially vulnerable to aphids, spider mites, and thrips. Always water thoroughly and deeply. Drip irrigation systems and deep mulches will help you keep on top of your watering. (You'll find more on both mulching and watering in "Mulching for More Roses" on page 90 and "Watering Wisely" on page 92.)

Watch How You Water

Blackspot and rust spores must be in water to germinate, so obviously it's important to keep rose foliage as dry as possible if these fungal diseases are a problem in your area. You can help keep your roses dry by spacing plants at least 3 to 4 feet apart in a site that gets full sun, pruning to create open centers, using drip irrigation or a bubbler head on the hose when watering so foliage is kept dry, and watering early enough in the day so foliage dries before evening.

On the other hand, powdery mildew spores often germinate best in dry conditions. If mildew is a problem in your area, keep it to a minimum by regularly washing the leaves. You can significantly reduce mildew by thoroughly spraying both upper and lower leaf surfaces with water in the early afternoon. Spray every three days for best control. Time these periods of spraying with new foliage growth spurts (tender, succulent leaves are most susceptible) and the ideal weather conditions for mildew: hot, humid, and airless.

Keep the Garden Clean

Check plants before you buy them or when they are delivered to your door, inspecting leaves, stems, and roots for insects, eggs, or diseases. On established roses, remove and destroy diseased leaves, stems, and flowers as they appear. Burn them, bury them 3 feet deep, or

Growth-Enhancing Sprays

The following three foliar sprays do not control pests, but they do improve growth because of the nutrients and hormones they contain, and they seem to help plants resist pests. Each of these materials is available from mail-order suppliers specializing in organic fertilizers or biodynamic preparations.

Stinging nettle: The coarse, hairy leaves of *Urtica dioica* cause a stinging reaction on bare skin, but a spray made from nettle leaves can help roses resist powdery mildew and aphids while providing trace elements. To make a concentrate, gather 1 pound of leaves, crush, and put in a jelly bag or old pillowcase. Submerge the bag or case in a gallon of unchlorinated water, cover, and let it sit in a warm place for a week. Store in a glass jar for up to a month. To spray, mix 1 part concentrate with 5 parts unchlorinated water. Spray roses once or twice a month.

Horsetail: A spray made from the leafless stems of *Equisetum arvense* helps to prevent fungal diseases. To make a concentrate, mix ⅛ cup of dried stems in 1 gallon of unchlorinated water, bring to a boil, then simmer for 30 minutes. Cool and strain, storing in a glass jar for up to a month. To make a spray, mix 1 part of concentrate with 5 to 10 parts of unchlorinated water. Spray roses every week or two.

Seaweed: An excellent source of micronutrients, seaweed or kelp also provides protection against diseases by enhancing growth. Since fish emulsion can encourage fungal diseases, don't use a concentrate that is a mixture of seaweed and fish emulsion. To use seaweed on healthy plants, follow manufacturer's recommendations, spraying once or twice a month. For sickly plants, use at half the recommended rate once a week.

send them to a landfill. Don't compost them; you might spread the disease all over your garden. As a final precaution, remove and destroy leaves and petals that fall to the ground year-round, as well as all prunings.

Prune for Disease Control

Good air circulation helps foliage dry quickly, which can prevent blackspot and rust. You can increase the air circulation within and around your plants by pruning roses to an open habit. Rose diseases can overwinter inside leaf buds and, to some extent, on or in canes. Fall pruning to remove infected parts helps to minimize diseases. If your roses had a lot of disease problems the previous summer, you may want to prune your roses to within 6 inches of the soil.

In mild climates with little or no dormant period, you can reduce diseases by creating a period that mimics dormancy. To do this, prune in mid-January, removing all leaves and infected canes.

Mulch for Disease Control

Mulching prevents overwintering disease spores on the ground from reaching your plants. After removing all fallen rose leaves in autumn, apply several inches of mulch. Put down another layer after the late winter/early spring pruning.

Biological Methods for Controlling Pests

Instead of fighting a time-consuming and costly battle against pests and diseases, it makes a lot of sense to let insect and disease allies take care of your problems instead—with a little encouragement from you. By encouraging beneficial insects to make their home near your roses, and by buying pest-specific microbial diseases and nematodes, you can tip the scales in favor of *really* natural control—the kind provided by Mother Nature herself. Let's look at some of the best biological controls.

Beneficial Insects

A healthy garden is naturally filled with a wide array of beneficial insects and other organisms that act as predators and parasites of destructive pests. To provide a haven for these beneficial species, you need diversity—a garden that's filled with many different types of plants and conditions.

Don't subject your garden to a blitzkrieg of poisons, either, since they can kill beneficial insects as well as harmful ones. Even the botanical poisons should be used only when absolutely necessary and only on the plants being damaged. It may take two to three years for enough predators and parasites to establish themselves and provide a counterbalance to foliage-eating pests.

If you want to introduce specific predators into your garden, the ones that are most worth the money and effort include aphid predatory midges, lacewings, and minute pirate bugs.

Besides providing a complex habitat in your garden, planting small-flowered plants rich in pollen and nectar will attract beneficial predators and parasites. Good plant choices include dill, caraway, fennel, lovage, parsley, Queen-Anne's-lace, catnip, hyssop, lemon balm, rosemary, thyme, coneflowers, daisies, yarrow, and goldenrod.

BT

Microbial insecticides that cause fatal diseases in target insects are another popular way to control pests. The most widely used biological control is *Bacillus thuringiensis,* or BT, a bacterial disease. Different strains of BT have been isolated for controlling specific pests. The strain of BT you need for rose pests is BTK (*B.t.* var. *kurstaki*), which infects caterpillars.

Unfortunately, BTK will infect all caterpillars, not just the tent caterpillars, webworms, and other pest larvae that eat rose foliage. To prevent butterfly caterpillars from being destroyed, spray only the rose bushes that show signs of caterpillars, webbing, or chewing damage (usually caterpillars chew large holes in leaves or skeletonize them).

Spray both the tops and bottoms of leaves with BTK as soon as you see caterpillars or larvae eating, following manufacturer's recommendations. Mix only enough spray mixture for a single application. You can also mix BT with other insecticide, soap, or oil sprays. BTK is sold under many brand names, including Caterpillar Attack, Dipel, and Thuricide.

Milky Disease

Milky disease (often called milky spore), caused by the bacteria *Bacillus popilliae* and

(continued on page 116)

Rose Pests and Diseases

Use this at-a-glance information to find out what's bugging your roses and what to do about it—fast!

PESTS

Aphids

Appearance and damage: Soft-bodied green, red, pink, brown, or black sucking insects about $\frac{1}{8}$ inch long. Most common in early spring on soft new growth, clustering on tips of young leaves and stems, flower buds, and blooms. Foliage and flowers may be dwarfed or disfigured. The honeydew-like substance excreted by aphids attracts ants and may develop sooty mold.

Controls: Prune off heavily infested parts and destroy them; use less nitrogen fertilizer; introduce lady beetles; wash off plants with strong sprays of water; spray with insecticidal soap; apply dormant oil in late winter or early spring to destroy eggs.

Beetles

Appearance and damage: Chewing insects with hard wings that eat rose leaves and flowers, and grublike larvae that feed on roots.

Diabrotica beetles: Also known as spotted cucumber beetles; small yellow-green beetles with six black spots on each wing; feed on flowers; worst in South and West.

Fuller rose beetles: Gray-brown weevils $\frac{1}{3}$ inch long, with white stripe on each side; feed at night, starting at the leaf edges; also eat flowers; root-eating larvae are yellow with brown heads; found mostly in South and Pacific Coast.

Goldsmith beetles: Hairy yellow inch-long beetles feed on foliage; root-eating larvae are white grubs; worst in Southwest.

Japanese beetles: Metallic green beetles $\frac{1}{2}$ inch long; curled larvae are 1-inch gray-white grubs with brown heads; voracious feeders on leaves and flowers.

June beetles: Large, $\frac{3}{4}$-inch red-brown to black beetles feed at night on leaves and flowers; root-eating large white grubs; worst in Midwest and South.

Rose chafers: Also known as rose bugs; long-legged, tan, $\frac{1}{3}$ inch long; feed on flowers and skele-tonize leaves; Northeast and Midwest.

Rose curculios: Weevils; eastern form is $\frac{1}{4}$ inch long and red with black curved beak; western form may be black and red or greenish-black; drills holes in buds; worst in Northern Plains.

Controls: Treat lawn areas with milky disease to destroy larvae in soil; this takes 3 years to significantly reduce population. Use traps placed 50 feet downwind from garden to destroy adult beetles, or pick off beetles by hand in early morning when they are inactive, dropping them into a can of water and kerosene or soapy water. Other means of controlling adult beetle populations include spraying with a mixture of 1 tablespoon isopropyl alcohol to a pint of pyrethrin mixture every 3 to 5 days and using rotenone spray or dust. Use sticky white traps for rose chafers.

Bristly Rose Slug

Appearance and damage: Light green, slug-like larvae of sawfly wasps, up to $\frac{1}{2}$ inch long. Rose slugs skeletonize rose foliage, eating on leaf undersides; especially destructive early in the growing season.

Controls: Spray foliage with insecticidal soap, or use rotenone for heavy infestations. If you hand-pick, wear gloves; touching bristly rose slugs can severely irritate bare skin.

Cane Borers

Appearance and damage: Larvae of various insects enter stems and canes from cut ends or by puncturing, causing shoots to wilt, be stunted, or die back. Damage is mainly cosmetic.

Rose stem sawflies: Wasplike insects with clear wings appear in early summer; larvae bore into canes, causing wilting and dieback.

Rose stem girdlers: Larvae spiral around inside canes, causing stems to swell and split; green-bronze beetles appear in summer.

Small carpenter bees: $\frac{1}{2}$-inch-long blue-green bees most often lay eggs in canes with cut ends; larvae bore out the soft center of stems.

Controls: Prune off the canes below the infested part and destroy; paint pruning cuts with wood glue or shellac.

Caterpillars

Appearance and damage: Chewing, wormlike moth or butterfly larvae skeletonize or completely eat leaves; may also eat buds and flowers.

Controls: Handpick caterpillars and destroy; spray weekly with BT (*Bacillus thuringiensis*) until pests are gone.

Leafhoppers

Appearance and damage: Green or brown, $\frac{1}{10}$- to $\frac{1}{2}$-inch-long, wedge-shaped insects that suck the juices from leaves, creating tiny pale spots on the foliage. Leaves eventually fall off. Hatch in late spring or early summer; found on undersides of leaves; hop quickly when disturbed.

Controls: Spray at three- to five-day intervals with a mixture of 1 tablespoon of isopropyl alcohol to each pint of prepared insecticidal soap mixture.

Leafrollers

Appearance and damage: Caterpillars that roll leaves around themselves, binding the leaf with weblike strands, then eat the leaves.

Controls: Handpick the curled leaves; spray with BT (*Bacillus thuringiensis*) just as first flower buds develop.

Rose Gall

Appearance and damage: Mosslike threads (in the case of mossy rose gall) or swellings on stems or roots (in the case of rose root gall) contain the larvae of wasps; usually appear in summer, most often on species roses.

Controls: Prune off infested stems and roots and destroy. Seal exposed canes with wood glue or shellac.

Rose Midges

Appearance and damage: White maggots of microscopic fly-like insects blacken and kill buds and leaves. Worst in midsummer.

Controls: Detect as early as possible, then remove and destroy infested growth.

Scale

Appearance and damage: Scale insects suck sap from plants. They have round or long and narrow white, gray, or brown hard shells about $\frac{1}{8}$ inch wide. Early signs include wilted and darkened leaves, then dropped leaves and stunted growth. In severe infestations, canes are encrusted with scales.

Controls: Treat light infestations by rubbing with a cotton swab dipped in isopropyl alcohol. For heavier infestations, spray plants every three days for two weeks with a mixture of 1 tablespoon of isopropyl alcohol to a pint of insecticidal soap. Prune off and destroy thickly encrusted canes.

Spider Mites

Appearance and damage: Microscopic red, brown, yellow, or green sucking mites that cause leaves to be stippled with yellow, red, or gray, to curl up, and to fall off. Webbing may appear on undersides of leaves. Worst in hot, dry weather.

Controls: Mites overwinter on weeds and garden trash, so clean up the garden well in fall or early spring. Destroy overwintering eggs with dormant oil spray in late winter. In hot, dry weather, wash foliage once or twice a week. If infestation is apparent, wash foliage three days in a row. For heavy infestations, spray with insecticidal soap every three to five days for two weeks.

Thrips

Appearance and damage: Tiny, yellow, black, or brown, piercing-rasping insects that feed on flower buds, causing petal edges to brown or buds to remain closed. New growth may be deformed, damaged, or mottled. Open buds and look at the base of the petals to identify. Worst during dry weather. Especially attracted to white and yellow roses.

Controls: Use yellow sticky traps four weeks after last frost for early detection. Spray with insecticidal soap, rotenone, sabadilla, or ryania every three days for two weeks. Predators include lacewings, lady beetles, benefical nematodes, and predatory mites.

DISEASES

Blackspot

Appearance and damage: Fungal disease forming black circles with yellow margins $\frac{1}{16}$ to $\frac{1}{2}$ inch in diameter, which may blend to form blotches

(continued)

Rose Pests and Diseases—Continued

on leaves and canes. In severe cases, entire leaf will yellow and fall. Leaves less than two weeks old are most susceptible. Optimum conditions for infection are temperatures of 64° to 75°F and continuous wetness for seven hours; symptoms manifest in three to ten days, with new spores produced every three weeks. Spores are dispersed by water, by contact with people, animals, or insects, and by wind. Spores overwinter on fallen leaves and in canes. Most common in areas with hot, humid summer climates such as the Northeast, the Southeast, and parts of the Midwest.

Controls: Plant disease-resistant cultivars. Monitor when temperatures are optimum and rainfall and humidity are high. At the first signs, prune off damaged foliage and begin treatment. Water with soaker hose or early in the day. Prune plants to improve air circulation. If necessary, spray every 7 to 14 days with fungicidal soap, antitranspirants, or wettable sulfur. Foliar feeding helps to prevent blackspot. Gather and destroy leaves and pruned canes in fall. Spray during dormancy with fungicidal soap or wettable sulfur, then dormant oil.

Canker

Appearance and damage: Fungal disease causing lesions or swollen, discolored areas on canes and, in worst cases, dieback from the tip. Enters plants through pruning cuts and insect wounds.

Controls: Prune off the canes below the infested part and destroy, dipping shears in disinfectant between cuts; paint pruning cuts with wood glue or shellac.

Crown Gall

Appearance and damage: Soilborne bacteria enter near the bud union or the roots and cause rough swollen growths; plant growth and flowering is poor.

Controls: Avoid wounding stems or roots. Check new plants for infection. Remove and destroy infected parts and seal wound with pruning paint. If necessary, remove and destroy entire plant, then remove and replace soil if replanting roses in the same spot, or select a different location.

Nematodes

Appearance and damage: Pale, deformed growth; knotty enlargements on roots with tiny white eggs inside. Caused by microscopic, soilborne eel-worms.

Controls: Remove and destroy plants; remove and replace soil or grow roses in another location. Incorporating plenty of leafmold in soil helps beneficial fungi to attack nematodes; a fish emulsion drench repels nematodes.

Powdery Mildew

Appearance and damage: Fungal disease starts on young growth as raised blisters and

B. lentimorbus, controls beetles in the grub, or larval, stage. Japanese beetles, a major pest of roses in the Northeast, can skeletonize rose leaves and damage buds and flowers. Other beetles that eat rose foliage or flowers include rose chafers, rose curculios, and rose leaf beetles.

Apply milky disease to the lawn, following manufacturer's directions, in spring after the danger of frost has passed. Although it may take several years before the beetle population is significantly reduced, the milky disease stays active in the soil for many years. It is most effective in areas where the soil temperature exceeds 70°F in the summer. Milky disease is sold as Doom and Japademic.

Nematodes

Nematodes that parasitize insects are an effective control for insects whose larval stage lives in the soil, such as Japanese beetles, rose chafers, June beetles, and cane borers. The two types of nematodes that are effective on these pests are *Steinernema carpocapsae* and *Heterorhabditis heliothidis.* The nematodes work by entering the larva's body and releasing toxic bacteria that paralyze and kill the pest within 24 to 48 hours.

To apply the microscopic nematodes, mix the nematodes (usually shipped dehydrated or in gel, a sponge, or moist peat and vermiculite) with water and spray on the soil around your causes leaves to curl; eventually new growth and flower buds are covered with thin, white, powdery substance and growth becomes deformed. Older growth is not usually affected. Optimum conditions include 60°F nights with high humidity and 80°F days with 40 to 70 percent humidity. Found in most locations, but worst in Pacific Coast and Southwest, where there is little rainfall. Spores overwinter inside leaf buds on canes and are spread by wind.

Controls: Start checking daily in spring for signs of disease; prune off infected parts immediately; when conditions are ideal for mildew, wash upper and lower leaf surfaces with a heavy spray of water in early afternoon every three days; spray plants weekly with fungicidal soap or wettable sulfur. In late winter, spray with fungicidal soap or wettable sulfur, then dormant oil. Buy mildew-resistant cultivars, and avoid mildew-prone cultivars like 'Tropicana', 'Papa Meilland', 'Europeana', and 'Mr. Lincoln'.

Rust

Appearance and damage: Fungal disease that appears in spring as small orange spots on undersides of leaves and light yellow spots on the upper side; long narrow spots may form on young canes. In summer, red-orange masses of spores form on the undersides of leaves, and upper surfaces will have dead spots surrounded by green or red. In fall, black spores appear in these spots. Leaves may drop in summer or fall. Optimum conditions include temperatures between 64° and 70°F and continuous moisture for two to four hours; reproduction occurs every 10 to 14 days in summer. Spores overwinter on leaves and canes and are distributed by wind and water. Infestations are worst on Pacific Coast; cold winters and hot summers limit the disease.

Controls: Start checking foliage in early spring and cut off diseased leaves. When conditions are ideal for rust, spray weekly with fungicidal soap or wettable sulfur.

Viruses

Description and damage: A number of viral diseases may attack roses. Leaves develop yellow-green mottling or odd patterns that bear no resemblance to chewing or sucking damage. Plants may be stunted.

Mosaic virus: Leaves develop circles of yellow or chartreuse, become streaked or mottled, or develop yellow netting; foliage may curl and growth may be stunted.

Controls: There is no cure for viral diseases; destroy infected plants immediately. Buy resistant cultivars when possible. Insects like aphids can spread viruses from plant to plant as they feed; controlling them may check the spread of the diseases.

roses or on the lawn according to package directions. Nematodes are most effective if you apply them to moist soil in the late afternoon or evening. You can also squirt the solution into borer holes in the rose canes with a syringe.

Physical Methods for Controlling Pests

One key to being a successful organic gardener is to be aware of pests and diseases as soon as they appear. It's a lot easier to control problems when the pest population and disease damage is small than waiting until you're confronted by an epidemic. Look at your roses carefully, checking both upper and lower leaf surfaces, flowers, buds, canes, and general appearance, every day or two. I like to check my plants in the early morning, when I can stroll around enjoying my garden at the same time. When you see a problem developing, the first line of defense is physical control.

The simplest type of physical control for pests is to handpick the insects and drop them into a pail of soapy water or water topped with kerosene. This method works best with large pests that are easy to spot and to pick up, like beetles. Wear gloves if you handpick the sluglike larvae of the rose sawfly, curled rose sawfly, and

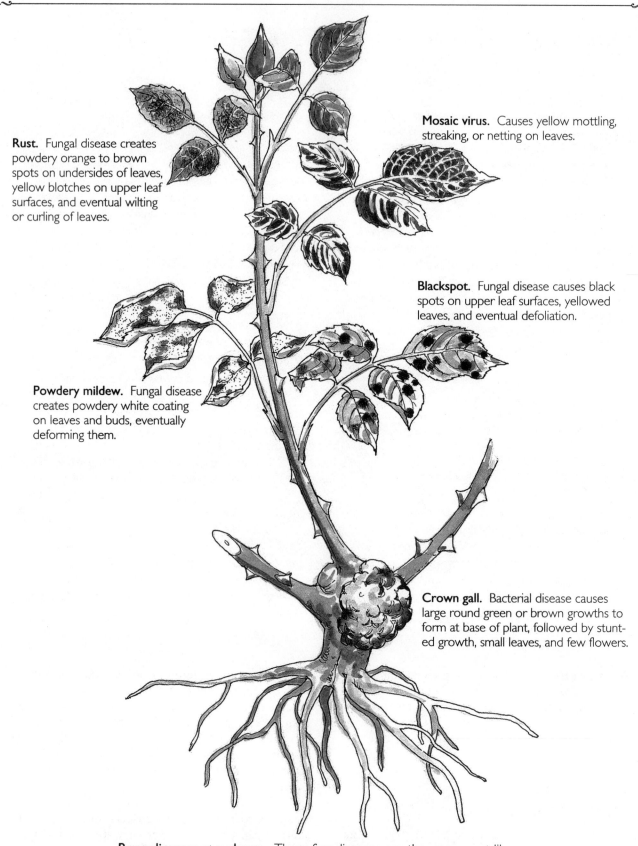

Rust. Fungal disease creates powdery orange to brown spots on undersides of leaves, yellow blotches on upper leaf surfaces, and eventual wilting or curling of leaves.

Mosaic virus. Causes yellow mottling, streaking, or netting on leaves.

Blackspot. Fungal disease causes black spots on upper leaf surfaces, yellowed leaves, and eventual defoliation.

Powdery mildew. Fungal disease creates powdery white coating on leaves and buds, eventually deforming them.

Crown gall. Bacterial disease causes large round green or brown growths to form at base of plant, followed by stunted growth, small leaves, and few flowers.

Rose diseases at a glance. These five diseases are the ones most likely to cause problems for your plants. When you see a disease on your roses, check here to find the cause. Then turn to "Rose Pests and Diseases" on page 114 to find a safe, effective control.

bristly rose slug (it's really an insect, not a slug); handling them can irritate bare skin.

Other physical controls are simple and effective, too. Spraying plants with with a stiff jet of water from the hose will get rid of small sedentary pests like aphids and spider mites. If you see disease symptoms on only a few leaves, it makes sense to pick off and destroy the infected foliage. This may be all it takes to keep the disease from spreading. The same is true of cutting off buds that are infested with rose midges and canes that are home to stem girdlers and cane borers. A sharp pair of pruners is also the best defense against botrytis blight and fungal cankers. If your rose has contracted a virus, removing and destroying the entire plant is really your only option.

Traps are another form of physical control. Traps attract insects through color, odor, or shape. You can use traps to monitor the arrival of a pest, lure pests away from plants, or reduce the pest population. Color-attractant traps lure pests to their surface, which is coated with a sticky substance that "glues" them to the trap. Yellow sticky traps attract aphids, whiteflies, and some thrips, while blue sticky traps monitor but do not control thrips. You can use white sticky traps to catch rose chafers.

You can buy sticky traps or make your own from ¼-inch plywood or Masonite boards. Paint them the appropriate color, coat one side with a sticky substance like Tanglefoot or petroleum jelly, and hang or stake them in the garden at foliage height with the sticky side facing the plants. When traps get full, clean them off with a paint scraper or a cloth soaked in baby oil or vegetable oil. Reapply the sticky coating after each cleaning.

The most well known traps as far as roses are concerned are Japanese beetle traps. Commercially available Japanese beetle traps use floral and fruit scents and sex pheromones as attractants. You can make your own traps with baits of wine, sugar, water, mashed fruit, and baking yeast. These traps do attract Japanese beetles—in fact, they can attract every beetle in your neighborhood. If you want to use Japanese beetle traps and don't want to draw beetles right to your roses, place the traps at least 50 feet downwind from your roses. You'll get the best control if you combine traps with frequent handpicking and an application of milky disease. Empty traps regularly—you may need to empty them daily at the height of the season.

As alternatives to Japanese beetle traps, you might consider floating row covers. Though they're unsightly in an ornamental garden, you only need to cover your plants during the two weeks or so that adult beetles are active. And if you weight the covers or use wire staples to hold them firmly in place, you'll keep your plants from being decimated by Japanese beetles. The lightweight synthetic fabric sold specifically for this use lets in more than 80 percent of sunlight and rain.

Slugs and snails can be serious pests on roses, too, feeding on leaves and flowers. Keep them off your rose bushes by putting a copper Snail-Gard band around the base of the trunk—snails and slugs coming in contact with the band will get an electric shock. Check for gray, pearly snail and slug eggs in and under the mulch around your plants.

You can also trap these pesky mollusks by setting out shallow pans of fermenting yeast and water, beer, near-beer, or yogurt. Straight-sided traps set in the ground around your plants are best—slugs and snails will crawl down the side for a drink and then drown. Commercial plastic traps are also available. If you use traps, empty and refill them regularly.

Organic Materials for Controlling Pests and Diseases

There are times when, even after you've made the best possible efforts to control pests and diseases with cultural, biological, and physical methods, your rose problem still isn't licked. As a last resort, there are sprays and dusts you can use in your organic garden. These differ from synthetic, petrochemical-based materials, in that they generally tend to affect only specific pests and diseases, and they break down quickly in the environment.

Unfortunately, pests can develop resistance to organic pesticides just as they do to other pesticides. To avoid this, try to use these methods as little as possible, target their use to the most effective life-cycle stage, and alternate controls rather than using the same one over and over.

It's most important to remember that even when using organic controls, you should use safety precautions. These include storing materials safely out of reach of children and pets, wearing protective clothing and a mask, and disposing of unused materials and containers safely. You'll find more safety tips for storing and using these materials in "Safety Guidelines for Using Pesticides" on page 120.

With these precautions in mind, review the controls on the following pages to familiarize yourself with all the available options for controlling rose pests and diseases organically. You'll feel more comfortable and confident when a problem does arise if you already know your options—and even more important, you can collect an assortment of materials beforehand so you'll have them when they're needed.

Alcohol

Isopropyl, or rubbing, alcohol can control aphids, mealybugs, scale, thrips, and whiteflies, but it can also burn foliage. Mix 1 quart of alcohol in 1 gallon of water, or substitute alcohol for half of the water when mixing an insecticidal soap spray. But before you spray your rose bush, test the alcohol spray on a few leaves and wait a day or so to check for leaf damage.

Ammonia

Household ammonia, which is a solution of ammonium hydroxide (containing hydrogen and nitrogen), can be effective as an insecticide when used at the rate of 3 tablespoons of ammonia in a gallon of water. It can control aphids, flea beetles, scale, thrips, and whiteflies. Like alcohol, ammonia can also burn foliage—test the spray on a few leaves before spraying the whole plant. To run the least risk of leaf damage, don't spray drought-stressed plants, and don't spray in really hot weather.

Antitranspirants

Antitranspirants like Wilt-Pruf, VaporGard, and ForEverGreen are normally sprayed on broad-leaved evergreens and conifers in winter to reduce water loss and to prevent the plants from being injured through drying out. But research has shown that these products also help prevent infection from fungal diseases, especially powdery mildew, by forming a barrier between the plant and disease spores. Because antitranspirants work as preventive controls, it's important to begin applying them before you see signs of mildew, and repeated applications are necessary to keep new growth protected. You'll also have to reapply the antitranspirants after each rain.

Baking Soda

A 0.5 percent solution of baking soda (sodium bicarbonate) has been shown to prevent blackspot on roses effectively, and it may pre-

Safety Guidelines for Using Pesticides

The sprays and dusts used by organic gardeners cause less environmental damage than petrochemical-based pesticides, both in their production and because they break down quickly into harmless compounds that don't accumulate in the food chain. Even so, they are still highly toxic for a brief period. Follow these basic guidelines whenever you apply pesticides:

1. Read the label when purchasing a product to be sure it is effective on the pest you want to control.

2. Keep the product in its original container. The label includes the active ingredients, mixing and application information, pests the product is registered for, and antidotes in case of poisoning.

3. Keep containers tightly closed in a cool, dry place, locked away from children and pets and far from food preparation areas.

4. Read the label again before you use a pesticide. Follow the recommended dosage, and measure and mix amounts accurately. Avoid breathing the dust from wettable powders when mixing. (Wear a mask if necessary.)

5. Wear protective clothing when spraying, including long pants and a long-sleeved shirt, shoes and socks, rubber or polyethylene gloves, and a face mask or respirator. If you're spraying for a long period, wear goggles. Wash sprayer, clothing, and skin thoroughly, and do so immediately after spraying.

6. Dispose of empty containers in sanitary landfills.

7. Never use a sprayer for pesticides that's been used to spray weed killers.

8. Wait until sprays have dried or dust has settled before going into treated areas.

vent other fungal diseases like powdery mildew as well. To make the solution, dissolve 4 teaspoons of baking soda in 1 gallon of water, adding 1 teaspoon of liquid dish soap or insecticidal soap to help it spread and stick to the leaves uniformly. Spray the plant thoroughly, including the undersides of the leaves. If disease symptoms have already appeared on your plants, try this solution from Cornell University: Mix 1 tablespoon of baking soda and 2½ tablespoons of horticultural oil in 1 gallon of water. Apply when symptoms appear and every two weeks thereafter until your plants are fungus-free.

Citrus Oils

Limonoid compounds in citrus peels have recently been found to kill or deter certain insects, including aphids, spider mites, and caterpillars. Look for citrus-based insecticides like Aphid-Mite Attack, and use following the manufacturer's recommendations.

Compost Tea

Here's a surprise—a foliar spray of compost tea can actually help protect your roses from fungal diseases like powdery mildew and botrytis blight even as it boosts their nutrient uptake. Make a "tea" solution by putting 1 gallon of finished compost in a 5-gallon bucket and filling the bucket with water. Stir the mixture well, and set it in a warm place for three days. Filter the finished tea through a porous cloth like cheesecloth or burlap, applying the solid compost around the base of your plants. Spray the compost tea on your roses in the evening for best results, repeating the application every three to four days until the disease is under control. Manure-based compost makes the most effective fungus-fighter.

Diatomaceous Earth

Composed of the fossilized silica shells of one-celled algae, diatomaceous earth (DE) is a talc-like substance that kills bugs by dehydration. It destroys all types of insects, including beneficial ones, but is not toxic to mammals. For roses, it's especially good for controlling slugs, snails, and thrips. Use only natural-grade DE. Apply when foliage is wet, dusting just the undersides of the leaves, never the blooms, and sprinkling DE on the soil in a circle around the plant. Use a dust mask when applying DE.

Garlic Oil

Combining garlic, mineral oil, and soap makes an effective control for mildew, aphids, and some caterpillars, bugs, and beetles. To make a stock solution, soak 3 ounces of minced garlic in 2 teaspoons of mineral oil for 24 hours. Slowly combine with 1 pint of water to which you've added 1 tablespoon of liquid dish soap or commercial insecticidal soap. Mix thoroughly, then strain and store in a tightly closed glass jar. To make a spray mixture, add ½ cup to 1 gallon of water. Test a few leaves for damage before spraying the entire plant. (Wait at least a day for signs of damage to appear.)

Horticultural Oils

A very small quantity of petroleum oil mixed in water kills insects by direct contact. There are two main types of horticultural oils, dormant and summer, differing in the degree of refinement. Neither type is poisonous to people. Horticultural oils can control scale, leafrollers, mealybugs, thrips, aphids, and mites on roses.

Apply dormant oils in late winter or early spring, when plants are leafless. Dormant oils destroy overwintering insects and their eggs. Prepare the spray according to manufacturer's recommendations, making sure the mixture is properly emulsified (that is, that the oil is adequately mixed into the spray solution). Spray on a calm day when no rain is forecast for 24 hours and temperatures will remain above 40°F.

Apply summer oils when plants are actively growing. Summer oils must be applied carefully to avoid leaf injury. Daytime temperatures should not be above 85°F or night temperatures below freezing. Don't use summer oils when the soil or air is dry, or a month before or after using sulfur spray or dust. Make sure your plants aren't drought-stressed when you spray them.

Hydrogen Peroxide

Spraying ½ cup of hydrogen peroxide per gallon of water on plants weekly produces dark, healthy leaves, larger flowers, and fewer pests. You can also use the mixture as a soil drench.

Neem

The seed of the neem tree (*Azadirachta indica*) from India yields an insecticide with very low toxicity to mammals and beneficial insects. Neem acts as both a repellent and an insect poison. Rose pests controlled include aphids, some beetles, caterpillars, mealybugs, spider mites, and thrips. Neem is commercially available as Bioneem; apply according to manufacturer's directions.

Pyrethrins

Extracted from dried flowers of the pyrethrum daisy (*Tanacetum cinerariifolium* and *T. coccineum,* formerly in the genus *Chrysanthemum*), pyrethrins kill many chewing and sucking insects on contact, including aphids, spider mites, and thrips. Pyrethrins also kill lady beetles, fish, aquatic insects, and small fish-eating animals but are not harmful to bees, birds, or mammals. Pyrethrins are available in pre-mixed sprays, liquid concentrates, and wettable powders, including Entire, Red Arrow (with rotenone), and Safer Yard and Garden Insect Killer.

You'll get the best control if you spray twice at two-hour intervals; cover all leaf and plant surfaces. Pyrethrins quickly lose their effectivness in light and heat, so store them in a cool, dark place. Don't use pyrethrins near a pond, water garden, lake, stream, or other body of water that might contain fish or other aquatic wildlife.

Quassia

Bark chips and shavings of the Latin American tree bitterwood (*Quassia amara*) yield a mild and very safe insecticide that does not harm lady beetles or honeybees but does control aphids and caterpillars. Quassia chips can be purchased in natural-food stores. To use them, crush, grind, or chop ½ cup of bark chips and soak them for one hour in 1 gallon of boiling water or overnight in cool water. Strain before using, spreading the soaked wood residue around the base of your plants. Use every three or four days when insects are eating leaves, spraying both upper and lower leaf surfaces.

Rodale's All-Purpose Spray

Try this formula, developed by the editors of *Organic Gardening* magazine, on leaf-eating pests: Chop, grind, or liquefy one garlic bulb and one small onion. Add 1 teaspoon of powdered cayenne pepper and mix with 1 quart of water. After steeping one hour, strain and add 1 tablespoon liquid dish soap or commercial insecticidal soap. Mix well and spray on both upper and lower leaf surfaces as needed; the mix will keep in a covered container in the refrigerator for up to a week.

Rotenone

Derived from the roots of a genus of South American legumes, rotenone is a paralyzing nerve poison that kills a number of insects. It is effective in the garden for about a week but persists longer in the environment. Very toxic to fish and birds, rotenone causes an allergic reaction in some people. On roses, rotenone can control most chewing insects, like Japanese beetles and rose chafers. Since both dust and spray forms leave a residue on leaves, choose the spray as it is usually safer to use. Select a wettable powder specifically formulated for mixing with water, buying just enough fresh stock for one season since it does not keep well. Thoroughly spray all leaf and plant surfaces. As with pyrethrins, don't use rotenone near any body of water where fish or other aquatic wildlife might live.

Ryania

Derived from the South American shrub *Ryania speciosa*, ryania is a contact and stomach poison. It controls a wide range of chewing and sucking insects, including beetles and caterpillars. Ryania is very stable—it will stay viable for at least five years if kept in a cool, dry, dark place. In the garden, it quickly loses its effectiveness with rain, overhead watering, or heavy dew. Ryania is available in both dust and spray formulations. It is highly toxic to mammals as well as fish and other aquatic life; apply with caution, and don't use ryania near any body of water where fish or other aquatic wildlife might live.

Sabadilla

The seeds of a Central and South American lily, *Schoenocaulon officinale,* are the source of sabadilla. This insecticide controls aphids, thrips, and many caterpillars, beetles, and bugs. Sabadilla will keep well in a dry, dark place, but it's unstable in light and quickly loses effectiveness in the garden. You'll get best results if you apply sabadilla weekly to wet leaf surfaces (as after a rain, or in the early morning when plants are dew-covered). Sabadilla is toxic to humans and honeybees, but it does not harm beneficial predators and parasites. It is available as Necessary Organics Sabadilla Pest Control and Veratran D; apply according to manufacturer's directions.

SilKaBen

This commercial preparation is a mixture of quartz minerals, bentonite clay, coral limestone, and trace elements. Mixed with water and sprayed on plants, it creates a thin, protective film that helps prevent fungal growth and deters sucking and chewing insects. Mix 1 ounce per 1½ gallons of water for a spray. Apply weekly or after a heavy rain.

Soap

The salts of fatty acids found in many soaps acts as contact insecticides. Sprays made from soap and water are most effective on soft-bodied insects such as aphids, mealybugs, scale, thrips, whiteflies, and mites. Soaps are not toxic to people, birds, or other animals, and they can be mixed with other insecticidal sprays to increase the coating power and effectiveness of the other pesticide.

You can use mild household soaps, like Ivory Snow, Ivory Liquid, or Shaklee's Basic H, mixing 1 teaspoon to 1 tablespoon of soap per gallon of water. Or try commercial insecticidal soaps like Safer Insecticidal Soap or Aphid-Mite Attack, applied at the manufacturer's recommended rate. Thoroughly spray all leaf and plant surfaces, preferably on overcast days, repeating every week to two weeks as needed.

Soaps may be ineffective with hard water. To test, add 3 tablespoons of soap to 1 quart of water, mix thoroughly, and let stand for 15 minutes; if a scum and milky-looking curds form, use bottled water to make your soap solution.

For control of fungal diseases like powdery mildew, try mixing sulfur in your soap solution (see "Sulfur" on this page), or buy Safer Garden Fungicide, which contains both soap and sulfur. There is also a commercial organic herbicide, SharpShooter, that uses soap to control weeds; it is most effective on young annual weeds rather than mature perennials. Again, apply according to manufacturer's directions.

Starch

Completely nontoxic to plants, animals, and people, this mixture of flour and water physically traps and suffocates insects. The most effective kind is potato starch, which controls aphids, spider mites, thrips, and whiteflies, and may also control powdery mildew and other fungal diseases. To make a homemade spray, mix ½ to 1 cup of potato starch (available from natural-food stores) in 1 gallon of water and add a teaspoon of liquid soap. This spray will cut down on photosynthesis and

won't add to the attractiveness of your rose bushes, so wash it off with water a few days after you've applied it.

Sulfur

Elemental sulfur controls fungal diseases like powdery mildew, rust, and blackspot by preventing fungal spores from germinating. To be effective, it must be on the leaf before the spores arrive, so repeated sprays are necessary. Sulfur also kills mites and some insects. Powdered sulfur distributes evenly and sticks to leaves well, but liquid formulations are easier to apply and less disruptive to beneficial insects. Don't use sulfur when temperatures exceed 80°F, or you'll injure your plants. Sulfur is available as Bonide Liquid Sulfur, Safer Garden Fungicide (with soap), and That Flowable Sulfur; apply according to manufacturer's directions.

MAKING MORE ROSES

Most people acquire their roses by buying plants either from a local source or by mail order. A more old-fashioned way is by starting roses from cuttings. When I was growing up, neighbors swapped cuttings of roses. For many people, especially those interested in the old garden roses, this method is just as valid today. It's also a great way to get free roses, if you need a number of plants on a limited budget. Other good reasons to propagate roses are to save plants that are about to be destroyed, to make gift plants from your own favorites, and to develop new cultivars. Also, roses growing on their own roots, such as those produced from cuttings or layering, are often more vigorous and hardier than those that are budded.

To understand plant propagation, the most important thing to know is the difference between sexual and asexual propagation. With sexual propagation, pollen from the (male) stamens pollinates the ovaries of the (female) pistils, with seeds resulting. (If you can't picture the parts of a flower, turn to "Basic Rose Anatomy" on page 5 for a look.) The plants resulting from the seeds may or may not resemble the parents, since both gene pools are available for the offspring to draw from. If both parents belong to the same species, the seedlings will be true to the species even if they're not exactly identical to their parents. With hybrids, including most available roses, the offspring will be very different from their parents. If you want to get more plants of a species or to hybridize new cultivars, try growing roses from seed. Bear in mind that it will take several years for the seedlings to reach flowering size.

Asexual propagation is the method to use when you want an offspring that is an exact genetic duplicate of its parent, as with a cultivar. (Of course, this technique works on species roses as well.) It involves taking a portion of the parent plant, then growing that portion into its own plant. The plant portion may be as small as a couple of cells, as with tissue culture; a single growth bud, when budding; or a length of stem, as with cuttings or layering. One advantage of asexual propagating techniques is that the new plants reach flowering size in a season or two—several years earlier than seedlings.

Because commercial rose producers want as many plants that are identical to the original plant as possible, since they're in the business of selling named cultivars, the most efficient method for them is to propagate by budding.

(Home rose propagators, take note: Most newly developed roses are patented, and these cannot be reproduced for sale without paying a royalty to the hybridizer. Patents are in effect for 17 years. However, you can propagate these plants for your own garden.) Gardeners can learn to bud, as I'll describe later, but propagating from cuttings or layering is much easier.

Roses from Cuttings

Although you can take cuttings at any time of the year, the best time is in fall, when night temperatures are between 50° and 60°F and days are not over 90°F. Choose firm, green stems that are about the diameter of a pencil, or about two months old. Cut the stem into 6- to 8-inch lengths, preferably with about five growth buds each. Using sharp, sterile pruners, make the cut at a 45-degree angle just below a leaf bud. Remove leaves from the lower half of each cutting. If you cannot plant the cuttings immediately, place them in a plastic bag with a piece of moistened towel

Rose Propagating Terms

You'll be more confident when following propagating instructions if you review these terms first. It's hard to bud a rose when you can't recall what they mean by a scion!

Budding: The standard commercial method of propagating roses by grafting an eye under the bark of a rootstock. A budded plant is propagated by budding.

Bud union: The swollen point where the bud is joined with the rootstock.

Crown: The point on the rose where the canes (basal shoots) sprout from the bud union.

Cutting: A piece of stem cut from a plant and allowed to root.

Grafting: The process of joining a stem or bud, called the scion, of one cultivar onto the rooted stem, called the rootstock, of another cultivar.

Mutation: A sudden change in the genetic make-up of a plant; see "sport."

Own-root roses: Roses grown from cuttings, rather than being budded onto a rootstock of another plant.

Rootstock: The host plant or root system onto which a scion or bud is grafted; also called understock.

Scion: The technical term for the bud grafted onto a rootstock.

Sport: A mutation or change in the genetic makeup of a plant expressed in a different characteristic or group of characteristics. For example, a rose with normally bushy growth might send out a long, climber-type cane, or a branch might bear a different color or shape of flowers. Sporting usually occurs only on a section of a plant.

Understock: The base of the plant, providing the root system, onto which the scion is grafted; also called rootstock.

around the ends. Wait no longer than a few days to plant them. Use separate bags for each cultivar, and label the cuttings.

Commercial rooting hormones are available, but these are not necessary for success. If used, follow manufacturer's directions. If you'd like to experiment with homemade rooting hormones, soak the bottom ends of your cuttings in a weak solution made from willow cuttings and water, or wrap the base of the cutting with a wad of lawn grass.

There are a number of places where you can stick your cuttings into the soil to root them. Some people put them under existing rose bushes or other shrubs. Other people develop a specific nursery area, incorporating builder's sand and vermiculite into the soil for a light, airy, well-drained soil. Still others plant the cuttings in pots with soilless potting mix. A greenhouse or cold frame is ideal, providing winter protection and increased humidity, but you can also make your own mini-greenhouse by inverting a large glass jar or plastic milk jug over each cutting, raising the jar or jug slightly off the ground with a pebble or stick to allow for air circulation. Remove the jar when temperatures are warm.

Whatever site you choose for your cuttings, the soil should be loose, rich in humus, and moist but well drained. Choose a site with bright but not direct light. Remove the leaves from the bottom half of the cutting, make a 3-inch hole in the soil with a pencil or dibble, and insert the cutting to half its length. Be sure that the cutting is "top-side up." (A trick of the pros is to make different cuts on the tops and bottoms of their cuttings, so you can tell at a glance which end is up. They usually make a slanting cut at the top and a straight cut at the bottom of each cutting.)

If you're making a row of cuttings, space them 8 inches apart. Label the cuttings with a waterproof tag and marker, stating the cultivar and the date you took the cutting. Firm the soil around each cutting, water well, and keep the cuttings adequately watered but not soggy. Roots normally develop in about six weeks.

Most gardeners making cuttings in the fall let them stay in the garden over winter, mulching around them. By the following spring, the cuttings will be putting out new growth. Transplant them to their permanent site in the spring, or feed and water during the growing season, then transplant them to their permanent location in the fall.

Roses from Layering

This method has a higher success rate than cuttings, but you can't create as many new plants. However, if you only want a few more roses, it's ideal. Layering works best with plants that have low and/or flexible canes. The best times of year for layering are early spring and mid-fall, when temperatures are mild and not freezing.

The layering technique is simple. Choose a cane that will reach the ground plus have an additional 8 to 12 inches of growth. With a sharp knife, make a small cut at an angle on the underside of the stem just above a growth bud. Put a toothpick or match stick in the cut to keep it open. Dig a hole 6 inches deep where the cut stem touches the soil. Place the "elbow" created by the cut in the hole, with the tip extending several inches above the soil. Fill in the hole with soil. If necessary, set a rock or brick on top of the hole to hold the stem in place, pin it in place with a U-shaped wire staple before you bury it, or mound up soil over the buried stem.

Roots should form in six to eight weeks. Two signs that your layer has rooted are active top growth on the new plant and a slight resistance when the tip is tugged. If conditions are not good for transplanting, leave the plant in place until they are. Otherwise, cut the plant from the mother cane and carefully transplant it to its permanent home.

Roses from Budding

Budding is a more complex technique than taking cuttings or layering. The first step in budding is to have a growing rootstock. A few mail-order nurseries carry the most commonly used rootstocks, which include *Rosa multiflora* and 'Dr. Huey', as well as *R. manettii* and *R. × odorata* in mild climates. You can experiment by using any hardy, vigorous rose as a rootstock, especially species and old garden roses. Start your rootstocks from cuttings in the fall or early spring, setting them 12 inches apart.

The best time to bud roses is from early to late summer. Budwood is the same as cuttings, or 6-inch pieces of stem about the diameter of a pencil. Remove all the leaves before cutting your buds from the piece of stem.

To prepare the bud, you will need a very sharp knife. Starting ½ inch below the bud, cut upward into the stem, just barely cutting into the wood below the bud. Then finish the cut ½

Rose Propagation at a Glance

Make more roses with these three simple techniques.

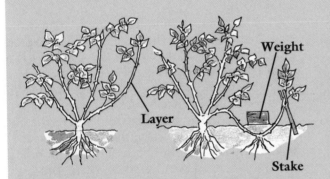

Layering. To layer, strip the leaves from the lower part of a young, supple cane and bend the cane to the ground. Where it touches the ground, dig a 6-inch-deep trench. To promote faster rooting, cut a notch in the underside of the cane where it will lie in the trench. Bend the cane into the trench, making sure that the notched area touches the ground. Fill in the trench, leaving the leafy tip of the cane aboveground, and put a rock or other heavy object on top of the soil to hold the buried cane in position. In six to eight weeks, tug gently on the cane; if it resists, it has rooted. Cut the rooted layer from the parent plant, and transplant it.

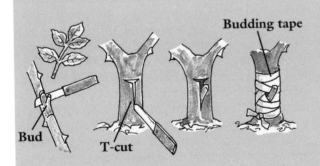

Budding. When you bud, you graft a desirable cultivar onto a hardy rootstock. First, prepare the budstock: Cut a 6-inch section of stem from the top of a healthy cane. Remove the leaves from this section, but leave a ½-inch stub at the base of the leaf stem—that's where the bud is. Cut off a bud with a sharp knife, making cuts in the bark ½ inch above and below the bud, then sliding the knife down about ⅛ inch deep under the bud from the top cut. Remove the bud and its surrounding bark, holding it by the leaf stub. Then make a T-shaped cut in the bark at the base of the rootstock, just above the ground. Make sure the T-cut is long enough to enclose the bud and its surrounding bark. Peel open the upper part of the T and slide the bud into it, making sure the bud is right-side up. Cut off any bark that protrudes above the bud. Use budding tape or a rubber band to wrap the bud securely to the rootstock, leaving the bud itself exposed. When the bud sprouts—usually the following spring—you'll know the graft has taken and you can remove the tape or rubber band. Prune off the top of the rootstock just above the bud, slanting the cut away from the bud.

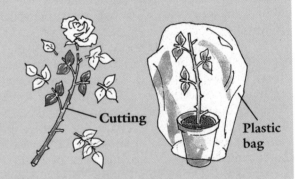

Taking a cutting. Take cuttings just as canes finish blooming. Cut a 6- to 8-inch section of stem from the top of a healthy cane. Remove the bottom leaves from the cutting. Insert the cutting in a container of sterile, moist soilless medium, pushing it in about 3 inches deep and firming the medium around it. (For faster rooting, use a rooting hormone.) Keep the cutting in a moist, humid atmosphere by putting a plastic bag over it, putting stakes in the container to hold the plastic away from the cutting. Put the cutting in a warm, bright place out of direct sunlight for three to eight weeks until it's rooted. When the cutting has rooted, remove the plastic bag and acclimate it to the outdoors before planting it in its permanent location. Cuttings may also be started in a cold frame or in the garden if covered with a glass jar or plastic jug.

inch above the bud, with about ⅛ inch of bark on each side of the bud. Very delicately, remove the woody part from the underside. With a young enough stem, this will be relatively easy.

Prepare the rootstock by pulling some soil away from the base to give you room to work and wiping the base of the plant clean with a rag. Make a T-shaped cut just above the soil line, with the vertical cut 1 inch long and the horizontal cut ½ inch long. Use the knife tip to carefully peel back the bark flaps. Slide the bud into the T-cut, making sure the bud remains upright. The bud should be touching the wood beneath the cut. Fold the bark over the bud, then wrap the T with budding tape, cut rubber bands, or electrical tape, being sure to leave the bud exposed. Put the soil back around the rootstock.

The bud will remain dormant until the following spring. When it sprouts, remove the tape or rubber band. Prune off the top growth of the rootstock at this time, cutting just above the bud. Remove any suckers that develop from the rootstock. Keep the budded plant fed and watered well during the growing season, and transplant the new plant to its permanent location in the fall or the following spring.

Roses from Seed

To propagate roses from seed, cut the hips from the plant when they are ripe. Cut each hip in half and carefully remove the seeds, then rinse and dry them. For best germination, rose seeds need a period of cold, called stratification. You can stratify the seeds by placing them between layers of moist paper towelling in a glass jar or plastic bag, then putting the jar or bag in the refrigerator for six to eight weeks. After this period, plant the seeds ¼ inch deep in a sterilized soilless seed-starting mix and label them. If you're not growing your seedlings in a greenhouse, cover the container with plastic or glass to maintain humidity. Provide temperatures of 50° to 55°F and bright but not direct light.

It may take three weeks to four months for the seeds to germinate. Remove the cover after germination, but keep the soil moist and the humidity high. When three sets of leaves have developed, transplant the seedlings to individual 2-inch pots. Move seedlings up to 4-inch pots when they're 4 inches tall. Transplant to their permanent site in the garden any time during the growing season when the plants are well developed. Give them the same care you would

any container-grown rose until the plants are established. (See Chapter 3 for more on planting a container-grown rose.)

If you want to learn more about how to hybridize roses, a 39-page booklet, *Rose Hybridizing for Beginners,* is available from the Rose Hybridizers Association. (See "Rose Resources" on page 280 for their address.)

WINTER PROTECTION

For many Northern gardeners, the worst aspect of rose-growing is winter protection. For years, there were two choices: unsightly rose cones covering your plants and marring your winter landscape, or the laborious task of mounding soil around roses in the fall, then painstakingly and back-achingly removing it the next spring. But, as in the case of other aspects of rose care, now you can have beautiful roses without tedious work or unsightly cones.

Having roses survive freezing temperatures with flying colors depends on a number of factors. These include the natural hardiness of the rose cultivar, whether it is a grafted plant or is growing on its own roots, how deeply you've buried the bud union of grafted plants, the vigor of the plants during the previous summer, how well you've hardened off the plants in the fall, wind and wind protection, winter precipitation, drainage, and freezing and thawing. Let's look at these more closely for successful care clues.

Hardy Cultivars

The first step in reducing the need for winter protection is to choose cultivars that are hardy in your climate. When you give it enough protection, you can grow just about any rose just about anywhere, but why create work for yourself? If you live where winter temperatures reach −20°F or lower (USDA Plant Hardiness Zones 4 and colder), make cold-hardiness a priority before you buy roses. There are a number of roses that will survive the rigors of low temperatures without protection. You'll find some of the best in "Roses for Special Situations" on page 24.

For gardens in the upper Midwest, the Great Plains, and much of New England as well as Canada, or areas with winter lows as cold as −50°F (Zone 2), some of the best choices are cultivars that were developed by the Canadian Department of Agriculture. Their roses not only

Winter protection. It's easiest for you and best for your plants if you grow roses that are hardy in your climate and don't need extra winter protection. But if you're determined to grow culti-vars that are slightly tender, here are three ways to increase their chances of survival.

Leaves

Trench

Trenching. Trenching is the best technique for tree or standard roses. After pruning the rose, remove the stake and loosen the soil around the plant's roots with a shovel. Dig a trench about 8 inches deep and long enough to fit the plant in. Slowly topple the rose into the trench, holding it by the middle of the trunk. Fill the trench with soil, mound-ing it over the plant. Add a foot or more of mulch—leaves and straw are best—on top for extra protection.

Straw

Canes pegged to ground

Pegging. Pegging is the preferred winter-protection technique for tender climbing roses. Just bend the canes to the ground and peg them in place with stakes or wire, then cover them with a foot of soil, leaves, or straw.

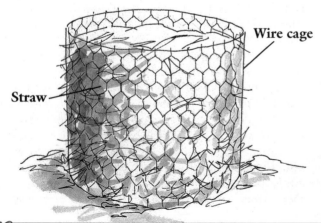

Wire cage

Straw

Caging. Mound about a foot of soil over the base of the plant for insulation. Then make a wire-mesh cylin-der around the plant, or use a tomato cage. Mound soil around the outside of the cylinder base to stabi-lize it. Fill the cylinder with a lightweight mulch of leaves or straw. In spring, remove the cylinder and mulch and gently wash off the extra soil.

are exceptionally hardy but also have a long blooming period and the ability to grow well on their own roots. That means they'll produce vigorous new growth and flowers even when killed to the ground the previous winter.

The Parkland series of roses from the Morden station in Canada have the native prairie wild rose *Rosa arkansana* in their lineage. Several of the Parkland cultivars resemble hybrid tea and floribunda roses. They are also exceptionally drought-tolerant.

The Explorer series of hardy roses were developed at the Ottawa and L'Assomption stations using *Rosa rugosa* as well as *R. × kordesii* and other hybrids. These roses have been selected for double flowers, long bloom period, and resistance to diseases. A number of shrubs and climbers in the Explorer series are available.

Roses that are hardy to at least –30°F (Zone 4) include the gallicas, albas, centifolias, multiflora ramblers, rugosas, and spinosissimas. Other hardy roses include the cultivars developed by Dr. Griffith Buck at Iowa State University, by the Brownells of Rhode Island in the 1930s and 1940s, by Wilhelm and Reimer Kordes and Mathias Tauntau in Germany, the Meidiland series from Meilland in France, and many of the miniatures, which also withstand temperatures in the –20° to –30°F range (Zone 4).

Grafted versus Own-Root Plants

In areas with a winter minimum between –20° and –50°F (Zones 4 to 2), it's important to choose roses that grow on their own roots (called own-root roses) rather than those that are grafted onto a rootstock. With own-root roses, if a plant is killed back to the ground in a bad winter, it can still send out new growth from the base. Even in areas with milder winters, it can be advantageous to have at least some of your roses growing on their own roots in case of a freak cold snap. I've listed some growers who specialize in own-root roses in "Rose Resources" on page 280.

Planting Depth

Although own-root roses have many advantages, the majority of roses for sale are grafted plants. If you have or want to buy these grafted cultivars, you must try to help them survive over winter. To protect the vulnerable graft area from cold, plant the graft, or bud union, below ground level, thus encouraging the top part of the plant to develop its own roots.

In climates with winter minimums lower than –10°F (Zones 5 and colder), set the bud union 2 to 4 inches below ground level, planting deeper the colder your zone is. In areas with minimum temperatures between 0° and –10°F (Zone 6), set the bud union an inch below ground level. In areas with winter minimums of 10° to 0°F, set the bud union right at ground level. In the Deep South and in California, set the bud union an inch or so above the soil level.

If temperatures tend to be erratic in your area, it's usually safer to set the graft union toward the deeper end of the range rather than the higher. Planting too deeply for your climate, however, can inhibit formation of new canes from the base of the plant.

Plant Vigor

The esteemed rosarian and author Dr. Cynthia Westcott said it over 40 years ago, and it continues to be true today: The absolute best winter protection is a healthy plant. A plant that has been stressed during the summer by drought, lack of fertilizer, or defoliation by insects and diseases is much more likely to perish during the following winter than a healthy plant. Follow the care tips I've given in this chapter to give your roses the best possible chance of making it through another season.

Hardening Off

Lush, tender new growth is vulnerable—it's going to be the first part of the plant that's injured by winter weather. To prevent winter injury, you've got to get this succulent new growth to harden off, or become woody, in time for winter. Harden your plants off by not giving them high-nitrogen fertilizer starting four to six weeks before the first fall frost, and gradually reduce watering over this period as well.

Wind and Wind Protection

We don't need television weather reporters to make us—or our roses—aware of the wind chill factor. Severe winds can cause canes to dehydrate and roots to loosen in the soil. Siting your rose beds in an area that is protected from prevailing winds lessens the risk of losing roses. Plant your roses near walls, fences, or wind breaks to moderate the force of the wind.

Pruning plants back in the fall and tying canes together loosely with twine help, too.

Winter Precipitation

Plants can be stressed by drought in winter as well as in summer. In areas where the soil either does not freeze or freezes and thaws, extra watering may be needed if precipitation is below normal. Areas with heavy snow cover often need less winter protection than those with only occasional snowfalls, because deep snows provide insulation for roses. If you are gardening in an area with minimum temperatures between –10° and –50°F (Zones 5 to 2) but very little snow, you'll have to grow hardier roses or provide more winter protection than someone gardening in an area with heavy snow.

Drainage

There is a clear correlation between poor drainage and winter injury. Roses will not tolerate wet feet during the winter. When choosing a site for your roses, be sure that the area drains well.

Freezing and Thawing

Many areas with minimum winter temperatures between 10° and –20°F (Zones 5 to 7) have warm weather alternating with freezing weather during the winter. These successive periods of freezing and thawing not only can literally uproot plants through frost-heaving, but can also affect their ability to withstand cold periods. Moderating soil temperatures with a winter mulch is the best way to help plants survive these conditions. Use mulch, not soil, for protection: When roses have the traditional soil mound in these climates, the warm weather builds up heat in the mound, providing ideal conditions for diseases.

If You Insist . . .

Sometimes there are certain roses we want to grow no matter what. In those instances, the only alternative is to provide winter protection. The standard method is to bring in topsoil from another area of the garden and mound it 6 to 10 inches high at the base of each rose. Then top the mound with 8 to 10 inches of oak leaves, pine boughs, or other loose mulch. You'll find mounding and other types of winter protection shown in "Winter Protection" on page 128.

ROSE CARE CALENDAR

Now that you know the basics of good organic rose care, you need to know when to feed, mulch, water, plant, prune, and do all the other things roses need to thrive. Here's a calendar that gives you month-by-month chores at a glance. I have divided the monthly chores by USDA Plant Hardiness Zones. (If you don't know your zone, check the map on page 279.) I've listed chores everyone should do first each month, followed by chores for specific areas. I suggest that you review the whole calendar quickly every month. That way, nothing can sneak up on you!

January

All climates:
- Plan your garden for the coming year; decide which roses you want to add.
- Compare catalogs and order roses.
- Purchase whatever new garden tools you need; clean, sharpen, and repair tools on hand.
- Check to make sure that winter protection remains in place.

Zones 8 to 10:
- Take soil samples and test for fertility and pH.
- Plant both container-grown and bareroot roses.
- Move any roses that would either look or grow better in another part of the garden.
- Prune roses to shape, to encourage new growth, or to remove dead, diseased, or damaged wood.
- Fertilize according to the soil test recommendations after pruning.
- Maintain adequate moisture with mulch and/or supplemental watering.
- Check plants for pests and diseases; control as necessary.

February

All climates:
- Continue to plan the garden for the coming year, and order roses.
- Maintain and repair tools and equipment as for January.

Zone 7:
- Prune roses to shape, to encourage new growth, or to remove dead, diseased, or damaged wood.
- Take soil samples and have them tested for fertility and pH.
- Fertilize according to the soil test recommendations after pruning.

Zones 7 to 10:
- Plant container-grown and bareroot roses, and transplant roses as necessary.

Zones 8 to 10:
- Maintain adequate moisture with mulch and/or supplemental watering.
- Check plants for pests and diseases; control as necessary.
- Weed and apply an organic mulch to control weeds and conserve moisture.

March

Zones 2 to 5:
- Make any adjustments to garden plans, and order roses.
- If you haven't already done so, purchase whatever new garden tools you need; clean, sharpen, and repair tools on hand.

Zones 6 and 7:
- Have soil tested for fertility and pH.
- Plant both container-grown and bareroot roses.
- Move any roses that would either look or grow better in another part of the garden.

Zone 6:
- Remove the winter protection from the plants.
- Prune roses to shape, to encourage new growth, or to remove dead, diseased, or damaged wood.
- Fertilize according to the soil test recommendations after pruning.
- Keep area around roses weeded.

Zones 7 to 10:
- Make an application of balanced organic fertilizer to the soil around roses, scratching it in lightly.
- Apply a foliar feeding of fish emulsion or liquid seaweed.

- Weed and apply an organic mulch if not done earlier.
- Check plants for pests and diseases; control as necessary.
- Water roses as necessary.
- Remove faded flowers and disbud side blooms on hybrid teas for larger, longer-stemmed blooms.
- In climates with a winter minimum of 10°F (Zone 7), apply an organic mulch to control weeds and conserve moisture.

April

Zones 2 to 7:
- Take soil samples and have them tested for fertility and pH.
- Plant container-grown and bareroot roses as weather permits and soil is dry enough.
- Move any roses that would either look or grow better in another part of the garden.
- Remove winter protection from plants as weather permits.
- Prune roses to shape, to encourage new growth, or to remove dead, diseased, or damaged wood.
- Fertilize according to the soil test recommendations after pruning.

Zones 7 to 10:
- Make an application of balanced organic fertilizer to the soil around roses, scratching it in lightly.
- Apply a foliar feeding of fish emulsion or liquid seaweed.
- Continue to weed and maintain an organic mulch to control weeds and conserve moisture.
- Check plants for pests and diseases; control as necessary.
- Water roses as necessary.
- Remove faded flowers and disbud side blooms on hybrid teas for larger, longer-stemmed blooms.
- Plant container-grown roses.
- Gather roses for bouquets for yourself and friends.
- Gather rose petals of fragrant once-blooming cultivars for potpourri.

May

All climates:
- Plant container-grown roses.
- Make an application of balanced organic fertilizer to the soil around roses, scratching it in lightly.
- Remove faded flowers and disbud side blooms on hybrid teas for larger, longer-stemmed blooms.
- Water as necessary.
- Visit public rose gardens and make notes about roses of particular interest.
- Gather roses for bouquets for yourself and friends.
- Gather rose petals of fragrant once-blooming cultivars for potpourri.

Zones 2 to 4:
- Plant bareroot roses as weather and soil conditions permit.

Zones 2 to 7:
- Check for pests and diseases; control as needed.
- Weed and apply an organic mulch to control weeds and conserve moisture.

Zones 7 to 10:
- Apply a foliar feeding of fish emulsion or liquid seaweed.
- Continue to weed and maintain an organic mulch to control weeds and conserve moisture.
- Check plants for pests and diseases; control as necessary.
- Water roses as necessary.
- Remove faded flowers.

June

All climates:
- Make an application of balanced organic fertilizer to the soil around roses, scratching it in lightly.
- Apply a foliar feeding of fish emulsion or liquid seaweed.
- Continue to weed and maintain an organic mulch to control weeds and conserve moisture.
- Check plants for pests and diseases; control as necessary.
- Water roses as necessary.

- Remove faded flowers and disbud side blooms on hybrid teas for larger, longer-stemmed blooms.
- Plant container-grown roses.
- Gather roses for bouquets for yourself and friends.
- Gather rose petals of fragrant once-blooming cultivars for potpourri.

July

All climates:
- Make an application of balanced organic fertilizer to the soil around roses, scratching it in lightly.
- Apply a foliar feeding of fish emulsion or liquid seaweed.
- Continue to weed and maintain an organic mulch to control weeds and conserve moisture.
- Check plants for pests and diseases; control as necessary.
- Water roses as necessary.
- Remove faded flowers and disbud side blooms on hybrid teas for larger, longer-stemmed blooms.
- Plant container-grown roses.

August

All climates:
- Plant container-grown roses.
- Make an application of balanced organic fertilizer to the soil around roses, scratching it in lightly.
- Apply a foliar feeding of fish emulsion or liquid seaweed.
- Continue to weed and maintain an organic mulch to control weeds and conserve moisture.
- Check plants for pests and diseases; control as necessary.
- Water roses as necessary.
- Remove faded flowers and disbud side blooms on hybrid teas for larger, longer-stemmed blooms.

September

All climates:
- Send off requests for catalogs.
- Plan new plantings.

Zones 2 to 6:
- Get new beds ready for spring planting, turning the soil over and working in organic matter.
- Stop removing faded flowers.

Zones 7 to 10:
- Send off orders for fall planting.
- Plant container-grown roses.
- Make an application of balanced organic fertilizer to the soil around roses, scratching it in lightly.
- Continue to keep garden areas weeded.
- Continue to check for pests and diseases; control as necessary.
- Water roses as necessary.

October

All climates:
- Send off requests for catalogs.
- Plan new plantings.

Zones 2 to 4:
- Prune roses; remove leaves from plants and from surrounding soil and destroy.
- Apply winter mulch.

Zones 6 to 10:
- Send off orders for fall planting.
- Plant container-grown roses.
- Continue to keep garden areas weeded.
- Continue to check for pests and diseases; control as necessary.
- Water roses as necessary.
- Stop removing faded flowers.

November

All climates:
- Send off orders for spring planting.

Zones 5 to 7:
- Prune roses; remove leaves from plants and from surrounding soil and destroy.
- Apply winter mulch.

Zones 6 to 10:
- Get new beds ready for spring planting, turning the soil over and working in organic matter.
- Plant container-grown and bareroot roses.
- Continue to check for pests and diseases; control as necessary.
- Stop supplying supplemental water.

December

All climates:
- Send off orders for spring planting.
- Use Christmas tree branches for compost or mulch.

Zones 7 to 10:
- Plant container-grown and bareroot roses as weather and soil permit.
- Move any roses that would either look or grow better in another part of the garden.
- Continue to check for pests and diseases; control as necessary.

Part Two

ROSE ARRANGEMENTS AND COUNTRY CRAFTS

Chapter 5

Designing Fresh Rose Arrangements

THROUGHOUT RECORDED HISTORY, people have been bringing fresh flowers indoors to beautify their homes, lift their spirits, and celebrate special moments. Roses, in particular, are valued for their silky texture, heady fragrance, and delightful range of colors. A rose carries a message of love and caring as no other flower can.

If you grow your own roses, you're lucky enough to be able to bring in armfuls of roses from your own garden! You can fill every room of the house and share your roses freely with family, friends, coworkers, neighbors, and churches. But no matter how many roses you grow, you will want to have these precious flowers last for as long as possible. To get the most enjoyment from your roses as cut flowers, it's important to cut and condition them properly so they have the longest vase life possible—nine days or more.

Next, you will want to be able to show them off. You could just stick a bunch of roses in a jelly jar—it's better than not having roses at all—but if you *arrange* them in that jelly jar, you can let your creative juices produce a display that does justice to your beautiful blossoms. Luckily, casual, simple arrangements are the style today, rather than the more stiff, formal, rule-bound arrangements of the past. Even so, to create the most satisfying arrangements you will need to pay attention to a few guidelines regarding size, balance, color, and shape. With a little practice, you'll be able to fashion romantic nosegays, corsages, and boutonnieres as well as beautiful vase arrangements.

Whatever your own personal taste or the style of your home, bringing roses indoors from the garden always enhances the beauty of your surroundings. And it's one of the most satisfying ways to savor the fruits of your gardening labors.

CHOOSING ROSES FOR THE LOOK YOU WANT

If having roses for cutting is a top priority for you, consider colors and form as you're selecting the roses for your garden. Plant at least two, preferably three, of each of your favorite cultivars to make sure you'll have enough for an impact in arrangements. Study the colors in your home and decide what shades of roses should predominate. Be careful in selecting pinks—the ones that tend toward coral can clash with others. The easiest arrangements to make are ones in the same color range, such as pinks with magentas or reds and oranges with yellows.

Colors also carry weight. The color red is very powerful and has a great deal of impact in an arrangement. If you use red, use a lot of it, because just one or two red flowers can throw an arrangement off-balance. White and yellow flowers tend to blend other colors together in an arrangement. You can also create an appealing blend by using several shades of the same color—try pastel versions of brighter colors for a harmonious arrangement.

Another aspect to consider in choosing roses for your arrangements is the formality implied by the shape of the rose. The high-centered hybrid tea rose—with its long, stiff, straight stem—has a very formal, geometric look. You can use this type of rose to form the structure for large, massed arrangements suitable for living and dining rooms with traditional furnishings. Interestingly enough, the geometric form of the hybrid tea rose also works well in very contemporary settings when used alone, without softening filler plant material.

If you are interested in roses with a more old-fashioned style, try true old roses or modern roses such as floribundas and shrub roses. These plants generally have shorter, thinner stems, often with multiple flowers per stem and cupped, single, or otherwise looser flower forms. These old-fashioned roses lend themselves to more informal arrangements and settings. Depending on the container and the shape of the arrangement, these roses fit beautifully in a variety of rooms, whether filled with yards of chintz, lace, gingham, country prints, unbleached muslin, or gauze.

LIVE ROSE ARRANGEMENTS

For the simplest rose arrangement of all, grow miniature roses as houseplants in decorative pots and set them wherever you'd like some color. Miniature roses offer a wonderful range of colors, shapes, sizes, and scents. Grow them on a sunny windowsill, in a sun room, or under plant lights, and enjoy them there; then, when they're at peak bloom, use them as centerpieces or accents around the house in places where they'll have the greatest impact.

If the pot you're growing your roses in is more functional than decorative, consider placing the functional pot in a decorative container. You can use a decorated flowerpot that's a size larger than the functional pot or you can use a handleless basket or a ceramic bowl or any number of other attractive containers that complement your decor. If the decorative container that you choose isn't watertight, line it with plastic or aluminum foil to keep water from damaging the container or the surface of the furniture or shelf that you set it on.

Growing Miniature Roses Indoors

To grow miniature roses indoors, you'll need to provide them with the same basic care you'd give potted herbs or other outdoor plants being grown inside. Roses need the right light, water, temperature, air circulation, humidity, soil, fertilizer, and pest prevention and control to grow and bloom well as houseplants.

Sunlight is one of the most critical factors in growing roses indoors. Miniature roses require at least five hours of bright sunlight to grow and bloom well indoors. A south- or west-facing window that gets full light is ideal. Miniature roses also do exceptionally well under fluorescent lights. The best setup is four 4-foot-long broad-spectrum tubes that are designed for plant growing. The lights should be on for 14 hours if they are the only light source. If your roses receive some natural sunlight as well, determine how many hours they receive and set timers on the fluorescent lights to add enough hours of light so the roses receive a total of 14 hours. Place the lights about 3 to 4 inches above the tops of the plants. Replace the tubes after a year.

The second most critical factor in indoor rose growing is soil moisture. Don't let your roses' soil dry out or the plants will wilt. Keep the soil evenly moist but not soggy. Any good-quality soilless potting mix will work well with miniature roses. If you want to make your own, combine 6 parts coarse sphagnum peat moss or sifted compost with 3 parts coarse perlite and 3 parts horticultural vermiculite. Be sure to moisten soilless mixes with warm water before using them for potting. When you pot them up, you can use either plastic or clay pots. Most miniature roses grow well in 4- to 5-inch-diameter pots.

Miniature roses bloom and grow best with night temperatures of 60° to 65°F and daytime temperatures of 70° to 75°F. Adequate humidity levels are also essential for healthy miniature roses. A relative humidity level of 50 to 60 percent is best. With these levels, spider mites, which thrive in low humidity, are less likely to bother plants, and the plants won't drop their leaves or produce small flowers.

To provide the high humidity levels that your roses need, group plants together on a

Roses indoors. You can make a lovely flower arrangement with nothing fancier than a blooming miniature rose in an attractive basket or pot. Remember that live roses need plenty of light. Place your rose where it will get direct sunlight, or move it back into the sun after you've displayed it for a few days.

metal or plastic tray filled with gravel or perlite and keep water in the tray. To keep the plants from extending roots into these trays, set pots on inverted clay saucers. As an alternative, you can use a cool-water humidifier in the room.

Feed miniature roses regularly with a complete organic fertilizer designed for indoor use, following the manufacturer's recommendations. If you use a water-soluble fertilizer, don't feed with every watering or the fertilizer may eventually burn the plant roots—a feeding every two weeks should be sufficient. You can also apply compost tea or liquid seaweed, which are mild enough to use every time or every other time you water.

Spider mites, aphids, whiteflies, blackspot, and mildew are the worst pests and diseases of indoor miniature roses. If you grow healthy plants with adequate light, water, humidity, fertilizer, and air circulation, these pests will seldom bother them. Be sure to quarantine new plants until you're sure they have no pests.

If you discover that your roses have aphids, control them with an alcohol-dipped swab. If the plants have a minor infestation of spider mites or whiteflies, spray the undersides of the leaves with a stream of water, such as from a sink sprayer; if your roses have a severe infestation, spray plants with insecticidal soap according to package directions. To prevent mildew and blackspot, expose your roses to fresh, moving air. The best way to keep air moving is to use a small fan and run it constantly.

CUTTING AND CONDITIONING ROSES

For the longest enjoyment from your rose arrangements, cut roses from your garden either in the evening or in the early morning. This is when the plants are most filled with water. Gather rosebuds as well as half-open flowers, but avoid fully open roses because they won't last long.

The general rule for picking roses is to cut stems at an angle just above a five-leaflet leaf. It's best if that leaf is facing outward because another shoot will grow from this point. Also consider the shape and size of the bush before cutting so that you don't destroy its form. One more important rule of thumb when cutting roses: use pruning shears, not scissors—they don't have enough leverage to cut cleanly

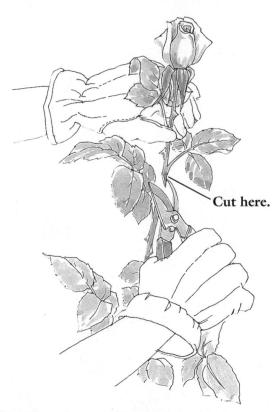

The right way to cut. Use sharp pruning shears to cut a rose at a 45-degree angle just above an outward-facing five-leaflet leaf. A new shoot will emerge from the cut stem to produce another flower.

through the woody stems. Once you've cut a rose, strip the foliage from the bottom 3 to 4 inches of its stem and cut off thorns in this area as well.

After you have chosen and cut your roses, you will need to condition them. Conditioning cut flowers saturates them with water then slows the uptake and release of water, thus producing stiff stems and firm petals. To condition roses, Kathy Noble, an award-winning American Rose Society rose arranger, recommends taking at least two plastic containers to the garden—one full of room-temperature tap water for recutting stems and the other with 3 inches of conditioning solution. (See "Solutions for Longer Cut-Flower Life" on the opposite page for information on conditioning solutions.)

After cutting the rose from the bush, immediately recut the stem underwater at an angle, removing ½ inch of stem. Transfer it to the container of conditioning solution, keeping a drop of water clinging to the cut end; this helps reduce air bubbles in the stem, which inhibit absorption of water.

When you've cut all of the roses you want, set the conditioning container in a humid, cool, dim place with no drafts for at least several hours, preferably overnight. If you do a lot of flower arranging, consider having a refrigerator just for conditioning, with the temperature at 34° to 38°F. Frost-free refrigerators tend to pull moisture out of flowers, so you will have to cover the flowers with plastic. Make sure that the plastic doesn't touch the blooms. To do this, cut several dowels or sticks to a few inches longer than your stems and insert them in the container before you cover it with plastic. Tightly seal the plastic against the container by putting a rubber band over the plastic just below the rim of the container.

Cut other flowers and foliage for your arrangement at the same time as you cut your roses and condition them, too. You can treat most cut flowers and foliage as you do roses. A few exceptions are hollow-stemmed flowers, such as delphiniums and large dahlias. Turn these upside down, fill the stems with cold water, and plug them with a bit of cotton. Plants that emit a milky substance, such as poppies and euphorbias, must have the stem end seared with a flame to seal it. Split the ends of woody stems so they can take up more water.

When you're ready to arrange the flowers, remove all leaves that will be below water or in floral foam. Recut the stems again underwater to the length needed for your arrangement.

Solutions for Longer Cut-Flower Life

Floral conditioners improve water uptake, inhibit stem decay, and reduce blockage in the stem. Preservatives, or cut-flower foods, are used after flowers are arranged. They contain substances that decrease the pH of the water, which inhibits bacterial growth. They also contain sugars that enhance bloom color and development. The sugars decrease water movement in stems, so don't use them for conditioning flowers. Most of the following conditioners include water. If your tap water is extremely alkaline or you have a water softener, use distilled water for the conditioning solution. Here are some floral conditioners you may want to try:

Listerine. Listerine or a generic substitute is a good floral conditioner. Dr. Jim Johnson, director of the Benz School of Floral Design at Texas A&M University, has found that mixing 2 tablespoons of this type of mouthwash per gallon of distilled water has both antibacterial action and a trace of nutrient value. Kathy Noble, an award-winning rose arranger, uses it as a simple, inexpensive material for both conditioning roses and maintaining rose arrangements. She changes the solution every three to five days, recutting the stems and washing the containers, then disinfecting them with a solution of ½ ounce of household bleach in 5 gallons of water.

Chrysal-RVB. Chrysal-RVB is a commercial flower conditioner used by wholesale florists. It is available from Pokon & Chrysal USA; for more information, call 1–800–CHRYSAL. Conditioning time is 4 to 12 hours, and flowers can be stored longer if kept below 50°F. Kathy Noble uses it mixed at the rate of ½ tablespoon per gallon of distilled water.

Aspirin. An aspirin tablet dissolved in water increases the acidity of the water but may damage the flowers. Test this technique on a few of the flowers you want to use before trying it on the actual arrangement.

Bleach. Household liquid bleach at the rate of ¼ teaspoon per gallon of water can inhibit bacterial growth for several days.

Sugar. Granulated sugar keeps flowers developing in arrangements. Add 1 tablespoon of granulated sugar per gallon of water. Use in conjunction with an antibacterial agent, such as bleach.

Tonic and soda. Tonic water and citrus-flavored soda increase acidity and supply sugar. Use 1 part soda or tonic water to 2 parts water.

Cut-flower preservatives. Commercial nutrient solutions, or cut-flower preservatives, inhibit bacteria and provide food. Florists and garden centers carry these preservatives in powder or liquid concentrate form. These usually need to be changed every three days, with containers cleaned and stems recut at that time. For best results, follow the directions on the package.

Preparing Containers

Make sure the container you choose for your fresh flower arrangement is clean to help reduce the bacteria that can clog plant stems. Wash it thoroughly with hot, soapy water, rinse with plain water, then rinse with a household disinfectant solution such as bleach, disinfectant household cleaner, or mouthwash. Rinse once more with plain water.

Caring for Your Arrangement

Fresh arrangements last longer if kept out of bright sunlight, high temperatures, and drafts. Another key to longevity is changing the water daily. When using floral foam, add water regularly to keep it from drying out. Sometimes, no matter how careful you are, flowers droop prematurely. Often, you can revive them by cutting off 1 inch of the stems and placing them in a container with several inches of hot water for ten minutes, then in cool water up to just below their blossoms for at least an hour. Or lay the entire flower and stem in tepid water for an hour or so.

FLOWER ARRANGING BASICS

Whether you're creating an elegant arrangement of roses in a silver urn as a centerpiece for a dinner party or casually arranging roses in a twig basket for a picnic, the same basic tools, supplies, and design principles apply. But don't rush out and purchase special items in order to begin arranging fresh roses—you probably already own many of the tools you'll need. After just a little practice, you can easily create arrangements of roses throughout your home, both for special occasions and for those no-occasion-at-all days.

Tools and Supplies

One of the best ways to make sure flower arranging is easy is to keep all of your tools and supplies in one place—a toolbox, a closet, a storage cabinet, or some other handy location. That way, you don't have to rummage around for an hour or try to make do without the proper supplies.

The tools and supplies that you'll need fall into three main categories: cutting tools, mechanics, and containers. The cutting tools

Garden-Fresh Roses in Winter

The cool weather of autumn brings a beautiful flush of bloom on many of the repeat-blooming roses. It's hard to watch them be decimated by the first hard freeze. Instead of cutting all of the flowers when a freeze is predicted, try this old technique that allows roses in bud to be stored for up to two or three months.

First, choose a deep, wooden box or large plastic or metal pan for storing your roses. (It should be as deep as you want the length of your rose stems to be.) Pick the roses as late in the year as possible, but before a killing frost. Choose fully developed buds that are showing some color. Use a sharp knife to make a long, slanting cut through the stem to sever it from the bush; cut the stems about as long as the depth of your box. Remove all leaves. Fill a container with warm water prepared with an antibacterial conditioner, and submerge the stems in it up to the flower heads. (See "Solutions for Longer Cut-Flower Life" on page 141 for details on conditioners.) Let stand for one hour.

Fill your box with wet sand to a depth that is about the same as the rose stem length. Use a thin dowel to make a hole in the sand and insert a rose stem, then pack the sand around it. Space stems as close as possible without letting the buds touch. Store the box in a cool, dark, humid place where the temperature does not go below 40°F, such as an unheated basement, root cellar, or shed. Check the sand periodically and keep it moist.

When you want some roses, remove them from the sand, recut the stem ends on a slant and place immediately in water that is heated to just below the boiling point. Let stand until the water cools. Use as desired.

you need are probably already in your possession; if not, you can buy them at hardware stores, discount department stores, or garden centers. Mechanics are items for holding and supporting the flower and foliage stems. You can purchase mechanics at craft stores, florists, or garden centers. As for containers, just about anything that holds water will do. The choices are limited only by your personal taste. (For the tools, mechanics, and containers used with dried-flower projects, see "Tools and Supplies" on the opposite page.)

Cutting Tools

Your cutting tools should be sharp and rust-free. Be sure to use the right tool for the job at hand. Here are some you will need to have handy.

Hammer. Use a hammer for smashing woody stem ends.

Knife. Use a knife for cutting and shaping floral foam and for slicing woody stem ends. A sharp, general-purpose paring knife will do, plus a long-bladed knife for cutting large foam blocks.

Pruning shears. Use pruning shears to cut thick, woody stems. Choose either the anvil or scissors type. Remember to dry them after each use and to oil and sharpen them periodically.

Scissors. Use scissors to cut thin, green stems. Choose either high-quality stainless steel household scissors or a special short-bladed florist's type.

Wire cutters. Use wire cutters, also known as side cutters, for cutting floral wire and wire mesh.

Tooling up. Keeping an assortment of flower-arranging tools on hand makes it easy to create beautiful arrangements whenever you feel like cutting flowers. Shown here are pruning shears, wire cutters, florist's scissors, floral clay, floral foam, floral tape, floral picks, floral wire, floral spikes, candle cups, and a pinholder.

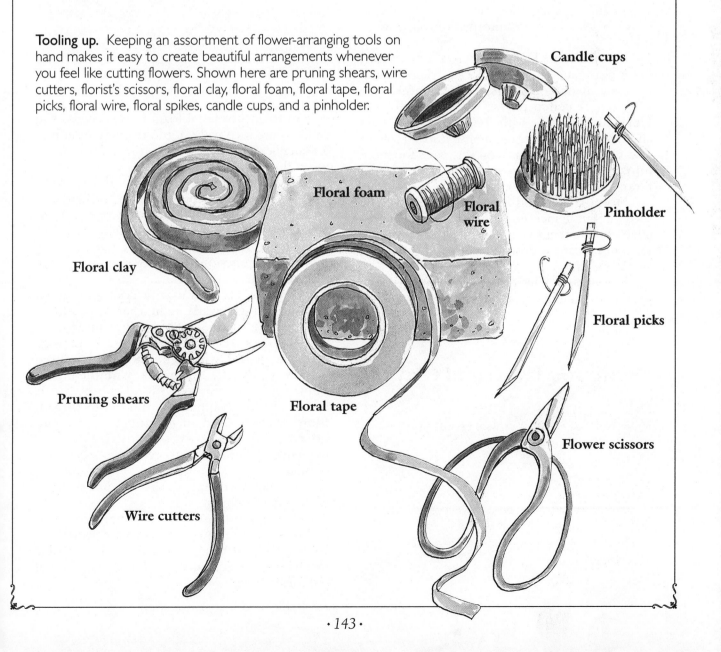

Candle cups

Floral foam

Floral wire

Pinholder

Floral clay

Floral picks

Pruning shears

Floral tape

Wire cutters

Flower scissors

Mechanics

Mechanics hold and support your floral materials in their arrangements. Choose mechanics that suit the flowers and container you're using. Here are the most common types you will use.

Candle cup. This is a specially made plastic bowl, usually with floral foam already in place, that fits into a taper-size candle holder, creating a pedestal for an arrangement. There are also taper-size candle cups with spikes on one end (also known as candle prongs), which, when inserted into floral foam, hold a candle.

Floral clay. This is a waterproof clay that resembles green modeling clay and is sold in bricks or flat coils. Use it to anchor pinholders or floral spikes to a container or to anchor a container within a container, such as a plastic saucer in a basket. (See "How to Use Floral Clay" below for more information on how to use it.)

Floral foam. Floral foam is a lightweight, fine-celled material sold in blocks, cylinders, and in ready-made containers. Don't confuse this with larger-celled polystyrene (Styrofoam). Floral foam for use with fresh flowers is green and is soaked in water before use. (See "How to Use Green Floral Foam" on this page for more information.) Floral foam for use with dried flowers is brown and nonabsorbent.

Floral spike. This is a four-pronged plastic spike, about 1 inch in diameter, that is used to attach floral foam to containers. Floral spikes are most often used with shallow or flat dishes, such as trays or saucers.

Floral tape. This coated-cloth tape is comparable to adhesive tape but is usually green. It

How to Use Green Floral Foam

To use green floral foam, submerge it in water until it's thoroughly soaked—when air bubbles no longer emerge. With a sharp knife, cut the foam so that it fits snugly into your container, with at least 1 inch extending above the rim. For shallow containers, the floral foam should be 1½ to 2 inches above the rim. To hold the foam in place, crisscross two pieces of green floral wrapping tape across the top of the foam and around the container. Do not reuse floral foam: New stems won't be the same diameter or length as the first stems you used, so the new stems won't be held securely in the foam or be in contact with moisture.

is used to anchor floral foam to containers. You can also use it to make a grid over the mouth of a container by crisscrossing strips ½ inch apart; insert flower stems in the spaces.

Thin, stretchy floral wrapping tape is ½ inch wide and available in green, brown, and white. Use it to wrap the floral wire that reinforces or replaces stems. Especially useful in corsages and boutonnieres, it may also be used in conjunction with larger, more elaborate nosegays.

Floral wire. Floral wire comes in green and silver and is available in a range of gauges (widths). It is usually sold either in 18-inch lengths or on reels, in which case it is called spool or paddle wire. The most widely used gauges are 18, 20, 22, and 24, with the higher numbers being thinner. Floral spool wire is also available wrapped in thin white thread. Floral wire is used in making corsages and boutonnieres and, occasionally, in arrangements. Use floral wire to reinforce stems and to make artificial stems. (See "Boutonnieres and Corsages" on page 154 for information on how to do this.)

Moss. Woodland moss, Spanish moss, sphagnum moss, and sheet moss are sometimes used either to hold stems or to hide other mechanics. Attach moss to a base with floral pins or hot glue.

How to Use Floral Clay

To use floral clay, make sure that the container and the object that you want to stick to it with clay are both thoroughly dry. Roll a piece of the clay between your palms and make a ¼-inch-diameter rope that is equal in length to the circumference of the object to be anchored. Place the rope around the perimeter of the object, then press it firmly onto the bottom of the container, twisting slightly.

Pebbles, marbles, gravel, shells, and sand. These materials provide an easy way of holding stems securely as well as hiding other mechanics. Use materials that have been purchased or collected from nature.

Pinholder. This is a small, heavy, metal base with sharp, closely spaced metal pins. It is best for use in small arrangements. Pinholders come in various shapes and sizes. Some are permanently attached to a small water-holding receptacle. Pinholders are especially useful for Japanese-style arrangements or for shallow containers. Use floral clay to attach a pinholder to its container.

Wire mesh. To use wire mesh, crumple your mesh and stuff it into a container. Arrange flowers by sticking them into it. Both chicken wire (with 1-inch mesh) and turkey wire (with 2-inch mesh) can be used this way. Or you can cut a piece of mesh slightly larger than your container and then bend the edges under and wedge the mesh into the top of the container for a snug fit.

Containers

When you think of containers for flower arrangements, especially rose arrangements, you may envision crystal vases, fine porcelain, or other formal flower holders. Yet there are infinite other possibilities. So, what criteria should you consider in choosing a container? First and foremost, the container should complement the flowers, not detract from them. Heavily ornamented or patterned containers usually call too much attention to themselves and distract your eye from the flowers. Containers that work best are those with the simplest designs or colors.

Second, the container should be in scale with the flowers. A handful of short-stemmed flowers is lost in a tall vase, but if you combine the same flowers with a few leaves in an antique teacup, the effect is perfect. The traditional rule of scale is that the arrangement should be 1½ times as tall as the container, but even that rule is often broken in this era of casual bouquets.

Although people have used unusual containers for many years, the advent of floral foam has made it even easier to turn an ordinary object into a serviceable vase. With the foam spiked or taped to a small plastic saucer, for example, it's quite easy to make a delightful arrangement in conjunction with almost anything.

Look around your house and see what wonderful containers you already have. You can choose from glass containers and baskets of every variety. All types of porcelain and pottery are possibilities, too. What you have on hand in your cupboards and drawers will provide a great many containers, but don't forget yard sales, craft stores, discount department stores, secondhand and thrift shops, and antique stores as sources for ingenious and inexpensive containers. The possibilities are endless.

Some of the most effective and unforgettable arrangements combine flowers and candles. Try putting an arrangement in the center of a candelabra by using a candle cup, or integrate one or more candles into an arrangement.

DESIGN BASICS

Flower-arranging styles, like styles of clothing, hair, architecture, music, and interior design, are continually evolving and changing. The highly stylized arrangements popular in the first half of the twentieth century, which were dependent on strong shapes, such as the S-curve and L-shape, are seen much less now. Instead, people favor impromptu natural arrangements that are highly individualistic and more fitting for today's lifestyle. However, when choosing a style for your arrangement, keep in mind that adaptations of the traditional triangular, fan, and circular mass arrangements never go out of style.

The Form of the Arrangement

In looking at the overall form, or shape, that a flower arrangement can take, three main types emerge: line, mass, and line-mass arrangements. Almost all arrangements fall into one of these categories.

Line Arrangements

Derived from the Japanese art of flower arranging called *ikebana,* line arrangements are mainly composed of linear plant material. These vertical or horizontal lines determine the overall form of the arrangement. The open space between the lines is critical to these arrangements.

Mass Arrangements

Mass arrangements have the form, or shape, filled in either solidly or in a more delicate manner. In either case, the silhouettes have very little open space. The most common shapes for mass arrangements are triangles, fans, circles, ovals, and squares. The current trend in mass arrangements is toward muted rather than starkly geometric forms.

Line-Mass Arrangements

Line-mass arrangements are a melding of the Western concept of the bouquet's solid, massed form and the Eastern influence of *ikebana* that relies strongly on linear elements. There are dominant lines, but these are partially filled in with other plant material. Geometric shapes, such as S-curves, crescents, columns, or exaggerated triangles, are most often used.

Forms within the Form

The shape of a mixed arrangement of flowers and plant material is determined by the interplay of four components: line materials, full materials, fine-textured materials, and materials for adding depth. Line materials, or tall stems of flowers and foliage, determine the height and shape of an arrangement. Bold, round, full flowers establish the focal point. Small, fine-textured flowers and foliage fill in between the other two. Other flowers, often of contrasting texture or color, are recessed into the arrangement to add depth.

If using only one type of flower in an arrangement, you can still use these four com-

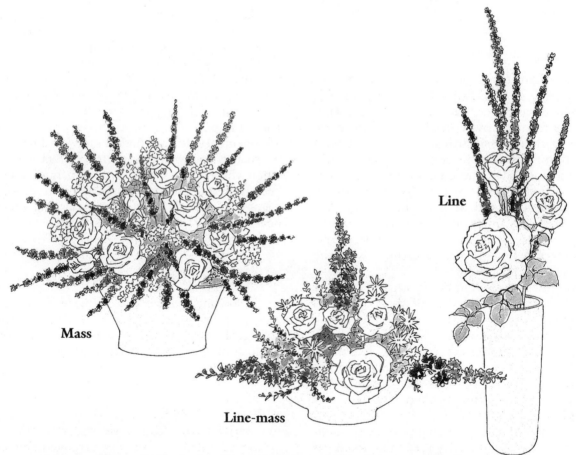

Mass

Line-mass

Line

Three distinct looks. You can create any style of arrangement using these three basic shapes. Line arrangements are tall and spiky, with lots of open space; mass arrangements are more dense, with little open space between flowers; and line-mass arrangements have the strong vertical element of a line arrangement and the fuller look of a mass arrangement.

ponents. Just use stems of different lengths and flowers at different sizes and stages of development to achieve the desired effect.

DESIGN PRINCIPLES

All flower arrangements, whether formal or informal, are based on design principles, or guidelines, to at least some degree. The extent to which you can bend the rules but still create an attractive design depends a great deal on your skill and experience. No one is born knowing how to arrange flowers; you learn with practice and the willingness to approach each arrangement with a fresh, relaxed outlook.

But before you can bend the rules, you need to know what they are and how to use them. The design principles used in flower arranging are basic to all design, be it furniture, fashion, or garden design. No matter what the medium or the style, the elements of balance, rhythm, scale, focus, and color determine how the design looks.

Finding a Balance

Your arrangement will look balanced when it seems secure and stable. One aspect of balance in an arrangement is the apparent weight on each side of an imaginary line drawn through the middle from top to bottom. Symmetrical, or formally balanced, arrangements have equal materials on each side. Asymmetrical, or informally balanced, arrangements have different items on each side, but there is still a sense of equal weight. You can also balance an arrangement by putting darker, larger, heavier flowers toward the center and lower part of the arrangement.

Reaching for Rhythm

Rhythm leads your eyes around the arrangement. Ideally, you are first aware of the focal point, then progressively aware of the outer points. To create rhythm in your designs, repeat the shapes of materials in arrangements or put larger and darker materials toward the center and base and smaller, lighter ones toward the edges. Or have the line of the arrangement flow in a continuum from the center to the edges either by creating a smooth sweep from the center down and out to the sides or by spoking out to the sides from a central hub. You can also create rhythm by using a gradation in size of flowers or foliage, or by using different textures, colors, heights, and sizes of twigs and branches to add punctuation to arrangements.

Staying in Scale

Scale, or proportion, is the size relationship of the various elements in the arrangement, including all of the plant materials, the container, and the location where you will be placing the arrangement. The basic guideline is for the height of the arrangement (from the bottom of the container to the tallest plant element) to be $1\frac{1}{2}$ to 2 times the height or width (whichever is greater) of the container.

Getting in Focus

The focus, or focal point, of an arrangement is the area to which your eyes are first drawn. Usually this area has the largest and darkest or most intensely colored flowers. Flowers and foliage farthest away from the focus should be lighter in color, smaller, and finer in texture. The focus is more apparent in arrangements with a definite front and back than in those that you can view from all sides.

Choosing Your Colors

If you don't have a sense of color relationships, find a color wheel where the three primary colors (red, yellow, and blue) are evenly spaced on a circle and the combinations resulting from mixing any two primary colors are shown in between. The safest color combinations are the ones that are close to each other on the color wheel, such as red and orange or blue and violet. Colors that are opposite each other on the color wheel are bold and dramatic, such as yellow and violet or orange and blue.

When considering the colors you will be using, don't forget green. The green of stems and foliage is the great unifier of a flower arrangement, and green goes with any other color. Use green lavishly in all of its many shades—from golden, gray, blue, and purple to deep, rich true green—as it is in nature. Generosity with foliage sets off the flowers and gives a natural look to arrangements.

Those are the basic design principles of flower arranging. Now all you have to do is practice working with them in arrangements until you're comfortable with them. You'll have a chance to use all of these guidelines in the projects that follow.

MATERIALS

6 fresh-cut roses

Tall, straight fresh-cut flowers, such as plumed cockscomb, gayfeathers, snapdragons, delphiniums, or foxgloves; or shrub branches, such as glossy abelia, spirea, or lilac

Fresh-cut filler material, such as baby's-breath, annual achillea, astilbes, spider flowers, or dusty miller

7 to 9 small fresh-cut flowers, such as roses, cornflowers, small zinnias, or love-in-a-mist (optional)

Sharp knife

Green floral foam

Watertight container

Green floral tape (optional)

Scissors

Formal Triangular Flower Arrangement

Sitting on a sideboard, an entrance hall table, or a mantel, a formally balanced, one-sided triangular mass arrangement is one you'll use more than any other. It's also the type of arrangement most often delivered from a florist. Because it follows a prescribed form, you will find it relatively easy to make.

1. Using the knife, cut the floral foam to fit securely into the container, allowing it to extend 1 inch above the container's rim. Anchor the foam with floral tape, if necessary.

2. Using scissors, cut your roses, flowers, filler, and plant material and condition them. (See "Cutting and Conditioning Roses" on page 140 for details.)

3. Establish the center and sides of the triangle with stems of the tall, straight flowers or branches. Use additional stems to create what looks from the front like one-half of a pyramid.

4. Use roses to form the outline of a second, smaller, triangle within the lines of the first. Use additional roses to fill in from the center outward.

5. Add filler material to soften the lines of the arrangement. If desired, use smaller roses or other flowers throughout the arrangement to add depth.

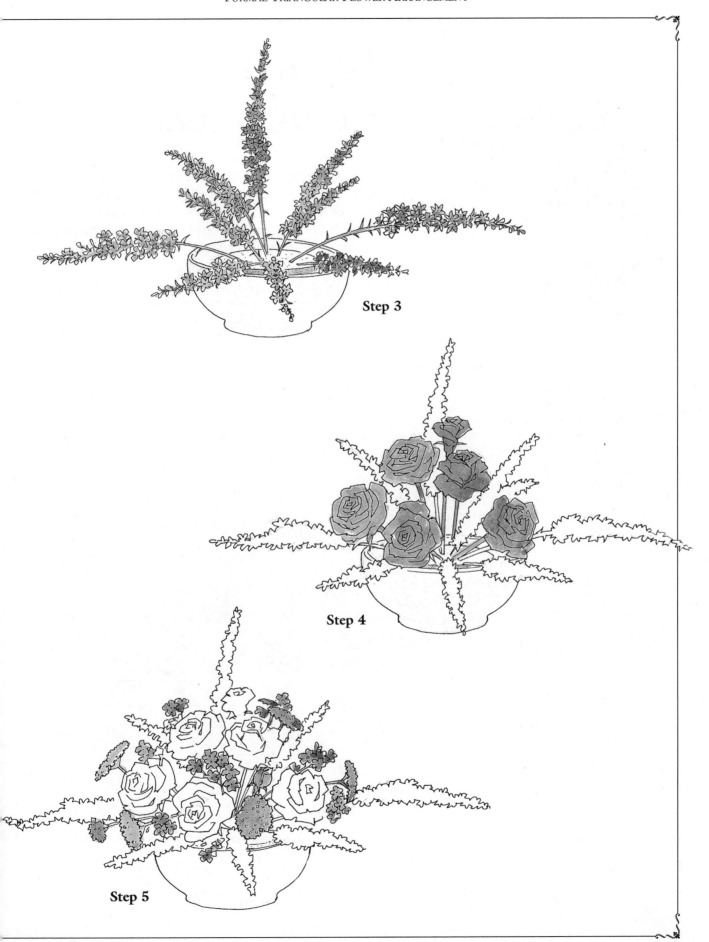

Step 3

Step 4

Step 5

MATERIALS

12 to 15 fresh-cut roses

Tall, straight fresh-cut flowers such as bells-of-Ireland, peach-leaved bell flower, lupines, and delphiniums; or vines and tree or shrub branches, such as forsythia, butterfly bush, and fothergilla

Filler material, such as catchfly, bee balm, or sweet rocket

7 to 9 small roses, cornflowers, small zinnias, or stems of love-in-a-mist (optional)

Sharp knife

Green floral foam

Watertight container

Green floral tape (optional)

Scissors

Formal Centerpiece

A centerpiece arrangement is made so that it looks attractive from all sides. A beautiful formal centerpiece lends elegant appeal to any coffee, end, library or dining room table. A centerpiece for a dining room table works best when it is arranged low enough so guests can see over it.

1. Using the knife, cut the floral foam to fit snugly into your container, anchoring it with floral tape, if necessary.

2. Using the scissors, cut your roses and other plant material and condition them. (See "Cutting and Conditioning Roses" on page 140 for details.)

3. Take long stems of your flowers and plant materials and insert them in the right and left ends of the floral foam, almost parallel to the tabletop. Place shorter stems at the front and back.

4. Next, insert shorter stems on each side, above the long ones and in front and back. Insert several stems straight up, then fill all sides with stems of varying lengths.

5. Use the roses as focus material, first following the shape established by the line material, then adding more roses to fill in.

6. Add filler material to soften the lines of the arrangement. If desired, add smaller roses or other flowers throughout the arrangement to add depth.

Informal Massed Arrangement

A bowl or shallow basket lined with plastic makes the perfect container for an informal rose arrangement. The only flowers and foliage you'll need for this simple but beautiful arrangement are your own healthy roses.

MATERIALS

18 to 24 fresh-cut roses
Basket
Plastic liner, to fit in basket
Sharp knife
Green floral foam
Green floral tape (optional)
Scissors

1. Place the plastic liner inside the basket. Using the knife, cut the floral foam to fit snugly into your container, anchoring it with floral tape, if necessary.

2. Using the scissors, cut your roses and condition them. (See "Cutting and Conditioning Roses" on page 140 for details.)

3. Insert the roses into the foam in the desired arrangement. The flowers can be loosely arranged for an open, airy look or tightly packed for a full, lush look.

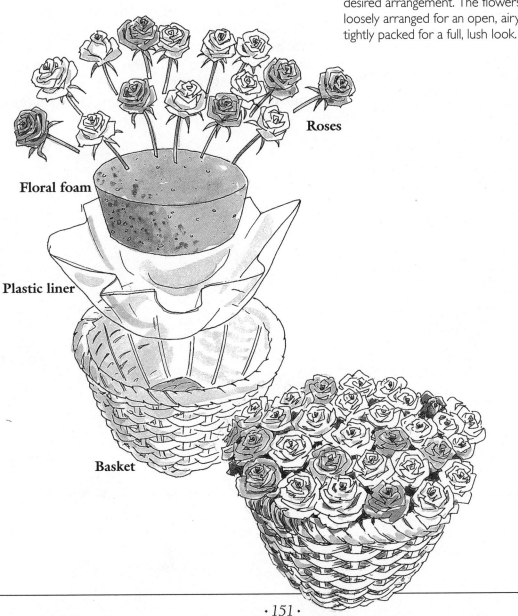

Roses

Floral foam

Plastic liner

Basket

MATERIALS

3 conditioned roses, stems cut to 4 to 6 inches

Assortment of conditioned flowers, herbs, and leaves, such as blue larkspur, German statice, miniature carnations, ferns, ivy, magnolia or salal leaves, stems cut to 4 to 6 inches

Rubber bands, string, or floral wire

Green floral wrapping tape

1 cotton ball, moistened with water

6-inch square of plastic wrap

6-inch square of white paper

White or clear tape or white craft or household glue

Green floral wire (optional)

Scissors

Paper doily, 6 inches in diameter

½-inch-wide French ribbon

Fresh Rose Nosegays

C alled tussie mussie, tussy-mussy, tutty, and turry, as well as posey or posie bouquet, the nosegay was originally a cluster of herbs used to ward off bad smells and diseases. Taken to their glorious height during the Victorian and Edwardian eras, nosegays traditionally had a perfect rose as the central flower. Other smaller or finer-textured flowers and herbs encircled the rose, then the bouquet was finished off with lace, ribbons, or other trim.

A nosegay is a delight to make both for yourself and for others, perhaps to carry to a party or to take as a gift for your hostess. It also looks lovely when used in place of a corsage for a wedding or special dance. Consider nosegays as gifts for anniversaries, birthdays, showers, christenings, and other celebrations and holidays.

1. Holding the roses in one hand, begin surrounding them with other flowers, herbs, and leaves. Use the rubber bands, string, or covered wire to help you hold the stems together, or wrap them in floral tape.

2. Place the moist cotton ball in the center of the piece of plastic. Fold the plastic around the stems, and wrap at the top with a piece of floral tape or wire. Wrap the stems with the white paper so the plastic and stems are completely covered. Use tape or wire to secure the paper.

3. Use the scissors to cut an X in the center of the paper doily. Insert the stems through the X so the doily frames the flowers.

4. Tie the French ribbon into a bow around the stems just beneath the doily. Tie on ribbon streamers, if desired.

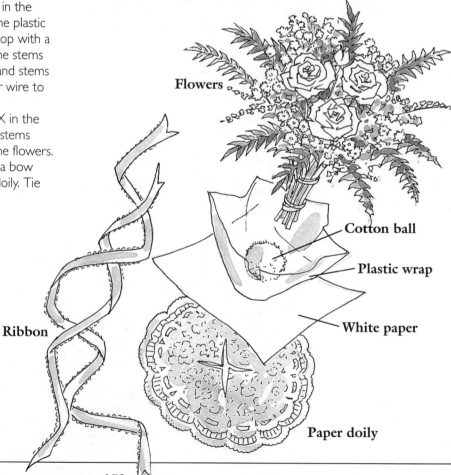

Flowers

Cotton ball

Plastic wrap

White paper

Ribbon

Paper doily

Much of the pleasure derived from a nosegay is in the scent, so choose your most fragrant roses. Old-fashioned roses are most appropriate for nosegays, but elegantly formed, high-centered hybrid tea rosebuds also make a stunning focus. For a tiny nosegay, perhaps to decorate a doll's house or a teddy bear's picnic, consider using miniature roses instead.

Because the roses and other flowers and foliage won't be in water, condition the material well so the nosegay stays fresh as long as possible. (See "Cutting and Conditioning Roses" on page 140 for a discussion of this technique.) To store your finished nosegay for a day or so, wrap it loosely in tissue paper, then put it in a plastic bag in the refrigerator.

A well-made nosegay will dry beautifully, so you can use it to decorate a table or shelf. To dry, simply hang it upside down, or set it in a dimly lit room where it will be undisturbed until dry. Keep it out of direct light so the floral materials will retain their colors.

Variations: Consider replacing the paper doily with some colorful tissue paper or perhaps a cotton doily. Trim the nosegay with wire-edged French ribbons tied in a simple bow. You can also cut ribbon streamers of various widths, tie knots in them, and glue small rosebuds onto the knots; attach the streamers to the nosegay. Or use lace for the bow and streamers, accompanied by streamers of colored ribbon. Experiment with different flowers and trim.

MATERIALS

1 conditioned rose
Assortment of conditioned plant
   materials, such as ferns, ivy leaves,
   lamb's-ears, variegated Solomon's
   seal, rhododendron, and holly (for
   Christmas corsages)
Scissors
Wire cutters
24-gauge floral wire
Green floral wrapping tape

1. Use scissors to cut the rose stem to an inch or so, then wire and tape it. To wire and tape a rose, take a 6-inch length of floral wire and insert it through the fat, rounded part of the rose, just below its petals. Center the wire horizontally. Gently bend down the wires on both sides. Starting just below the rose petals, take the floral tape and wrap it around the bent wires, twirling and stretching the tape downward as you work to form an artificial stem.

2. Use the scissors to trim the foliage stems to 1 inch long. Wire and tape the leaves by bending a 6-inch length of floral wire into a hairpin shape and inserting it through the leaf or laying it against the stem. Wrap the wire "stem" with the floral tape, twirling and stretching as you work.

3. Arrange the wired and taped rose and foliage in one hand. With your other hand, wrap all of the stems together with floral tape, twirling and stretching as you work. Use the wire cutters to trim off any excess wire stems. To wear, insert the "stem" through a buttonhole of a suit jacket or pin on the lapel.

Boutonnieres and Corsages

Boutonnieres and corsages most often make a showing at formal occasions like weddings, dances, and anniversary celebrations, but it's fun to surprise someone with one for no occasion at all. And there's no reason why you can't get into the habit of wearing flowers yourself, any time.

Corsages are merely overgrown boutonnieres, so once you've mastered the basics of wiring and taping, the rest is up to you—to mix, match, and create to your heart's desire. Fern fronds or ivy leaves are often used as the foliage, but other leaves will work equally well. Combine other flowers with roses if you're so inclined. The most difficult part of corsage making is not getting carried away and making it too large. It's better to make a corsage that's a little too small than to make one that's big and heavy.

Rose Corsage: To make a corsage, use 3 to 5 roses, placing the smallest bud at the top and arranging the remaining according to size, ending with the largest. Wrap all of the stems together with floral tape. Work foliage or filler flowers in among the roses, attaching each component with floral tape to the main stem. Bend each stem slightly so the flowers will face the viewer when worn, rather than pointing upward. When all of the flowers and foliage have been arranged and taped together, finish it off with several more windings of tape. Add a bow, if desired, and use wire cutters to cut off any excess wire stem. Insert a corsage pin through the stem.

Informal Vase of Roses

MATERIALS

10 to 12 fresh-cut roses
Fresh-cut foliage, such as ferns,
   ornamental grasses, viburnum,
   or leucothoe
Scissors
Cylindrical, watertight container

1. Using the scissors, cut your roses and other plant material and condition them. (See "Cutting and Conditioning Roses" on page 140 for details.)

2. Add water to the container until it is two-thirds full. Arrange the foliage in a semi-circular shape.

3. Carefully insert the roses throughout the foliage. Fill in the arrangement on all sides if it will stand alone or on three sides if it will be placed against a wall.

Its simple design is what makes this informal arrangement so attractive. Using only floral materials and a vase, you can show off your roses without any fuss. Very little or no mechanics are needed with most tall, cylindrical containers if you arrange the foliage first in a roughly semicircular shape then carefully insert roses and other flowers throughout the foliage.

Step 3

Chapter 6

How to Dry Roses

*I*F YOU ARE ACCUSTOMED TO THE silken texture and vibrancy of fresh roses, using dried roses throughout your home may seem unthinkable. Yet those who know will eagerly testify that dried flowers have their own particular charm—a beauty that goes beyond being a stopgap measure during the fall and winter months. The colors, shapes, and scents of dried flowers are useful year-round for creating exquisite bouquets, wreaths, and other projects.

THE MANY METHODS OF DRYING FLOWERS

Drying flowers, like any type of craft, is both an art and a science. The techniques and methods that make up the science of flower drying include air drying, desiccant drying, microwave drying, and freeze drying. The artistry of drying flowers comes from your individual touch, your choice of flowers, your adaptation of the techniques, and the new techniques you will discover as you dry flowers. Below you will find the basics on the different methods of flower drying. The artistry is up to you.

The most basic flower-drying technique involves simply hanging flowers upside down to dry. At a home furnishings or florist's shop, roses dried this way may sell for more than $24

a dozen. What fun to grow and dry your own and have them practically free! Air drying is obviously the cheapest and easiest method of drying, but it has a drawback: You would never mistake air-dried roses for fresh ones. (Other drying methods such as desiccant drying result in roses that look more like fresh-cut flowers.) See "Air Drying: It's Easy" on page 158 for more information on how to air dry flowers.

For an only slightly larger investment of time and money, you can dry roses with a water-absorbing material, or desiccant. Examples of desiccants include clean sand, cornmeal, borax, and silica gel. You can be even more modern and combine silica gel with a microwave oven for almost instant gratification. Roses dried with desiccants closely resemble fresh flowers. For more information, see "Desiccant Drying: It's Dependable" on page 159 and "Microwave Drying: It's Miraculous" on page 161.

Another twentieth-century technique called freeze-drying creates almost perfectly fresh-looking dried roses. Unfortunately, this requires special—and very expensive—equipment; a home freezer won't produce the same result. For now, the expense tends to prohibit everyone except professionals from freeze-drying flowers, but in the future, smaller and more affordable freeze-driers may be made available, enabling anyone to use this technique.

Another method of drying flowers is pressing them until they are flat and dry. Pressing flowers is a time-honored technique that is easy and inexpensive. Victorian ladies created intricate and elaborate pictures with pressed flowers, but you can use them in any number of less time-consuming ways. Although flowers lose their third dimension and scent when pressed, you can use pressed flowers to create one-of-a-kind decorated objects such as picture-frame mats and note cards. To learn how to press roses perfectly, see "Pressing: It's Picture-Perfect" on page 162.

Before you plant, pick, or dry your roses, remember that drying flowers tends to change their color. If you need a particular color of rose for a project you're making, keep the following information mind: Reds darken, sometimes almost to black; yellows may change to beige or brown; white turns to cream or beige; and oranges often become red, with 'Tropicana' being best known for the wonderful shade it turns. Pink shades generally retain their color the best.

PICKING ROSES IN THEIR PRIME

No matter which drying technique you choose or what you plan to do with the dried roses, the goal remains the same: to remove the moisture as quickly as possible so that the form and color are as close as possible to fresh. To meet that goal, pick flowers when there is no dew or other water on them. The best time for picking is late morning, after the flowers are thoroughly dry but not water-stressed from the heat.

Always choose the most perfect roses possible and pick them at several stages of development, from buds to not-quite-fully-opened flowers. Since roses almost always continue to open as they dry, avoid drying flowers that have been open for several days.

For best results, you should start your chosen drying procedure immediately after picking. If that isn't possible, put the roses in a bucket of lukewarm water and set them in a cool, dark place until you're ready.

As you read the sections that follow, remember that the techniques described can be used for all of your flowers. You'll probably want to dry annuals and perennials to use with the roses in arrangements, wreaths, potpourri, and other projects.

AIR DRYING: IT'S EASY

Almost any area that is warm, dark, and dry can be used to air dry roses. Ideally, the spot should also have gently moving air. A garage, attic, garden shed, unused room, or large closet will usually meet all of these requirements. A small fan or dehumidifier is often helpful in speeding up the drying process. If you don't have an area that is dark, place a paper bag, with the bottom cut out, over the cluster of drying stems.

Suspending Your Roses

One way to air dry roses is to hang them upside down from the ceiling. To do this, you will need to set up a framework for hanging your roses. Put nails or hooks in the rafters or ceiling joists. Or, if you're lucky enough to have one, use an old-fashioned floor-standing wooden clothes-drying rack. You can also hang a pipe, dowel, wire, or heavy cord from the ceiling. Next, make S-shaped hooks from 3-inch lengths of 9-gauge wire. You will use the hooks to suspend the flowers from your flower-hanging framework.

To prepare your roses for air drying, make sure that there is no water on the flowers or foliage, and remove all thorns as well as leaves near the base of the stems. Group the flowers in bunches of four to six stems, staggering the flower blossoms so that each one has space around it. Wrap a rubber band once or twice around the stem or stems, then run one end of the rubber band through the other and pull up snugly. Loop the rubber band over a nail or S-hook so that the blossoms are hanging upside down. You can also tie the stems with string or twist ties, but rubber bands have the advantage of contracting as the stems dry and shrink so that your flowers don't wind up falling to the floor.

If you're drying hybrid teas or other roses with one or two blooms per stem, hang the roses upside down in bunches of four to six stems. The air-drying method works best with double or semidouble flowers in bud. Roses that bloom in clusters, such as floribundas, do not usually dry well this way—the flowers will droop and dry at odd angles. Also, if the bunches are too big, the flowers and foliage will dry too slowly and will get moldy, or they may crush each other. Experiment with different flowers in different amounts to see what works best for you.

Roses will usually dry in one to three weeks, depending on the humidity and temperature. Your roses are dry when the stems snap easily and the leaves and petals are crisp.

Drying Rosebuds

When drying tiny rosebuds that will be used without their stems, you have two choices of air-drying methods. One method is to cut the clusters when most of the flowers are in bud, air dry them upside down as described in "Suspending Your Roses" on the opposite page, then cut the buds off when dry. The second method is to cut the buds just before they begin to open and spread them out on a wood-framed screen or a cookie sheet. The screen is better because it allows air to reach the underside of the flowers

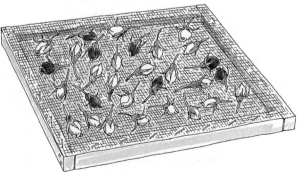

Air drying. When air drying roses and other flowers by hanging, tie the stems with a rubber band. It will continue to hold them tightly as they dry and shrink. Use a screen to dry rosebuds. It allows air to reach all sides of the flowers for faster drying.

Air Drying at a Glance

1. Gather four to six single-stemmed roses, removing all thorns and any leaves near the base. Make sure there is no surface moisture, such as rain or dew.

2. Stagger the stems so that each blossom has space around it. Wrap a rubber band once or twice around the stems, then run one end of the rubber band through the other and pull up snugly.

3. Hang the roses in a warm, dark, dry, well-ventilated place. Roses should be dry and ready to store or use in one to three weeks.

for faster, more even drying. Place the screen or cookie sheet in a gas oven with a pilot light or in any warm, dark, well-ventilated place. If using the oven, check about every four hours until the material is dry.

Storing Air-Dried Roses and Buds

You can use roses and rosebuds as soon as they are thoroughly dried, or store them loosely in boxes lined with tissue paper. Place tissue paper between flower layers, and never make more than three layers so the flowers are not crushed. Add a few mothballs to repel moths and rodents, then seal the box with masking tape and label it with the name of the rose cultivar, the flower color, and the date. Store the boxes in a dry location. Before storing or using the roses and rosebuds, you can spray them with hairspray, clear plastic craft spray sealer, or clear lacquer spray to prevent shattering.

DESICCANT DRYING: IT'S DEPENDABLE

Particular materials have the ability to draw moisture out of flowers or to speed the evaporation of moisture from flowers, thereby drying and preserving them. These substances, called desiccants, produce a dried rose that has better color and shape than one that is air-dried. Unfortunately, desiccants have some disadvantages: Desiccant drying is more costly than air drying; when using desiccants, you usually have to remove the natural floral stems and replace them with wire; the desiccant may damage the flower's petals; and the flowers may reabsorb moisture and droop when out in the air. Still, there are many times when this method yields roses that are perfect for a certain project. For example, desiccant drying is the best technique for drying single roses, and desiccant drying is good if you want to dry roses that are beyond the bud stage.

Making Your Own Desiccant

If you want, you can mix up your own desiccant at home. You can use cornmeal, sand, or borax to dry flowers and plant materials, but a mixture of the three is more effective. To make this mixture, combine 1 part of white cornmeal or fine, well-washed river sand with 2 parts of borax. To increase color retention in the flowers, add 3 tablespoons of noniodized salt per quart of either desiccant mixture. Unfortunately, these homemade mixtures are apt to cake or stick to the petals. With either mixture, drying time is usually one to two weeks.

Drying with Silica Gel

The best desiccant available is silica gel. Resembling white sand, silica gel absorbs up to 40 percent of its weight in water. It is lightweight, so it doesn't damage delicate flowers, and it acts quickly, so flowers may dry in as little as two days. Silica gel doesn't cake or stick to petals, and it dries flowers with superior color and form. The disadvantages are its bulk and the expense: You usually need 5 to 10 pounds to get started, but it's a one-time expense since you can reuse silica gel.

To dry roses using silica gel or a homemade desiccant, you will need airtight containers such as cake tins, plastic food-storage containers, or cardboard boxes and masking tape. You'll also need an artist's or makeup brush, wire cutters, and an assortment of floral wire in gauges from 22 to 26.

Gather roses late in the morning when they're thoroughly dry. Choose unblemished flowers in various stages of development. Cut the stems to 1 inch long. Cut a 6-inch-long piece of floral spool wire or floral wire. (Use 22-gauge wire for large roses, 24- or 26-gauge for

Desiccant drying. After wiring the stems of your roses or other flowers, nestle them in 1 inch of silica gel, then drizzle the gel over each flower until it's buried. Cover each flower with ½ to 1 inch of desiccant.

tiny roses like sweethearts). Insert the wire crosswise through the rose hip (the fat part of the rose just beneath the petals), as shown in the illustration on page 164. Center the wire.

Spread a 1-inch layer of desiccant on the bottom of your drying container. Nestle the wired roses into the material, allowing at least several inches of space between each flower. Single roses or semidouble cultivars with few petals are best dried face-down. When all of the flowers are in place, gently cover each one by letting the desiccant slowly flow in a fine, thin stream from your fist. If necessary, use a toothpick to work the gel into all of the little nooks and crannies. With practice, you'll be able to have each flower maintain its natural shape. Cover the roses with ½ to 1 inch of desiccant.

Seal the container and label with the date and contents. In two or three days, check the flowers by gently tilting the container until a few petals are exposed. When the petals are crisp and papery, the flowers are dry. Carefully pour the desiccant into another container, then gently remove each flower. Use a soft makeup or artist's brush to remove any desiccant clinging to the petals. Transparent spots on the petals indicate that there were water droplets on the flowers before preserving. To protect the flowers from humidity, spray them with a dull-finish clear plastic craft spray sealer or hairspray.

Sometimes large rosebuds may not be totally dry when the petals of open roses are. Staying too long in the desiccant can overdry and shrivel the petals, so remove the open flowers but leave the buds in the open container of desiccant for several days.

Reusing Silica Gel

Silica gel is sold under various brand names at garden centers and craft stores and from mail-order craft suppliers. Its white crystals have blue cobalt chloride crystals interspersed among them as moisture indicators. When these turn light blue, pink, or white, the silica gel cannot absorb any more water. To reactivate it, remove any flowers and spread the silica gel in a shallow baking pan. Reheat for several hours in a 250°F oven or microwave for 2 to 5 minutes on high power, or until crystals turn bright blue. Store in airtight containers. Silica gel can be reused indefinitely.

Desiccant Drying at a Glance

❧

1. Spread a 1-inch layer of desiccant in the bottom of an airtight container, such as a cake tin or plastic food-storage container.

2. Cut each rose stem to 1 inch long and insert a 6-inch piece of floral spool wire through the hip.

3. Nestle the rose into the desiccant and slowly drizzle more desiccant around and over the flower until it is covered by at least ½ inch of desiccant. Seal and label the container.

4. After two or three days, inspect the flower. If petals are crisp, then gently pour off the desiccant into a storage container.

Storing Desiccant-Dried Roses

If you are ready to use the dried roses immediately, proceed with the steps described in "Wiring and Taping Dried Roses" on page 164. Because desiccant-dried flowers reabsorb moisture from the air, you may not want to use them in humid weather unless you have air conditioning. To store desiccant-dried flowers, set them upright in an airtight lidded container that has a layer of dry sand or silica gel in the bottom. Alternatively, fold the wires down along the stems and stick these into a block of polystyrene, then store in an airtight container with a layer of desiccant in the bottom.

MICROWAVE DRYING: IT'S MIRACULOUS

Combining that modern miracle, the microwave oven, with silica gel gives the freshest-looking, most colorful flowers possible by any method other than freeze-drying. Several days or weeks of drying time are reduced to several minutes. This method allows you to dry a lot of flowers in a short period of time with less silica gel. The disadvantages are that it is labor-intensive because you can dry only one or two flowers at a time and it is difficult to judge the correct drying time.

Drying Roses

You will need small, deep, microwave-safe containers such as glass measuring cups or microwave cook-and-serve dishes. Each container should be deep enough to allow 2 inches of space from the gel-covered rose to the top of the container.

Pour silica gel into one of these containers and preheat it in the microwave for 1 minute on high power. Pour a 1-inch layer of preheated gel in the bottom of a separate microwave-safe dish. Place the rose inside, facing up if it has double blooms and down if it has a single bloom. Gently cover the rose by letting the desiccant slowly flow in a fine, thin stream from your fist. If necessary, use a toothpick to work the gel into all of the little nooks and crannies. With practice, you'll be able to have each flower maintain its natural shape. Cover the roses with ½ to 1 inch of desiccant. Remember to keep 2 inches of space from the surface of the gel to the top of the container.

Microwave Drying at a Glance

<small>❧</small>

1. Preheat silica gel in the microwave for 1 minute on high power.

2. Pour a 1-inch layer of the preheated gel in a small, deep, microwave-safe container. Place a rose with a 1-inch-long stem into the silica gel. Gently cover the flower with more silica gel.

3. Cook for 2 minutes on high, using a turntable or rotating the container one-half turn every 30 seconds. Let the container cool for 20 to 30 minutes.

4. Carefully pour off the silica gel and check the condition of the flower. If too "done," cut the cooking time in half for the next rose. Wire and tape the flower to use immediately, or store it.

Use a turntable or rotate the container one-half turn every 30 seconds. A large, many-petaled rose will need to be cooked for about 2 minutes on high power. After this time, let the container stand for 20 to 30 minutes, then gently pour off the silica gel. Use a soft makeup or artist's brush to remove any desiccant clinging to the petals. If the flower has turned beige or brown, it has been cooked too long, was past its prime, or was low in water. Try cutting the cooking time in half for the next flower.

Immediately wire and tape each dried flower as described in "Wiring and Taping Dried Roses" on page 164. Use the dried roses now or store them for later use as described in "Storing Desiccant-Dried Roses" on page 161.

Drying Rose Foliage

To dry rose foliage in the microwave, simply put one or several leaves either inside a paper napkin, with two layers of napkin above and below, or inside a piece of folded paper towel, with one layer above and one below. Place the wrapped foliage in the microwave, and set a microwave-safe cup or glass on top to keep the leaves from curling. (When using this method, always put a small container of water in the microwave along with your plant material. Drying in paper towels or napkins without water may damage your microwave.) Cook on high power for 2 minutes. Check; if the leaves are dry and crisp, they are done. If they are almost dry, let them sit in the napkin overnight. If they're still damp, cook them another minute or so. If the leaves are too dry, try again with new leaves and halve the cooking time.

PRESSING: IT'S PICTURE-PERFECT

The best roses for pressing are the single roses such as the once-blooming species roses or repeat-bloomers like 'Dainty Bess', 'Betty Prior', or 'Golden Wings'. You can also press some of the semidouble roses, the buds of miniature roses, and the buds of single cultivars.

Making a Flower Press

You can press your flowers with something as uncomplicated and inexpensive as an old telephone directory. But a directory or other printed paper can stain the flowers with ink. For only a little more effort and money, you can buy stacks of unprinted newspaper stock. (If you use printed newspapers, place layers of blank typing paper on either side of the flowers to avoid getting ink on them.) Blotter paper is another excellent choice for pressing flowers. Don't be tempted to use such common household items as facial tissue, paper towels, or cardboard: Facial tissue is too thin, and the wafflelike texture of paper towels and corrugated cardboard will wrinkle flowers.

To maintain even pressure on the paper and plant materials, use bricks, concrete blocks, books, or other heavy objects to weigh down the stack of paper. You can make a simple but effective flower press with two pieces of ½-inch-thick unpainted plywood held together with three strips of webbing that have Velcro fasteners at their ends. Or drill a hole in each corner of the plywood and use screws and wing nuts to adjust the pressure, as shown in the illustration on the opposite page.

Pressing Roses

To press roses, gather them on a dry, sunny day, preferably in late morning after the dew has dried. Place the roses on the drying paper,

Pressing flowers. Using a simple plywood press with screws and wing nuts lets you adjust the pressure for a tight fit and evenly pressed flowers.

Wiring and Taping Dried Roses

Often, the finishing touch to air-dried, desiccant-dried, or microwave-dried roses is creating stems for them. Air-dried roses with long stems may be used as is, but you may be frustrated by the inflexibility of the stems. If you need flexible stems or are using the short-stemmed desiccant-dried roses, make replacement stems with floral wire and floral wrapping tape.

Green floral wire is available in a variety of gauges; gauges 22 to 26 are the ones most often used with roses. Floral wrapping tape is a thin, stretchy ½-inch-wide tape that is used to wrap the floral wire so that it resembles a stem. It is sold in green, brown, and white. To make replacement stems for your roses, use the following steps:

1. Use wire cutters or household scissors to cut a 6-inch length of floral wire. Insert the wire through the rose hip—the fat part of the flower just below the petals—and center the wire. (If you have used desiccants to dry your flowers and have already inserted a wire, you will not need to do this step.)

2. Gently bend the wire down on both sides and squeeze together or overlap the two wires to form one "stem." Place a 12-inch length of floral wire alongside the short wire stem.

3. Place the end of a roll of green floral wrapping tape alongside the wires and against the rose hip. Twirl the wires and wrap them together with the tape, stretching the tape as you go along and creating one 12-inch-long stem. Tear off the tape at the base of the stem.

Note: For projects not requiring long stems, simply tape the folded wire and flower, eliminating the second wire.

Pressing at a Glance

❧

1. Place roses on paper, arranging petals and leaves as you like them. Do not let flowers overlap; do not let leaves lie on top of stems.

2. Put several layers of blotter paper or a ½-inch stack of newsprint between each layer of flowers.

3. Weight the stack with books, bricks, or concrete blocks, or use a plywood press with Velcro straps or bolts and wing nuts.

4. Check the roses in several weeks. Store them in the press or in shallow boxes or drawers.

arranging the petals in an attractive way. Press flowers at different stages of development, with some head-on and others in profile. If pressing head-on, place the rose face-down. Do not let flowers overlap. Thin out foliage, if necessary, and don't let leaves lie on top of the stem. Choose some roses with curved stems and others that are straight. You can advantageously place tiny pieces of masking tape on stems to help create a particular curve or to position leaves and flowers where you want them. Do not put tape directly on leaves and flowers.

If you're using a telephone directory or stack of newspaper, allow a ½-inch layer of paper between each layer of plant material. For blotter paper, you only need to use several sheets between layers. When the stack is ready for drying, put it in a warm, dry place with good air circulation. Avoid areas with damp floors or high humidity. Put weights on top of the stack or fasten the webbed straps or bolts and wing nuts.

Check the press in several weeks. Drying time depends on the plants, temperature, and humidity. Dried, pressed flowers and leaves can be left in the press or stored in thin, flat boxes or drawers.

Now that you've mastered the basic techniques of drying and pressing roses and other flowers, you can start collecting dried materials to use in the delightful projects in Chapters 7 through 9. Look in Chapter 7 for dried arrangements, baskets, pressed-flower pictures, and many other projects. Chapter 8 provides a wealth of lovely wreath and garland projects. And Chapter 9 features an array of potpourris, candles, jewelry, and beauty products like soaps and lotions. Have a wonderful time working with your dried flowers!

Chapter 7

Using Dried Roses

*I*F YOU ENJOY HOME DECORATING OR just like to give your rooms a new touch now and then, dried rose projects are for you. Using dried roses opens up almost unlimited possibilities for decorating your home, providing unique and lovely gifts, and indulging yourself in a creative and pleasurable pastime. And best of all, you can continue to enjoy your creations for months or even years.

You can use dried roses in so many ways that the projects in this chapter represent only a small sampling of the possibilities. There are styles ranging from the unconventional, sophisticated arrangements seen in New York or London boutiques to the traditional formal bouquets of Williamsburg and the sweetly romantic Victorian or country-style creations. In this chapter, you will find projects in several different styles accompanied by basic, easy-to-follow instructions. They will provide a springboard for you to produce creations in a style all your own.

TOOLS AND SUPPLIES

Dried rose crafts require some special equipment in addition to the tools used to make fresh rose arrangements. (See "Tools and Supplies" on page 142 for descriptions of the tools used in making fresh arrangements.) To make dried rose crafts, your toolbox should also include the tools described below. In addition to the tools, you will need mechanics, which are items for holding and supporting the flower and foliage stems. You can purchase mechanics at craft stores, florists, or garden centers. Last, you will need containers to hold your dried arrangements. Just about anything can be used as a container. The choices are limited only by your personal taste.

Tools

Artist's brush. Use this type of paintbrush for dusting desiccants from flower petals.

Needles. Use a collection of various-size darning and knitting needles for making holes in polystyrene; poultry skewers also come in handy.

Tweezers. Use tweezers to handle pressed flowers and small dried flowers. The best tweezers are the ones used by stamp collectors—they have rounded heads and textured grips.

Mechanics

A variety of items, collectively called mechanics, help support flower and foliage stems in arrangements or aid in arranging and using dried flowers in crafts. While these items are not necessary for every project in this chapter, they do broaden the scope of what you can do. In addition to the materials listed in "Mechanics" on page 144, the following materials—available from local craft stores, florists, or mail-order suppliers— are useful for dried crafts. (See "Rose Resources" on page 282 for addresses of craft suppliers.)

Clear plastic adhesive paper. Use this type

of paper to seal pressed-flower projects. It is available in rolls or sheets.

Floral foam. Use hard brown foam bricks for thick stems and branches; use softer brown foam for thinner stems.

Floral pick. This is a wooden pick about 3 inches long with one end sharpened to a point and a length of very fine floral wire attached to the other end. Floral picks are painted green. To use, attach individual flowers, groups of flowers, or other items to the pick with the wire and then insert the loaded pick into an arrangement, wreath, or other project. You can make small, homemade picks with toothpicks and floral wire.

Floral pin. Floral pins, also known as greening pins, resemble flat-topped hairpins. They are used to attach moss, flowers, ribbons, corn-husks, or other materials to floral foam, poly-styrene, or wreath forms.

Glue. Use white craft or household glue for many tasks, such as gluing fabric or ribbon. For gluing pressed flowers, use white craft or house-hold glue. For jobs where quick setting is important, such as placing dried flowers on a wreath, hot glue dispensed from a glue gun is best. You can also use spray adhesive to attach one flat surface to another, such as fabric or paper to the side of a box.

Plaster of paris. Use plaster of paris to add base weight for a top-heavy arrangement or to hold a topiary trunk upright in a container. Mix the plaster with just enough water to make it the consistency of thick cake batter. You can also buy a type of mixable foam to support topiaries, but this has the disadvantage of being light in weight.

Polystyrene. Use polystyrene, also known as Styrofoam, as a base on which you glue flowers, or insert wire stems or very tough stems directly into the polystyrene. White or green polystyrene comes in a variety of precut shapes, or you can buy a block of it and cut it to the shape you need. Polystyrene is harder than floral foam.

Raffia. Use raffia to tie moss or hay to a container or to create a simple bow. Braid or tie it into swags, ropes, or wreaths.

Ribbon. Use ribbon to tie bows or make streamers. All manner of sizes, colors, and pat-terns of ribbon are available. Besides the various fabric ribbons, there is crinkled paper ribbon as well as French ribbon, which has fine wires along each edge. For a craft project displayed outdoors, be sure to use a weather-resistant ribbon.

Surface finish. Use clear plastic craft spray sealer or hairspray to prevent dried flowers from shattering. For an attractive finish on nuts and

Tips for Using Glue Guns

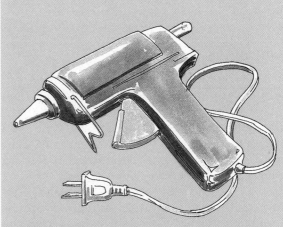

Hot glue guns are one of the most useful craft tools you'll ever buy. When you go to purchase one, be sure to get one that has a self-advancing glue stick, and follow package directions for usage and care. Here are a few other tips you'll want to keep in mind when choosing and using a glue gun:

• Choose a glue gun with a stand; otherwise you'll need to set aside a plate or other non-flammable object to hold the glue gun when it's hot.

• Whenever possible, use clear glue sticks.

• Cover your work surface with several layers of newspaper.

• After applying glue, hold small items in place for 20 to 30 seconds; hold larger, heavier items in place for up to a minute.

• Fine, thin strands of glue will form as you pull the glue gun away; remove these later when they dry.

• Hot glue may melt polystyrene or floral foam; test a small area first. If the foam melts, use floral pins or white craft or household glue instead of the glue gun.

• Never leave hot glue unattended, especially with children around.

• When finished with the glue gun, unplug it immediately.

• Keep a bowl of ice water and a tube of burn ointment near your work area for quick treatment of burns.

seedpods, spray them with a transparent gloss, such as a quick-drying polyurethane varnish. Most people prefer to leave dried flowers in their natural colors, but you may want to add a bit of silver or gold glitter or spray paint for Christmas holiday decorations.

Containers

The containers and other objects you can use to display dried roses and other dried flowers are as wide-ranging as your imagination. Since holding water is not a consideration, you need to focus only on whether or not a particular item will complement the dried roses and other plant materials. Spend time looking around your home as well as at yard sales, craft shops, flea markets, thrift shops, antique stores, and anywhere else you might come across the curious, the beautiful, or the unusual.

All types of baskets seem to enhance the look of dried flowers. But don't overlook containers made of other materials, including wood, glazed or unglazed pottery, pewter, silver, brass, copper, aluminum, tin, steel, porcelain, ironstone, clear or colored glass, and terra-cotta.

What really broadens the scope of decorating with dried roses is the fact that the base doesn't actually have to be a container. With various readily available craft supplies, you can transform items as far-ranging as slaw cutters or shoe lasts by attaching dried flowers to them. If you're looking for a container, don't just look at vases; consider soup tureens, bowls, compotes, teapots, teacups, pitchers, jugs, brandy snifters, wine glasses, seashells, bonsai pots, ginger jars, clocks, bookends, and antique bobbins. Other objects you can decorate include a slice of tree trunk, a picture frame, a breadboard, a butter paddle, a flat slab of stone, a piece of felt-covered plywood, a hatbox lid, a hand mirror, a comb, a lamp base, or a tin tray.

PREPARING CONTAINERS AND BASES

The two most popular materials used to hold dried flowers in an arrangement are brown floral foam and chicken-wire mesh. When using floral foam, you must make the foam as secure as possible in the container. First, press either the opening or the base of the container into the foam surface to make a slight indentation. To shape the foam to the container, cut around the indentation with a sharp knife. The foam block should be tall enough that it extends at least 1 inch above the rim of the container. (For shallow containers, the floral foam should be 1½ to 2 inches above the rim.) You need this extra foam height so that stems can be inserted horizontally and upward, with heads facing downward.

To use less foam and add stabilizing weight to a deep container, try filling the base of the container with gravel or sand. For shallow containers, impale the foam on one or more floral spikes that are attached to the bottom of the container with floral clay or glue; secure the foam to the top of the container with floral tape. To provide additional support for heavy stems inserted into floral foam, stretch chicken wire over the top of the foam and tape it to the container with floral tape before inserting the stems.

For arrangements made on an object rather than in a container, first sculpt the floral foam into a rounded shape. Next, attach it to the surface of the base with floral spikes, glue, or floral tape.

To use floral foam in glass containers, cut the foam smaller than the container and attach it to the container's bottom with floral spikes. To conceal the foam, fill in around it with potpourri, moss, marbles, smooth pebbles, or some other attractive materials.

To use chicken wire to hold flowers, you'll need a pair of sturdy work gloves and some wire cutters. First, cut a piece of chicken wire several times larger than the surface area of the container. Then crumple the wire and force it into the container. Another technique is to cut the chicken wire only a few inches larger than the container's diameter, fold the edges down, and wedge the wire snugly inside the container.

Basket arrangements look best with the flowers massed in either a rounded or triangular shape. You can construct either of these two simple massed styles to be seen either from all sides or from one side only. For more information on shapes of arrangements, see "Design Basics" beginning on page 145. As for roses in basket arrangements, you can use either long-stemmed air-dried roses or desiccant-dried roses with artificial wire stems. For instructions on how to dry roses and wire them with artificial stems, see Chapter 6.

Many aspects of arranging dried flowers are the same as for arranging fresh. The styling principles of balance, rhythm, scale, and color are equally valid for both. For more information on these aspects of flower arranging, see "Design Principles," beginning on page 147.

Rose Basket Arrangement

There's nothing quite so charming as a basket brimming with dried roses and other colorful flowers. Handmade, antique, ethnic, brightly colored, or subtly natural, baskets filled with flowers fit almost any decor. The number of roses needed obviously depends on the size of the basket and how many other flowers you use.

MATERIALS

Dried tall, straight flowers, such as mealycup sage, bells-of-Ireland, or delphiniums

Dried roses

Assortment of dried round-headed flowers, such as strawflowers, hydrangeas, and zinnias (optional)

Dried filler material, such as baby's-breath or German statice

Basket

Brown floral foam or wire mesh

Sharp knife

Brown floral tape (optional)

Sturdy work gloves (if using wire mesh)

Wire cutters

Pruning shears

Scissors

Green floral wire

Green floral wrapping tape

1. To prepare the basket, use the knife to cut the floral foam to fit inside the basket. If desired, secure the foam to the top of the basket with crossed strips of brown floral tape. Or put on the work gloves and use wire cutters to clip and crumple wire mesh to fit inside the basket.

2. Wire and tape the flowers as necessary. (See "Wiring and Taping Dried Roses" on page 164 for complete instructions.)

3. Using the tall, straight flowers, form a rounded or pyramidal outline. Use scissors to cut stems to different lengths to give depth to the arrangement.

4. Next, fill in with roses. Again, use stems of different lengths for depth. If desired, add other dried round flowers.

5. To soften the transition between the linear and round materials, add dried filler material.

Variations: Use roses of all one color for a monochromatic look. Or mix roses of several different colors for variety. Try using roses in different stages of development—some in bud and others more fully open. Even minor changes such as these can create a totally different look.

MATERIALS

5 stems of dried long-stemmed wheat

35 stems of dried long-stemmed
lavender

12 air-dried long-stemmed roses with
foliage

Dried moss

Heavy cord

Scissors

4-inch-diameter terra-cotta pot

French ribbon

Massed Arrangement in a Clay Pot

Often there is the greatest elegance in simplicity, be it a single strand of pearls, a classic blue blazer, or a bunch of dried roses tied with a single ribbon bow. This easy-to-make arrangement is at home with rustic antiques as well as with sleek modern decor. Terra-cotta pots (preferably darkened with age), natural baskets, or wooden boxes are ideal containers. French ribbon is the customary counterpart to these arrangements. For a stunning effect, make up several different pots and baskets and display them together.

1. Gather together the stems of wheat, arranging them so all of the heads are the same height. With heavy cord, securely tie together the stems one-third of the way from the bottom. Use the scissors to trim the stem ends to the same length.

2. Arrange stems of lavender around the wheat, so that the lavender heads are all the same height and start just below the heads of wheat as shown in the illustration. With heavy cord, securely tie together the stems of lavender and wheat one-third of the way up and use the scissors to trim the stem ends to the same length.

3. Use scissors to cut all of the rose stems to the same length; they should be long enough so that when placed next to the lavender, the rose heads start just below the lavender heads. Stand the lavender and wheat in the center of the pot. Place a single ring of roses around the outside. Stuff moss into the pot to keep all of the plant stems in place.

4. Tie a length of French ribbon loosely around the stems of the arrangement, making a simple bow.

Everlasting Centerpiece

A centerpiece on the dining table makes even the most ordinary meal seem special. It shows that you care about the people with whom you're sharing the meal. Also, use centerpieces to adorn a sideboard, coffee table, or wherever a bit of beauty will brighten your day.

MATERIALS

Assortment of preserved foliage, such as beech, rose leaves, and grasses
10 to 12 dried roses
Assortment of dried plant materials, such as delphiniums, annual statice, German statice, strawflowers, cones and pods, and 'Victoria' mealycup sage
Brown floral foam
Low or flat container or base, such as a dish, platter, or cork mat
Floral spikes
Floral clay or white craft glue
Dripless candles (optional)
Pruning shears
Scissors
Green floral wire
Wire cutters
Green floral wrapping tape

1. Plan to make the centerpiece low enough to allow guests to see one another across the table. To hold the arrangement, attach floral foam to the container or base using floral spikes held in place with floral clay. Or for a more permanent arrangement, glue the foam to the container. If you're using candles, insert them into the foam.

2. Wire and tape the foliage and flowers as necessary. (See "Wiring and Taping Dried Roses" on page 164 for complete instructions.)

3. Insert the foliage into the foam first to build up the outline of the arrangement.

4. Add the wired and taped roses, cones, pods, or other flowers, as desired.

Christmas Dinner Centerpiece: Use fresh evergreens, dried red roses, gilded pinecones or poppy seedpods, and dried German statice for a festive holiday centerpiece. Add a candle or two and some ornaments for a special holiday glow.

Harvest-Time Centerpiece: For a fall arrangement, combine polished walnuts, glycerin-preserved leaves, wheat, and orange or yellow roses.

Colors-of-Spring Centerpiece: For spring, consider a pastel palette of pink roses, pale yellow yarrow, and sky blue larkspur.

MATERIALS

Assortment of dried plant materials, such as bare branches, ferns, Chinese lanterns, poppy or lotus pods, foxtail, globe thistles, larkspur, and yarrow

3 dried roses

Large dried leaves (optional)

Low, flat platter, bowl, or vase

Floral clay

Pinholder

Pruning shears

Scissors

Green floral wire

Wire cutters

Green floral wrapping tape

Assortment of small, smooth pebbles (optional)

1. To prepare the low container, use floral clay to attach a pinholder to the container.

2. Wire and tape the foliage and flowers as necessary. (See "Wiring and Taping Dried Roses" on page 164 for complete instructions.)

3. Place the longest branch of plant material vertically in the pinholder. Next add an intermediate-size branch. Place the final branch in the pinholder either horizontally or downward so the branch line directs the eye from the center of the arrangement. If you desire, add large leaves placed horizontally from the center of the arrangement and covering the pinholder.

4. Incorporate an odd number of dried roses near the convergence of the three lines formed by the tall, straight plant materials. The roses should serve as a focal point as well as an extension of one of the three lines.

5. For a *moribana* arrangement in which the pinholder is not covered with leaves, you may choose to cover the pinholder with smooth pebbles arranged in an attractive pattern.

Oriental-Style Arrangement

Japanese flower arranging appeals to many of us who enjoy simplicity and clean lines. Traditional oriental arrangements blend nicely with contemporary interiors, and some also complement more rustic or traditional rooms. Another allure of these arrangements is that they require only a small amount of plant material, sometimes only a few branches and a single flower.

The apparent simplicity of Japanese flower arranging, called *ikebana*, belies complex symbolism and nuances of meaning that have evolved over centuries. Although people spend years studying and practicing *ikebana*, beginners can make very basic but satisfying arrangements with only a rudimentary understanding of the principles involved.

Traditionally, there are three major elements in *ikebana:* the longest, usually upright, stem represents heaven; the next highest denotes man; and the lowest, usually horizontal or downward hanging, depicts Earth. As *ikebana* has been practiced over many centuries in Japan, several different traditional styles have developed, including *moribana* and *haika. Moribana*-style arrangements feature a low container fitted with a pinholder for securing plant material. Depending on the choice of the arranger, the pinholder may be hidden by leaves or shiny black stones. With arrangements in the *haika* (tall-vase) style, branches are wedged into the vase in a way that makes mechanics unnecessary. Alternatively, you may construct a simple triangle from a folded woody stem or sliver of bamboo. Wedge this triangle inside the tall vase to serve as a simple mechanic for holding branches in place. With either style, black or dark-colored containers are traditional.

Although *ikebana* arrangements are not traditionally created from dried flowers, contemporary enthusiasts readily adapt this style to use preserved material. As an ideal way to use a few perfect specimens combined with a small amount of foliage or other plant material, *ikebana* opens up new possibilities for using dried roses creatively.

Haika Arrangement: For this type of arrangement, you can use the same plant materials as in the *moribana* arrangement, but you will need a tall cylindrical vase. If you like, prepare the vase by folding a woody stem or sliver of bamboo into a triangle and inserting it into the vase. Place the longest branch of plant material in the container. Next, add an intermediate-size branch. Finally, insert a branch or stem bent downward. Incorporate an odd number of dried roses near the convergence of the three lines formed by the tall, straight plant material. The roses should serve as a focal point as well as an extension of one of the three lines.

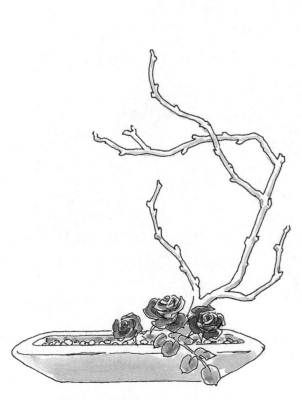

Moribana-Style Arrangement

Haika-Style Arrangement

Rose Bouquet

Bouquets and bunches of dried flowers are remarkably versatile, as well as fun and easy to make. You can use them to decorate a wall, door, or beam, or to nestle in the arms of a bride. Larger than nosegays, bouquets are usually flat-backed and tied with a ribbon close to the base of the stems. When creating a bouquet, coordinate the scale and final size of the arrangement, as well as the colors, to make a piece that looks good where you plan to use it.

1. Gather together the stems of the dried flowers and leaves, making an attractive arrangement. Holding the stems in one hand, place the longer stems first, then add the shorter stems at the top and sides. Put the most beautiful blooms near the top center. Cut the stems to the lengths necessary.

2. When the arrangement is to your liking, tie the stems together with heavy cord. Hide the cord with a ribbon tied in a simple bow. Cut a V-shape out of each end of the ribbon ends to finish.

Innovative Arrangement

Ever wonder how you could fix up that old lamp, use that strange piece of bark in an ingenious way, or add a little pizzazz to that boring pair of bookends? The answer is with dried roses, of course. Even though there is no one set way of creating arrangements on such a diverse lot of items, here are basic guidelines that will show you how easy it is to do.

For most items, cut a block of floral foam to fit the portion of the object to be decorated and tape it to the object with floral tape. This works even with unusually shaped items; for instance, with a columnar lamp base or candlestick, cut a round ball of foam in half, carve out the middle of each half to fit around the item, then tape the two halves together where you want the arrangement.

MATERIALS

6 to 8 dried roses
Assortment of dried flowers and plant materials, such as strawflowers, statice, ageratums, 'Silver King' artemisia, and yarrows
Dried filler material, such as baby's-breath or statice
Sharp knife
Brown floral foam
Floral clay or white household glue
Jar with jar lid
Pruning shears
Scissors
Green floral wire
Wire cutters
Green floral wrapping tape

1. With a knife, shape the block of floral foam to fit the jar lid, rounding the outer edges. Attach the foam to the lid with floral clay or white household glue.

2. If necessary, wire and tape stems of plant material to have flowers with the proper stem length. To have fewer stems to insert into the foam, you may create small clusters of dried flowers by wiring and taping several stems together to form one stem. (See "Attaching Accent Materials" on page 224 for complete instructions.)

3. To create your arrangement, establish the outline first with stems or bunches of dried materials. Next, fill in with dried roses. Then fill in with other dried material, such as baby's-breath or statice.

Rosebud-Covered Objects

MATERIALS

100 to 125 dried rosebuds
Extruded polystyrene wreath base,
    5 or 6 inches in diameter
Hot glue gun with clear glue sticks,
    or white craft or household glue
Clear plastic craft spray sealer
Ribbon and lace (optional)

Tiny, perfect rosebuds epitomize the romantic quality of roses. Favorite rosebuds for drying are the exquisite little buds of the 'Sweetheart' rose, more correctly named 'Cecile Brunner'. Pale shell pink with a high, pointed center, the buds of 'Cecile Brunner' are no more than ½ inch long.

Covering objects with dozens upon dozens of beautiful little rosebuds romantically transforms them into beautiful accessories and gifts. You can make small circular or heart-shaped wreaths, picture and mirror frames, kissing balls, and diminutive topiaries. Add lace and ribbon as your muse dictates.

1. Using the hot glue gun or white craft or household glue, glue individual rosebuds to the wreath base, tucking them close together.

2. When the glue is completely dry, spray the completed wreath with clear plastic craft sealer to keep the dried material from shattering or absorbing moisture.

3. Add ribbon or lace decorations, if desired.

Rosebud-Covered Ornament: Glue rosebuds to a 3- or 4-inch-diameter extruded polystyrene ball, covering its entire surface. (If you want to add a ribbon loop for hanging, glue the loop of ribbon at the top of the ball before applying the roses.)

Rosebud-Covered Ornament

Rosebud-Covered Wreath

Rosebud Necklace and Earrings

MATERIALS
(FOR A 28-INCH-LONG NECKLACE)

17 fresh rosebuds, each about ½ inch across and just beginning to open
1 yard of ⅛-inch-wide satin ribbon
Scissors
Darning needle
18 pearl beads, 5 mm in diameter
Large safety pin

A necklace of pearl beads, satin ribbon, and rosebuds is a wonderful gift for your favorite little girl. This necklace is quick and easy to make, and the roses will dry in place on the ribbon. For the earrings, all you'll need are rosebuds, a pair of purchased earring backs, and some glue. For best results, gather rosebuds early in the morning after the dew has dried, cutting the stems just below the hip. You can vary the length of the necklace as desired. You may admire the necklace you made for your daughter, granddaughter, or niece so much you can't resist making a longer version for yourself. Wear it with a romantic white dress to an afternoon tea, or enjoy it draped on an antique linen-covered table adorned with potpourri, family photos, and a stack of nineteenth-century novels.

1. Tie a single knot in one end of the ribbon, or where you want the beads to begin. Use the scissors to trim off the end at an angle.

2. Thread the ribbon through the needle. String one pearl bead onto the ribbon, sliding it to the knot.

3. String a rosebud onto the ribbon, piercing it through the center, from side to side.

4. String one pearl bead, leaving about ¼ inch of space between the rosebud and the first bead.

5. String another rosebud onto the ribbon, leaving about ¼ inch of space between it and the last bead.

6. Repeat the pattern and spacing of a rosebud, then one bead, until all rosebuds and beads have been strung. Then tie off with a single knot. Trim the end at an angle, ½ inch from the knot.

7. Insert a large safety pin into one end of the strand and use this to hang the necklace in a dark, dry, well-ventilated place. When dry, tie the ends together.

Rosebud Earrings: To make the earrings, you will need two dried rosebuds and two purchased earring backs. Hot glue one rosebud to each earring back.

Rosebud Earrings

Rosebud Necklace

Dried Rose Nosegay

MATERIALS

1 dried rosebud, stem cut to 6 inches
3 to 5 dried roses, stems cut to 4 to 6 inches
Assortment of dried flowers and foliage, mealycup sage, German statice, mini-carnations, ferns, ivy, and magnolia or salal leaves, stems cut to 4 to 6 inches
Pruning shears
Scissors
Green floral wire
Wire cutters
Green floral wrapping tape
Paper doily, 6 inches in diameter
Ribbon

1. Wire and tape the flowers and foliage as necessary. (See "Wiring and Taping Dried Roses" on page 164 for complete instructions.)

2. Holding the flowers in one hand, start with a central rosebud and arrange roses and other flowers around it. When satisfied with the design, wrap the stems together with a length of floral wire.

3. Use the scissors to cut an X in the center of the paper doily. Insert the stems through the X so the doily frames the flowers, and wrap the stems with floral tape, stretching it as you twirl the nosegay in your hand.

4. Finish with a ribbon bow tied just under the doily. Add ribbon streamers, if desired.

Nosegays had their heyday in the Victorian era, when people conveyed elaborate messages through the flowers they chose for their nosegays. (For more information on the meanings of roses and other flowers, see "A Floral Dictionary" on page 233.)

Today, we can still take pleasure in carrying nosegays or in having them in our homes. A pair of nosegays make lovely curtain tiebacks. A dinner party takes on added spirit with a nosegay at each place setting or hanging from the back of each chair. One nosegay in a teacup or several placed together in a crystal bowl make an instant arrangement. A single nosegay simply set on a table or shelf provides a lasting remembrance of summers past. They also make thoughtful and charming gifts for birthdays, Valentine's Day, Mother's Day, anniversaries, bridal or baby showers, and christenings. Use them to thank a hostess or send a get-well message.

You can make dried nosegays with dried flowers or you can use fresh flowers and allow them to dry in the bouquet. Begin the nosegay with a perfectly formed rosebud as the central flower. Add other flowers from the center outward, either in concentric rings or casually arranged. Mix a variety of flowers and leaves, or use only roses and a few leaves and filler flowers. If desired, include sweet-smelling herbs.

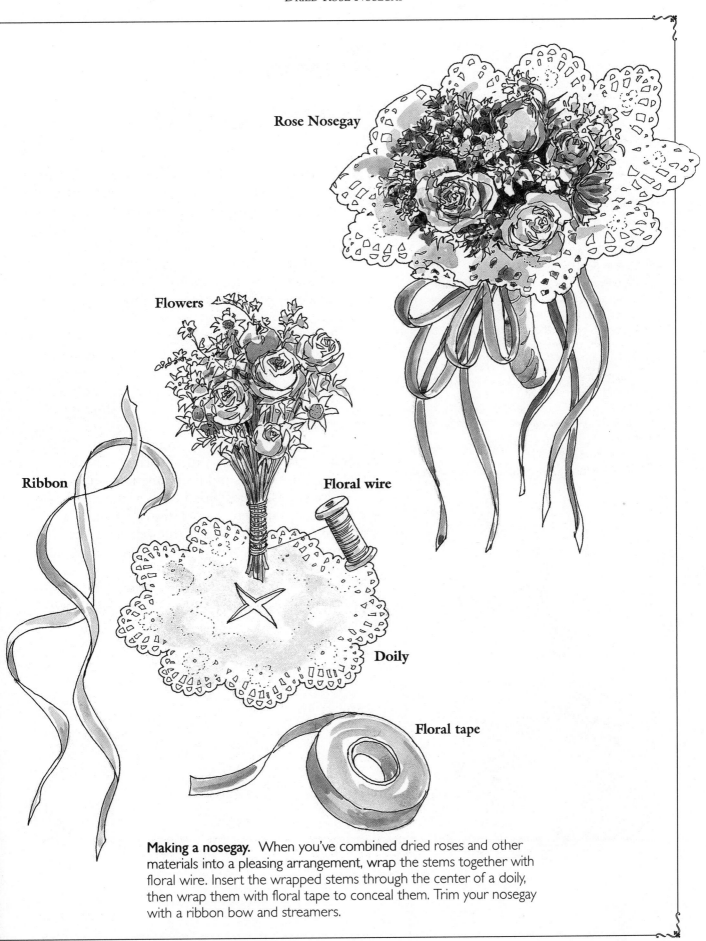

Rose Nosegay

Flowers

Ribbon

Floral wire

Doily

Floral tape

Making a nosegay. When you've combined dried roses and other materials into a pleasing arrangement, wrap the stems together with floral wire. Insert the wrapped stems through the center of a doily, then wrap them with floral tape to conceal them. Trim your nosegay with a ribbon bow and streamers.

Roses under Glass

MATERIALS

Assortment of dried flowers and plant materials, such as strawflowers, 'Victoria' mealycup sage, and lady's-mantle flowers

6 to 8 dried roses

Filler material, such as baby's-breath or statice

Dried Spanish or sphagnum moss

Pruning shears

Scissors

24-gauge floral wire

Wire cutters

Green floral wrapping tape

Decorative fabric, such as velvet, satin, or lace (optional)

Glass dome with wooden base

Hot glue gun and clear glue sticks, or white craft or household glue

Glossy enamel paint (if using glass jar)

Sharp knife

Round piece of brown floral foam

Floral spikes and floral clay (optional)

Floral pins (optional)

Clear silicone tub sealer and caulking gun (optional)

¼-inch-wide velvet ribbon (optional)

I n Victorian times, bell jars were used to display and keep dust and humidity from the rarest and finest dried flower arrangements. Few of us have access to antique bell jars, but reproductions are available in various sizes. Look for these glass domes with wooden bases at jewelry, import, and craft stores. They still make lovely display cases and will keep your own treasured arrangements dust-free.

An inexpensive alternative to the traditional domed bell jar is a glass jar, especially a small one, fitted with a miniature arrangement. These make wonderful fund-raising projects. They're also easy-to-make craft items for older children. Choose jars with as wide a mouth as possible and without words or numbers imprinted on the bottom. Other decorative glass containers that work nicely include ginger jars, fishbowls, and hurricane lampshades.

Use your loveliest dried roses and other flowers and leaves for these special displays. Create an arrangement to fit the season, the occasion, or a color theme. For a wedding present, design an all-white bouquet; make a pink or blue one for a mother and new baby; or for an autumn gift, combine yellow or orange roses with cones, nuts, seedpods, and grasses.

1. Wire and tape the foliage and flowers as necessary. (See "Wiring and Taping Dried Roses" on page 164 for complete instructions.)

2. If desired, cut and glue fabric to cover the wooden base of the glass dome. If using an old jar, paint the lid.

3. Use the knife to cut the floral foam so that it is ½ to 1 inch thick and 1 inch less in diameter than the inside of the glass cover or slightly smaller than the diameter of the jar lid. Attach the foam to the wooden base with floral spikes held in place with clay, or glue the foam to the base. Cover the foam with the moss, attaching with hot glue or floral pins.

4. If your arrangement will be viewed from all sides, place the tallest plant material at the center of the foam. If the arrangement will be viewed from one side only, place the tallest flowers at the back of the foam. As you add material, make sure the dome or jar will fit over the arrangement without touching it.

5. Add flowers, placing the larger, rounder flowers toward the center and lower part of the arrangement and the smaller flowers toward the top.

6. Fill in around the arrangement with filler, such as baby's-breath or statice.

7. When the arrangement is complete, put on the glass cover or carefully screw the glass jar to its lid. If desired, use the silicone sealer and caulking gun to run a narrow bead of sealer around the base of the cover. Hide the seal with a length of velvet ribbon hot glued in place.

Step 3

Step 4

Step 5

Rose and Flower Topiary

MATERIALS

Dried Spanish or sphagnum moss
15 to 20 dried roses, stems cut off
Assortment of dried flowers and plant materials, such as German statice, caspia, hydrangeas, sweet Annie, and strawflowers
Pruning shears
Scissors
22-gauge green floral wire
Wire cutters
Green floral wrapping tape
Old bowl, bucket, or disposable container
Plaster of paris
Water
Decorative waterproof container or decorative container with a waterproof liner
Grapevine, branch, or dowel with the diameter in proportion to the container and top
Extruded polystyrene ball or cone, or floral foam cut to desired shape
Hot glue gun with clear glue sticks
Floral pins (optional)
Thin knitting needles (optional)
Ribbon (optional)

Growing roses as topiaries has been popular since the nineteenth century. A topiary, or standard, is a shrub pruned and trained to a single stem so that it resembles a small tree. Today, the concept of topiaries has evolved into exquisite, richly detailed dried flower designs that sell for hundreds of dollars in New York and London. A single magnificent topiary is a striking accent; a perfectly matched pair is a symmetrical foil to French doors or a mantel. A cluster of topiaries makes an attractive centerpiece for a buffet table, while diminutive ones made of tightly packed rosebuds could mark place settings or add a graceful touch to a very feminine room.

The range of topiary designs is remarkable. Besides choosing from an array of containers and colors, you can arrange the flowers informally or you can tightly space them, perhaps in geometric patterns, for a formal look. Form the topiary "trunk" from a dowel wrapped in ribbon, a natural plant stem, or even a contorted piece of driftwood. The most popular shapes for topiaries are spheres or cones.

1. Wire and tape the foliage and flowers as necessary. (See "Wiring and Taping Dried Roses" on page 164 for complete instructions.)

2. Using an old bowl or other container, mix the plaster of paris with just enough water to give it the consistency of thick cake batter. Mix enough to fill the decorative container to within 1 inch from the top.

3. Pour the wet plaster of paris into the decorative container, let it thicken slightly, then insert the grapevine, branch, or dowel in the center. Make sure the "trunk" stays straight or at the desired angle until the plaster completely hardens. Wash out the mixing bowl as soon as possible. Complete curing of the plaster may take several days, but you can work on the topiary within an hour.

4. When the trunk is firmly established in the dry plaster of paris, push the polystyrene or foam form onto the top of the trunk. Remove the form, put hot glue into the hole, and replace the form on the trunk.

5. Cover the form with Spanish moss, attaching it with hot glue or floral pins.

6. You may decorate the moss-covered form in one of two ways. Either insert natural stems or wired-and-taped stems directly into the form, using knitting needles to create holes for the stems, or hot glue statice or other fine-textured flowers to the moss, covering the form, then hot glue on larger flowers, like roses. Build up layers of dried material, with flowers at different depths. For an airy touch, insert very thin twigs that extend beyond the rest of the flowers.

7. Use ribbon for various effects, either as loops among the flowers, as a bow at the top, or as a bow and streamers at the base of the form. If you used a dowel as your trunk, wrap it in ribbon to disguise it.

8. To camouflage the plaster of paris, cover the plaster surface with moss or flowers, using hot glue to attach.

Dried Rosebud Topiary: To make topiaries covered with closely spaced dried rosebuds, follow the instructions above through Step 4, then decorate by hot gluing rosebuds in a tightly spaced pattern around the form.

Rose and Flower Topiary

Rosebud Topiary

Rose Topiary Spiral

MATERIALS

Dried Spanish or sphagnum moss
15 to 20 dried roses, stems cut off
Sheet moss (optional)
Old bowl, bucket, or disposable container
Plaster of paris
Water
Decorative, waterproof container or decorative container with water-proof liner
Wire topiary form, about 15 inches tall
Hot glue gun with clear glue sticks
Clear fishing monofilament
¼-inch-wide ribbon (optional)
Scissors

B esides the ever-popular globe shape most often associated with topiary, garden centers and specialty mail-order suppliers offer other wonderful wire topiary shapes, including spirals (one of the most popular) as well as other geometric and animal shapes. Most topiary enthusiasts train ivy or other plants to the form. To use dried roses with topiary forms, attach the flowers to follow the outline of the wire frame.

Set your topiary form in an attractive container to fit the season, occasion, or setting, and trim it in whatever colors strike your fancy. The one shown here is quite simple—a moss-covered frame trimmed with roses and ribbons. You could make a more elaborate topiary by starting with a background of small, fine flowers such as grass heads, German statice, or baby's-breath, then adding roses and other flowers. You don't have to cover all of the wires on a topiary frame with dried flowers; if desired, you may wrap ribbon around some of the wires instead. You can also make your own simple forms, including a spiral, from 9-gauge galvanized wire.

Large rose-trimmed topiary forms are striking in a foyer or hall, while smaller ones are perfect for a buffet table, sideboard, mantel, or coffee table. Even smaller topiaries make imaginative markers for place settings or perfect accents where you want just a bit of color.

1. Using an old bowl or other container, mix the plaster of paris with just enough water to give it the consistency of thick cake batter. Mix enough to fill the decorative container to within 1 inch from the top.

2. Pour the wet plaster of paris into the decorative container, let it thicken slightly, then insert the base wire of the topiary form into the center. Make sure the wire base stays straight until the plaster completely hardens. Wash out the mixing bowl as soon as possible. Complete curing of the plaster may take several days, but you can work on the topiary within an hour.

3. Working on a small section at a time, coat the wire frame with hot glue and attach a clump of Spanish or sphagnum moss. Use moss to cover as much of the frame as desired, then lightly wrap the clear fishing line around the moss-covered sections to further secure them. To give the topiary a fuller look, you can hot glue flat sheet moss over the sphagnum. If desired, leave part of the frame undecorated, or wrap it with ¼-inch-wide ribbon, glued in place.

4. Hot glue on the roses in a pattern of your choosing. Include small bows in your design, if desired.

5. To camouflage the plaster of paris, cover the surface with Spanish or sphagnum moss, using hot glue to attach it.

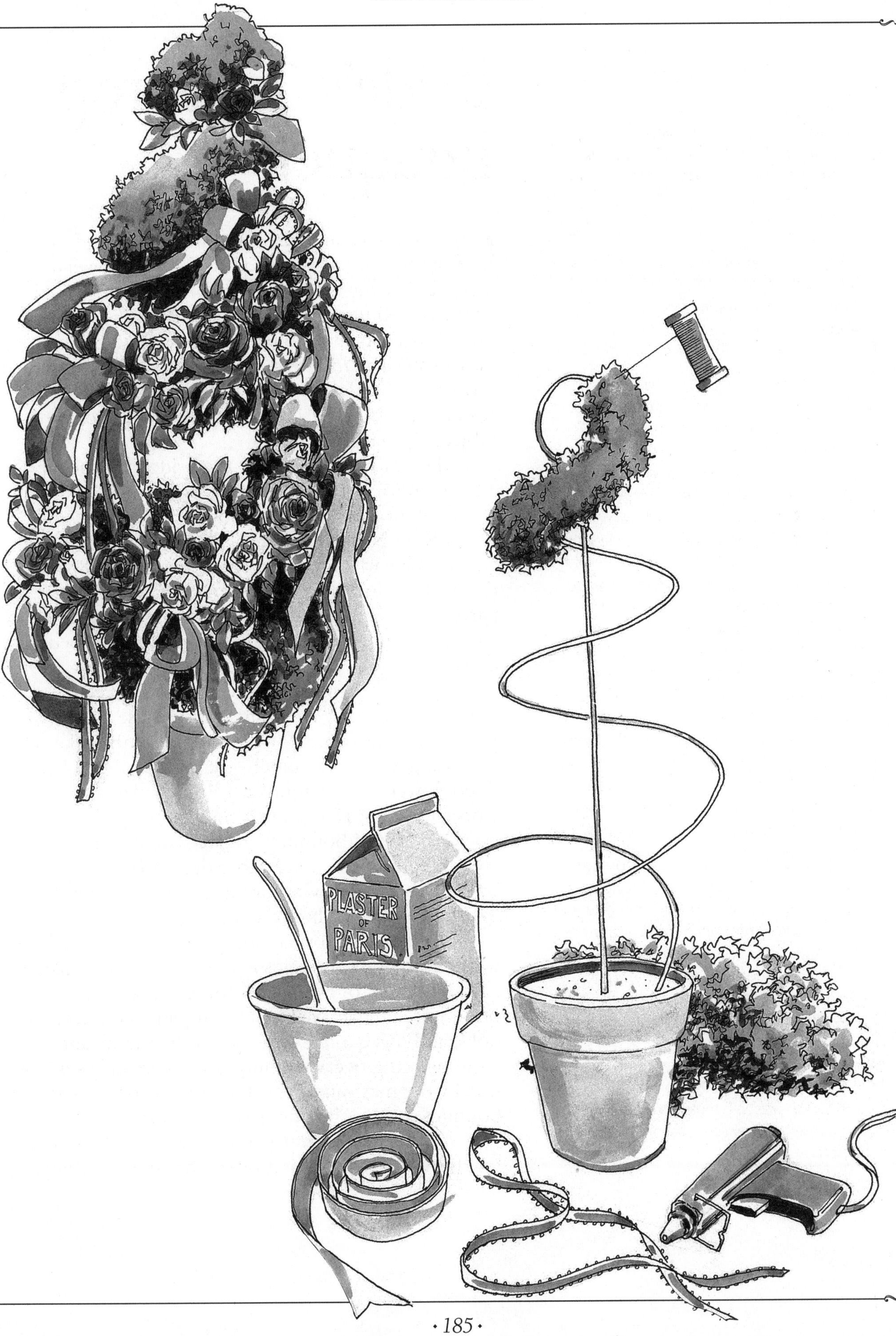
PLASTER
OF
PARIS

1. Wire and tape all of the foliage and flowers. (See "Wiring and Taping Dried Roses" on page 164 for complete instructions.) Wire and tape small flowers into clusters.

2. Hold the wire stems in your non-dominant hand and bind each wire stem into the cluster with floral wire. Start by making a flat-backed spray three-quarters the length of the bouquet; this will be the long, pointed tip. Add more stems, gradually broadening and rounding out the shape at the top and bending the wire stem handle as you go. Since wired stems are covered with sticky floral tape, you won't have to bind in every stem with wire, but you will want to wrap wire around every couple of stems added.

3. Add wired and taped ribbon loops throughout the bouquet, if desired. You may also add a ribbon bow and streamers directly behind the bouquet at the top of the handle. Wrap the completed handle in ribbon.

Variation: If using a plastic bouquet handle fitted with a foam block, begin at the center and work outward, with the bouquet densest at the center and lighter and more open at the edges. Create a teardrop shape, somewhat broader at the top and using longer stems for the bottom of the bouquet. Add wired and taped ribbon loops throughout the bouquet, if desired. You may also add a ribbon bow and streamers directly behind the bouquet at the top of the handle and slide the plastic handle through an X cut in the center of a large piece of gathered tulle netting.

Bride's Teardrop Bouquet

One spectacular way to use dried roses and other flowers is in weddings. Dried flowers make lasting mementos that can be enjoyed long after the wedding day. There are many ways to use dried flowers in a wedding. The bride and bridesmaids can carry informal bouquets, or they can carry Rose Bouquets (page 174), Rose Basket Arrangements (page 169), or Rosebud-Covered Objects (page 176).

For a formal wedding, the bride may choose a large, more intricately made arrangement, like the one described here, with the bridesmaids carrying Dried Rose Nosegays (page 178). A circlet of flowers may be part of a Rose Headdress (page 188) for the bride or for all of the women in the wedding party. Attendants may also wear combs decorated with dried flowers, using the technique described in Rose-Trimmed Objects (page 190).

Use swags of dried flowers with matching bows positioned at the points of the Rose and Herb Garlands (page 240) to ornament the cake and add grace and beauty to the buffet table. Use dried flower combinations for Boutonnieres and Corsages (page 154) and to encircle the punch bowl. Use dried bouquets to decorate the ends of church pews and as candelabra decorations. If the bride wishes to keep her bouquet, you can make a special nosegay for her to toss.

At one time, bridal bouquets were made of white flowers, but today the flowers are just as likely to be pastels or even jewel tones if that's the bride's preference. Make the bouquet so it's easy to hold, and make it large enough to be significant without being overwhelming. Eighteen inches is usually the maximum length of a teardrop, or spray, bouquet such as the one described here.

There are two types of mechanics you can use for this bouquet. One is a plastic bouquet handle fitted with a small block of florist's foam, available at craft stores and florist supply houses. The second mechanic is to wire and tape each stem, combine the wires into clusters, and use the wire clusters to form the handle. This second method takes longer, but it allows you greater design flexibility so that is the one described. For a bouquet made with a purchased bouquet holder, see the variation.

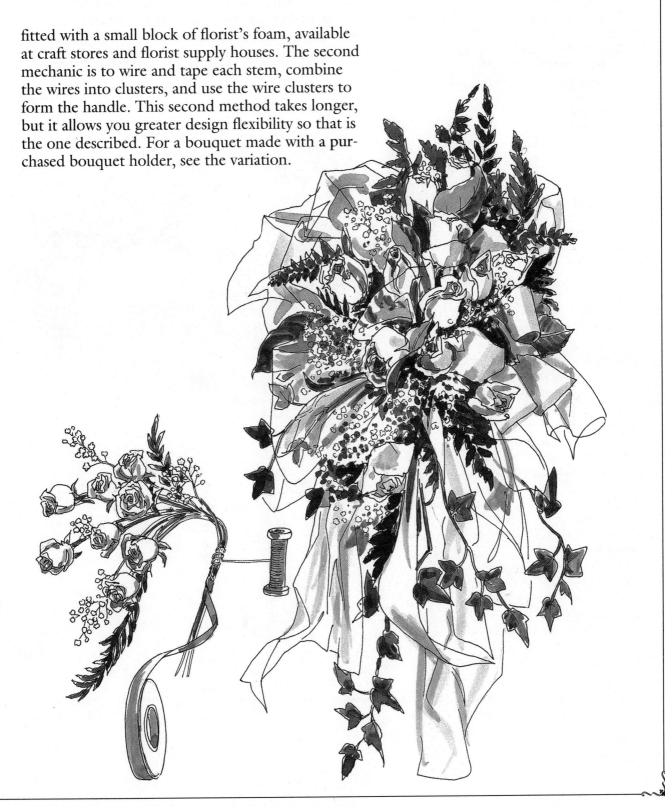

Rose Headdress

A circlet of flowers is a lovely crowning touch in a wedding embellished with dried flowers. The headdress can be worn alone with ribbon streamers or a veil can be attached to the wire before you add the flowers.

MATERIALS

20 to 30 dried roses
Assortment of dried flowers and plant
   materials, such as ferns, ivy,
   baby's-breath, and statice
Flexible cloth tape measure
18-gauge floral spool wire
Wire cutters
Green floral wrapping tape
Bridal veil (optional)
Sewing needle and white thread
   (optional)
Pruning shears
Scissors
22-gauge floral wire
Ribbon

1. Use the tape measure to measure the circumference of the wearer's head. Use the wire cutters to cut two lengths of 18-gauge floral wire, each about equal in length to the head circumference. Make a bend 2 inches from one end of each piece of wire. Interlock the two pieces at the bends, and twist tightly to secure.

2. Add 2 inches to the head circumference measurement and trim the joined wires to this final measurement by removing equal amounts of wire from either end of the whole length. Make a small loop, or "eye," at one end of the wire and a hook at the other. (Do *not* put the hook through the eye yet.) Cover the entire length of wire with floral tape.

3. If desired, attach a veil to the taped wire using a needle and thread.

4. Using the 22-gauge floral wire, wire and tape small bunches of dried flowers, containing at least one rose plus other flowers and foliage in each bunch. (See "Attaching Accent Materials" on page 224 for complete instructions.)

5. Using the 22-gauge floral wire, attach a flower bunch about 1 inch in from one end of the long taped wire, then wrap it with a length of floral tape. Place a second bunch so its flowers cover the stems of the first bunch, and wrap it with floral wire then floral tape to secure. Continue along the length of the long wire, keeping the bunches tightly packed so that no wire shows. When you reach the end, make sure that about 1 inch of uncovered wire still shows.

6. Add ribbon bows and streamers at each end of the wire, where it is bare of floral material. Bend the wire into a circle and connect the hook into the eye.

Roses in a Heart-Shaped Container

MATERIALS

Dried Spanish or sphagnum moss
30 dried roses (or enough to fill your container)
Ribbon (optional)
Hot glue gun with clear glue sticks
Heart-shaped container
Scissors

Roses, more than any other flower, are symbolic of love. In the Victorian language of flowers, more than three dozen different roses had specific love messages or connotations. Even if we no longer recognize these meanings, almost everyone understands the loving message of a gift of roses.

Whether it's a present for yourself or for someone special in your life, a gift combining hearts and roses is appropriate for Valentine's Day, birthdays, anniversaries, Mother's Day, or any time you want to let someone know how much you care.

Be on the lookout for heart-shaped containers. Baskets of various materials and sizes, boxes of china, tin, or wood, coeur à la crème molds, cast-iron muffin pans, and cake pans are the most obvious examples. Once you've filled them with roses, they can be hung on the wall or set on tables, counters, and shelves.

1. Attach a ribbon for hanging, if desired, by either tying or hot gluing a loop of ribbon onto the back of the container. (The method of attachment will depend on the container you have chosen.)

2. If the arrangement is to be permanent or will be hung, hot glue the moss into the container. If the arrangement will be displayed horizontally on a flat surface, just fill the container with moss.

3. Cut the rose stems off just below the heads and hot glue the roses to the moss.

4. Add ribbon bows, if desired.

Rose-Trimmed Objects

One of the most popular ways to use dried flowers is to trim various objects with them. The possibilities are limitless, and you can hot glue materials to a variety of objects. The rose-trimmed basket, napkin ring, and hat shown in the photos on pages 198, 201, and 206 are all fairly simple to make and are perfect for showing off your prize dried roses.

1. Apply a thin layer of moss in a circle around the crown of the hat, attaching with hot glue. Although not strictly necessary, a moss background provides a visually pleasing base for attaching the flowers. (A length of tulle netting attached with hot glue is an attractive alternative to the moss.)

2. Hot glue the filler flowers and foliage onto the moss or tulle, then add the roses and rose leaves in the design of your choice.

3. Hot glue a ribbon bow and streamers onto the back of the hat.

Rose-Trimmed Basket: Apply a thin layer of moss along the top and inside of the basket rim, attaching with hot glue. Hot glue flowers, plant materials, and roses to the moss. Tie a bow to the basket handle, if desired.

Rose-Trimmed Napkin Ring: Hot glue a thin layer of moss to one small section of a napkin ring; this will become the top of the ring. Hot glue filler flowers and plant materials to the center of the moss. Hot glue a single rose to the center.

Objects for Trimming

In gathering objects to trim with roses, use this list to stimulate your thinking:

Basket rims and handles
Bellpulls
Earrings
Garlic or raffia braids
Hair combs
Hand mirrors
Hats
Keepsake boxes
Lampshades
Light-switch covers
Mirror frames
Napkin rings
Picture frames
Pinecone swags
Wall plaques

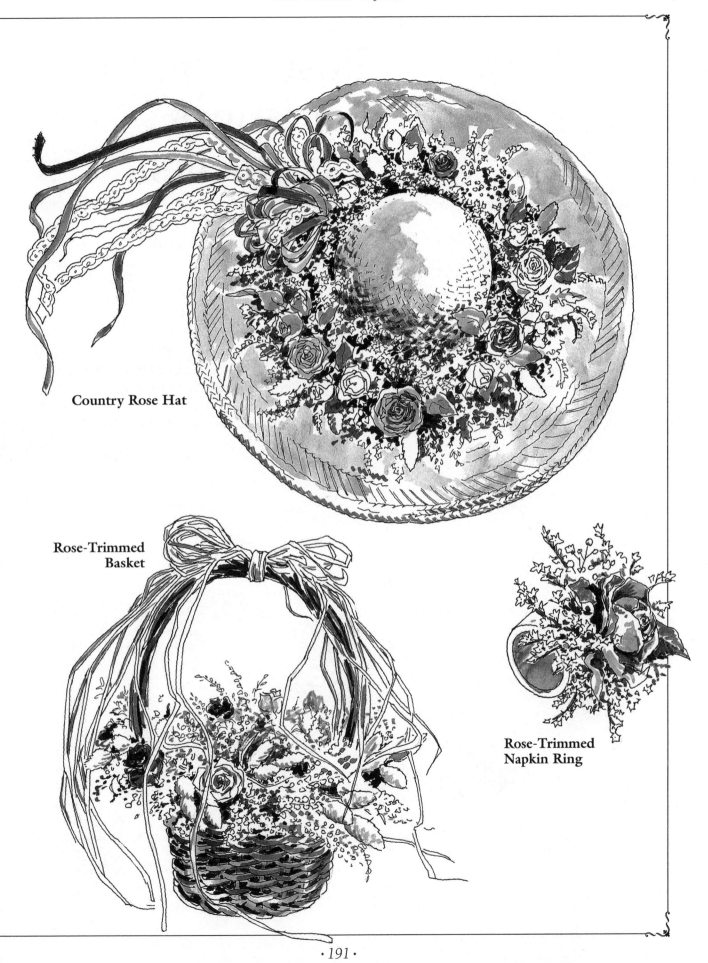

Country Rose Hat

**Rose-Trimmed
Basket**

**Rose-Trimmed
Napkin Ring**

Rose-Trimmed Christmas Ornaments

MATERIALS

Dried rosebuds

Assortment of dried floral materials, such as baby's-breath, German statice, and lamb's-ears

Ribbon

Object to trim, such as a tiny twig wreath, pinecone, pomander, or wooden ornament

Hot glue gun with clear plastic glue sticks

Scissors

Clear plastic craft spray sealer

1. Hot glue a small ribbon loop at the top of the object for hanging.

2. Hot glue the rosebuds and other dried materials onto the object.

3. Spray the completed ornament with the clear plastic craft sealer to keep the dried material from shattering or absorbing moisture.

Variation: You can trim all sorts of objects using the directions above. Try trimming lotus pods, wooden rocking horse ornaments, traditional glass balls, crocheted and starched stars, cookie cutters, tiny wrapped packages, and metallic bows.

For a variation on the standard Christmas tree, you can plan to have a tree that features only handmade rose-trimmed ornaments. Or have holiday visitors choose a handmade ornament as a gift when they stop by. For a thoughtful present, give a box of a dozen rose ornaments to a friend or relative. These ornaments are also good items for children's school projects or church projects, for fund-raising bazaars, or for the whole family to make together at holiday time. For other ornament projects, see Spice Ornaments (on the opposite page), Pasta Angel (page 194), and Pressed-Rose Egg Ornament (page 216).

Spice Ornaments

Spice ornaments are delightfully scented rose-bud-trimmed tree decorations. These spice ornaments can not only be hung on the Christmas tree but also make attractive package trimmings. Or set them around the house to add a spicy fragrance to your rooms.

MATERIALS
(FOR **12** SPICE BALLS)

Dried filler material or foliage, such as German statice, baby's-breath, lamb's-ears, or dusty miller
12 dried rosebuds
1/4 cup of ground cinnamon
1/4 cup of ground cloves
1/4 cup of nutmeg
Glass or stainless steel bowl
Applesauce
Wax paper
1/8-inch-wide ribbon
Scissors
Hot glue gun with clear glue sticks, or white craft or household glue

1. Combine the spices in the bowl. Add just enough applesauce so the mixture reaches the consistency of stiff cookie dough.
2. Shape the mixture into balls about 1 1/2 inches in diameter. Place the balls on wax paper and leave them in a warm place to dry. Turn them over once a day for five to ten days, until completely dry.
3. When fully dry, glue a ribbon loop onto each ball for hanging it.
4. Glue filler material or foliage to the ball, then glue a rosebud in the center of the filler material.

Pasta Angel

You've seen porcelain angels, plastic angels, wire angels, and straw angels. As Christmas approaches, you can find angels everywhere, made of every conceivable material. But here's one you won't find on the store shelves—an angel made entirely of pasta pieces, trimmed with rosebuds and ready to delight all who set eyes upon her. Your friends will be amazed at your inventiveness, but this project is simple enough for a child to do with some adult supervision. Note: Do not use white craft or household glue, which causes the pasta to crack. Pasta will also crack if exposed to cold temperatures.

1. Hot glue a pasta wheel to the wooden ball to form the angel's head and collar.

2. Hot glue a piece of rigatoni vertically beneath the pasta wheel to form the body.

3. To create hair on the angel's head, spread a thin layer of hot glue over the top, sides, and back of the wooden ball and carefully roll it in the soupettes.

4. Hot glue a bow pasta to the back of the rigatoni piece for wings.

5. Hot glue a piece of straight macaroni to the front of each wing to form the arms.

6. Use spray paint to paint the angel white and allow it to dry.

7. Tie the ribbon around the neck of the angel, and then make a loop for hanging.

8. Make a tiny arrangement of rosebuds plus filler flowers, hot gluing the flowers to the arms of the angel, so she looks as though she's holding a bouquet.

Pressed-Rose Glass Hanging

Light is anathema to pressed or dried flowers, causing them to lose their color, and usually we're told to display pressed flower pictures in subdued light. Yet the whole reason for glass hangings is to have sunlight radiate through the rich, vibrant colors of the translucent petals. So take pleasure in the fleeting beauty of a pressed rose glass hanging. By the time the colors fade, you'll probably be inspired to try a new design.

Commercial pressed-flower glass hangings usually have the edges bound by copper foil or lead. Use this method if you have the skill or have access to classes that teach these techniques. Otherwise, use this fun and easy method for creating pressed-rose glass hangings.

MATERIALS

2 to 3 small pressed roses
Assortment of pressed foliage, such as ferns and herb leaves
2 glass microscope slides
Tweezers
Cuticle scissors or fine embroidery scissors
Camel's hair artist's paintbrush or small makeup brush
White craft or household glue
Small saucer
Toothpick
⅛-inch-wide ribbon

1. Placing a microscope slide vertically, develop a design with pressed roses and leaves. Use the tweezers and artist's paintbrush to move the plant material around on the slide. To keep the arrangement as flat as possible, use sharp cuticle scissors or fine embroidery scissors to cut away stems and plant parts that are hidden beneath other floral material. Put the other slide on top and, holding tightly together, turn over.

2. The design is now face-down and can be transferred to the first slide. Squeeze the glue into the saucer. If necessary, thin the glue with water to the consistency of light cream. Use a toothpick to dab tiny amounts of glue on the backs of the flowers and foliage. Place them on the slide, following the design you've planned.

3. Cut a 5-inch length of ribbon. Make a loop with the ribbon and glue it to the top of the flower-decorated slide.

4. Put a drop of glue in each corner of the decorated slide and gently place the second slide on top.

5. When the glue between the slides has dried, put a thin layer of glue around the raw edges of the glass and cover with ribbon. Put a small bow at the base of the glass hanging, if desired.

Candles Trimmed with Pressed Roses

MATERIALS

3 to 7 pressed roses
3 to 5 pressed rose leaves
Assortment of pressed foliage and
    flowers
Tweezers
1 white candle, at least 2 inches in
    diameter
Cuticle scissors or fine embroidery
    scissors
White craft or household glue
Small saucer
Small artist's paintbrush
Water (optional)
½-inch-wide artist's paintbrush

Candlelight weaves its magic spell even more brightly through the translucent glow of rose petals. For this project, use small, delicate pressed miniature roses. Place most of the flowers near the base of the candle. Some people prefer white candles, but experiment with different colors and sizes to see what suits you. For a dramatic effect, display many candles together.

1. Using tweezers to lift and arrange the delicate dried flowers and leaves, place the plant material on the candle in a pleasing design. To keep the arrangement as flat as possible, use sharp cuticle scissors or fine embroidery scissors to cut away stems and plant parts that are hidden beneath other floral material.

2. Pour some glue into a saucer. If necessary, thin it with water to the consistency of light cream.

3. Working with only one piece at a time, lift each flower and leaf with tweezers and lightly brush the underside with glue, using the small artist's paintbrush. Attach to the candle. Continue until you have glued down your original design. Let dry, preferably overnight.

4. After the design is completely dry, cover it with a protective coating of glue. To coat with glue, make up a mixture of glue thinned with water and use the ½-inch paintbrush to paint it over the pressed flowers, extending the glue slightly beyond the pressed material. The glue will dry clear.

Rose Crafts
from Your Garden

Rose crafts from the heart. It's easy to make beautiful Valentine's Day gifts or household accents with roses from your garden. Create a country or Victorian look with a Heart-Shaped Twig Wreath with Roses (page 236), Rose Sachet (page 260), or Roses in a Heart-Shaped Container (page 189).

▲ **Dressing up a dressing table.** Give your bath or bedroom table a new look with this Rose Sachet (page 260) and Rose-Trimmed Basket (page 190). This elaborate-looking basket is actually easy to make when you glue Spanish moss to the basket rim, then attach colorful dried flowers to the moss.

▶ **A stunning centerpiece.** Whether you use fresh or dried roses with other flower accents, the basics of centerpiece design are the same. Find out how to make this colorful Everlasting Centerpiece on page 171.

▲ **Bouquets aren't just for brides.** The color and drama of this dried Rose Bouquet (page 174) can turn a plain door into a focal point. Surprisingly, it's the scarlet-orange roses like 'Tropicana' that dry to this clear red color, rather than red roses, which often darken to purple-black.

▲ **Give your hearth a festive look.** Make your hearth the center of your home with this Rose and Herb Garland (page 240). Use a garland to add color to a plain mantel. You can make different garlands for each season, or add special touches for holiday appeal.

◀ **Roses for party time.** This Twig Bundle with Roses (page 225) is the perfect accent for a table at parties, tea time—or anytime! It looks lovely over a door or window, too.

▶ **A romantic dinner.** Rose-Trimmed Napkin Rings (page 190) and a Mirror Centerpiece Wreath (page 226) set the mood for a meal to remember. You can also hang the wreath, trimmed with roses and colorful dried flowers, to create a mirror that's as beautiful as it is functional.

▲ **A closet full of fragrance.** Spice up your linen drawers and closets with fragrant Rose Sachets (page 260), pomanders, and cinna-
mon-stick bundles (see Rose-Trimmed Christmas Ornaments on
page 192). A Raffia Braid with Roses (page 242) would look as beautiful hanging in a hall, framing a mirror, or making a welcoming statement by a door as it does in this wardrobe. And a ribbon-trimmed
Moss Wreath with Roses (page 239) adds a festive touch wherever
you choose to display it.

▲ **Give this wreath a whirl.** An exciting Starburst Wreath (page 237) adds a swirl of color to a country wall. You could cover the whole wreath with dried roses and other bright flowers, but by covering only half, the contrast between the simple twig-and-moss framework and the dynamic flowers adds sparkle and energy to the arrangement.

▲ **Informal wreaths for all occasions.** Two variations of the basic Vine and Rose Wreath (page 228) show some of the many design possibilities with this easy, versatile style. You can vary the basic wreath shape, as in the figure-eight wreath on the bottom shelf, or vary the amount of wreath base you cover with flowers, as in the pastel-trimmed wreath on the top shelf.

▶ **Making the most of moss.** Use moss as a background to set off dried roses. The Moss Wreath with Roses (page 239) uses moss to accent a bundle of dried roses, lavender, and wheat. Using a moss wreath base, you can create endless variations, like this little bird's-nest wreath with its mock "bird." Cover a picture frame with moss and a tiny rose bouquet (see Rose-Trimmed Objects on page 190) to continue the theme.

◀ **A rose wreath for Christmas.** Roses and evergreens make wonderful holiday partners. Use pastel roses with gilded magnolia leaves and dried boxwood for a southern touch, or mix red roses with fresh pine and fir branches. You'll find more variations on this Rose and Evergreen Wreath on page 234.

▲ **A dried rose wedding.** As beautiful as if they were made from fresh flowers, this Bride's Teardrop Bouquet (page 186) and Rose-Trimmed Hat (page 190) are made from dried garden roses, creating lasting keepsakes. If the bride in your family would prefer to wear flowers in her hair, you'll find instructions for a Rose Headdress on page 188.

▼ **Romance in bloom.** Add a Victorian touch to your bedroom with these lovely, romantic Dried Rose Nosegays (page 178) and Rose Sachets (page 260). To create an attractive assortment, vary the color of the roses, the combinations of other dried flowers, the type of ribbons, and the material used to make the sachets. An old-fashioned brass bouquet holder adds the perfect finishing touch.

▲ **What a way to say "welcome."** There's nothing like a wreath to make a warm and welcoming statement about your home. This Herbal Friendship Wreath (page 232) adds a country look to a rustic door. Dried roses, hydrangea, pearly everlasting, German statice, and other colorful flowers set off an abundance of fragrant herbs like mint, rosemary, and artemisia.

▶ **A wealth of rose crafts.** This dresser shows off some of the many ways you can use roses. Make jewelry (see pages 177 and 264) to wear with your Rose-Trimmed Hat (page 190). You and your friends will love fragrant Rose Petal Candles (page 262). Pressed-Flower Pictures and Wooden Objects Trimmed with Pressed Roses (page 213), like this box, make delightful accents.

◀ **Crafts that reflect your taste.** You'll enjoy projects most if the finished crafts suit your personal style. If you like a formal look, try the Rosebud Pattern Wreath (page 238). If "country" means you, make a Rose-Trimmed Basket (page 190). And if you love to try something different, make an Innovative Arrangement (page 175) like this bouquet in a jar.

▲ **Ornaments and decorations.** Hang these delightful decorations on the Christmas tree, then display them in other seasons on shelves or a table, or in a knicknack cupboard like this. There are dozens of ideas for rose-trimmed ornaments in this book, including the Pasta Angel (page 194), Spice Ornaments (page 193), and Rose-Trimmed Christmas Ornaments (page 192).

A touch of elegance. Dress up your windowsill with a Rose and Flower Topiary (page 182), Dried Rosebud Topiary (page 183), or Massed Arrangement in a Clay Pot (page 170). For the ultimate in refined beauty, place a matching pair on the mantel, sideboard, or dining table.

Wooden Objects Trimmed with Pressed Roses

Decorating furniture and other wooden pieces with pressed flowers is an old craft that offers a simple, inexpensive way to dress up ordinary items. Pressed rose designs complement almost any object, from an antique pine box to a contemporary black lacquer tray. In your attic or basement, at flea markets, or in unfinished-furniture shops, you'll find a wealth of objects to decorate with pressed flowers. Consider mirror and picture frames, bookends, wastebaskets, clocks, jewelry boxes, plaques, napkin holders, light-switch covers, and coasters. You can also decorate metal items, such as trays, canisters, and boxes.

Whether you choose to decorate an object as is or to refinish it before decorating, make sure the final surface is completely smooth, clean, and dry before applying pressed roses. Also use the flattest possible pressed plant material because it will require the least amount of clear sealer to thoroughly cover and protect the design.

MATERIALS

Pressed roses
Pressed rose leaves
Assortment of pressed foliage and
 flowers, such as ferns, grasses,
 herbs, violets, and pansies
Wooden object
Clear lacquer
Fine-quality natural-bristle paintbrush
Sheet of smooth cardboard
Tweezers
Cuticle scissors or fine embroidery
 scissors
Very fine grit sandpaper
Fine steel wool
Tack cloth
Old can or cup (for cleaning brush)
Lacquer thinner

1. To seal the surface of the wood, brush on one coat of lacquer and let it dry.

2. On a separate sheet of smooth cardboard, create the pressed-rose design you wish to impose on the piece. Move and place the flowers and foliage with tweezers. To keep the arrangement as flat as possible, use sharp cuticle scissors or fine embroidery scissors to cut away stems and plant parts that are hidden beneath other floral material.

3. Lightly sand the surface of the wooden object and then rub with fine steel wool. Wipe the piece with a tack cloth, then apply a second coat of lacquer. While the lacquer is still wet, use tweezers to gently move each flower and leaf from the cardboard to the surface of the piece until you have re-created your original design. Let dry.

4. Apply a third coat of lacquer over the entire object, including the pressed materials. Let dry. If some of the pressed roses or other plants protrude, rub the lacquered surface lightly with fine steel wool, being careful to avoid the protruding plants. Brush with a tack cloth and then apply a fourth coat of lacquer.

Variation: Instead of lacquer, you can use decoupage coating or a vinyl resin kit. Just follow the directions on the packaging, adding the pressed roses and other materials at the step suggested by the manufacturer.

Pressed-Rose Picture

MATERIALS

3 to 7 pressed roses

Assortment of pressed plant materials, such as ferns, herbs, and grass seed heads

White or off-white posterboard

X-acto or utility knife

Frame with glass

Tweezers

Camel's hair artist's paintbrush or small makeup brush

Cuticle scissors or fine embroidery scissors

Polaroid camera or paper and pencil

Sheet of stiff cardboard (optional)

White craft or household glue

Small saucer

Toothpick

Glass cleaner and paper towels

Small hammer

Small picture nails or glazing points

Masking tape

Aluminum foil

Brown craft paper

Self-leveling picture hanger or 2 picture-frame screw eyes and picture wire

A pressed-rose picture makes a delightful gift for a friend, especially if the flowers are from his or her garden. Wild roses gathered on vacation and pressed, then added to a pressed picture later, make a charming memento of the trip. For a lovely keepsake, incorporate wedding or party invitations, birth announcements, or special photographs into pressed-flower designs.

Picture-perfect step-by-step. When you create a pressed-flower picture, design it first, then glue it down. Start with the background foliage, then add the roses and other pressed flowers. Finally, add the frame to make sure the picture looks perfect.

1. Use the X-acto or utility knife to cut the posterboard background to size, using the glass from the frame as a guide.

2. Envision your design. Use the tweezers and artist's paintbrush to move the plant materials around on the background. Begin by placing the outer, or framing, flowers and leaves first, using the lightest colored and textured materials, such as tiny rosebuds pressed in profile, single miniature roses pressed flat, fern fronds, grass heads, or other fine, light plant materials. Incorporate larger, darker flowers toward the center and base of the design. Keep the size of the flowers and leaves in scale with each other and the overall size of the picture. To keep the arrangement as flat as possible, use sharp cuticle scissors or fine embroidery scissors to cut away stems and plant parts that are hidden beneath other floral material.

3. Once the design is complete, you may either make a sketch or take a Polaroid photograph and then disassemble the arrangement, or turn the entire design upside down onto a separate sheet. If choosing the latter, place a sheet of stiff cardboard on top of the design, hold the cardboard and the backing tightly together, and turn them over. Carefully remove the background sheet, leaving the reversed rose design on the cardboard.

4. Squeeze the glue into the saucer. If necessary, thin the glue with water to the consistency of light cream. Use a toothpick to dab tiny amounts of glue on the backs of the flowers and foliage. Place them on the background, following the design you've planned. Let the picture dry thoroughly (at least overnight) before framing.

5. Wipe both sides of the frame's glass with glass cleaner and dry well, checking carefully for smudges and lint particles. Lay the glass in the frame. Next, gently lay the pressed-rose picture into the frame. Using the hammer, carefully tap in small picture nails or glazing points to hold the picture in place. Apply masking tape to seal the edge where the cardboard and frame meet.

6. To help seal out moisture, cut a piece of aluminum foil to fit inside the frame and tape it in place with masking tape. Then cut a piece of brown craft paper to cover the back and glue it on.

7. To make a hanger, either attach a single self-leveling hanger at the top back of the frame, or attach two picture-frame screw eyes about one-third of the way down from the top of the back of the frame and thread picture wire between the screws.

Variations: Instead of plain white posterboard, choose the background in a color that complements the roses. Posterboard is an inexpensive choice. Slightly more upscale is mat board, used in picture framing. Or try rice paper and other handmade or unique papers. Also, choose a frame that complements the pressed-flower colors and shapes, the flower design, and the background.

Fabric-Background Pressed Roses: Instead of posterboard or mat board, you can use fabric such as velvet, wool, burlap, felt, grasscloth, matte-finish silk, or moiré as a background for your pressed-flower picture. First cut stiff cardboard to the correct background size, using the glass from the frame as a guide. Then mount the fabric on it by applying a continuous, very narrow bead of white craft or household glue right on the edge of the cardboard and attaching the fabric. Or apply fabric to the cardboard using artist's spray adhesive, which is available at art or craft stores.

MATERIALS

3 to 5 pressed miniature roses

Assortment of pressed flowers and foliage, such as violets, pansies, ferns, and grasses

Assortment of dried flowers and foliage, such as German statice, annual statice, baby's-breath, rose leaves, ferns, and grasses (optional)

Clean eggs

Corsage or hat pin

Bowl

Egg dye (optional)

Hot glue gun with clear glue sticks (optional)

White craft or household glue

Scissors

¼-inch-wide ribbon or decorative braid

Small saucer

Water (optional)

Tweezers

Small artist's paintbrush or toothpick

Thin gold cording

Clear plastic craft spray sealer

Pressed-Rose Egg Ornament

Whether decorated, painted, or filled with miniature scenes, blown eggs have been highly prized for centuries. Perhaps you have access to duck or goose eggs or lovely pale blue Araucana chicken eggs. No matter—even plain white grocery-store eggs become unique ornaments when trimmed with pressed roses and other flowers and leaves. (And don't forget that you can always dye the eggs first!) Egg ornaments can be part of a rose decorating theme at Christmas, the basis of an exceptional Easter-egg tree, or treasured gifts for any occasion.

Miniature roses are in their glory when pressed for this relatively diminutive work. Press them at different stages of development, from bud to full bloom. Also, press some of them with the flowers laid on their sides (in profile) and others face-on. Single roses like 'Single's Better' are ideal for this. Curve stems at different angles and press the tiny leaves, too.

For best results, use eggs that aren't too fresh. Eggs that are a few weeks old are easier to blow than fresh eggs. If you're intimidated by working with eggshells because they seem too fragile, consider using egg gourds instead.

1. Allow eggs to come to room temperature. With the pin, make a ⅟₁₆-inch-wide hole at one end of the egg. Make a ³⁄₁₆-inch-wide hole at the other end. Pierce the yolk with the pin and shake the egg.

2. Place your mouth over the smaller hole and blow the white and yolk into a bowl. Rinse the egg by filling the empty shell with water, shaking, and blowing out the water. Set the shell upright in an egg carton to dry. If you plan to dye the eggs, do so now, following package directions, then dry them before proceeding to Step 3.

3. Use the scissors to cut a piece of ribbon or braid long enough to go around the egg lengthwise. Using either the hot glue or white craft glue, glue the ribbon or braid lengthwise around the egg, covering the holes.

4. Pour some white craft glue into a saucer. If necessary, thin the glue with water until it is the consistency of light cream. With tweezers, lay the pressed flowers on the egg in a pleasing design. With a brush or toothpick, lightly coat the underside of the dried materials and attach them to the front and back of the egg, using tweezers to handle the flowers and leaves, until you have re-created your original design. Let the egg dry thoroughly, preferably overnight.

5. Cut a 6-inch length of the gold cord, make a loop with it, and hot glue the loop to the top of the egg as a hanger. If desired, trim the top of the egg with dried flowers and herbs, attached with white glue or hot glue.

6. Spray the entire surface of the egg with clear plastic craft sealer.

Pressed-Rose Stationery and Bookmark

MATERIALS

Assortment of pressed miniature roses, rosebuds, and rose leaves

Assortment of pressed flowers and leaves

Plain note cards, paper, or heavy stock

Cuticle scissors or fine embroidery scissors

Pencil (optional)

White craft or household glue

Small saucer

Water (optional)

Tweezers

Small artist's paintbrush

Clear self-sticking plastic sheets (optional)

Scissors

1. On the paper you've selected, place the pressed flowers in your own design. To keep the arrangement as flat as possible, use sharp cuticle scissors or fine embroidery scissors to cut away stems and plant parts that are hidden beneath other floral material. Use a ruler and pencil, if necessary, to mark the placement of the flowers.

2. Pour some white craft glue into a saucer. If necessary, thin the glue with water until it is the consistency of light cream. Use tweezers to gently lift each flower and leaf and lightly brush the back with diluted white glue. Set the plant material in place. Allow the decorated paper to dry thoroughly, preferably overnight.

3. You can use the paper as is or protect it with clear plastic. To do so, cut a piece of clear, self-sticking plastic $\frac{1}{2}$ inch or so larger than the decorated paper. Remove the backing from the self-sticking plastic, center it over the project, and press it in place. Trim the edges with scissors. (Note: If you decide to cover it with clear plastic, you will either have to write on it before covering it with the plastic or you will have to use a permanent marking pen to write on top of the plastic.)

Handmade greeting cards for special occasions, notepaper, trimmed envelopes, bookmarks, and place cards readily become one-of-a-kind heirlooms and treasured gifts when trimmed with pressed miniature roses, other flowers, and leaves. To enhance the item even more, add a message or quote in calligraphy.

A box of plain notepaper is a good starting point. Create designs across the top, along the side, or at the bottom, making a nosegay, swag, crescent, right-angle, or straight-line design.

Before decorating note cards for mailing, make sure they follow postal size restrictions. Put the design on the front of the note cards or cut out a window for showcasing the design. If you'd like to decorate place cards, the traditional size is 3 by 2 inches, folded to 1½ by 2 inches. An average size for a bookmark is 1½ by 5 inches. Craft, art supply, and stationery stores have a variety of beautiful papers and card stocks. (For mail-order suppliers, see "Rose Resources" beginning on page 282.)

For a gracious finishing touch on a gift of rose-decorated stationery, trim the stationery box or writing portfolio to match the contents. Or decorate a heart-shaped candy box to hold stamps and return-address labels.

Pressed-Rose Bookmark: Cut a 2- by 6-inch piece of heavy-stock paper and fold it in half lengthwise. Using a hole puncher, punch a hole through both layers near the top. Glue the bookmark shut and create your pressed-rose design on the front, gluing on the materials as described above. If you like, cover both the front and back with clear self-sticking plastic to make it durable. Tie a 2-inch-long piece of ribbon through the hole.

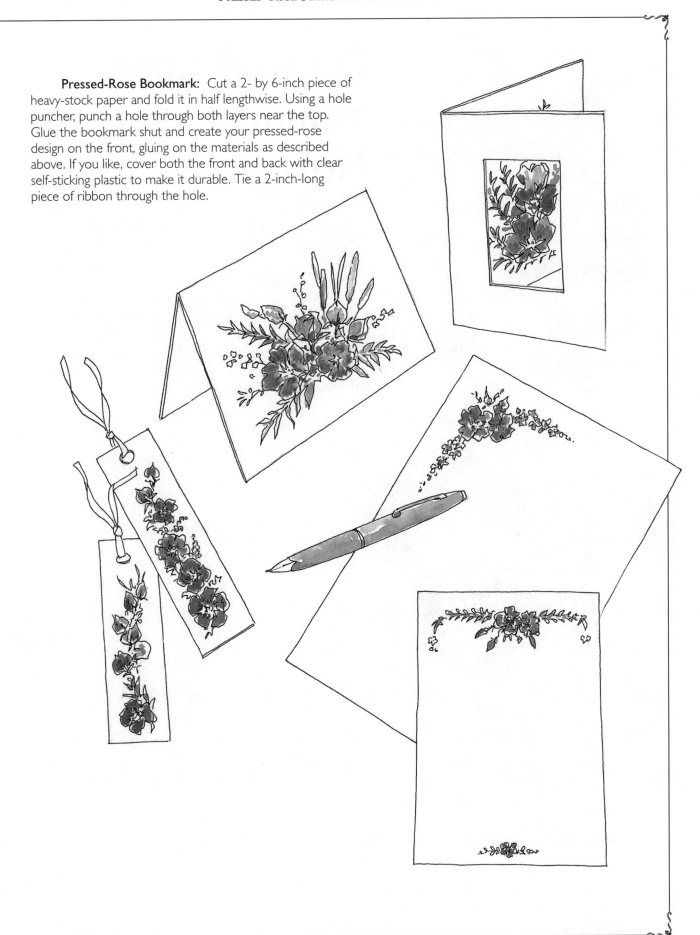

MATERIALS

Assortment of pressed miniature
    roses, rosebuds, and rose leaves
Assortment of pressed flowers and
    foliage, such as violets, pansies,
    ferns, and grasses
Heavy card stock
Mat or X-Acto knife
Metal ruler
Artist's template of circles and ovals
    or a compass
Scissors
Pregathered lace
Parchment or rice paper
Pencil
White craft or household glue
Small saucer
Water (optional)
Small artist's paintbrush or toothpick
Clear acetate

Pressed-Rose Valentine and Nosegay Cards

Roses and Valentine's Day are the perfect romantic match. Your loved ones will treasure a handmade valentine, perhaps framing the card to display and enjoy for years to come.

    With the range of papers available, especially by mail-order, as well as the assortment of lace, tulle netting, and other trims offered at craft and fabric stores, you don't ever have to make two cards alike. Feel free to experiment and try different shapes, sizes, and colors.

Pressed-Rose Valentine

Pressed-Rose Nosegay Card

1. Use the knife and metal ruler to cut a 7- by 14-inch piece of card stock. Crease and fold it in half. Using the template or a compass, draw a 4½-inch diameter circle in the center of the front. Cut this out with the knife.

2. Use the scissors to cut a length of pregathered lace to fit around the circumference of the opening. Glue in place on the outside of the card.

3. Cut a piece of parchment or rice paper the same size as the card. Crease and fold it in half. Slide it inside the card stock and, with a pencil, lightly draw a heart shape on the parchment or rice paper so that it is centered in the card's circular window. Remove the parchment or rice paper.

4. Pour some white craft glue into a saucer. If necessary, thin the glue with water until it is the consistency of light cream. Using an artist's brush or toothpick to apply glue, attach several rows of pressed miniature rosebuds along the heart outline, adding other pressed flowers and leaves as desired.

5. Cut a 5-inch diameter circle of acetate. Run a bead of glue along the circumference and place the acetate behind the window on the inside of the card stock.

6. Glue the front of the rosebud-decorated parchment to the inside of the card stock, making sure that the heart design is visible through the acetate window. Leave the right-hand parchment page loose.

Pressed-Rose Nosegay Card: Use the knife and metal ruler to cut a 6- by 12-inch piece of card stock. Crease and fold it in half. Then cut a 3½-inch square from the center of the card. Cut a piece of parchment or rice paper the same size as the card, and crease and fold it. Slide it inside the card stock and, with a pencil, lightly draw a square on the parchment so that it is centered in the card's window. Remove the parchment. Cut a 4-inch square of white tulle. Run a bead of glue around the perimeter and place the tulle behind the window on the inside of the card stock. Following the directions above, glue the pressed miniature roses, flowers, and leaves to the center of the square marked on the parchment, creating a small nosegay arrangement. Glue a bow and streamers made from ⅟₁₆-inch-wide ribbon just below the nosegay. Glue the front of the rose-decorated parchment to the inside front of the card stock, making sure the nosegay is visible through the tulle-covered window. Leave the right-hand parchment page loose.

MATERIALS

Assortment of pressed roses, rosebuds, and rose leaves

Assortment of pressed flowers and foliage, such as violets, pansies, ferns, and grasses

Tweezers

Lampshade

Cuticle scissors or fine embroidery scissors

White craft or household glue

Small saucer

Water (optional)

Small artist's brush or toothpick

Clear plastic craft spray sealer

Pressed-Rose Lampshade

If you're tired of looking at plain-Jane lampshades in your home, create a lovely new look by trimming them with pressed roses and other flowers. Some mail-order catalogs even offer lampshades and other objects specifically made for decorating with pressed flowers, including vanity sets, clear glass paperweights, wooden and glass trays, trinket boxes, decorative doorplates, and jewelry. (For addresses of mail-order suppliers, see "Rose Resources" beginning on page 282.) You can also find some of these items at local craft stores. The directions here are for a decorated lampshade, but you can follow the same instructions to decorate any of the objects mentioned above. Spray lampshades and jewelry with clear plastic craft sealer when done. For information on decorating and finishing wooden objects, see "Wooden Objects Trimmed with Pressed Roses" on page 213.

1. With tweezers, place the pressed roses, leaves, and other flowers on the lampshade in a pleasing design. To keep the arrangement as flat as possible, use sharp cuticle scissors or fine embroidery scissors to cut away stems and plant parts that are hidden beneath other floral material.

2. Pour some white craft glue into a saucer. If necessary, thin the glue with water until it is the consistency of light cream.

3. Use tweezers to gently lift each flower and leaf and lightly brush the back with diluted white glue. Set the plant material in place. Allow the decorated lampshade to dry thoroughly.

4. Spray the entire surface of the lampshade with clear plastic craft sealer.

Chapter 8

Rose Wreaths and Garlands

ROM ANCIENT PAINTINGS AND sculptures, we know that wreaths and garlands—particularly those that feature roses—have been around for a very long time. Wreaths are still among the most popular flower crafts. As either a pastime or a vocation, many people enjoy the inventive aspects of making wreaths—creating beautiful and original decorations with their own hands. Wreaths and garlands now adorn every room of the house at every season of the year. Whether you prefer wreaths that are simple and classic or ones that are intricate and elaborate, you will find that making wreaths and garlands sparks your creativity and allows you to enjoy the beauty of flowers year-round.

To make an endless array of different wreaths and garlands, all you need are a few basic tools and supplies combined with step-by-step instructions on the core techniques involved. You can make exact copies of the wreaths and garlands shown in this chapter, or you can use them as a springboard for your imagination.

As you explore the craft of wreathmaking, be open to new ideas and experimentation. Look for ideas from a variety of sources, such as magazines, books, craft and decorating shops, art and craft shows, and window displays. Keep a notebook with suggestions and sketches. Consider trying unusual combinations of colors and materials. You will find that

your experiments lead to the creation of something beautiful and unique.

TOOLS AND SUPPLIES

The tools and supplies you'll need to make wreaths and garlands include pruning shears, scissors, a knife, wire cutters, a hot glue gun with clear glue sticks, white craft or household glue, floral spool (paddle) wire, floral wrapping tape, floral picks, and an assortment of ribbons. You can substitute waxed twine, specially made for winding wreaths, for the floral spool wire. (See "Tools and Supplies" on page 142 for detailed descriptions of these items.)

You can buy wreath bases—the forms you attach plant materials to—or make them at home. Commercially available wreath bases come in a range of sizes and materials, including straw, excelsior, vine, wire, extruded foam, and polystyrene. Most wreath bases are round, but heart-shaped ones are also popular. Moss-trimmed wire wreath bases and raffia braids are usually made at home. If you have a garden or have access to woods, it's easy to make your own vine, twig, and evergreen wreath bases, too. To make garlands, you don't need to buy or make bases at all. Just attach your clusters of dried flowers or leaves directly to a piece of rope or wire, and you're done!

Prepare the roses you'll use to decorate wreaths and garlands by air drying or desiccant drying. (For a detailed discussion of these techniques, see Chapter 6, beginning on page 157.) You can choose any number of other flowers, leaves, cones, seeds, pods, and additional items to make your creations one-of-a-kind. For suggestions on the best plants to use for wreath-making, see page 226.

USING WREATHS AND GARLANDS

In addition to the obvious places for wreaths, such as on doors and over mantels, think about other places where a wreath would enhance your environment. How about including a wreath as part of a grouping of pictures or as a frame for a picture or a mirror? Let the wreath design and placement evoke moods. Be whimsical.

Don't forget that wreaths set flat on a table can encircle a hurricane-shaded candle or a punch bowl. You can even use candles as an accent piece, attaching them to the wreath itself.

Besides putting garlands on mantels and over doors and windows and looping them around staircase banisters and finials, try one at the head of a bed draped on the headboard or hanging on the wall. Use a garland to frame a grouping of pictures or a seating area; drape one around a mirror; festoon ceiling beams with a garland or hang it around a chandelier. As a table decoration, a garland may be laid on the table as a centerpiece or attached in swags around the perimeter of the table. A dried garland is especially lovely around the perimeters of buffet tables at weddings and other parties.

Attaching Accent Materials

You can attach accent materials to a wreath in several ways. In addition to the simple method of hot gluing flower heads and small pods and cones directly, there are two other methods that are particularly useful: picking and wiring.

Picking is useful when you have large and/or heavy accent materials. To attach such materials to the wreath base, you simply wrap the wire of a floral pick around the base or stem of the accent material, and, if desired, wrap with green floral wrapping tape to bind the wire, stems, and pick together. Insert the pick into the wreath base. To secure the pick, put a small amount of hot glue around the pick where it meets the wreath base. Floral picks are also handy when you want to group several flowers into small bouquets.

Wiring is best for flowers with delicate stems or stems that have been cut too short. With this method, you will build a new stem for the flower with wire and floral tape. First, determine how long you want your new stem to be, and cut a piece of 22-gauge floral wire that is twice as long. Bend the wire into a hairpin shape. Either insert the wire through the base of the flower, down through the center, or lay it alongside the base. Then, starting at the base of the flower, begin wrapping the wire with green floral wrapping tape. Twirl the new "stem" and stretch the tape as you work. Tear off the tape when you reach the end of the stem. To attach the wired flower to the wreath base, just stick the wire stem into the base. To secure it, put a small amount of hot glue around the stem where it meets the base.

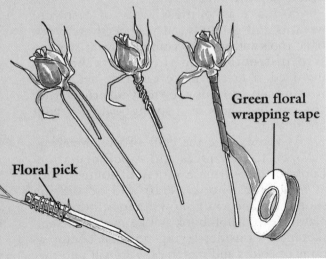

Green floral wrapping tape

Floral pick

Twig Bundle with Roses

Homemade twig bundles give you the opportunity to use branches from a variety of trees and shrubs. For uniqueness, look for interesting or colorful bark, unusually shaped branches, or other pleasing features. Some favorite trees and shrubs for twig bundles include river and white birches, contorted willow, contorted hazelnut, larch, alder, and poplar.

Twig bundles are a fast and free way to make a base for dried flowers, and they look as if you spent either lots of money or lots of time. Because of their versatility, you can use them just about anywhere, from highlighting a doorway or picture to accenting a mantel, tabletop, sideboard, or shelf.

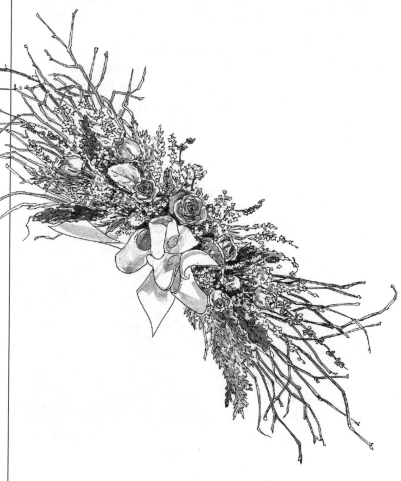

MATERIALS

30 to 40 twigs or branches, about 12 to 18 inches long

Assortment of dried filler material, such as artemisia, baby's-breath, statice, goldenrod, pearly everlasting, wheat, and ornamental grass seed heads

10 to 12 dried roses

Assortment of dried flowers, such as globe amaranths, strawflowers, celosia, and cockscomb

22-gauge floral wire

Wire cutters

Scissors

Hot glue gun with clear glue sticks

Ribbon

Clear plastic craft spray sealer

1. Make two equal bundles of twigs or branches. Overlap the cut ends, meshing the bundles together. Arrange so the outer ends form an open, airy, three-dimensional shape. Use floral wire to securely wire the cut ends together. Trim the ends of the wire with the wire cutters.

2. To make a hanger for your twig bundle, cut a 6-inch length of floral wire and bend it into a hairpin shape. Twist the ends together, creating a loop. Continue twisting until the loop is only about 1 inch long. Attach the cut ends of the wire behind the center where the bundles overlap.

3. Use the scissors to trim the stems of the filler material to the length you desire. To decorate the bundles, hot glue or wire the background of filler material onto the twig bundle. Accent this with the roses and other plant materials, attaching with hot glue.

4. Tie a bow and attach with glue in the center of the bundle, as shown in the photo on page 200. For complete instructions on how to make a bow, see "How to Tie a Perfect Bow" on page 243.

5. Spray the completed project with clear plastic craft sealer to keep the dried material from shattering or absorbing moisture.

MATERIALS

Enough dried Spanish or sphagnum
   moss to cover wreath base

12 to 18 dried rosebuds

Dried strawflowers and other
   everlastings

Dried German statice, baby's-breath,
   or asparagus fern

Heart-shaped extruded polystyrene
   wreath base, 6 to 10 inches across

Hot glue gun with clear glue sticks

Scissors

Ribbon (optional)

Lace (optional)

Clear plastic craft spray sealer

Dried Rose and Everlasting Wreath

Few floral creations are as beautiful as a wreath made of a wealth of dried roses and other colorful dried flowers. Everlastings are flowers that are naturally papery so that very little time or effort is needed for drying. Some of the most widely grown and used everlastings include strawflower, globe amaranth, love-in-a-mist seedpods, bells-of-Ireland, cockscomb, statice, hydrangea, baby's-breath, Chinese lantern, globe thistle, sea holly, heather, money plant, immortelle, pearly everlasting, starflower, winged everlasting, golden ageratum, and yarrow. These, combined with dried roses, provide a marvelous palette of colors and textures with which to work.

In choosing roses to use, keep the size in scale with the other flowers. This wreath can be made in various sizes and shapes. You can also use the same floral materials in topiaries, picture and mirror frames, kissing balls, and other covered items.

1. To soften and conceal the wreath base, lightly cover it with pieces of moss, attaching them with hot glue.

2. Use scissors to cut the stems from the rosebuds and single-blossomed flowers. For cluster-type flowers such as baby's-breath, break or cut the heads into pieces. Break foliage such as the asparagus fern into small pieces.

3. Starting on the inside of the wreath, begin hot gluing the flowers and foliage in place until plant material covers everything but the back.

4. Trim the wreath with ribbon, lace, or other materials, if desired. If desired, surround the outside of the wreath with pregathered lace and hot glue it to the back. Then attach a bow made of lace and ribbons in complementary colors. (For complete instructions on how to make a bow, see "How to Tie a Perfect Bow" on page 243.)

5. Spray the completed wreath with clear plastic craft sealer to keep the dried material from shattering or absorbing moisture.

Mirror Centerpiece Wreath: Glue an extruded polystyrene wreath base onto the same size round mirror. Decorate as described above. This wreath can be used as a table centerpiece or hung on a wall.

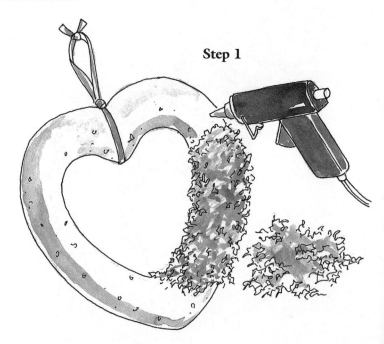

Step 1

Step 3

Heart-Shaped Wreath

Mirror Centerpiece Wreath

MATERIALS

Vine trimmings, about 30 to 40 feet
    total length
Dried roses
Assortment of dried flowers and plant
    materials, such as annual statice,
    baby's-breath, asparagus fern,
    and yarrows
Large tub or sink of warm water
Pruning shears
Bucket or other cylindrical object
    (optional)
22-gauge floral wire (optional)
Wire cutters (optional)
Hot glue gun with clear glue sticks
Ribbon (optional)

Vine and Rose Wreath

Grapevines form the basis for the most easily made and inexpensive wreaths. You can also use other vines to make wreaths: Honeysuckle is good for small, fine-textured wreaths, while wisteria has more bulk so it's good for larger wreaths.

If you grow grapes, you can gather material for your grapevine wreaths when you prune your grapes in mid- to late winter before the sap begins to flow. Save the trimmings to use throughout the year as needed. If wild grapes grow on your property, you can collect their vines in the same manner. If you don't have grapes growing on your property, ask around. Many people would be happy to let you cut wild vines. And people who grow grapes for the fruit are often happy to part with their trimmings.

Although vine wreaths can be covered completely with flowers, as straw wreaths usually are, they are often more attractive and elegant if the wreath base shows through. You can combine flowers, cones, seedpods, ribbon, and grasses together on a vine wreath in countless ways.

1. Soak the vines for 30 minutes in the warm water to increase pliability.

2. Make a 12-inch circle with a vine, adding more pieces as necessary to get the thickness you want—about 12 times around is the average. Use the pruning shears to cut the individual vines to the length you need. If you have trouble making a perfect circle, wrap the vines around a bucket or other cylindrical object. Tuck in the vine ends to secure, or tie in several places with the floral wire, using the wire cutters to trim off the ends.

3. Attach wired clusters of roses and other dried flowers at intervals around the wreath, or decorate by hot gluing roses and flowers to vine wreath as desired.

4. Finish by trimming the wreath with a fancy bow, if desired. (For complete instructions on how to make a bow, see "How to Tie a Perfect Bow" on page 243.)

Wheat and Roses Wreath: Tie small bunches of wheat and informal clusters of roses to the wreath with raffia.

Bird's Nest Wreath: Tuck small pieces of moss, rose leaves, and roses in among the vines, putting most near the bottom. Then attach a found or purchased bird's nest to one side with several wooden or marble eggs in the nest.

Ribbons and Roses Wreath: Attach a bow to the wreath and thread and loop a length of ribbon in and out of the vine stems. Attach clusters of roses, baby's-breath, and other dried flowers at intervals around the wreath.

Baby Roses Wreath: Dry clusters of polyantha roses, such as 'The Fairy', or small-flowered floribundas like 'Eutin', keeping some of the foliage attached. Then attach them to the base with hot glue or floral wire in a loose, open, informal manner.

Festive Christmas Wreath: For the Christmas holidays, spray the wreath white, gold, or silver. Attach a length of tinsel stars along a thin wire and intertwine them with the vine, or glue on airy painted seed heads. Make small nosegays of roses and other flowers backed with gold doilies and tied with gold ribbon. Attach some of the nosegays around the wreath, adding various glass ball ornaments as well. Tiny wrapped packages and glitter-sprayed baby's-breath may also be used.

Simple Flowered Vine Wreath: Use two crisscrossing pieces of wire to attach a small block of brown floral foam to the wreath. Cover the foam with dried Spanish or sphagnum moss, and create a design extending across the base of the wreath.

Rosy Heart Wreath: Decorate a purchased or homemade heart-shaped vine wreath with moss, ferns, roses, sprigs of rose hips, and flowers, placing a cluster at the throat of the heart, another to one side of the point, and a third halfway up the other side. Thread ribbons around the wreath.

Autumn Hues Wreath: Wire and attach small gourds, sprigs of rose hips, Chinese lanterns, roses, cockscombs, or other fall-inspired items to a vine wreath.

Royal Vine Wreath: For a delicate effect, wire clusters of dried 'Silver King' artemisia and flat-leaved eucalyptus to the wreath and accent with roses and assorted flowers.

Wonderful One-Color Wreath: Make a monochromatic wreath with dried grasses, bleached pods and cones, and cream-colored roses.

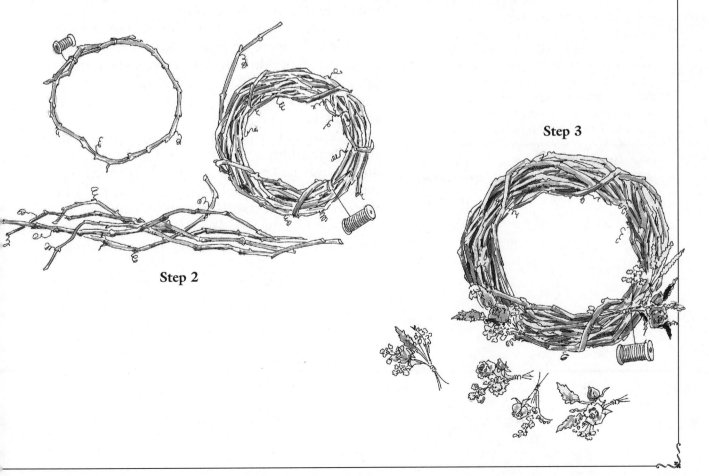

Step 2

Step 3

Yarrow and Rose Wreath

1. To make a hanger for the wreath, put a dime-size blob of hot glue on the back of the wreath base. Stick a floral pin through the glue and into the base at an angle, with the curved side up. Leave about ½ inch of the pin sticking out of the wreath. Allow to dry.

2. Use scissors to cut the stems from the yarrow flower heads to 1 inch or shorter. You can use floral pins to attach the flower heads to the wreath, or you can use one of the methods described in "Attaching Accent Materials" on page 224. Overlap the flower heads slightly. Cover as much of the wreath with yarrow as desired, staggering the heads so that they do not end up in rows.

3. Decorate with roses and assorted plant material as desired. (See "Attaching Accent Materials" for methods of attaching them.) Trim with a bow, if desired. (For complete instructions on how to make a bow, see "How to Tie a Perfect Bow" on page 243.)

4. Spray the completed wreath with clear plastic craft sealer to keep the dried material from shattering or absorbing moisture.

People have used yarrow as a healing herb for more than 2,500 years. Supposedly, Achilles used yarrow leaves during the Trojan War to stop the bleeding of his soldiers' wounds. Today, some people still recommend the herb as a wound treatment, but many gardeners grow this perennial simply as an ornamental plant. A low-maintenance plant, yarrow withstands a wide range of soil types and thrives in full sun and dry soil. Insects and diseases are seldom a problem.

Best of all for those who love garden crafts, yarrow yields an abundance of flowers that look beautiful in both fresh and dried arrangements. Yarrows bear large, flat clusters of tiny flowers in shades of white, rose, pink, peach, cerise, red, bronze, lavender, yellow, and gold atop 2- to 4-foot-tall stems. The pungently scented foliage is usually gray-green and fernlike.

To dry yarrow, pick the flowers just as they become fully open, tie them in loose bunches, and air dry them upside down in a dark, well-ventilated place. Yarrows bloom in June and July, and if you cut the flower heads, the plants will often bloom again later.

Although yarrow's long, sturdy stems make it a welcome addition to bouquets, yarrow's large flowers also are excellent for quickly covering the surface of a wreath. Red, orange, yellow, and white roses combine spectacularly with the golden yarrows, while the wonderful new pastel cultivars of yarrow blend with just about every color of rose.

Step 2

Step 3

Herbal Friendship Wreath

MATERIALS

Dried 'Silver King' artemisia, baby's-breath, German statice, goldenrod, and/or pearly everlasting
12 to 16 dried roses
8 to 12 stems of dried hydrangea
Assortment of dried herbs, leaves, and flowers, such as mint, oregano, marjoram, rosemary, thyme, and parsley
Straw wreath base, 12 inches in diameter
Hot glue gun with clear glue sticks
Floral pins
Floral picks (optional)
22-gauge floral wire (optional)
Green floral wrapping tape (optional)
Scissors
Clear plastic craft spray sealer

1. To make a hanger for the wreath, put a dime-size blob of hot glue on the back of the wreath base. Stick a floral pin through the glue and into the base at an angle, with the curved side up. Leave about ½ inch of the pin sticking out of the wreath. Allow to dry.

2. Use scissors to cut the stems of the artemesia, baby's-breath, German statice, goldenrod, or pearly everlasting to 3 inches long. Gather into bundles composed of three to five stems. Use all one plant material or a combination.

3. Attach each bundle of plant material to the wreath base with a floral pin or by inserting a floral pick or wire stem. (See "Attaching Accent Materials" on page 224.) Start on the inside of the wreath and work in one direction, using the flowers of one cluster to overlap and cover the stems of the previous cluster. When you arrive at your starting place, gently lift the first cluster and tuck in the stems of the last. Cover the front of the wreath and, finally, the outside edge, following the same procedure.

4. Add the roses, hydrangeas, herbs, and any other dried plant material as desired, using hot glue.

5. Spray the completed wreath with clear plastic craft sealer to keep the dried material from shattering or absorbing moisture.

Much of our fascination with herbs and roses comes from their lovely or intriguing fragrance. And for centuries, people have been beguiled by the symbolic meanings of these plants. The Medieval, Renaissance, and Victorian eras each contributed meanings to the language of flowers. For example, in Victorian times, the rose symbolized love and beauty and a purple violet told another, "You occupy my thoughts."

Today, it's easy and fun to create herb-and-flower wreaths that will fill a room with subtle fragrance as well as convey thoughtful sentiments. Lush and lavish, these wreaths adorned with dried roses and herbs not only will enhance your home but also will carry messages of love, loyalty, devotion, or whatever emotion you wish to express to friends near or far. They will make treasured gifts for birthdays, anniversaries, weddings, and housewarmings.

A Floral Dictionary

People have always spoken to each other with flowers. We send flowers to cheer loved ones who have taken ill, to romance the special person in our life, and to congratulate friends on their special accomplishments. But in the 1800s, each flower had its own special meaning, and people gave specific flowers to express specific thoughts. By far the rose had the most meanings. If you'd like to make a wreath with a built-in message, use the following list from the 1857 classic *Language of Flowers* to find the meanings of some of the flowers and herbs most often used in wreathmaking today.

Rose: Love

Cabbage rose: Ambassador of love.

Full red rose: Beauty.

Full white rose: I *am* worthy of you.

Deep red rose: Bashful shame.

Red rosebud: You are young and beautiful.

Burgundy rose: Unconscious beauty.

Yellow rose: Jealousy; decrease of love.

Carolina rose: Love is dangerous.

Austrian rose: Thou art all that is lovely.

Bridal rose: Happy love.

White and red rose together: Unity.

Ambrosia: Love returned.

Coriander: Concealed merit.

Dahlia: Instability.

Globe amaranth: Unchangeable.

Lavender: Distrust.

Love-in-a-mist: Perplexity.

Marjoram: Blushes.

Mint: Virtue.

Money plant, honesty: Honesty; sincerity.

Peony: Shame; bashfulness.

Rosemary: Your presence revives me; remembrance.

Rue: Disdain.

Sage: Esteem; domestic virtues.

Thyme: Activity.

Vervain: Enchantment.

Zinnia: Thoughts of absent friends.

Materials

Dried filler material, such as artemesia, baby's-breath, statice, goldenrod, wheat, or ornamental grass seed heads (optional)

8 to 12 dried roses

Assortment of dried plant materials, such as cones and seedpods (optional)

Scissors

22-gauge floral wire

Wire cutters

Boxwood, fir, pine, spruce, or juniper wreath, 14 inches in diameter

5 to 7 Christmas ornaments (optional)

Wire ornament hangers (optional)

Ribbon (optional)

Rose and Evergreen Wreath

This year, jazz up your traditional evergreen wreath with roses. One festive rose-and-evergreen wreath is described below, but there are plenty of beautiful alternatives. Whatever design you choose, roses will add a splash of color and uniqueness to your holiday wreath. Hang it on your front door to welcome friends and family into your home.

1. If desired, add filler material to the wreath before accenting it with roses. To do this, begin by cutting the stems of the filler material to 3 to 5 inches long, using the scissors. Separate the stems into bundles of three to five stems.

2. Using wire cutters, cut several 3- to 5-inch lengths of floral wire. To attach each bundle of filler to the wreath, wrap a piece of floral wire around the stems and around a piece of the evergreen wreath, then twist the ends of the wire together in the back of the wreath to secure. Tuck the wire ends into the evergreen to hide them, making sure the ends of the wires can't be seen from the front of the wreath.

3. Accent the wreath with roses. Add pinecones and other materials, if desired. (See "Attaching Accent Materials" on page 224 for methods of attaching them.)

4. For a festive look, wire on ornaments. To do this, slip a 3- to 5-inch-long piece of floral wire through each ornament's hanging loop and wrap the ends around a "branch" of the evergreen wreath. Twist the ends together and conceal them as described in Step 2. If the wreath will be hung where it won't be jostled, you can attach ornaments with wire ornament hangers instead of floral wire.

5. Finish by trimming the wreath with a fancy bow, if desired. (For complete instructions on how to make a bow, see "How to Tie a Perfect Bow" on page 243.)

Ringed-with-Roses Wreath: Let roses encircle an evergreen wreath, perhaps combined with some pinecones.

Nosegay Rose Wreath: Top an evergreen wreath with gilt-painted twigs, tuck rosebuds and rose hips in among them, then put a nosegay of roses at the center of a long-streamered bow.

Old-Fashioned Garland Wreath: For another fun twist on the traditional theme, wrap an evergreen wreath with garlands of popcorn or cranberries, then add dried roses as ornaments around the wreath.

Golden Memories Wreath: For a more elegant look, wrap a garland of gold beads around an evergreen wreath. Highlight it with golden glass ornaments, gold bells, and yellow roses. Trim with a metallic gold bow.

Christmas Cheer Wreath: You can create a simple red, white, and green evergreen wreath by tucking sprays of polyantha or floribunda roses and baby's-breath in among the branches of evergreen. Complement them with red-and-white-striped candy canes.

Rose and Holly Wreath: For a natural look, tuck sprigs of plain or variegated holly leaves, rose hips, artemisia, and roses in among the evergreens.

Classic Evergreen Wreath: Use two crisscrossing pieces of wire to attach a block of brown floral foam to the wreath so that the foam extends across the entire base of the wreath. Adorn with an arrangement of dried roses and other plant material, covering the entire block of foam. Trim with a colorful bow, if desired.

Heart-Shaped Twig Wreath with Roses

MATERIALS
(FOR A 14-INCH-LONG HEART)

8 to 10 willow, alder, or birch
　branches, each 36 inches long
Dried Spanish moss
6 to 10 dried roses
Assortment of dried flowers and plant
　material, such as statice,
　strawflowers, 'Silver King'
　artemesia, and celosia
Large tub or sink of warm water
22-gauge floral wire
Wire cutters
Pruning shears
Hot glue gun with clear glue sticks
Ribbon or lace (optional)

Although the circle symbolizes unending life and is the most typical form for wreaths, many people also like heart-shaped wreaths. You can often find vine or twig heart-shaped wreaths at craft stores, but it's easy and inexpensive to make them at home.

Start by gathering trimmings from grapevines or other vines such as honeysuckle or clematis. Or you can use twigs from trees and shrubs with long, thin, pliable branches; for instance, consider using willow, alder, or birch branches. Steps 1, 2, and 3 describe how to form your trimmings into a heart-shaped wreath base.

You can trim your heart wreath with a variety of materials, choosing a style that suits your decor. Some people prefer a sparse, airy effect, while others prefer a more frilly treatment complete with lace and ribbons. Whichever you prefer, a heart-shaped wreath will lend romantic appeal to any room of your house.

1. Soak the branches for 30 minutes in the warm water to increase pliability.

2. Gather the branches together, with the ends even, and secure about 2 inches from the end with a piece of floral wire. Use wire cutters to trim off the ends of the wire. This is the throat of the heart.

3. With the wired end closest to you, split the the branches into two equal sections, and curve them to form a heart shape. Cross the ends of the two bundles (as shown in the illustration) to form the point of the heart. Securely wire the bundles in place and trim the wire. The ends of the branches should extend several inches past the point of the heart. Use pruning shears to trim any branch ends that seem too long.

4. Hot glue a cluster of Spanish moss to the throat of the heart. Then glue the roses and other accent materials on top of the moss.

5. Glue Spanish moss at the point of the heart, and hot glue on roses and other flowers so they cascade down the trailing branch ends as shown.

6. Trim with a ribbon or lace bow, if desired. (For complete instructions on how to make a bow, see "How to Tie a Perfect Bow" on page 243.)

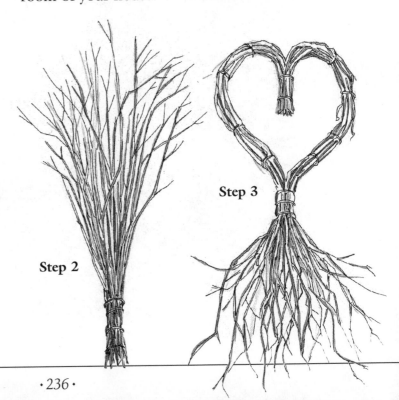

Step 2

Step 3

**Heart-Shaped
Twig Wreath
with Roses**

Starburst Wreath: You can also make a beautiful circular twig wreath in the shape of a starburst. To make one, you'll need a special wreath base called a Hillman wreath form, which is a wire form with pairs of open wire clamps evenly spaced around the circle. To use a Hillman wreath form, position a bundle of about six twigs so their ends lie in one of the wreath form's clamps. Using pliers, bend over the clamp wires one at a time so they hold the twigs securely. Position another bundle of twigs in the clamp above the first clamp so the branches of the second bundle conceal the first clamp. Continue around the wreath. Finish the starburst wreath by hot gluing on roses and other flowers.

**Hillman
Wreath Form**

Starburst Wreath

MATERIALS

Enough dried Spanish or sphagnum
     moss to cover wreath base
20 to 30 dried pink rosebuds
30 to 40 stems of dried globe
     amaranth
30 to 40 dried love-in-a-mist seedpods
5 to 10 stems of dried celosia
16 to 20 dried strawflowers
5 to 10 stems of dried annual statice
Extruded polystyrene wreath base,
     12 inches in diameter
Hot glue gun with clear glue sticks
Ribbon
Scissors
Clear plastic craft spray sealer

Rosebud Pattern Wreath

If you're looking for a strikingly different look in wreaths, try this! The solid bands of dried rose-buds and other flowers circling the wreath make it very distinctive. This bold design makes good use of rosebuds and everlastings like strawflowers, globe amaranth, statice, and celosias. Be sure to pack the materials in tightly for a full, lush look. The love-in-a-mist seedpods and use of comple-mentary colors create a dramatic effect.

1. To soften and conceal the wreath base, lightly cover it with pieces of moss, attaching them with hot glue.

2. To make a hanger for the wreath, tie a ribbon around the top of the wreath, then tie the ends together, forming a loop.

3. Use scissors to cut the stems from the rosebuds and single-blossomed flowers. For cluster-type flowers such as celosia and annual statice, break or cut the heads into pieces.

4. Decorate the wreath base in bands, grouping the rosebuds, strawflowers, celosia, annual statice, globe amaranth, and love-in-a-mist seedpods as shown in the photo on page 210. To do this, start on the inside of the wreath and begin hot gluing the flowers in place. Put the flowers as close together as possible. Continue gluing on flowers until plant material covers everything but the back.

5. Spray the completed wreath with clear plastic craft sealer to keep the dried material from shattering or absorbing moisture.

Variations: If you wish, you can deco-rate your wreath with geometric patterns or spiraling rows instead of bands. For a slightly different look, you can trim the wreath with ribbon, lace, or other dried materials. Experiment with different designs and trims and see what you come up with!

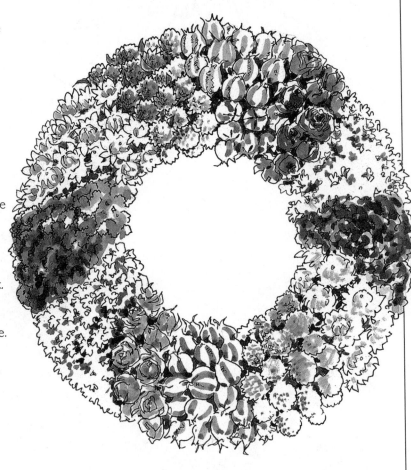

Moss Wreath with Roses

This small wreath, only 10 inches across, can highlight long-stemmed air-dried roses, combined with dried wheat and lavender. Dried Spanish and sphagnum moss both produce a soft, natural background for dried roses and are especially appealing with old-fashioned roses. For a summer memory, use shells from a beach trip and pale pink roses to contrast with the soft moss.

MATERIALS

Enough dried Spanish or sphagnum moss to cover wreath base
5 to 9 long-stemmed air-dried roses
7 to 10 stems of dried lavender
5 to 9 stalks of dried wheat
Wire wreath form, 10 inches in diameter
20-gauge floral wire or clear fishing monofilament
Wire cutters
Scissors
1-foot length of string
2-foot length of French ribbon
Hot glue gun with clear glue sticks
Clear plastic craft spray sealer

Step 2

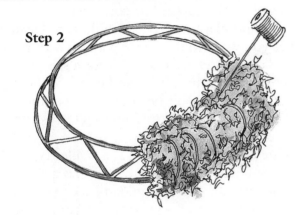

Steps 3 and 4

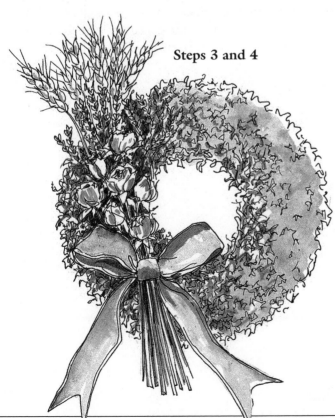

1. Attach the floral wire or monofilament to the wreath form.

2. Take an ample clump of moss and lay it along the top, upward-curving side of the form. Bind it firmly in place by winding the floral wire or monofilament around and around the moss and form. Continue adding clumps of moss and attaching securely. When done, the moss should be firm and about 1 inch thick. Be careful to keep the thickness even. When completed, secure the end of the wire or monofilament to the frame. If using wire, trim the ends with wire cutters; if using monofilamant, trim with scissors.

3. Gather the roses, lavender, and wheat into a bouquet and tie it with the string, trimming the ends. Tie the French ribbon into a bow around the bouquet and hot glue the bouquet onto the wreath as shown.

4. Using scissors, trim the bow streamers to the desired length, cutting a V into each end and arranging the streamers in a pleasing shape.

5. Spray the completed wreath with clear plastic craft sealer to keep the dried material from shattering or absorbing moisture.

MATERIALS
(FOR A 42-INCH GARLAND)

8 to 16 dried roses
Assortment of dried flowers and plant
    materials, such as artemisia, baby's-
    breath, hydrangea, peppergrass,
    love-in-a-mist, and strawflowers
Scissors
18-gauge floral wire
22-gauge floral wire
Wire cutters
Hot glue gun with clear glue sticks
    (optional)
Ribbon

1. Separate the roses and other flowers into bundles of three to five stems. Use a scissors to trim the stems of each bundle to 5 inches long. Secure the bundles by wrapping their stems with 22-gauge floral wire.

2. Using wire cutters, cut a 48-inch length of 18-gauge floral wire to serve as the base or "backbone" for your garland. At each end, bend 3 inches of wire back, twisting the end to secure, to form loops for hanging. Starting at one end of the wire base, position the first floral bundle with stems pointing toward the opposite end of the wire base. Secure to the base with 22-gauge floral wire. Position a second floral bundle so that its blossoms cover the stems of the first bundle. Wire it to the base.

3. Continue adding floral bundles as described in Step 2 until you reach the end of the wire base.

4. Attach accent flowers and plant materials with hot glue or wire, if desired.

5. Trim with bows at either end. (For complete instructions on how to make a bow, see "How to Tie a Perfect Bow" on page 243.)

Rose and Herb Garland

Whether you call them garlands or swags, ropes of dried flowers festooning your home or acting as a party decoration create a glorious, graceful effect. Although making garlands is time consuming and requires a lot of dried flowers, there's nothing like garlands of flowers for beauty and floral impact.

Before you start, consider where you're going to place the garland so you can determine the colors and plant materials you'll need. Decide whether you want to trim your garland with ribbons or lace. If you are making it for a special occasion, let the colors in the garland enhance the colors of the season. Don't be afraid to experiment with different colors and different materials. Be inventive!

The bulk of most garlands is a filler-type material, such as baby's-breath. You can attach accent flowers either as the garland is created or after the filler material is in place. Usually, a length of wire forms the "backbone" of a garland. You can use rope to make heavier garlands, but for most rose garlands, wire is best.

Festive Autumn Swag: Combine roses in a fall garland of miniature Indian corn, bittersweet, and wheat. Use accent materials in orange, gold, and russet to enhance the autumn feel.

Quick and Easy Christmas Garland: You can readily find evergreen garlands during the Christmas season, but it's easy to make your own from tree prunings. Use your evergreen base to make quick creations by just wiring on some red roses and baby's-breath. Accent with golden bows and tree ornaments for a touch of holiday magic.

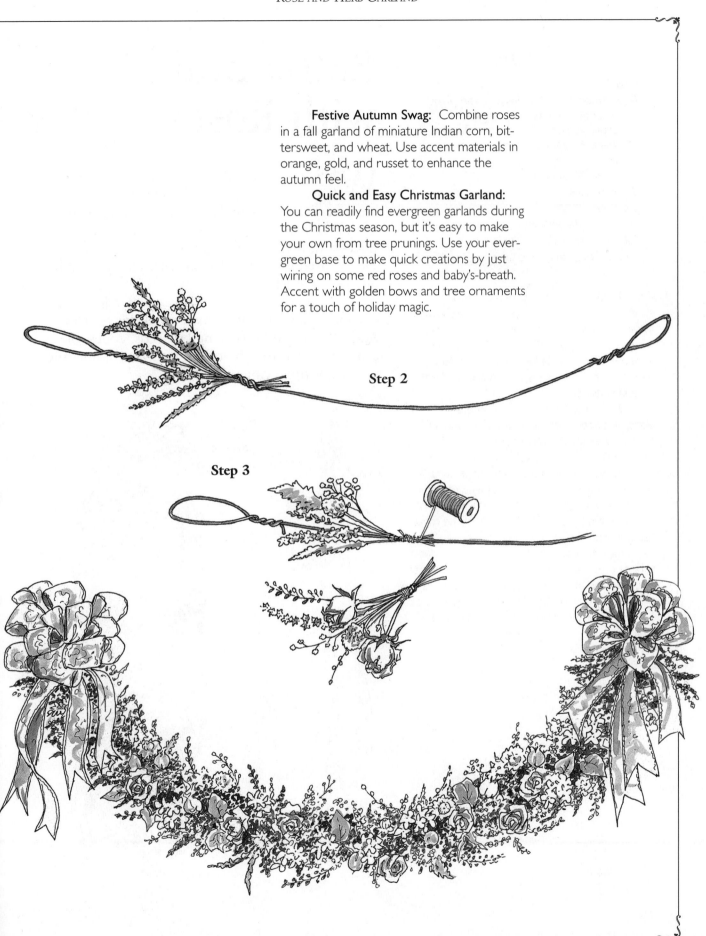

Step 2

Step 3

Raffia Braid with Roses

While garlands are usually draped in a curve between two points, a braid is more often hung vertically, much like a bellpull. You can also hang braids in pairs, with one on either side of a sideboard, fireplace, or door. Of course, they can also be used lying on a flat surface, such as a table, mantel, or shelf.

Plenty of ribbons and clusters of dried roses enhance the simple attractiveness of this project. Add other dried flowers, herbs, seeds, cones, or other materials to suit your mood, your home, the season, or the recipient.

1. Gather a thick bunch of raffia strands. Wire one end together securely with floral wire. Fold in half. Use a piece of floral wire to secure the raffia 3 inches from the folded end. The raffia loop at the end forms a hanger. If you wish, hang on a nail to make the braiding easier.

2. Divide the raffia into three equal sections, and alternately braid the right and left section over the center section; keep the braid taut.

3. When the braid is the length you desire, tie it off securely with a piece of floral wire. Use wire cutters to trim off the ends of the wire. If needed, trim the ends of the raffia using scissors.

4. Decorate the braid with three clusters of dried roses and other flowers, one at the top, one at the center, and one toward the end, hot gluing the flowers in place. Add a ribbon or raffia bow at each cluster, hot gluing in place.

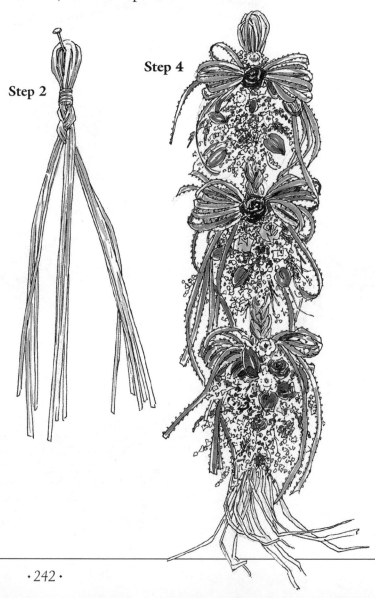

Step 2

Step 4

How to Tie a Perfect Bow

Often, the finishing touch to a wreath or other craft project is a lavish ribbon. Craft and florist shops will usually make these bows for you for a fee, but it's easy to learn to make them yourself. The same craft and florist shops usually sell ribbon by the yard, and you'll have gingham, satin, plaid, solids and prints, and many others to choose from.

Once you have chosen the ribbon you want, you'll need to purchase 2½ yards of ribbon for the bow and 1 additional yard if you want matching streamers. You'll also need a chenille stem (long pipe cleaner) in a color that matches your ribbon. The directions and illustrations will tell you the details of bow making. Here's what to do:

1. Hold the ribbon between your thumb and forefinger with the right side of the ribbon facing you. The end should extend several inches above your fingers. Gather the ribbon tightly between your thumb and forefinger, as you would gather fabric by hand. (As you work through the rest of these steps, be sure to keep the right side of the ribbon facing you at all times. To do this, you will have to twist the ribbon where you are holding it between your fingers.)

2. Keeping the right side of the ribbon toward you, form the first lower loop by bringing the long end of the ribbon up underneath the piece you are holding. As the ribbon is brought under

your thumb, pinch it against the first gathering and make a second gathering as shown.

3. Next, make the first upper loop, bringing the ribbon down and under your thumb in the same manner, pinching and gathering it as shown and twisting the ribbon to keep the right side out. Make three upper and lower loops, keeping each firmly gathered between your thumb and forefinger.

4. Next, you will make a set of loops perpendicular to the ones made in Step 3. Giving the ribbon a twist to keep the right side out, form a loop over your thumb slightly smaller than the previous loops and pinch it under your thumb and on top of the first loop you made in Step 3. Gather as before. To make the lower loop, bring the long end of the ribbon around behind the last loop you made in Step 3, and gather it under your forefinger. Repeat twice more.

5. Run a chenille stem through all of the loops made in Step 4. Pull the ends of the stem around to the back of the bow, twisting tightly.

6. If desired, fold an additional yard of ribbon in half and attach it to the back of the bow by twisting the chenille stem around it.

7. Pull on the loops to spread them out and open them up so the bow looks attractive.

8. Use scissors to trim the ends of the ribbon at an angle.

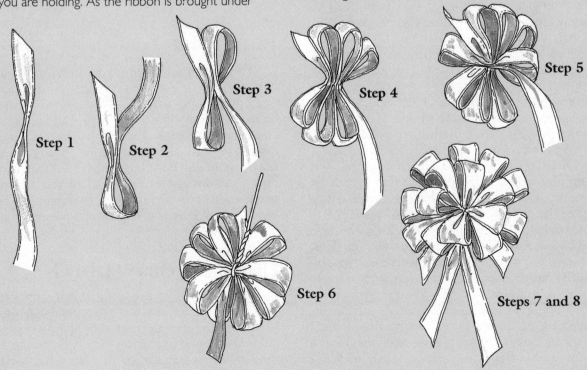

Step 1 Step 2 Step 3 Step 4 Step 5 Step 6 Steps 7 and 8

Chapter 9

Rose Crafts
for Scent and Beauty

RAGRANCE HAS ENCHANTED PEOPLE
since the beginning of time. The
word *perfume* is a derivation of
the Latin *perfumare,* to fill with
smoke; burning scented wood was a primitive
method of perfuming rooms. Early records indicate that the Egyptians used plant oils in religious services, to embalm the dead, and to
sweetly scent their homes and their bodies.

Ancient Greek and Roman civilizations
learned the art of perfumery from the
Egyptians, but with the fall of the Roman
Empire, most use of scent was restricted to
burning incense in the church. During this period, however, people in the Middle East perfect-
ed the process of distillation of essential oils,
altering the course of perfumery forever.

Distillation provided larger quantities of
more intensely scented oils than had ever been
possible. The first plant oil to be distilled was
that of the damask rose, or "attar of roses."

Meanwhile, in Europe, fragrant flowers and
herbs were mainly grown in monastery gardens,
principally for medicinal purposes. By the six-
teenth century, scented plants were part of many
larger households as well. Whether strewn on
the floors, used in the laundry, made into furniture polishes, placed among linens, or just held
up to the nose, scented plants were becoming a
component of everyday life for their pleasant
effects as well as their medicinal uses. It was not

until two centuries later that mixtures of flowers, herbs, and spices came to be known as potpourri. Literally translated from the French as
"rotten pot," in reference to the damp mixtures
of rose petals pickled or preserved with salt and
spices, the term today includes both moist and
dry medleys.

POTPOURRI

Today, potpourri refers to both moist and
dry blends of flowers, herbs, and spices.
Sometimes other materials, such as bits of wood
or dried pieces of fruit, are also added. These
basic plant materials along with a fixative and an
essential oil are the three important ingredients
necessary in any potpourri. After you read about
how to choose and prepare all of the materials
needed for potpourri making, try whipping up a
batch of your own using the recipes on pages
254 and 255.

Flowers and Other Materials

From the beginning, the most important
potpourri ingredient was rose petals. A quick
perusal of the species roses as well as the earliest
cultivars shows that these are still among the
most intensely fragrant of all roses. High on the
list are 'Apothecary's Rose', 'Autumn Damask',

Best Roses for Potpourri

When choosing roses for potpourri, roses from the Alba, Bourbon, Centifolia, Damask, Moss, Musk, and Rugosa classes are all good choices, as is 'Apothecary's Rose.' The following cultivars also keep their fragrance especially well when dried:

'Belle de Crecy'

'Cerise Bouquet'

'Chaucer'

'Chrysler Imperial'

'Comte de Chambord'

'Fair Bianca'

'Fragrant Cloud'

'Heritage'

'Honorine de Brabant'

'Madame Isaac Pereire'

'Mister Lincoln'

'Nymphenburg'

'Stanwell Perpetual'

'Variegata di Bologna'

is to have these oils last as long as possible. At one time, fixatives were often of animal origin, such as musk, civet, ambergris, and castor. Now, three plant-derived fixatives—orris root, calamus root, and oak moss—are preferred because of their plant origins. All three are available at craft shops and potpourri suppliers, but you can grow orris root and calamus root in your garden. For dry potpourris, use the fixatives in chopped form. The powdered form is better for moist potpourris and pomanders. (See "Preparing Plant Materials" on page 246 for information on preparing homegrown orris and calamus root for use in potpourri.)

Calamus root. This fixative is made from the roots of sweet flag (*Acorus calamus*), a plant for boggy ground. It fuses well with spicy, earthy, and vanilla-scented potpourris.

Oak moss. This fixative is a lichen—*Evernia pranastri*. It blends wells with lavender, gives freshness to citrus and floral blends, and adds depth to potpourris containing patchouli, vetiver, vanilla, and tonka bean.

Orris root. This fixative is made from the roots of the Florentine iris (*Iris × germanica* var. *florentina*), a member of the iris family. It has a delicate, violetlike scent and blends particularly well with woodsy and oriental-type mixtures. Some people have an allergic reaction to orris root, so test it on yourself before using it in sachets and pillows.

'Celsiana', 'Celestial', and 'White Rose of York'.

While rose petals and other scented flowers and petals are the primary ingredient in potpourris, you can also use fragrant wood, roots, seeds, barks, herbs, and spices. The combination sets the tone of the mix. Today, people tend to experiment with scents other than florals, such as musky, fruity, woodsy, or oriental fragrance medleys.

You don't have to limit yourself to scented flowers; you can also include unscented blossoms to enhance the beauty of your potpourri. Some people use pressed as well as dried flowers, while others add brightly colored dried seeds, berries, or fruits. You can color-coordinate potpourri to a room, an event, or a season.

Fixatives

A fixative is the ingredient in potpourri that holds the perfume of the plant materials and their essential oils. Since the fragrance in potpourri is released as the oils evaporate, your goal

Essential Oils

An essential oil provides extra, intense fragrance in a potpourri. Usually, you would choose an oil that is the same as the plant material used in the greatest quantity—for instance, you would use rose oil if your potpourri features roses. If you don't have that type of essential oil, use a scent that has a fragrance that complements the scent of the predominant plant material. Never use more than three different essential oils in one batch of potpourri.

You can purchase essential oils at craft or perfume shops or by mail order. (See "Rose Resources" beginning on page 282 for addresses of mail-order suppliers.) Many oils sold today are synthetic and of varying quality. When possible, smell the oils and read the labels carefully before purchasing.

In her book *Potpourri... Easy as One, Two, Three!* Dody Lyness suggests that the gum resins, such as gum arabic, gum benzoin, frankincense, myrrh, and gum styrax, act as fusing agents, uniting all of the fragrances in the mixture. Her recommendation is to add 2 tablespoons of one of them to each gallon of potpourri.

Preparing Plant Materials

One of the surprises of making potpourri is that what seems like a large amount of fresh flowers becomes so much smaller when dried. You may have to dry flowers and herbs over several months to have enough of what you want for a certain blend. (Note that, unlike for dry potpourri, you don't really dry flowers and herbs for moist potpourri—you just dry them out a little, until they're limp and leathery. For more on this technique, see "Moist Potpourri" on page 249.)

As when working with other dried flower projects, gather your roses and other flowers and herbs after the dew has dried but before the midday heat has evaporated the fragrant oils. It is best to harvest on a morning following a few days of clear, dry weather. Pick flowers just as they begin to open. Harvest herbs that you want to dry for foliage just before they start to flower.

Roses are mainly used as individual petals in potpourri. After harvesting your roses, pull the

Herbs for Potpourri

Herbs aren't just for cooking. Add some of these fragrant herbs to your next potpourri, and enjoy them for their scent instead of their flavor. You can use both their leaves and their flowers.

Angelica	Marjoram
Anise hyssop	Myrtle
Bay	Orange mint
Bergamot	Pennyroyal
Catmint	Peppermint
Catnip	Rosemary
Chamomile	Sage
Cinnamon basil	Santolina
Clary sage	Scented geranium
Costmary	Southernwood
Fennel	Spearmint
Holy basil	Summer savory
Hyssop	Sweet basil
Lavender	Sweet woodruff
Lemon balm	Tansy
Lemon basil	Tarragon
Lemon grass	Thyme
Lemon thyme	Wormwood
Lemon verbena	Yarrow

Fragrant Flowers for Potpourri

Try a combination of these fragrant flowers in your next potpourri:

Citrus	Magnolia
Daffodil	Meadowsweet
Elder	Mignonette
Carnation	Mock orange
Flowering tobacco	Peony
Heliotrope	Pinks
Honeysuckle	Stock
Hyacinth	Sweet pea
Jasmine	Sweet rocket
Lilac	Tuberose
Lily-of-the-valley	Violet
Linden	Wallflower

petals from the flowers and spread them out to dry. To make a dry rose potpourri more attractive, you can also dry a few tiny rosebuds, such as those from miniature roses or from 'Bonica' or 'Cecile Brunner'. For other flowers, trim off the stems. If the stalks are large but have many smaller florets, as with delphiniums, cut the individual florets from the stalks.

To dry roses and other flowers, spread petals and flowers in a single layer on cheesecloth, a nonmetal screen or tray, or a cookie sheet with a nonstick coating. Put in a dark, dry, well-ventilated place to dry. If you use a solid tray or sheet, stir occasionally.

To dry herbs for potpourri, hang them upside down in small bunches held together with rubber bands. Another drying method is to carefully pull away the leaves or snip them off with scissors, and lay them in a single layer to

Equipment

You won't need any special apparatus for making potpourri. Almost everything you need is probably already in your kitchen. For measuring and mixing potpourri, you'll need to have a 6-quart glass, enamel, ceramic, or stainless steel bowl; measuring cups; measuring spoons; and a long-handled wooden spoon.

To crush spices, a mortar and pestle is useful, but a rolling pin and a paper bag work just as well. You can also use a food processor, coffee grinder, or blender, but clean them well between making potpourri and preparing food.

You will also need two glass jars. One is the aging jar, which you'll store the potpourri in until it is ready for use. You can use any wide-mouthed glass jar with an airtight, screw-top lid for your aging jar, but for most batches of potpourri you'll want a gallon-size jar. You should be able to obtain one from a restaurant; they often throw away jars this size. The other jar you'll need is a 6- to 8-ounce jar, which you'll use for preparing the oil-and-fixative mixture.

dry, as you would flower or rose petals. The disadvantage of the second method is that it must be done very gently since the more you handle the leaves, the more fragrant oil is released.

Drying is complete when the flowers, leaves, or herbs are crackly crisp. You can speed up the drying time by placing the herbs on a cookie sheet in an oven set on the lowest possible temperature. A gas oven with a pilot light also works very well.

If you're growing and drying your own orris or calamus root, dig out the roots and scrub them thoroughly. Dice them into ¼-inch pieces, and allow the root to dry thoroughly in a warm, dark, well-ventilated place. When they are dry, use them in chopped form or grind them into powder using a mortar and pestle, coffee grinder, or blender.

If using spices in your potpourri, purchase whole spices and lightly crush them with a mortar and pestle. Ground spices do not work as well in potpourri because they settle to the bottom and quickly lose their scent.

When they're thoroughly dry, you can store flowers and leaves in glass containers with airtight, screw-top lids. Place each flower and herb in a separate container and label it. Store the jars in a dark place. After a few days, check the jars for mold or a musty smell—both are signs that the material wasn't completely dry. If you catch these symptoms early enough, you can sometimes salvage a batch by drying it again before returning it to the jar.

USING AND DISPLAYING DRY POTPOURRI

Because it's easy to make potpourris look as beautiful as they smell, there's no reason to tuck them away in some obscure corner. Bring out your prettiest china or glass bowls, dishes, con-

Flowers for Potpourri Color

Add flowers to your potpourri for color, not just scent. Below you'll find blue, yellow to orange, pink to purple, white, and red to wine. When choosing which to use, consider the season or the color scheme of a certain room, and pick flowers in colors that are complementary.

Yellow to Orange

Blanket flower
Buttercup
Calendula
Chinese lantern
Chrysanthemum
Cockscomb
Coneflower
Daffodil
Forsythia
Golden ageratum
Jerusalem sage
Lady's-mantle
Marigold
Mullein
Nasturtium
Pansy
Poppy
Primrose
Statice
Strawflower
Tansy
Yarrow

Pink to Purple

Aster
Bougainvillea
Clematis
Cockscomb
Columbine
Geranium
Globe amaranth
Heather
Hydrangea
Immortelle
Larkspur
Lobelia
Mallow
Pansy
Poppy
Statice
Violet

Blue

Borage
Cornflower
Cupid's dart
Delphinium
Forget-me-not
Hydrangea
Love-in-a-mist
Mealycup sage
Pansy
Periwinkle
Primrose
Violet

White

Ammobium
Globe amaranth
Heather
Immortelle
Money plant
Pearly everlasting
Queen-Anne's-lace
Statice
Strawflower
Yarrow

Red to Wine

Bergamot
Bougainvillea
Cardinal flower
Cockscomb
Fuchsia
Hibiscus
Hollyhock
Poppy
Primrose
Snapdragon
Strawflower
Sweet William

tainers, baskets, large seashells, teacups and saucers, ceramic mustard crocks, ginger jars, soup tureens, antique wooden bowls, glass-lined serving dishes, gourds, and apothecary jars. Search through your cupboards and nose around at yard sales, flea markets, and antique shops. Don't hoard your potpourri—it's a welcome gift, too.

Some people prefer to use closed containers for potpourri, opening them only occasionally to release the scent. Others enjoy leaving the potpourri in an open dish where they can see and smell it all of the time, replacing it every couple of months. Use whichever style suits your potpourri preferences.

But don't limit yourself to potpourri in containers. Sew potpourri into small cloth bags, plain or fancy, to make sachets for scenting drawers, cabinets, and closets. Fill larger sacks with potpourri for bath bags, decorative pouches for hanging on doorknobs, and sleep pillows. Use diminutive net bags filled with potpourri to scent nosegays, garlands, wreaths, clothes hangers, and dried arrangements. Layer stationery with potpourri, and store soaps in closed containers of it so that the soap absorbs the scent. Or fashion kissing balls covered with potpourri to use as ornaments on your Christmas tree or hanging in a window.

Rejuvenating Dry Potpourri

As potpourri ages, especially in an open container, colors fade and fragrance dissipates. Often it's more fun to just create a new batch of potpourri rather than rejuvenate the old one, but if you have a particular blend you want to keep around, here are three ways to bring it back to life:

1. Sprinkle a few drops of brandy on the potpourri.

2. Add 10 to 12 drops of 90 to 96 percent pure grain alcohol to each cup of potpourri, then put it in a 1-gallon glass aging jar. Put the jar in a warm, dark place. About twice a week, turn the jar end for end and shake gently to redistribute the ingredients. The potpourri should be rejuvenated in about four weeks. (This is more time consuming than the brandy method, but it is more effective.)

3. Sprinkle a few drops of essential oil on the potpourri. It's best to use the same essential oil as you used when originally mixing the potpourri. (This method will create the strongest scent.)

MOIST POTPOURRI

Moist potpourri dates back to the ancient Egyptians and Greeks, who made it by slowly fermenting rose petals and salt in earthenware crocks. While moist potpourri is not as attractive as dry, its scent is more intense and long lasting, which is why it is still popular today. Some people claim that moist potpourris can hold their fragrance for 50 years!

Moist potpourris are made up of ingredients similar to those used in dry potpourris, except moist potpourris also contain coarse, noniodized salt with no additives. Both types of potpourri often include sweet spices, such as cinnamon and cloves. Some moist-potpourri recipes include sugar and brandy for extra sweetness. There are two main differences between moist and dry potpourris: how the ingredients are prepared and how they are combined. For moist potpourri, you will only want to dry the plant materials until they are leathery but still pliable, not dry and crisp. For instructions on how to combine materials for moist potpourri, see "Moist Potpourri with Sugar and Brandy" on page 253.

Pick the roses in the morning after the dew has dried. Choose roses just before they are fully open. Gather them in a box, basket, or paper bag, but never plastic, which causes them to get too hot and lose much of their oils. Immediately bring them inside, pull off the petals, and place them on drying racks, ideally in a single layer. If you must put more than a single layer of petals on your rack, stir them several times a day. Put in a warm, dry, well-ventilated place until they are leathery but still pliable, or about two to three days. If they become fully dry and crisp, use them in dry potpourri instead.

BEAUTY FROM ROSES

Should it come as any surprise that flowers as beautiful and beloved as roses can enhance our beauty as well? Definitely not, if you take a look at herbal cosmetics and aromatherapy down through the ages. Rose oil has long been considered one of the safest of healing substances, said to improve circulation, strengthen capillaries, and soothe sore throats and stomach disorders. It also relaxes us, relieving tension and buoying our dispositions. Rose water is an excellent skin toner and eye wash, with a tonic effect on dry, sensitive, or aging skin.

You can add rose oil or rose water to all manner of beauty preparations. Try them in moisturizers and creams; soaps; hair shampoos and conditioners; bath bags, salts, and bubble baths; facial steams and astringents; and body powders. You'll find that they're therapeutic to both body and spirit.

Homemade beauty preparations are a pleasure to use and they contribute to a safe, natural look and lifestyle. The scent will be light and delicate, not harsh and abrasive. Since these preparations use little or no preservative chemicals, they don't last as long as commercial products, but they contain no harsh or harmful ingredients.

Making, using, and sharing herbal beauty

An elegant assortment. Start to collect attractive bottles and jars now so that when you make rose lotions, colognes, vinegars, and creams, you'll have beautiful containers for them. You can purchase apothecary bottles in various colors from some garden catalogs, or you can look for especially pretty perfume bottles at flea markets.

preparations is an adventure of exploration. Besides concoctions from roses, you can use beauty products made with many other flowers and herbs. If your interest is piqued, read more about beauty from plants in *Gifts and Crafts from the Garden* by Maggie Oster or in any of the books by Jeanne Rose, such as *Kitchen Cosmetics* or *Jeanne Rose's Herbal Body Book*.

Rose Water, Oil, Vinegar, and More

Rose water, oil, and infusions have been part of life since ancient times, and they are just as popular today. Commercially available concoctions are made using an elaborate distillation process. Although the home crafter can't duplicate these techniques, it is still possible to make quite pleasing rose water, oil, and infusions at home. With any of these concoctions, always

use glass, stainless steel, or enamel containers, bowls, and pots, and use natural spring or distilled water. To make your own rose-scented toiletries, see the recipes on pages 266 to 278.

Rose Moisturizers and Creams

For rose-scented skin, try some of the lotions and creams from the recipes that follow. In addition to a popular lotion made from rose water and glycerin, other more elaborate preparations with rose water and various emollients can leave your skin feeling as pampered and cared for as any treatment at the most expensive spa.

You can purchase most of the ingredients in the following recipes at drugstores or supermarkets. Specialty items are available from mail-order sources. All of these preparations use either commercially available rose water or homemade infusions or extractions. As you practice making these lotions and creams, keep in mind that you can vary the proportions to a certain extent; by experimenting, you'll find the ratios that work best for you. All of these cosmetics are relatively short-lived, lasting several weeks if kept in the refrigerator. To try your hand at making your own rose creams and moisturizers, see the recipes on pages 271 to 273.

Rose Soaps

For some people, soap is soap, but to others soap takes on many forms. With different scents, textures, and qualities, there can be soaps to fit seasons and moods, as well as suit different uses, just as with other handmade crafts. While making soap from scratch is a laborious process, there are shortcuts that give you tantalizingly scented, uniquely individual soaps with very little effort.

Your handmade rose soaps start with either glycerin soap or castile soap as a base. Glycerin soaps are the purest and mildest soaps, containing the least amount of alkaline. Castile soap is a generic term for another delicate soap, usually with an olive oil base. Using one of these as a base, you can add rose oil or water as well as fresh or dried chopped rose petals. Other ingredients, such as coarsely ground oatmeal or bran, may be added, too. Make your own rose-scented soaps using the recipes on pages 273 and 274.

Shaping rose soaps. Get a head start on soap making by using unscented glycerin or castile soap as a base for your creations. Make rose soaps in an assortment of shapes, colors, and textures, from fragrant soap balls for guests to rose-oatmeal soap for deep cleaning or rose gel soap for dry or delicate skin.

MATERIALS

4 cups (about ¼ to ⅓ pound) of dried roses, other flowers, and herbs

2 to 4 tablespoons of chopped orris root or calamus root; or 1 cup of oak moss

6- to 8-ounce glass jar with lid

10 to 20 drops of essential oil

Long-handled wooden spoon

1 to 3 tablespoons of crushed spices

6-quart glass, enamel, ceramic, or stainless steel bowl

1½ teaspoons of powdered gum resin (optional)

½ cup of dried, crushed citrus peel (optional)

½ cup of cedar or sandalwood chips (optional)

1-gallon glass jar with airtight screw-top lid

Basic Dry Potpourri

There are lots of methods and variations for making potpourri, and almost all of them work. Don't feel that there is a right or wrong way. This basic dry potpourri recipe gives proportions that should serve as standard guidelines for creating your own special mixtures. The method described here should consistently produce potpourri with a long-lasting fragrance. For variations on this basic recipe, see "A Medley of Rose Potpourris" on page 254.

1. Prepare for potpourri making at least two days in advance by placing the fixative (orris, calamus root, or oak moss) in the small glass jar, sprinkling the essential oil over it and capping tightly.

2. Combine the dried flowers, dried herbs, and crushed spices in the bowl. Add gum resin, citrus peel, and wood chips, if desired.

3. Sprinkle on the two-day-old oil-and-fixative mixture and stir in thoroughly, using the wooden spoon.

4. Pour the mixture into the 1-gallon aging jar and cap tightly. Be sure there's room in the jar for the potpourri to be shaken.

5. Put the jar in a warm, dark place. About twice a week, turn the jar end for end and shake gently to redistribute the ingredients. In about four weeks, the potpourri should be well-blended and no longer "raw" smelling.

Moist Potpourri with Sugar and Brandy

T his recipe for moist potpourri isn't quite as hard to make as some moist potpourris, and it smells heavenly! Display in a closed container, opening when you want to enjoy the scent or use an open-work container to enjoy the fragrance every day, but for a shorter time.

MATERIALS

4 cups of partially dried rose petals
2 cups of partially dried, fragrant flowers
1 cup of partially dried, fragrant leaves, such as rose geranium, lemon verbena, rosemary, or lemon thyme
2 large glass, ceramic, or stainless steel bowls
Long-handled wooden spoon
1 tablespoon of chopped orris root
¾ cup of pure, coarse salt
¼ cup of crushed allspice berries
¼ cup of crushed cloves
¼ cup of brown sugar
2 crushed bay leaves
Straight-sided earthenware, glass, china, or stainless steel container, such as a crock, canister, wide-mouthed jar, or bucket
2 tablespoons of brandy
Plate or other flat object that fits snugly inside the container
Weight, such as a brick or a jar of sand or pebbles

1. In one of the large bowls, combine the rose petals with the fragrant flowers and leaves. Using the wooden spoon, toss the petals and leaves with the orris root.

2. In the other large bowl, combine the salt, allspice, cloves, brown sugar, and bay leaves.

3. In the straight-sided container, alternate layers of petals and herbs with layers of salt and spices. Sprinkle on the brandy. Cap tightly with a plate. Weight the "lid" with the brick or jar of sand or pebbles.

4. Stir daily with a wooden spoon for a month.

A Medley of Rose Potpourris

Use any of the potpourri recipes below in the crafts described on pages 257, 258, and 260. To make any of the potpourris that follow, use the directions given for Basic Dry Potpourri on page 252, substituting the ingredients listed here. For all of the following recipes, you will need a 6- to 8-ounce glass jar with lid, a long-handled wooden spoon, a 6-quart glass, enamel, ceramic, or stainless steel bowl, and a 1-gallon glass jar with airtight screw-top lid. Remember that the essential oil mentioned in Step 1 of the directions can be rose oil, lavender oil, carnation oil, or any of the other oils mentioned in the ingredients listed below. If there is more than one essential oil listed in the ingredients list, add them all at once.

ROSE POTPOURRI

4 cups of dried rose petals and buds
2 cups of dried rose geranium flowers and leaves
1 teaspoon of crushed cloves
1 teaspoon of crushed allspice berries
1 teaspoon of crushed cinnamon stick
10 to 20 drops of Rose Oil (page 266)
¼ cup of chopped orris root or calamus root; or 1 cup of oak moss
2 teaspoons of powdered gum resin

COTTAGE GARDEN POTPOURRI

8 cups of dried rose petals and buds
4 cups of dried flowers for scent, such as honeysuckle, violets, pinks, stocks, peonies, and bergamot
2 cups of dried flowers for color, such as delphiniums, cornflowers, pansies, and borage
½ cup of chopped orris root or calamus root; or 2 cups of oak moss
30 drops of Rose Oil (page 266)
2 tablespoons of powdered gum resin

ROSE AND HERB POTPOURRI

4 cups of dried rose petals and buds
1 cup of dried rose geranium leaves
1 cup of dried lavender flowers
½ cup of dried lemon verbena leaves

½ cup of dried sweet woodruff leaves
½ cup of dried bergamot flowers
½ cup of dried rosemary leaves
¼ cup of dried marjoram
¼ cup of dried hyssop
¼ cup of dried bay leaves
¼ cup of dried angelica leaves
1 tablespoon of crushed cinnamon stick
1 teaspoon of crushed angelica seeds
1 teaspoon of crushed cloves
1 teaspoon of crushed allspice berries
1 tablespoon of powdered gum resin
¼ cup of chopped orris root or calamus root; or 1½ cups of oak moss
10 drops of Rose Oil (page 266)
10 drops of bergamot oil
10 drops of rosemary oil

ROSE AND LAVENDER POTPOURRI

4 cups of dried rose petals and buds
3 cups of dried lavender flowers
1 cup of dried rosemary flowers and leaves
¼ cup of dried, crushed lemon peel
15 drops of Rose Oil (page 266)
10 drops of lavender oil
¼ cup of chopped orris root or calamus root; or 1½ cups of oak moss
1 tablespoon of powdered gum resin

SPICY ROSE POTPOURRI

4 cups of dried rose petals, such as 'Duchesse de Brabant'; musk roses 'Cornelia', 'Penelope', and 'Vanity'; myrrh-scented English roses 'Fair Bianca', 'Chaucer', 'Hero', and 'Wife of Bath'; and tea-scented English roses 'Graham Thomas' and 'Perdita'
1 cup of dried lemon verbena leaves
1 cup of dried pinks
1 cup of dried rose hips
½ cup of crushed coriander seeds
½ cup of crushed allspice berries
½ cup of crushed anise seeds
½ cup of chopped dried gingerroot
½ cup of crushed juniper berries
½ cup of dried, crushed lemon peel

1 tablespoon of crushed cinnamon bark
1 tablespoon of crushed star anise
1 tablespoon of crushed cloves
¼ cup of chopped orris root or calamus root,
 or 1½ cups of oak moss
15 drops of Rose Oil (page 266)
15 drops of carnation oil
1 tablespoon of powdered gum resin

WINTER POTPOURRI

4 cups of dried deep-red rose petals and buds,
 such as myrrh-scented 'Chaucer' or
 'The Yeoman'
2 cups of dried balsam, juniper, or spruce tips
2 cups of cedarwood shavings
2 cups of dried rose hips or red berries
1 cup of crushed juniper berries
1 cup of broken dried bay leaves
1 cup of hemlock cones
1 cup of dried red flowers
¼ cup of crushed frankincense
¼ cup of crushed myrrh
½ cup of crushed star anise
1 teaspoon of crushed cloves
1 teaspoon of crushed cinnamon stick
1 teaspoon of crushed nutmeg
½ cup of chopped orris root or calamus root,
 or 2 cups of oak moss
15 drops of Rose Oil (page 266)
15 drop of balsam, cedar, or spruce oil
10 drops of frankincense oil

CINNAMON-CITRUS-ROSE POTPOURRI

6 cups of dried rugosa rose petals and buds
2 cups of dried calendula petals
2 cups of dried bergamot flowers and leaves
1 cup of dried orange mint leaves
1 cup of dried cinnamon basil leaves
1 cup of dried orange flowers
1 cup of dried, crushed orange peel
¼ cup of crushed cinnamon stick
½ cup of chopped calamus root
15 drops of Rose Oil (page 266)
15 drops of cinnamon oil
15 drops of orange blossom oil
2 tablespoons of powdered gum resin

MOTH- AND INSECT-REPELLENT POTPOURRI

2 cups of dried rose petals and buds
6 cups of dried moth- and insect-repellent herb
 flowers and leaves, such as tansy, wormwood,
 southernwood, santolina, pyrethrum,
 pennyroyal, clary sage, mint, cedar, lemon
 verbena, pot marjoram, and lavender
¼ cup of dried, crushed lemon peel
1 tablespoon of powdered gum resin
⅓ cup of chopped orris root or calamus root;
 or 1½ cups of oak moss
10 drops of cedar oil
10 drops of lavender oil
10 drops of lemon oil

FRUITY ROSE POTPOURRI

2 cups of dried rose petals and buds, preferably
 with a fruity scent, such as 'Madame Hardy'
 (lemony scent), 'Adam Masserich' and 'Cerise
 Bouquet' (raspberry scent), and 'Nymphenburg'
 (apple scent)
2 cups of bergamot flowers and leaves
3 to 4 cups of fruit-scented herb leaves, such as
 lemon-scented geranium, lemon verbena,
 lemon balm, lemon thyme, tangerine-scented
 southernwood, pineapple sage, apple mint,
 pineapple mint, and orange mint leaves
Dried, crushed peel of a lemon, lime, orange,
 tangerine, or grapefruit
1 cup of dried sliced kumquats
1 cup of dried yellow flowers
1 tablespoon of crushed coriander seeds
1 tablespoon of crushed cloves
1 tablespoon of crushed cinnamon stick
1 tablespoon of powdered gum resin
⅓ cup of chopped orris root or calamus root;
 or 1½ cups of oak moss
10 drops of Rose Oil (page 266)
10 drops of orange oil
10 drops of bergamot oil

MATERIALS

2 cups of dried rose petals and buds

2 cups of dried lemon verbena or mint leaves

Large glass, ceramic, or stainless steel bowl

½ cup of whole allspice

½ cup of broken cinnamon sticks

½ cup of star anise

½ cup of whole cloves

½ cup of ginger root

½ cup of orange peel

Long-handled wooden spoon

30 drops of Rose Oil (page 266)

Large glass jar with airtight, screw-top lid

1. In the bowl, combine the allspice, cinnamon, anise, cloves, ginger root, orange peel, dried rose petals and buds, and dried lemon verbena or mint leaves. Stir with a wooden spoon.

2. Sprinkle the rose oil on as much of the different ingredients as possible.

3. Until ready to use, store in the large jar, capping it tightly.

Simmering Potpourri

This form of potpourri is so popular that there are many different simmering pots and mixtures commercially available. In addition, simmering potpourri can be put in a small pot on the stove or on a piece of foil in the oven with the door open. However you use this type of potpourri, you'll love the way the scent permeates your house. Making your own simmering potpourris allows you to combine your favorite spices with delightful roses and herbs. To use, place ½ cup of the potpourri mix in 2 cups of water in a heatproof container and simmer on the stove or over a candle, adding water as needed. The potpourri can be simmered several times before the scent is gone.

Plants and Spices for Simmering Potpourris

To add your own personal touch, try experimenting by adding some of the following ingredients when you mix up your next batch of simmering potpourri:

Allspice berries	Lavender flowers
Apple slices	Myrrh
Cedar shavings	Peppermint leaves
Cinnamon bark	Pine needles
Citrus peel	Rosemary leaves
Cloves	Sandalwood shavings
Eucalyptus leaves	Savory leaves
Frankincense	Thyme leaves
Juniper berries	

Potpourri-Filled Embroidery Hoop Hanging

MATERIALS

6 to 10 dried roses or rosebuds

Assortment of dried flowers and herbs, such as baby's-breath, annual statice, yarrow, sage, and mint (optional)

Enough dry potpourri to fill embroidery hoop

Embroidery hoop, 4 inches in diameter

2 squares of lace or eyelet fabric, each 6 by 6 inches

Pencil

Scissors

Hot glue gun with clear glue sticks, or white craft or household glue

Ribbon

½- to 1-inch-wide lace or eyelet ruffling, pregathered and bias-bound

Heat releases essential oils. One way to get fragrance intensity from dry potpourri is to encase it in lace and hang it in a window so the heat from the sun can release the fragrance. These embroidery hoop hangings can also be used in other ways around the house—hang them in closets, around doorknobs, and on the backs of chairs. The hoop hangings are pretty as well as fragrant, since you can see the colorful potpourri glowing through the lace.

Many different sizes of embroidery hoops are available at craft and fabric stores. Try the little 1½- or 2-inch-diameter hoops for potpourri-filled Christmas ornaments, package trims, and necklaces. Use the 3-, 4-, or 5-inch-diameter hoops for displaying around the house and as gifts. Trim the hoops with dried roses and other flowers to fit the room or season, and vary the type and color of fabric as well.

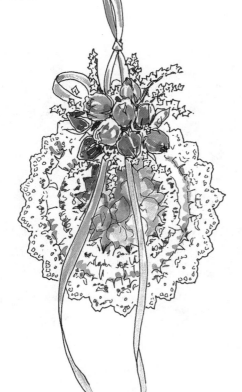

1. Open the embroidery hoop and lay the inner hoop on one square of fabric. With the pencil, draw a circle ½ inch beyond the outside of the hoop. Use the scissors to cut this out.

2. Lay the outer hoop on the other square of fabric. Use the pencil to draw a circle around the outer hoop, outlining it. Use the scissors to cut this out.

3. Placing the fabric so the right side will face out when the hoop is put together, center the larger fabric circle over the inner hoop, then lay the outer hoop on top and tighten the screw.

4. Lay the hoop on a flat surface, fabric-side-down, and fill it with potpourri.

5. Attach the second circle of fabric to the back of the hoop with glue, then glue on a ribbon loop at the back for hanging.

6. Cut a length of pregathered, bias-bound ruffling to fit the circumference of the circle. Glue it to the fabric on the back of the hoop (the side that will face the window rather than the room), positioning it as shown in the photo.

7. Trim by gluing a bow and dried roses and any other flowers and herbs in a cluster at the top front of the hoop, near the hanging loop.

Potpourri-Covered Forms

MATERIALS

Dry potpourri
Dried roses or rosebuds
Assortment of dried flowers and
    herbs, such as annual statice,
    German statice, strawflowers,
    lamb's-ears, and lavender (optional)
Food processor, coffee grinder,
    blender, or plastic bag and rolling pin
White craft or household glue
Small saucer
Water (optional)
½-inch wide paintbrush
Polystyrene form
Ribbon (optional)
Hot glue gun with clear glue stick

O nce you've gotten into potpourri making, you may find that you have more than enough to share with friends. One great way to use up some of your abundance of potpourri is to grind or crush it and glue it to various forms, such as polystyrene wreaths and balls.

    Small potpourri-covered polystyrene balls make great pomanders and ornaments. Be sure to glue on a ribbon or lace loop for hanging. Larger polystyrene balls covered with potpourri can become topiaries with the addition of a stem and a pot. Another simple, inexpensive way of using up some potpourri is to use it as covering for a straw wreath base or a ready-made basket, or make a miniature basket out of a peat pot with a bent-twig handle glued inside, then cover it with crushed potpourri.

1. Process, grind, blend, or roll potpourri to a coarse texture. (You can still use it even if you overdo it.)

2. Pour some glue into a saucer. If necessary, thin it with water to the consistency of light cream.

3. Using the paintbrush, paint the form with glue, then sprinkle the potpourri on, as thickly as possible. Build up layers, if desired.

4. Decorate with the dried roses and rosebuds. Accent with other flowers, herbs, and a ribbon bow, if desired.

Rose Pastilles

Scenting the air with fragrant smoke is an ancient ritual. Long used in religious ceremonies, as well as for purifying the air to ward off sickness, the burning of herbs and flowers was thought to affect both our spirits and our bodies. Recipe books from the Middle Ages mention making rose petals and herbs into a paste and forming them into pastilles, which were burned to freshen the air in a room.

To make your own room-freshening pastilles, follow the directions below. To release the scent, just heat a pastille in a small cast-iron skillet over very low heat or use a simmering potpourri holder over a candle.

MATERIALS

¼ cup of loosely packed, fresh, fragrant rose petals
2 tablespoons of dried lavender flowers, crushed to a powder
Small glass, ceramic, or stainless steel bowl
Wooden spoon
Mortar and pestle, blender, food processor, or coffee grinder
1 tablespoon of powdered orris root
1 tablespoon of powdered gum benzoin
Rose Water (page 266)
Wax paper

1. Thoroughly mash the rose petals using a mortar and pestle, blender, food processor, or coffee grinder. Put the mashed petals in the bowl, and use a wooden spoon to stir in lavender, orris root, and gum benzoin. Mix thoroughly.

2. Add rose water until the mixture forms a thick paste.

3. Shape the mixture into marble-size balls and flatten. Place on wax paper in a sunny window and let dry, turning occasionally. (Wait until pastilles are thoroughly dry before heating them to release their scent.)

Sachets

MATERIALS

Crushed dry potpourri
Dried rosebuds and leaves
2 rectangles of fabric, each 3 by 6
  inches
Sewing needle
Scissors
Thread to match fabric
Ribbon
Hot glue gun with clear glue sticks

1. Put the right sides of the fabric rectangles together and sew up the two long sides and one of the short sides. Clip corners.

2. Turn the fabric pouch right-side-out and fill halfway with crushed potpourri. Tie the top of the pouch with a ribbon bow.

3. Decorate by gluing on dried rosebuds and leaves.

Variations: The appearance of your sachets can be as varied as you like. Some materials you might consider using include satin, lace, moiré, silks, linen, voile, gingham, muslin, batiste, calico, organdy, burlap, pillow ticking, crocheted doilies, tea towels, and handkerchiefs. Adorn and enhance the cases with embroidery, needlepoint, appliqué, ribbon, lace, pressed flowers, satin flowers, beads, and sequins. Make squares, ovals, rectangles, circles, hearts, birds, butterflies, or whatever shape you fancy.

Potpourri Car Sachet: To make a car freshener, sew only the two long sides. Tie one end tightly with ribbon, and fill the pouch with potpourri. Tie the other end tightly with ribbon. If desired, make a ribbon loop for hanging it from your rearview mirror, or just place it over a vent in the car.

Sachets are little cases of fabric seldom larger than 3 by 4 inches and filled with crushed potpourri. Because there is only a small amount of potpourri in each sachet, you may want to add extra essential oil to intensify the fragrance. You can place sachets among bed and bath linens, sweaters, scarves, underwear, and handkerchiefs.

Don't limit your sachets to such conventional sites, though. Put them in closets, armoires, desks, cupboards, bookshelves, blanket chests, pockets, purses, and boxes of stationery; on clothes hangers, chair backs, doorknobs, ceiling beams, dressing tables, and bedposts; under bed or sofa pillows; or over the air vents in automobiles. Sachets with a masculine bent, such as those with a woodsy, citrusy, or spicy aspect, are most appropriate for men's dresser drawers and clothes closets.

Rose Sachet Powder

Some people prefer to compose botanical mixtures that are slightly different from regular potpourri. These usually are made with fewer ingredients and have a more concentrated fragrance. All ingredients should be thoroughly dried before mixing. Grind the dried mixture to a powder in a blender, coffee grinder, or food processor, or use as is. Add the oils to the dried powder and store in a closed container, shaking once a day for a month. Here are some possible rose sachet combinations:

Lavender-Rose Sachet Powder

- 3 cups of dried rose petals
- 1 cup of dried lavender flowers
- 10 drops of Rose Oil (page 266)
- 5 drops of lavender oil

Carnation-Rose Sachet Powder

- 2 cups of dried rose petals
- 2 cups of dried carnation petals
- 1 cup of crushed cloves
- 10 drops of Rose Oil (page 266)
- 5 drops of carnation oil

Tea Rose Sachet Powder

- 3 cups of dried hybrid tea rose petals
- 1 cup of dried jasmine tea
- 2 crushed patchouli leaves
- 10 drops of Rose Oil (page 266)
- 5 drops of sandalwood oil

Bergamot-Rose Sachet Powder

- 3 cups of dried rose petals
- 1 cup of dried bergamot petals and leaves
- 10 drops of Rose Oil (page 266)
- 5 drops of bergamot oil

Violet-Rose Sachet Powder

- 2 cups of dried rose petals
- 2 cups of dried violets
- 1 cup of dried sweet myrtle leaves
- 10 drops of Rose Oil (page 266)
- 5 drops of violet oil

Potpourri-Filled Pillows

Although the term aromatherapy may be fairly new, the practice of using aromas to affect your mood is centuries old. The scent of lavender promotes relaxation, while a lemon scent refreshes us. And these are just two examples of the effects of fragrance on the human psyche.

If you'd like to try a little aromatherapy of your own, make a few potpourri pillows. Traditionally, the pillows, or cushions, which are at least 6 by 8 inches, are pinned to a chair back or laid under a bed pillow to induce sleep, relieve headaches, or affect dreams.

As a soporific, hops is the dominant ingredient. Mints and bee balm or bergamot soothe an aching head, while lemon balm is said to keep dreams sweet and pleasant. Combine rose petals with any of these herbs for a distinctive fragrance. Although orris root is a typical ingredient in potpourri, some people are allergic to it, so it is advisable to leave it out of potpourri that you plan to use in pillows.

Choose a washable fabric for your pillow covers, and be sure to put the potpourri in a muslin case that fits inside the cover rather than directly in the cover itself. You can make special covers to celebrate a birthday, anniversary, wedding, or other occasion. Or sew a small pocket into a boudoir pillow or small throw pillow for holding a sachet. If you have knitted pillow covers, insert a muslin bag filled with potpourri for an especially soft and comforting cushion.

Potpourri-Filled Objects

You can use potpourri in place mats, pincushions, stuffed toys, tea cozies, hot pads, tissue box covers, nightdress cases, clothes hangers, shoe shapers, hot water bottle covers, and fabric mobiles.

For quick little presents for tucking in a gift basket, putting in with a gift of clothing, or adding to a Christmas stocking, recycle greeting cards by putting crushed potpourri inside them and gluing or sewing them shut.

Rose Petal Candles

MATERIALS

Fresh, highly scented rose petals, snipped into small pieces, or finely ground rose potpourri
Pressed roses (optional)
Candle mold, found or purchased
Cooking brush
Vegetable oil
Scissors
Candle wicking
Pencil, small stick, or dowel
Water
1 or 2 double boilers
Knife
Paraffin
2 old saucepans or large tin cans
Stearin
Candy thermometer
Commercial candle coloring or crayons (optional)
Rose Oil, page 266 (optional)
Toothpick
Cotton ball

S ince roses are the flowers of love, what could be more idyllic than combining them with romantic candlelight in the form of handmade rose-scented candles? These candles have a much more natural, soft, pleasing scent and appearance than store-bought versions. To make rose candles, you can use either dry rose potpourri ground to a fine powder or fresh rose petals. For a more intense scent, you can also add essential oil.

You'll need very little equipment and only a few supplies to make candles. You can use ordinary paraffin from the grocery store, or you can buy 10-pound slabs of paraffin from craft suppliers. Because pure paraffin candles drip a lot when burning, another wax called stearin is added. One caution—stearin cannot be used with rubber molds. A rule of thumb is to add 2 to 3 teaspoons of stearin to 1 pound of paraffin.

Craft shops have candle molds available in clear plastic, rubber, glass, or metal. Molds can also be improvised from "found" objects such as waxed milk cartons, tin cans, salad molds, cardboard tubes, or plastic soft drink bottles.

Ordinary household cord can be used for the wick, but special candle wicking costs very little and works much better. Made from cotton yarn, candle wicking comes in various thicknesses. Generally, the thicker the candle, the thicker the wick.

As for color, you can purchase commercial candle coloring at a craft shop or you can use crayons.

1. To prepare the mold, use the cooking brush to lightly brush the inside of the mold with vegetable oil.

2. To prepare the wick, use the scissors to cut the candle wicking so it is about 2 inches longer than the mold is tall. Tie one end of the wicking to a pencil, stick, or dowel and set it on top of the mold so the wicking hangs in the center of the mold and touches the bottom with an extra inch of wick bent against the bottom of the mold.

3. Put water in the bottom of a double boiler and bring to a boil; reduce heat to simmer. With a knife, grate the paraffin into an old saucepan or tin can set inside the top of the double boiler and bring to 180°F. Melt stearin in a separate pan or can, using the same double boiler if there is room or a separate one if not. Use 2 to 3 teaspoons of stearin for each pound of paraffin.

4. Add color to the stearin, if desired, using candle coloring by adding grated crayons. If you're using the rose oil, add it to the stearin. Then add the stearin to the paraffin.

5. To scent your candles, add the pieces of rose petal to the parrafin mixture when it has reached 180°F. If using potpourri, add it to the melted paraffin.

6. Slowly pour the melted, scented wax into the mold that has been prepared with wicking.

7. As the wax cools, a depression will form around the wicking. Lightly break the surface with a toothpick and fill in with more melted wax until level.

8. Allow the candle to harden thoroughly, about 5 hours. Tear or cut away disposable molds. Remove candles from reusable molds by holding the mold in hot water briefly or running hot water over it. Trim the wick to ½ inch long.

9. To give your candles a shine, wipe them with a cotton ball dipped in vegetable oil. Trim with pressed roses, if desired. (See "Candles Trimmed with Pressed Roses" on page 196 for instructions on decorating candles with pressed roses.)

Beeswax Candles: Beeswax candles are fun to make if you can find a beekeeper with wax to sell. Beeswax candles have a slow, steady burning; bright light; a smooth, glossy finish; and a sweet honey scent. Stearin can also be added to beeswax, and paraffin and beeswax can be mixed as well. Beeswax candles need slightly thicker wicks than paraffin candles.

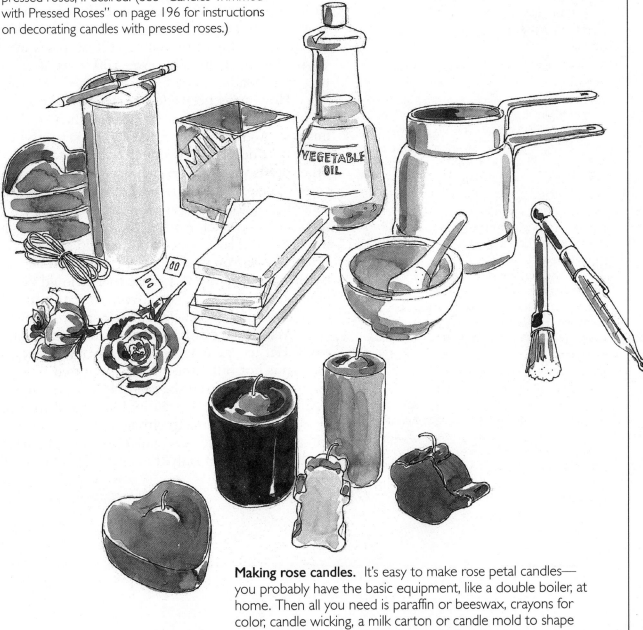

Making rose candles. It's easy to make rose petal candles—you probably have the basic equipment, like a double boiler, at home. Then all you need is paraffin or beeswax, crayons for color, candle wicking, a milk carton or candle mold to shape the candles, and, of course, rose petals!

Rose Bead Necklace

MATERIALS

Grocery sack full of fresh, fragrant rose petals, with tough, white parts cut off

Food processor, meat grinder, or large mortar and pestle

Large, black cast-iron skillet

Fork

Rose Oil (page 266)

Stainless steel T-pins or hat pins

Block of polystyrene

Jewelry bead thread, button thread, clear fishing filament, or thin satin cord

Gold, silver, pearl, or glass beads (optional)

Jewelry catch

W ho knows what prompted the first person who ground up rose petals, aged them in an iron pot, and made beads of the fragrant, black mixture. Whatever it was, we can be grateful because the process has been passed down from generation to generation for centuries. Although variations have evolved through the years, the end result is still dark beads that release the delicate, elusive fragrance of fresh roses when warmed against the skin, even 100 years after they were made.

How many petals does it take to make a necklace? It takes a great many more than you'd imagine. A grocery sack full is a good starting point for a short necklace. Combining rose beads with other beads—gold, silver, pearl, glass, or whatever—will help extend your rose petal supply. On the other hand, you may want to make matching earrings and a bracelet. And friends may start to hint for a rose necklace, too. Both the pulp and the beads can be stored, so it's okay to make small batches at a time. In fact, since there should be as much contact as possible between the pan and the pulp during aging, smaller batches are preferable.

Make rose beads from your most fragrant roses. Gather the petals in early morning before the sun is hot but after the dew has dried. You can pluck the petals from the plant, leaving the hips to develop, or remove the entire bloom and trim the petals from the stem. In either case, use scissors to trim off the tough white part of the petals near the base. You want only the tenderest portion of the petals.

1. Using the food processor, meat grinder, or mortar and pestle, grind the rose petals as finely as possible. The finer the texture of the rose pulp, the smoother and more refined looking the finished bead will be.

2. Place the pulp in a black cast-iron skillet and, with the fork, pat the pulp against the bottom and sides of the pan so that as much of the pulp is against the iron as possible. Let sit for 3 to 4 hours, then stir the mixture, mixing thoroughly. Re-place against the sides and bottom of the skillet again. Let sit overnight.

3. Repeat the stirring and spreading out against sides and bottom daily for one to two weeks. This is the aging and curing process. Continue until every last bit of pulp is completely dull and black. The pulp can be reground at any time during this process if it doesn't seem fine enough.

4. Add at least 3 to 5 drops of rose oil to the cured pulp and mix in thoroughly.

5. Form beads slightly larger than the size desired because they will shrink. Roll the beads between your fingers or in the palm of your hands until they are smooth and well-rounded. Add a little rose oil to your hands as you work.

6. Pierce the rose beads through the center so there is a hole for stringing. To do this, place each bead on a large pin, then stick the pin into the polystyrene. (For other methods of piercing holes in beads, see the variation below.) Allow the beads to dry completely, from four days to two weeks, depending on the weather.

7. Thread the rose beads on the jewelry thread, filament, or cord, alternating with gold, silver, pearl or glass beads, if desired. Be sure to leave some space at either end of the thread for the jewelry catch.

8. Attach the jewelry catch to the ends of the jewelry thread to complete your necklace.

Variation: In addition to the pin-and-polystyrene method, there are several methods of piercing a hole in each rose bead. You can also space the beads on meat skewers or darning needles, then stick them into the polystyrene. Or you can string them on dental floss or heavy thread, hung from a nail and turned once a day. Be sure to hang the thread so that the beads are not touching anything. Whichever method you choose, let the beads dry completely before using them to make jewelry.

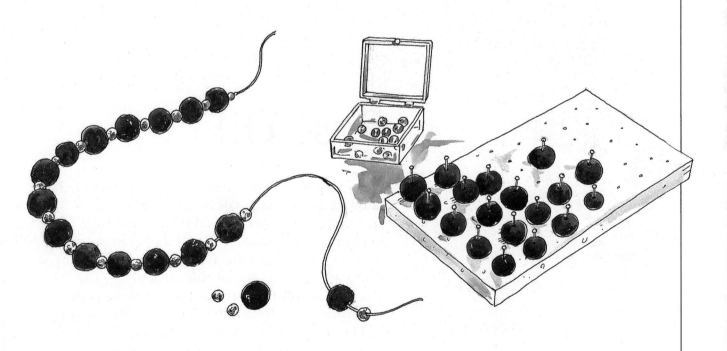

Rose Water

MATERIALS

2 cups of fresh rose petals
2 cups of natural spring or distilled
   water
Clean glass quart jar with lid
¼ to ¾ cup of vodka
10 drops of Rose Oil (below)
Strainer
Clean glass storage bottles with caps
   or stoppers
Label and permanent marking pen

Rose water has been around since ancient times. People have used rose water for various things, including medicinal purposes, but today people most commonly use rose water in the manner of the ancient Egyptians—as a perfume. Commercially, rose water is prepared by mixing distilled rose essence with distilled water, but you can prepare your own using a somewhat less elaborate distillation process. Store your homemade rose water at room temperature. It will be strongest during the first month but will be usable for three months.

1. Pour the water into the jar. Add the vodka, then the petals and the rose oil.

2. Cap tightly and let stand in a cool, dark place for at least a week. Strain and put into storage bottles; cap and label.

Variation: If you prefer, you can boil the water, then pour it over the petals. Then add the vodka and rose oil. The advantage of this method is that it will decrease steeping time by several days.

Rose Oil

MATERIALS

Fresh rose petals, crushed
Glass jar with lid
Mild cooking oil, such as almond,
   avocado, or sunflower
Strainer
Clean glass storage bottles with caps
   or stoppers
Large glass, ceramic, or stainless steel
   bowl
Label and permanent marking pen

In antiquity, the perfume of roses was extracted by steeping rose petals in oils of other substances. The rose-scented oil that resulted was used in baths. Today, most of the oil we purchase as rose oil is a synthetic of some type with varying quality. Although you will not be able to duplicate the elaborate distillation process used to make commercial rose oil, by making your own rose oil you will be assured that it is both natural and of good quality. Use your homemade rose oil in your bath water and in other homemade concoctions such as potpourri. Rose oil will last for up to one year if refrigerated; if stored at room temperature, it will last only three to six months.

1. Pack the petals loosely in the jar, filling it.

2. Fill the jar with oil and cap tightly. Set in a warm, dark place.

3. After 24 hours, strain the rose oil into the bowl and discard the used petals. Fill the now-empty jar with fresh petals, and pour the rose oil over it. Cap tightly.

4. Repeat Step 3 daily for a week or two, or until the desired fragrance is attained.

5. After the final straining, store the oil in tightly stoppered glass bottles, and label.

Basic Rose Infusion

An infusion is an extract made by steeping flowers, leaves, herbs, or stems in water. It is made like a tea, but in infusions the concoction steeps longer, making the end result stronger. Herbal infusions have been used for centuries as medicinal remedies for various ailments. Some modern herbals recommend an infusion made with rose hips as a drink to help get rid of colds and flu. This particular infusion's uses are almost endless: It's an astringent to cleanse your face, a fragrant addition to bath water, a rosy hair rinse, a revitalizing body splash . . . and you can even cook with it!

MATERIALS

1 to 2 cups of fresh rose petals
Saucepan
2 cups of natural spring or distilled
   water
Glass, stainless steel, or enamel bowl
Strainer
Clean glass storage bottles with caps
   or stoppers
Label and permanent marking pen

1. Pour the water in the saucepan and bring it to a boil.

2. Put the rose petals in the bowl and pour the boiling water over them. Let stand for 15 minutes to several hours, depending on the strength desired.

3. Strain and put into storage bottles; cap and label. Store at room temperature and use within several days, or store in the refrigerator and use within two weeks.

Variation: Instead of Step 2, you can bring the water to a boil and add the petals or start with cool water and petals and bring both to a simmer. Simmer the water and petals together, covered, for 30 minutes. Allow to cool. This process makes the infusion stronger. Strain and bottle the liquid as described above.

Strong-Scented Rose Infusion

MATERIALS

2 pounds of fresh, fragrant rose petals
Food processor, blender, or mortar
   and pestle
Large stainless steel or enamel pot
Natural spring or distilled water
Strainer
Glass jar with lid
Clean glass storage bottles with caps
   or stoppers
Label and permanent marking pen

For an infusion with a more pervasive scent, try the one described at left. Use it as you would the Basic Rose Infusion (page 267). It will serve the same purpose, but the fragrance will be more noticeable. Use the infusion as is or dilute it with spring or distilled water.

1. Puree 1 pound of rose petals in a food processor or blender, or use a mortar and pestle. Transfer the puree to the pot and let the puree sit for 5 hours.

2. Cover the puree with water. Puree the other pound of rose petals as before, and add it to the pot. Let sit for 24 hours.

3. Bring the mixture to a boil and strain. You can run the remaining rose water through a simple still (see below) or put it into a lidded glass jar and set it in a cool, dark place to age for one week.

4. Once it has aged, transfer the rose infusion to storage bottles; cap and label. Store at room temperature and use within several days, or store in the refrigerator and use within two weeks.

A Do-It-Yourself Still

To give your rose water a stronger scent, you'll need to make your own still. You can make a simple distillation unit by placing a small heat-proof bowl inside a 6- to 8-quart pot with a domed lid. Put Rose Water (page 266) or Strong-Scented Rose Infusion (above) into the pot, surrounding the bowl, or use fresh petals and 2 cups of hot water. Invert the lid and put it on top of the pot. Fill it with ice cubes and cold water. Bring the water in the pot to a simmer; do not let it boil. As the steam rises, it will condense against the lid and drop into the bowl. Take a peek every once in a while and continue the simmering until most of the water in the pot has disappeared. Do not let the pot boil dry. Store the condensed liquid in sterilized bottles in the refrigerator.

Rose Extraction

Alcohol extractions, or tinctures, are essentially colognes or floral waters that are produced commercially by distillation. You can make them at home by steeping flowers in pure grain spirits or 100-proof vodka. After straining, the extract may be diluted with distilled or scented water. Glycerin is sometimes added as a softening agent. A few drops of tincture of benzoin acts as a preservative, but it may make the mixture cloudy. (Tincture of benzoin is available at herb suppliers and some drugstores. See "Roses Resources" beginning on page 282 for addresses of mail-order suppliers who carry it.)

Extractions have a drying, toning effect on the skin, tightening pores, removing excess oils, and clearing the skin. They also help to normalize the pH of the skin. Use as a splash after bathing, or add 1 cup to bath water. You can also use a rose extraction to add fragrance to a room by pouring it into finger bowls, simmering it on the stove, or simply leaving the bottle open. This extraction will last for six months if stored at room temperature and for one year if refrigerated.

MATERIALS

Fresh rose petals
Chef's knife
Pint or quart jar with lid
Pure grain spirits or 100-proof vodka
Blotter paper
Strainer
Glycerin
Tincture of benzoin
Clean glass storage bottles with caps
    or stoppers
Label and permanent marking pen

1. Using the chef's knife, coarsely chop enough rose petals to fill a pint or quart jar halfway.

2. Add enough grain spirits or vodka to cover. Screw the lid on tightly. Shake daily for several weeks.

3. After several weeks, check the scent by dipping a small strip of blotter paper in the extract and letting it dry. Then sniff to see how strong the scent is. If the fragrance is not as strong as you would like, strain the alcohol and repeat the process, pouring the rose-scented alcohol over fresh, chopped petals.

4. When the desired fragrance is attained, strain the alcohol, then add 2 teaspoons of glycerin for each cup of alcohol, along with several drops of tincture of benzoin.

5. Transfer the rose extraction to storage bottles; cap and label.

Rose Vinegar

MATERIALS

I cup of fresh rose petals
Glass jar with lid
2 cups of apple cider vinegar or white wine vinegar
Strainer
Clean glass storage bottles with caps or stoppers
Label and permanent marking pen

Vinegars scented with rose petals have been used as beauty aids for centuries. Used as a skin toner, rose vinegar refines the skin's pores and restores the natural acid balance of the skin after washing. Added to bath water, it vitalizes and refreshes, softening the skin. As a compress on the brow, dabbed on the temples, or held under the nose, it's said to provide relief from headaches and stress. Rose vinegar can also be added to the rinse water for hand laundry, and it makes an excellent hair rinse.

Simple to prepare, rose vinegar has a fragrance similar to an infusion, but its shelf life is longer. Use a good-quality cider or white wine vinegar for best results. To use rose vinegar, dilute either by adding several tablespoons to the water in the sink when you rinse your face, or by combining equal parts of vinegar and an infusion or plain distilled water. Store this vinegar at room temperature; it will last for six months.

1. Put the petals in the glass jar and cover with vinegar.

2. Put the lid on the jar and set it in a cool, dark place. Shake the jar daily for several weeks. When the fragrance is strong enough, strain the vinegar.

3. Pour the rose vinegar into storage bottles; cap and label.

Rose Water and Glycerin Lotion

MATERIALS

I cup of Rose Water (page 266)
½ cup of glycerin
Glass, stainless steel, or enamel bowl
Long-handled wooden spoon
Clean glass storage bottle with cap or stopper
Label and permanent marking pen

This lotion is not only one of the most popular moisturizers but also is one of the simplest and best. This traditional mix from the Victorian era is a highly effective basic moisturizer and hand lotion. Although readily available in drugstores, mixing your own rose water and glycerin lotion allows you to vary the ingredient proportions to fit the season and your skin. The directions here are for a lotion for normal skin, with variations given for oily and dry skin. Lotions will last for one to three months if stored at room temperature.

1. In the bowl, use the spoon to stir together the rose water with the glycerin until the mixture is smooth and creamy.

2. Pour the lotion into a storage bottle; cap and label.

Lotion for Oily Skin: Instead of ½ cup of glycerin, use only 3 tablespoons. Be sure that the label indicates that it is for oily skin.

Lotion for Dry Skin: Instead of ½ cup of glycerin, use I cup. Be sure that the label indicates that it is for dry skin.

Refreshing Rose Lotion

Treat yourself or a friend to the luxury of this homemade rose lotion. Give a bottle as a gift to your mother, a special aunt, a close friend, or yourself. Choose a pretty bottle, tie a pretty lace and ribbon bow around its neck, and label it with the lotion's name and the date. For a special touch, use a calligraphy pen to write the label. Store this lotion at room temperature; it will last for one month.

MATERIALS

Glass, stainless steel, or enamel bowl
Long-handled wooden spoon
½ cup of Rose Water (page 266)
¼ cup of glycerin
2 tablespoons of witch hazel
1 tablespoon of mild cooking oil, such as almond, avocado, or safflower
½ teaspoon of borax
Clean glass storage bottle with cap or stopper
Label and permanent marking pen

1. In the bowl, use the spoon to mix together the rose water, glycerin, witch hazel, oil, and borax.

2. Pour the lotion into a storage bottle; cap and label. Shake well before using.

Rose Lotion with Vitamin E

Vitamin E has long been championed as a healing and rejuvenating agent for skin. This fragrant lotion combines the sweet scent of rose water with the moisturizing powers of this wonderful vitamin. Store this lotion at room temperature; it will last for one month.

MATERIALS

2 stainless steel, enamel, or nonstick saucepans
1 cup of apricot kernel, almond, avocado, or safflower oil
1 tablespoon of vitamin E oil
1 tablespoon of liquid lecithin
1 cup of Rose Water (page 266)
Whisk or electric mixer
Rose Oil, page 266 (optional)
Clean glass storage bottle with cap or stopper
Label and permanent marking pen

1. In one saucepan, combine the two oils and the lecithin, and heat until just hot to the touch.

2. Using the second saucepan, heat the rose water to a simmer. Remove from the heat.

3. Slowly pour the warm oil into the rose water, beating slowly with a whisk or electric mixer until creamy. Add a few drops of rose oil, if desired, for a stronger fragrance.

4. Pour the lotion into a storage bottle; cap and label. Store in the refrigerator. If mixture separates, shake before using.

Rose Facial Moisturizing Jelly

Many of us care more about moisturizing the skin on our faces than anywhere else on our bodies. Here is a wonderful moisturizing jelly formulated specifically for your face. Use it every day for a healthy, youthful glow. Store this lotion at room temperature; it will last for one month.

1. Fill one of the saucepans halfway with water. Heat it to simmering. Place the glycerin in the small bowl, and set it in the saucepan. Add the arrowroot powder to the glycerin and stir it with the wooden spoon, making a smooth, thick cream.

2. Warm the rose water in a separate saucepan and gradually stir it into the arrowroot mixture. Continue heating gently until the mixture clears.

3. Remove from the heat and let cool.

4. Transfer the jelly to the jar; cap and label.

Lemon and Rose Cream

Although lemon juice has traditionally been used as a hair rinse, here it is added to rose water, oil, and other natural ingredients to create a refreshing moisturizer. Use it wherever your skin feels dry. Try it on your elbows and the soles of your feet to smooth out the rough spots. Store this lotion at room temperature; it will last for one month.

1. Heat the lemon juice, beeswax or cocoa butter, and oil in a saucepan.

2. In a separate saucepan, combine the rose water and the borax, and heat until the borax is dissolved. Remove the oil mixture from the heat and slowly add the rose water mix, stirring with a wooden spoon until the cream is smooth.

3. Remove from the heat and let cool.

4. Transfer the cream to the jar; cap and label.

Aloe and Rose Cream

Herbalists have long known about the healing powers of aloe vera gel. People use it to soothe wounds and burns, including sunburn. The aloe plant is also well-known for the moisturizing quality of its gel. To make her skin shine, Cleopatra rubbed her skin with this wonderful gel. This recipe combines the wonders of aloe and rose water to create a lotion fit for a queen. If refrigerated, this cream will last for up to one year; stored at room temperature, it will last for three to six months.

MATERIALS

Whisk or electric mixer
1 tablespoon of aloe vera gel
½ cup of mild cooking oil, such as almond, avocado, or safflower
Small bowl
2 tablespoons of white beeswax
2 tablespoons of cocoa butter
Double boiler
3 tablespoons of Rose Water (page 266)
Rose Oil (page 266; optional)
Long-handled wooden spoon
Glass or ceramic jar with lid
Label and permanent marking pen

1. Using a whisk or electric mixer, thoroughly mix the aloe gel and the oil in a small bowl; set aside.

2. Melt the beeswax with the cocoa butter in the top of a double boiler. Slowly whisk or beat in the oil mixture.

3. Remove from the heat and whisk or beat in the rose water and rose oil, if desired. Continue to stir the mixture with the whisk or a wooden spoon until it cools and thickens. Before it gets too stiff, pour it into the jar; cap and label.

Rose Gel Soap

This sweetly scented soap is easy to make and fun to use. If you like, you can purchase an attractive ceramic or pottery soap dispenser and fill it with the gel when company is coming. Just be sure that you don't leave it out too long with only the pump "capping" it. To make the soap last longest, you should routinely keep it in a tightly closed jar.

MATERIALS

Saucepan
1½ cups of Rose Water (page 266)
1 cup of grated unscented glycerin soap
¼ cup of borax
Long-handled wooden spoon
Rose Oil (page 266)
Small wide-mouthed glass or ceramic jars with lids
Label and permanent marking pen

1. In the saucepan, heat the rose water to a boil, then add the soap and borax.

2. Using the wooden spoon, stir and boil for 3 minutes, then stir in a few drops of rose oil for more fragrance.

3. Let cool, then pour the soap into jars; cap and label.

Rose Soap Bars

MATERIALS

¼ cup of Rose Water (page 266)
Rose Oil (page 266)
2 tablespoons of finely chopped fresh
  rose petals or 1 tablespoon of finely
  ground dried rose petals or rose
  potpourri
Double boiler
2 cups of grated glycerin soap or
  castile soap
Long-handled wooden spoon or whisk
1-quart empty milk carton
Knife

Bar soap doesn't have to be boring or smell like deodorant. Use this recipe to make soap with the scent of rose petals instead! If you want to give some of your soap as a gift, take three bars and wrap each one in pastel-colored plastic wrap. Then, stack them one on top of the other, making sure that the bars on the top and bottom have the raw edges of the wrapping facing the middle bar. Take a length of wide lace or velvet ribbon in a color that complements the tissue paper, and tie a large bow around the stack. If you desire, you can hot glue dried roses and baby's-breath to the top of the bow for a romantic touch.

1. Combine the rose water, oil, and petals or potpourri in the top of a double boiler. Heat the mixture until simmering.

2. Add the soap and stir or whisk until well-mixed.

3. Pour the liquid soap into the empty milk carton. When the soap has hardened, peel off the carton and use the knife to slice the soap into bars.

Rose Soap Balls: To make soap balls, wait until the liquid soap has cooled about 15 minutes, stir, and then roll the soap into balls about 1½ inches in diameter. Set the soap balls on waxed paper or plastic wrap and let dry.

Rose Soap Shapes: Don't limit yourself to bars or balls of soap. You can pour the liquid soap into individual salad molds, egg poaching cups, or other small containers lined with wax paper, plastic wrap, or dampened cheesecloth. Candy mold tins with shapes of animals and hearts also make nice molds for soap. When the soap has hardened, lift up on the edges of the liner to remove the soap from the container.

Rose Body Powder

MATERIALS

Blender or food processor
5 tablespoons of ground dried rose
    petals or rose potpourri
8 ounces of arrowroot or cornstarch,
    or a blend of both
4 ounces of baking soda
Rose Oil (page 266)
Storage container with lid
Label and permanent marking pen

Beautifully scented rose body powder makes summertime much more tolerable as it soothingly absorbs moisture from the skin. It is particularly delightful after taking a bath conditioned with homemade Rose Vinegar (page 270), Rose Bath Salts (page 278), Rose Bubble Bath (page 278), or a Rose Bath Bag (page 276). You can make body powders quickly and easily from ingredients readily found in the garden and supermarket.

Arrowroot and cornstarch are the customary bases for body powders; avoid talcum powder because it may contain asbestos. Baking soda enhances the deodorant effect of the mixture. Ground orris root can be added as fixative, but because some people are allergic to orris root, it's best to add this cautiously.

Store and display this wonderful handmade powder in a lovely antique tin box or cut-crystal powder bowl with a silver lid. Add a powder puff from the drugstore.

1. Using a blender or food processor, combine the rose petals or potpourri, arrowroot and/or cornstarch, baking soda, and rose oil until well-blended.

2. Transfer to the storage container; label. Keep the container closed when not using.

Hair Care with Roses

For shiny hair with the fragrance of roses, treat your hair to Rose Oil Conditioner, Rose Shampoo, and a Rose Rinse.

Rose Oil Conditioner

Used once a week, a warm oil conditioner is especially good for dry, brittle, or unmanageable hair. To make your own Rose Oil Conditioner, warm 2 tablespoons of Rose Oil (page 266) in a saucepan over low heat. Rub it thoroughly into your scalp and then through your hair. Cover your hair with a plastic shower cap and then with a towel dampened with very hot water and wrung out well. Leave on for 30 minutes. Remove the towel and cap and then shampoo.

Rose Shampoo

Treat your hair with a rose shampoo and be rewarded with silky, shiny hair perfumed with roses. To make Rose Shampoo, combine equal parts of Rose Water (page 266) and liquid castile soap or baby shampoo. Label and store in a plastic dishwashing liquid bottle. Use it after the Rose Oil Conditioner or on its own. Apply a final Rose Rinse, if desired.

Rose Rinse

To make a Rose Rinse for your hair, first make an infusion by pouring 1 cup of boiling water over ¼ cup of fresh rose petals. Let steep for 20 minutes. Strain and pour over hair that has been washed and then rinsed with plain water. Work the final rinse in well.

Rose Bath Bags

A rose beauty bath is just the cure for a stressful day. Hang a bag filled with rose petals under the tap, filling the tub with warm water that flows through the bag. Then sink in and relax. Note: If you use fresh rose petals and plant materials, you must use the bath bags right away.

1. Place the rose petals and other floral materials, if desired, inside the muslin bag.

2. Draw the bag closed and hang it by the drawstring under the tap so the water runs through it.

Variation: If you don't have a muslin bag, you can use a washcloth instead. Just place the rose petals in the middle of the washcloth, then gather the cloth and tie it with string or a rubber band. Hang it under the tap by the string or rubber band (or tie on another piece of string to hang it from), and let the water run through it.

Bath Basics

❦

The basics for your own private beauty-spa treatment include first taking a quick soap-and-water shower, then filling the tub with water at 90° to 98°F. If your muscles are especially sore, use slightly warmer water. As the tub fills, add a Rose Bath Bag (above), Rose Bath Salts (page 278), or Rose Bubble Bath (page 278). Shut out the rest of the world for at least 15 to 20 minutes. This gives you time to enjoy the full effect of the warm water and the bath ingredients; any longer than that will dry out your skin. In addition to the bags, salts, or bubble bath, try these bath treats:

• Make a strong infusion of 1 cup of fresh rose petals in a quart of water; simmer for 20 minutes and steep for 30 minutes. Strain the petals and add the water to the bath.

• Add 1 cup of powdered milk, ¼ cup of sea salt, or ⅓ cup of honey to the bath water.

• Use ½ to 1 cup of Rose Vinegar (page 270) in your bath to soften and soothe skin and muscles.

Rose Bath Salts

Disappear into your own beauty spa as often as you wish by gathering together a few common household items and your homemade rose beauty products, shutting the bathroom door, and entering a leisurely, relaxing world of your own making. You'll feel refreshed and energized.

MATERIALS

Large bowl
2 cups of borax or Epsom salts
1 cup of baking soda
1 cup of dried rose petals or rose potpourri, finely ground
Rose Oil (page 266)
Large glass jar with lid
Label and permanent marking pen

1. In the bowl, combine the borax or Epsom salts, baking soda, dried rose petals or potpourri, and as much rose oil as desired.

2. Transfer to the jar; cap and label.

3. To use in the bath, add 2 to 4 tablespoons of the bath salts to warm running water as you fill the tub.

Rose Bubble Bath

There's nothing like a nice hot bubble bath to melt your tensions away. The fragrance of this bubble bath creates the perfect atmosphere for luxuriating in the bathtub by candlelight with a glass of champagne and the strains of "Claire de Lune" softly playing.

MATERIALS

1 cup of natural spring or distilled water
½ cup of fresh rose petals or ¼ cup of dried rose petals
Saucepan with lid
Strainer
1 cup of liquid castile soap
Large bowl
2 teaspoons of Rose Oil (page 266)
Long-handled wooden spoon
Plastic or glass storage bottle with cap
Label and permanent marking pen

1. Combine the water and rose petals in the saucepan and bring to a boil. Cover and simmer for 30 minutes. Strain the rose water into a bowl, pressing down on the petals. Let cool.

2. Add the liquid soap to the cooled rose water. Add the rose oil and mix well, using the wooden spoon.

3. Transfer the bubble bath to the storage bottle; cap and label.

4. To use, add a capful or two under warm running water for a bubbly rose bath.

U.S.D.A. Plant Hardiness Zone Map

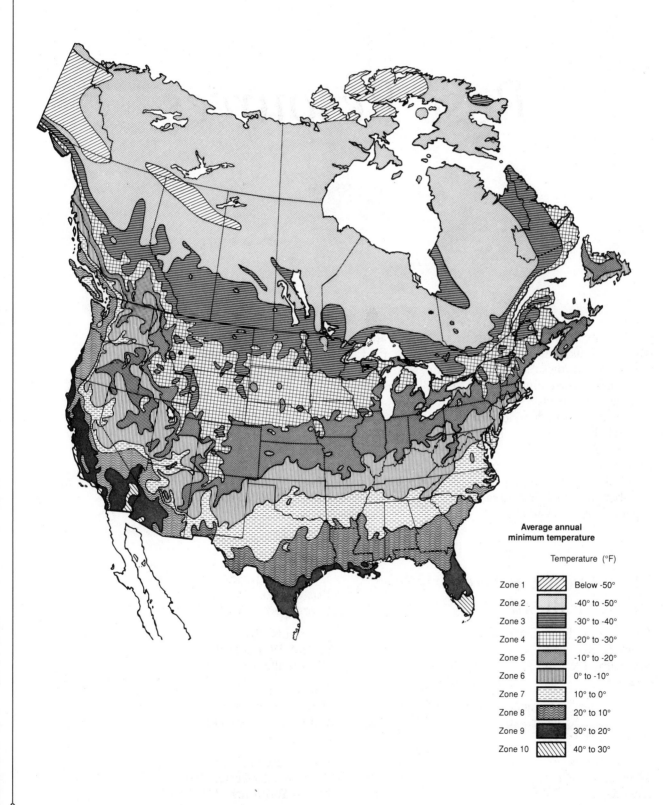

Average annual
minimum temperature

Temperature (°F)

Zone 1		Below -50°
Zone 2		-40° to -50°
Zone 3		-30° to -40°
Zone 4		-20° to -30°
Zone 5		-10° to -20°
Zone 6		0° to -10°
Zone 7		10° to 0°
Zone 8		20° to 10°
Zone 9		30° to 20°
Zone 10		40° to 30°

Rose Resources

This resource guide was designed to let you get the most out of rose growing, rose crafts, rose gardens, and rose societies. You'll find mail-order sources of roses, rose crafts materials, and organic gardening supplies, as well as public rose gardens to visit (listed by state), rose societies and groups, newsletters and journals, and even where to get more information on entering your own roses in shows. So run down the list until you find the category and resource you want. Remember that prices for catalogs and memberships may increase—call before sending money. Happy browsing!

MAIL-ORDER SOURCES OF ROSE BUSHES

The Antique Rose Emporium
Route 5, Box 143
Brenham, TX 77833
Catalog $5

Blossoms and Bloomers
11415 East Krueger Lane
Spokane, WA 99207

Bridges Roses
2734 Toney Road
Lawndale, NC 28090

Butner's Old Mill Nursery
806 South Belt Highway
St. Joseph, MO 64507

Carroll Gardens
Box 310, 444 East Main Street
Westminster, MD 21157
Catalog $2

Corn Hill Nursery, Ltd.
Rural Route 5
Petitcodiac, New Brunswick
Canada E0A 2H0

Country Bloomers Nursery
Route 2 Box 33
Udall, KS 67146

Donovan's Roses
Box 37800
Shreveport, LA 71133-7800

Edmunds' Roses
6235 S.W. Kahle Rd.
Wilsonville, OR 97070

Forestfarm
990 Tetherow Road
Williams, OR 97544-9599
Catalog $3

Forevergreen Farm
70 New Gloucester Road
North Yarmouth, ME 04097

Garden Valley Nursery
P.O. Box 750953
Petaluma, CA 94975

Giles Ramblin' Roses
2966 State Road 710
Okeechobee, FL 34974

Gloria Dei Nursery
36 East Road
High Falls Park
High Falls, NY 12440

Greenmantle Nursery
3010 Ettersburg Rd.
Garberville, CA 95442
(send a #10 SASE)

Ingraham's Cottage Garden
Box 126, 370 C Street
Scotts Mills, OR 97375

Heirloom Old Garden Roses
24062 Riverside Drive N.E.
St. Paul, OR 97137
Catalog $5

Henry Field's Seed and Nursery Company
415 North Burnett
Shenandoah, IA 51602

Heritage Rosarium
211 Haviland Mill Road
Brookeville, MD 20833
Catalog $1

Heritage Rose Gardens
Tangle Wood Farms
16831 Mitchell Creek Drive
Fort Bragg, CA 95437
Catalog $1.50

High Country Rosarium
1717 Downing Street
Denver, CO 80218

Historical Roses
1657 West Jackson Street
Painesville, OH 44077
(send a #10 SASE)

Hortico, Inc.
723 Robson Road, R.R. 1
Waterdown, Ontario
Canada L0R 2H1

Howertown Rose Nursery
1657 Weaversville Road
Allen Township
Northampton, PA 18067

Jackson & Perkins Company
One Rose Lane
Medford, OR 97501-0702

Justice Miniature Roses
5947 S.W. Kahle Road
Wilsonville, OR 97070

J. W. Jung Seed Company
335 South High Street
Randolph, WI 53957-0001

Kimbrew-Walter Roses
Route 2, Box 172
Grand Saline, TX 75140

Lowe's Own Root Roses
6 Sheffield Road
Nashua, NH 03062
Catalog $2

Magic Moment Miniatures
P.O. Box 499
Rockville Centre, NY 11571

Mendocino Heirloom Roses
Box 670
Mendocino, CA 95460

Michigan Miniature Roses
45951 Hull Road
Belleville, MI 48111

Milaeger's Gardens
4838 Douglas Avenue
Racine, WI 53402-2498

The Mini-Rose Garden
Box 203
Cross Hill, SC 29332

Mini-Roses of Texas
P. O. Box 267
Denton, TX 76202

Nor'East Miniature Roses
Box 307
Rowley, MA 01969

Oregon Miniature Roses
8285 S.W. 185th Avenue
Beaverton, OR 97007-5742

Pickering Nurseries
670 Kingston Road, Highway 2
Pickering, Ontario
Canada L1V 1A6
Catalog $3

Pixie Treasures Miniature Rose Nursery
4121 Prospect Avenue
Yorba Linda, CA 92686

Richard Owen Nursery
2300 East Lincoln Street
Bloomington, IL 61701

Roseberry Gardens
Box 933, Postal Station F
Thunder Bay, Ontario
Canada P7C 4X8

Rosehaven Nursery
8617 Tobacco Lane S.E.
Olympia, WA 98503

Rosehill Farm
Gregg Neck Road
Galena, MD 21635

The Roseraie at Bayfields
Box R
Waldoboro, ME 04572

The Rose Ranch
Box 10087
Salinas, CA 93912

Roses Unlimited
Route 1, Box 587
Laurens, SC 29360
(send a SASE)

Roses of Yesterday & Today
802 Brown's Valley Road
Watsonville, CA 95076
Catalog $3

Schumacher's Hill Country Gardens
588 FM Highway 1863
New Braunfels, TX 78132

Sequoia Nursery
Moore Miniature Roses
2519 East Noble Avenue
Visalia, CA 93277

Stanek's Garden Center
2929 27th Avenue East
Spokane, WA 99223

Stark Bro's Nurseries
Box 10
Louisiana, MO 63353-0010

Tate Nursery
10306 FM Road 2767
Tyler, TX 75708-9239

Taylor's Roses
Box 11272
Chickasaw, AL 36671-0272

Thomasville Nurseries
Box 7
Thomasville, GA 31799

Tiny Petals Nursery
489 Minot Avenue
Chula Vista, CA 92010

Vintage Gardens
3003 Pleasant Hill Rd.
Sebastopol, CA 95472

V. Kraus Nurseries Ltd.
Box 180
Carlisle, Ontario
Canada L0R 1H0

Wayside Gardens
1 Garden Way
Hodges, SC 29695-0001

White Flower Farm
Litchfield, CT 06759-0050

A World of Roses
Box 90332
Gainesville, FL 32607

York Hill Farm
271 N. Haverhill Road
Kensington, NH 03833

Mail-Order Sources of Rose Craft Materials

Activa Products
P.O. Box 1296
Marshall, TX 75671-0023
(glycerin and silica gel)

A Little Bit Crafty
135 Duggan Road
Central Point, OR 97501
Catalog $5

Aphrodisia
264 Bleecker Street
New York, NY 10014
Catalog $2.50

Aroma-Vera
2728 South Robertson
Los Angeles, CA 90034
(essential oils)

Attar
Playground Road
New Ipswich, NH 03071
Catalog 25¢
(dried herbs, spices, oils, and potpourri supplies)

Boericke & Tafel
1011 Arch Street
Philadelphia, PA 19107
(cosmetic supplies)

Bolek's Craft Supplies
P.O. Box 465
Dover, OH 44622
Catalog $1.50

The Carolina Biological Supply Company
Burlington, NC 27215
or
The Carolina Biological Supply Company
Gladstone, OR 97027
(flower press)

Caswell-Massey
21 Fulton Street
South Street Seaport
New York, NY 10038
(potpourri, oils, cosmetics, and toiletries)

Century Florist Supplies
P. O. Box 32562
Detroit, MI 48232-2562
Catalog $5

Cottage Gardens
9120 Blowing Tree Road
Louisville, KY 40220
(dried flowers and herbs, many unusual colors; decorated wreaths, baskets, and arrangements)

Curtis Woodard
4150 Boulevard Place
Mercer Island, WA 98040
(dried materials, cones, exotic pods, grains, and fillers from United States, Africa, and Australia)

Dorothy Biddle Service
U. S. Route 6
Greeley, PA 18425-9799
(wide selection of supplies and tools for fresh and dried flower arranging; books)

The Essential Oil Company
P.O. Box 88
Sandy, OR 97055
(essential oils)

Frontier Cooperative Herbs
Box 299
Norway, IA 52318
(essential oils, wreathmaking supplies)

The Ginger Tree
P.O. Box 1882-P2
Schenectady, NY 12301
Catalog $1
(essential oils)

Gingham 'N' Spice, Ltd.
P.O. Box 88
Gardenville, PA 18926
Catalog $2
(oils and fragrance products)

Herbal Bodyworks
Suite P, 219 Carl Street
San Francisco, CA 94117
Catalog $1
(essential oils)

Herbal Endeavors and Tisserand Oils
3618 South Emmons Avenue
Rochester Hills, MI 48063
(essential oils)

Herb Garden Fragrances
3744 Section Road
Cincinnati, OH 45236
(send a #10 SASE)
(essences for potpourri)

The Herb Greenhouse
Box 22061
Louisville, KY 40222
(dried herbs, potpourri and supplies, oils, books, seasonings, seeds, and plants)

Indiana Botanic Gardens
P.O. Box 5
Hammond, IN 56324
Catalog $1

The Keth Company
Box 645
Corona del Mar, CA 92625
(floral foam, pinholders, containers, candlestick cups, shears, pebbles, raffia, floral wire, tape, clay, pins, silica gel, and books)

Lavender Lane
P.O. Box 7265
Citrus Heights, CA 95621-7265
Catalog $2
(fragrance and essential oils, jars for creams and salves)

Ledet Oils
P.O. Box 2354
Fair Oaks, CA 95628
(essential oils)

Lee Wards Creative Crafts
200 St. Charles Street
Elgin, IL 60120
(wide selection of craft supplies)

Lorann Oils
P.O. Box 22009
Lansing, MI 48909
(Request Food, Apothecary, & Home Crafting catalog)
(oils and supplies for soap and candlemaking)

McFadden's Vines and Wreaths
Route 3, Box 2360
Butler, TN 37640
Catalog $1

Robert Moffitt
Box 3597
Wilmington, DE 19807
(silica gel, floral foam, tape, wire, pins and clay, dried flowers and leaves, books, preservative spray, candle adapters, and butterflies)

Mountain Farms
Box 108
Candlewood Isle
New Fairfield, CT 06812

Nature's Finest
P.O. Box 10311
Burke, VA 22015
Catalog $2
(oils and products for the bath, cosmetic supplies)

Nature's Florist Supplies
Route 4, Nesco
Hammonton, NJ 08037
(dried wild plants, cones, pods, cattails, grasses, grains, and flowers)

Nature's Products
20020 Conant
Detroit, MI 48234
(essential oils)

Nature's Symphony
10 N.E. First Avenue
Boca Raton, FL 33434
(essential oils)

Nichols Garden Nursery
1190 North Pacific Highway
Albany, OR 97321
(silica gel)

On the Wind
Route 1, Box 188E
Mountain View, MO 65548
(dried flowers, herbs, and garlic braids; decorated wreaths and baskets)

Original Swiss Aromatics
P.O. Box 606
San Rafael, CA 94915
(essential oils)

Penn Herb Company
603 North Second Street
Philadelphia, PA 19123
Catalog $1
(dried herbs and spices, extracts, oils, incense, gums, waxes, books, toiletries, and vitamins)

Santa Fe Fragrance
P.O. Box 282
Santa Fe, MN 87504

Seventh Heaven Herb Products
856 12th Avenue South
Onalaska, WI 54650

Tom Thumb Workshops
Box 332
Chincoteague, VA 23336
(dried flowers, herbs spices, pods, cones, oils, fixatives, potpourri, books, silica gel, wreath forms, moss, and floral wire)

SOURCES OF ORGANIC AND NATURAL GARDENING SUPPLIES

Age-Old Garden Supply
P.O. Box 1556
Boulder, CO 80306

Bargyla Rateaver
9049 Covina Street
San Diego, CA 92126
(send a #10 SASE)

Bonide Chemical Company
2 Wurz Avenue
Yorkville, NY 13595
(send a #10 SASE)

Bricker's Organic Farm
832 Sandbar Ferry Road
Augusta, GA 30901
Catalog $1

Earlee, Inc.
2002 Highway 62
Jeffersonville, IN 47130-3556

Earthly Goods Farm & Garden Supply
Route 3, Box 761
Mounds, OK 74047

Full Circle Garden Products
Box 6
Redway, CA 95560
Catalog $2

Gardener's Supply Company
128 Intervale Road
Burlington, VT 05401

Green Earth Organics
9422 144th Street East
Puyallup, WA 98373

Growing Naturally
Box 54
149 Pine Lane
Pineville, PA 18946

Harmony Farm Supply
Box 460
Graton, CA 95444
Catalog $2

Holland's Organic Garden
8515 Stearns
Overland Park, KS 66214

The Natural Gardening Company
217 San Anselmo Avenue
San Anselmo, CA 94960

Necessary Trading Company
One Nature's Way
New Castle, VA 24127
Catalog $2

Nitron Industries
Box 1447
Fayetteville, AR 72702

Ohio Earth Food
13737 Duquette Avenue N. E.
Hartville, OH 44632

Organic Control, Inc.
Box 781147
Los Angeles, CA 90016

Organic Pest Management
Box 55267
Seattle, WA 98155

Peaceful Valley Farm Supply
Box 2209
Grass Valley, CA 95945
Catalog $2

Pinetree Garden Seeds
Route 100
New Gloucester, ME 04260

Plants of the Southwest
930 Baca Street
Santa Fe, NM 87501
Catalog $1.50

Ringer Corporation
9959 Valley View Road
Eden Prairie, MN 55344-3585

PUBLIC ROSE GARDENS

ALABAMA

Battleship Memorial Park
Battleship Memorial Parkway
Mobile, Ala.

Bellingrath Gardens Rose Garden
12401 Bellingrath Gardens Road
Theodore, AL 36582
205-973-2217

David A. Hemphill Park of Roses
Springdale Mall, Airport Boulevard
Mobile, AL 36606
205-479-3775

ARIZONA

Gene C. Reid Park
900 South Randolph Way
Tucson, AZ 85716
602-791-4873

ARKANSAS

State Capitol Rose Garden
State Capitol Building
Little Rock, AR 72201
501-371-5176

CALIFORNIA

Inez Parker Memorial Garden
Balboa Park
Park Boulevard
San Diego, CA 92112
619-525-8200

Bella Rosa Winery
Pond Road & Highway 99
Delano, CA 93216

Capitol Park Rose Garden
1300 L Street
Sacramento, CA 95814
916-445-3658

Descanso Gardens
1418 Descanso Drive
La Cañada Flintridge, CA 91011
818-952-4400

Exposition Park Rose Garden
Exposition Boulevard and Figueroa
Los Angeles, CA 90037
213-748-4772 or 213-485-5529

Fountain Square
7115 Greenback Lane
Citrus Heights, CA 95621
916-969-6666

Golden Gate Park Rose Garden
Golden Gate Park
San Francisco, CA 94117
415-666-7200

Huntington Botanical Gardens
1151 Oxford Road
San Marino, CA 91108
818-405-2100

Mission Historical Park Rose Garden
Upper Laguna and Los Olivos Streets
Santa Barbara, CA 93103
805-564-5433

Morcom Amphitheater of Roses
700 Jean Street
Oakland, CA 94610
510-658-0731

Rose Hills Memorial Park
3900 South Workman Mill Road
Whittier, CA 90601
213-699-0921

San Jose Municipal Rose Garden
Naglee and Dana Avenues
San Jose, CA 95126
408-287-0698 or 408-277-4661

Tournament of Roses Wrigley Garden
391 South Orange Grove Boulevard
Pasadena, CA 91184
818-449-4100

Westminster Civic Center
8200 Westminster Boulevard
Westminster, CA 92683
714-895-2860

COLORADO

Roosevelt Park
700 Longs Peak
Longmont, Colo.

War Memorial Rose Garden
5804 South Bemis Street
Littleton, Colo.

CONNECTICUT

Elizabeth Park Rose Garden
150 Walbridge Road
West Hartford, CT 06119
203-722-6543

Norwich Memorial Rose Garden
Rockwell Street and Judd Road
Norwich, CT 06360
203-886-2381, Ext. 210

FLORIDA

Florida Cypress Gardens
Box 1
Cypress Gardens, FL 33884
813-324-2111, Ext. 217

Sturgeon Memorial Rose Garden
Serenity Gardens Memorial Park
13401 Indian Rocks Road
Largo, FL 34644
813-595-2914

Walt Disney World
Box 10000
Lake Buena Vista, FL 32830
407-824-6987

GEORGIA

Atlanta Botanical Garden—Rose Garden
Piedmont Park at the Prado
Atlanta, GA 30309
404-876-5859

The State Botanical Garden
2450 South Milledge Avenue
Athens, GA 30605
404-542-1244

Rose Test Garden
Thomasville Nurseries, Inc.
1840 Smith Avenue
Thomasville, GA 31792
912-226-5568

ILLINOIS

Cantigny Gardens
1 South 151 Winfield Road
Wheaton, IL 60187
708-668-5161

Chicago Botanic Garden
Lake Cook Road
Glencoe, IL 60022
708-835-5440

Cook Memorial Park
413 North Milwaukee Avenue
Libertyville, Ill.

George L. Luthy Memorial Botanical Garden
2218 North Prospect Road
Peoria, IL 61603
309-686-3362

Nan Elliott Memorial Rose Garden
4550 College Avenue
Alton, IL 62002
618-463-3580

Merrick Rose Garden
Lake Avenue and Oak Street
Evanston, IL 60201

Sinnissippi Rose Garden
2400 North Second
Rockford, IL 61107

Washington Park Botanical Garden
Box 5052
Corner of Fayette and Chatham Roads
Springfield, IL 62705
217-787-2540

INDIANA

Lakeside Park Rose Garden
1500 Lake Avenue
Fort Wayne, IN 46805
219-427-1253

IOWA

Bettendorf Municipal Garden
2204 Grant Street
Bettendorf, IA 52722
319-359-0913

Dubuque Arboretum and Botanical Gardens
3125 West 32nd Street
Dubuque, IA 52001
319-556-2100

Greenwood Park Rose Garden
48th Street and Grand Avenue
Des Moines, IA 50317
515-271-4708

Iowa State University Horticulture Garden
Haber Road and Pammel Drive
Ames, IA 50011
515-294-0042

Noelridge Park Garden
4900 Council Street NE
Cedar Rapids, IA 52402
319-398-5101

State Center Rose Garden
300 Third Street SE
State Center, Iowa

Vander Veer Park Municipal Rose Garden
215 West Central Park Avenue
Davenport, IA 52803
319-326-7818

Weed Park Memorial Rose Garden
Muscatine, IA 52761
319-263-0241

KANSAS

Reinisch Rose Garden
Tenth and Gage Streets
Topeka, KS 66604
913-272-6150

KENTUCKY

Kentucky Memorial Rose Garden
Kentucky Fair and Exposition Center
Louisville, KY 40232
502-366-9592

LOUISIANA

American Rose Center
8877 Jefferson-Paige Road
Shreveport, LA 71119
318-938-5402

Hodges Gardens
Box 900, Highway 171 South
Many, LA 71449
318-586-3523

MAINE

Deering Oaks Park
227 Park Avenue
Portland, Maine

MARYLAND

Brookside Gardens
1500 Glenallan Avenue
Wheaton, MD 20902
301-949-8230

MASSACHUSETTS

Kelleher Rose Garden
Park Drive
Boston, MA 02215

Stanley Park
400 Western Avenue
Westfield, MA 01085
413-568-9312

MICHIGAN

Frances Park Memorial Garden
2600 Moores River Drive
Lansing, MI 48910
517-483-4227

Michigan State University
Horticultural Demonstration Gardens
Horticulture Department
Plant and Soil Sciences Building
East Lansing, MI 48823
517-355-0348

Wayne County Cooperative Extension Center
Rose Garden
Wayne County Extension & Education Center
5454 Venoy Road
Wayne, MI 48184

MINNESOTA

Lyndale Park Municipal Rose Garden
4125 East Lake Harriet Parkway
Minneapolis, MN 55409
612-348-4448

MISSISSIPPI

Hattiesburg Area Rose Society Garden
University of Southern Mississippi
Hattiesburg, MS 39401
601-583-8848

MISSOURI

Capaha Park
Broadway and Perry
Cape Girardeau, MO 63702

Jacob L. Loose Memorial Park
52nd Street and Pennsylvania Avenue
Kansas City, MO 64112
816-333-6706

Missouri Botanical Garden
4344 Shaw Boulevard
St. Louis, MO 63110
314-577-5100

MONTANA

Missoula Memorial Rose Garden
600 and 700 block of Brooks Street
Missoula, MT 59801

NEBRASKA

Antelope Park
2740 A Street
Lincoln, NE 68502

Father Flanagan's Boys' Town Constitution
Rose Garden
Boys Town, NE 68010
402-498-1104

Memorial Park Rose Garden
57th and Underwood
Omaha, NE 68132

NEVADA

Reno Municipal Rose Garden
2055 Idlewild Drive
Reno, NV 89509
702-334-2270

NEW HAMPSHIRE

Fuller Gardens
10 Willow Avenue
North Hampton, NH 03862
603-964-5414

NEW JERSEY

Brookdale Park
1259 Victor Avenue
Union, NJ 07083

Rudolf W. van der Goot Rose Garden
Colonial Park
RD #1, Mettler's Road
Somerset, NJ 08873
908-234-2677

Jack D. Lissemore Garden
Davis Johnson Park
137 Engle Street
Tenafly, NJ 07670
201-569-PARK

Lambertus C. Bobbink Memorial Rose Garden
Thompson Park
Newman Springs Road
Lincroft, NJ 07738
908-842-4000

NEW MEXICO

Prospect Park Rose Garden
8205 Apache Avenue NE
Albuquerque, NM 87111

NEW YORK

The Cranford Rose Garden
Brooklyn Botanic Garden
1000 Washington Avenue
Brooklyn, NY 11225
718-622-4433

Central Park Rose Garden
Central Parkway
Schenectady, NY 12309
518-382-5152

Maplewood Park
100 Maplewood Avenue
Rochester, N.Y.

The Peggy Rockefeller Rose Garden
The New York Botanical Garden
Southern Boulevard
Bronx, NY 10458
212-220-8700

Old Westbury Gardens
Old Westbury, N.Y.

Queens Botanical Garden
43–50 Main Street
Flushing, NY 11355
718-886-3800

Sonenberg Gardens
151 Charlotte Street
Canandaigua, NY 14424
716-394-4922

Edmund Mills Memorial Rose Garden
Thornden Park
Syracuse, NY 13220
315-473-4336

United Nations Rose Garden
42nd Street at the East River
New York, NY 10017
212-963-6145

NORTH CAROLINA

Biltmore Estate
One North Pack Square
Asheville, NC 28801
704-255-1776

Fayetteville Tech Community College
Fayetteville Rose Garden
Box 35236
Fayetteville, NC 28303
919-323-1961

Raleigh Municipal Rose Garden
301 Pogue Street
Raleigh, NC 29607
919-821-4579

Wake Forest University
Reynolda Rose Garden
100 Reynolda Village
Winston-Salem, NC 27106
919-759-5593

Tanglewood Park Rose Garden
Route 158, Box 1040
Clemmons, NC 27012
919-766-0591

OHIO

Cahoon Memorial Park
Bay Village, OH 44140

Columbus Park of Roses
3923 North High Street
Columbus, OH 43214
612-445-3350

Kingwood Center
900 Park Avenue West
Mansfield, OH 44906

Stan Hywet Hall and Gardens
714 North Portage Path
Akron, OH 44303
216-836-0576

OKLAHOMA

J. E. Conard Municipal Rose Garden
Honor Heights Park
42nd Street and West Okmulgee Avenue
Muskogee, OK 74401
918-684-6302

Charles E. Sparks Garden
Will Rogers Park
3500 Northwest Thirty-sixth Street
Oklahoma City, OK 73112
405-495-6911

Tulsa Municipal Rose Garden
Woodward Park
21st Street and Peoria Avenue
Tulsa, OK 74114
918-747-2709

OREGON

Avery Park Rose Garden
Avery Park Drive
Corvallis, OR 97333
503-757-6918

International Rose Test Garden
400 Southwest Kingston Avenue
Portland, OR 97201
503-823-3636

Owen Memorial Rose Garden
300 North Jefferson Street
Eugene, OR 97401
503-687-5334

Shore Acres State Park
13030 Cape Arago Highway
Coos Bay, OR 97420
503-888-3732

PENNSYLVANIA

Malcolm Gross Memorial Garden
2700 Parkway Boulevard
Allentown, PA 18104
215-437-7628

Hershey Gardens
Hotel Road
Hershey, PA 17033
717-534-3492

Longwood Gardens
Route 1, Box 501
Kennett Square, PA 19348
215-388-6741

Morris Arboretum
9414 Meadowbrook Avenue
Philadelphia, PA 19118
215-247-5777

Robert Pyle Memorial Rose Garden
Routes 1 and 796
West Grove, PA 19390
215-869-2426

SOUTH CAROLINA

Edisto Memorial Gardens
200 Riverside Drive
Orangeburg, SC 29115
803-533-5870

SOUTH DAKOTA

Rapid City Memorial Rose Garden
444 Mount Rushmore Road
Rapid City, SD 57702
605-394-4175

TENNESSEE

Warner Park
1254 East Third Street
Chattanooga, TN 37404
615-757-5056

TEXAS

Brown Center of Lamar University
4205 West Park Avenue
Orange, TX 77630

Fort Worth Botanic Garden
3220 Botanic Garden Boulevard
Fort Worth, TX 76107
817-870-7686

Houston Municipal Rose Garden
1500 Hermann Drive
Houston, TX 77044
713-529-3960

El Paso Municipal Rose Garden
1702 North Copia
(Copia and Aurora Streets)
El Paso, TX 79904
915-598-0771

Riverside Park
Victoria, Tex.

Samuell-Grand Municipal Rose Garden
6200 East Grand Boulevard
Dallas, TX 75223
214-670-8281

Tyler Municipal Rose Garden
420 South Rose Park
Tyler, TX 75702
903-531-1213

UTAH

Nephi Federated Women's Rose Garden
100 East 100 North
Nephi, UT 84648
801-623-2003

House Park
Municipal Rose Garden
1602 East 2100 South Sugarhouse Park
Salt Lake City, UT 84106
801-467-0461

Territorial Statehouse, State Park
50 West Capitol Avenue
Fillmore, UT 84631
801-743-5316

VIRGINIA

American Horticultural Society River Farm
7931 East Boulevard Drive
Alexandria, VA 22308

Bon Air Park
Bon Air Memorial Rose Garden
850 North Lexington Street
Arlington, VA 22205
703-358-3317

Norfolk Botanical Garden
Airport Road
Norfolk, VA 23518
804-441-5831

WASHINGTON

Chehalis Municipal Rose Garden
80 Northeast Cascade Avenue
Chehalis, WA 98532

Fairhaven Rose Garden
Chuckanut Drive
Bellingham, WA 98226
206-676-6801

Rose Hill
Manito Park
4 West 21st Avenue
Spokane, WA 99203
509-456-4331

Point Defiance Park
54th & North Pearl
Tacoma, Wash.

WASHINGTON, D.C.

George Washington University
G & H, 20th & 21st Streets NW
Washington, DC 20052

WEST VIRGINIA

Ritter Park Rose Garden
1500 McCoy Road
Huntington, W.Va.

WISCONSIN

Boerner Botanical Gardens
5879 South 92nd Street
Hales Corners, WI 53130
414-425-1130

Olbrich Gardens
3330 Atwood Avenue
Madison, WI 53704

ROSE ORGANIZATIONS AND PUBLICATIONS

Akron Rose Society
Peter Schneider
P.O. Box 677
Mantua, OH 44255
Monthly newsletter
Annual dues $10

American Rose Society
P.O. Box 30,000
Shreveport, LA 71130
Monthly magazine and a soft-bound annual
Annual dues $32

Bev Dobson's Rose Letter
Beverly R. Dobson
215 Harriman Road
Irvington, NY 10533
Bimonthly newsletter
Subscription $12 per year

The Canadian Rose Society
Anne Graber
10 Fairfax Crescent
Scarborough, Ontario
Canada M1L 1Z8
Quarterly journal and an annual
Annual dues $18 (individual) or $20 (family)

Combined Rose List
Peter Schneider
P.O. Box 677
Mantua, OH 44255
Complete source list of roses in commerce and cultivation
$18 (Ohio residents add 7% sales tax)

Dallas Area Historical Rose Group
Mrs. Betty Taylor
9125 Leaside
Dallas, TX 75238
Monthly journal
Annual dues $15

The Heritage Roses Foundation
Mr. Charles A. Walker, Jr.
1512 Gorman Street
Raleigh, NC 27606
Quarterly newsletter
Annual dues $10

Heritage Roses Group
Quarterly *Heritage Roses Letter*
Annual dues $5, sent to regional coordinator nearest you:

NORTH/EAST
Ms. Lily Shohan
R.D. 1, Box 228
Clinton Corners, NY 12514

SOUTH/EAST
Ms. Jan Wilson
1700 South Lafayette Street
Shelby, NC 28152

NORTH/CENTRAL
Dr. Henry Najat
6365 Wald Road
Monroe, WI 53566

SOUTH/CENTRAL
Mr. Conrad Tips
1007 Highland Avenue
Houston, TX 77009

NORTH/WEST
Ms. Judi Dexter
23665 41st Avenue South
Kent, WA 98032

SOUTH/WEST: INITIALS A TO F
Ms. Betty L. Cooper
925 King Drive
El Cerrito, CA 94530

SOUTH/WEST: INITIALS H TO O
Ms. Marlea Graham
100 Bear Oaks Drive
Martinez, CA 94553

SOUTH/WEST: INITIALS P TO Z
Ms. Frances Grate
472 Gibson Avenue
Pacific Grove, CA 93950

Rose Hybridizers Association
Mr. Larry D. Peterson
425 Wheaton Road
Horseheads, NY 14845
Quarterly newsletter
Annual dues $7

The Royal National Rose Society
Chiswell Green
St. Albans, Hertfordshire
England AL3 3NR
Quarterly journal and tickets to their rose show
Annual dues $17 (U.S.)

Southern California Heritage Roses Group
Roland & Debbie Mettler
3637 Empire Drive
Los Angeles, CA 90034
Quarterly newsletter
Annual dues $7.50

Texas Rose Rustlers
Mrs. Margaret P. Sharpe
9426 Kerrwood Lane
Houston, TX 77080
Quarterly newsletter
Annual dues $7

ENTERING YOUR ROSES IN A SHOW

For *Guidelines for Judging Roses,* send check or money order for $7.20 to American Rose Society, P.O. Box 30000, Shreveport, LA 71130, or call (318) 938-5402 if Visa or MasterCard purchase. *The Rose Exhibitors' Forum,* a quarterly journal for rose exhibitors devoted to all aspects of rose exhibiting and rose growing, is also available from the above address for $10.00.

Recommended Reading

ROSES

Austin, David. *The Heritage of the Rose*. Woodbridge, England: Antique Collectors' Club, 1988.

Beales, Peter. *Classic Roses*. New York: Holt, Rinehart and Winston, 1985.

——. *Twentieth-Century Roses*. London: Collins Harvill, 1988.

Browne, Roland A. *The Rose-Lover's Guide*. New York: Atheneum, 1983.

Burke, Ken, ed. *All About Roses*. San Francisco, Calif.: Ortho Books, 1983.

Christopher, Thomas. *In Search of Lost Roses*. New York: Summit Books, 1989.

Edwards, Gordon. *Wild and Old Garden Roses*. Newton Abbot, England: David & Charles, 1975.

Fearnley-Whittingstall, Jane. *Rose Gardens*. New York: Henry Holt and Co., 1989.

Fisher, John. *The Companion to Roses*. Topsfield, Mass.: Salem House, 1986.

Fitch, Charles Marden. *The Complete Book of Miniature Roses*. New York: Hawthorn Books, 1977.

Gault, S. Millar, and Patrick M. Synge. *The Dictionary of Roses in Colour*. London: Michael Joseph Limited, 1971.

Gibson, Michael. *Growing Roses*. Portland, Ore.: Timber Press, 1984.

——. *Roses*. London: The Royal Horticultural Society, 1989.

Griffiths, Trevor. *The Book of Classic Old Roses*. New York: Viking Penguin, 1986.

——. *The Book of Old Roses*. New York: Viking Penguin, 1983.

Harkness, Jack. *How to Grow Roses*. St. Albans, England: The Royal National Rose Society, 1988.

Hessayon, Dr. D.G. *The Rose Expert*. Herts, England: pbi Publications, 1981.

Jekyll, Gertrude, and Edward Mawley. *Roses*. Salem, N.H.: The Ayer Co., 1983 (originally published as *Roses for English Gardens*).

Krussman, Gerd. *The Complete Book of Roses*. Portland, Ore.: Timber Press, 1981.

Le Rougetel, Hazel. *A Heritage of Roses*. Owings Mills, Md.: Stemmer House, 1988.

McCann, Sean. *Miniature Roses For Home and Garden*. New York: Prentice Hall Press, 1985.

Nisbet, Fred J. *Growing Better Roses*. New York: Alfred A. Knopf, 1973.

Oster, Maggie. *10 Steps to Beautiful Roses*. Pownal, Vt.: Storey Communications, 1989.

Pesch, Barbara B., ed. *Roses*. Brooklyn, N.Y.: Brooklyn Botanic Garden, 1990.

Phillips, Roger, and Martyn Rix. *Roses*. New York: Random House, 1988.

Ray, Richard, and Michael MacCaskey. *Roses*. Tucson, Ariz.: HPBooks, 1985.

Reddell, Rayford Clayton. *Growing Good Roses*. New York: Harper & Row, 1988.

Reilly, Ann. *Enjoying Roses*. San Ramon, Calif.: Ortho Books, Chevron Chemical Co., 1992.

Scanniello, Stephen, and Tania Bayard. *Roses of America*. New York: Henry Holt & Co., 1990.

Steen, Nancy. *The Charm of Old Roses*. Washington, D.C.: Milldale Press, 1987.

Taylor's Guide Staff. *Taylor's Guide to Roses*. Boston: Houghton Mifflin Co., 1986.

Thomas, Graham Stuart. *Climbing Roses Old and New*. London: J.M. Dent & Sons, 1983.

——. *The Old Shrub Roses*. London: J.M. Dent & Sons, 1983.

——. *Shrub Roses of Today*. London: J.M. Dent & Sons, 1980.

Toogood, Alan. *Roses in Gardens*. Topsfield, Mass.: Salem House, 1987.

Warner, Christopher. *Climbing Roses*. Chester, Conn.: The Globe Pequot Press, 1987.

Welch, William C. *Antique Roses for the South*. Dallas, Tex.: Taylor Publishing, 1990.

GARDENING

Ball, Jeff and Liz. *Rodale's Flower Garden Problem Solver*. Emmaus, Pa.: Rodale Press, 1990.

Brickell, Christopher. *Pruning*. New York: Simon and Schuster, 1979.

Browse, Philip McMillan. *Plant Propagation*. New York: Simon and Schuster, 1979.

Coughlin, Roberta M. *The Gardener's Companion*. New York: HarperCollins, 1991.

Ellis, Barbara W., and Fern Marshall Bradley, eds. *The Organic Gardener's Handbook of Natural Pest and Disease Control*. Emmaus, Pa.: Rodale Press, 1992.

——. *Rodale's All-New Encyclopedia of Organic Gardening*. Emmaus, Pa.: Rodale Press, 1992.

Foster, Catherine Osgood. *Organic Flower Gardening*. Emmaus, Pa.: Rodale Press, 1975.

Hessayon, Dr. D.G. *The Bio Friendly Gardening Guide*. Herts, England: pbi Publications, 1990.

——. *The Garden Expert*. Herts, England: pbi Publications, 1986.

Hill, Lewis. *Pruning Simplified*. Pownal, Vt.: Storey Communications, 1986.

Kreuter, Marie-Luise. *The Macmillan Book of Organic Gardening*. New York: Macmillan Publishing Co., 1985.

Roth, Susan A. *The Four-Season Landscape*. Emmaus, Pa.: Rodale Press, 1993.

DRIED FLOWERS, HERBS, AND POTPOURRI

Black, Penny. *The Book of Potpourri*. New York: Simon and Schuster, 1989.

Conder, Susan. *Dried Flowers*. Boston: David R. Godine, 1988.

Cormack, Alan, and David Carter. *Flowers*. New York: Crescent Books, 1987.

Culpeper, Elizabeth. *Heritage Roses & Old Fashioned Crafts*. Kenthurst, Australia: Kangaroo Press, 1988.

Diamond, Denise. *The Complete Book of Flowers*. Berkeley, Calif.: North Atlantic Books, 1990.

Duff, Gail. *Natural Fragrances*. Pownal, Vt.: Storey Communications, 1989.

Hillier, Malcolm, and Colin Hilton. *The Book of Dried Flowers*. New York: Simon and Schuster, 1986.

Jacobs, Betty E.M. *Flowers That Last Forever*. Pownal, Vt.: Storey Communications, 1988.

Joosten, Titia. *Flower Drying with a Microwave*. Asheville, N.C.: Lark Books, 1988.

Kollath, Richard. *Wreaths*. Boston: Houghton Mifflin, 1988.

Laking, Barbara, ed. *Dried Flower Designs*. Brooklyn, N.Y.: Brooklyn Botanic Garden, 1974.

Michael, Pamela. *All Good Things Around Us*. New York: Holt, Rinehart and Winston, 1980.

Moffitt, Roberta. *The Step-by-Step Book of Dried Bouquets*. Wilmington, Del.: Roberta Moffitt Designs, 1981.

——. *The Step-by-Step Book of Preserved Flowers*. Wilmington, Del.: Roberta Moffitt Designs, 1982.

Newdick, Jane. *Betty Crocker's Book of Flowers*. New York: Prentice Hall, 1989.

Newnes, Mary. *Arranging Everlasting Flowers*. New York: Henry Holt and Co., 1987.

Ohrbach, Barbara Milo. *The Scented Room*. New York: Clarkson N. Potter, 1986.

Oster, Maggie. *Gifts & Crafts from the Garden*. Emmaus, Pa.: Rodale Press, 1988.

Pinder, Polly. *Scents & Fragrances*. London: Search Press, 1978.

Pulleyn, Rob, and Claudette Mautor. *Everlasting Floral Gifts*. New York: Sterling Publishing Co., 1990.

Reader's Digest Editors. *Magic and Medicine of Plants*. Pleasantville, N.Y.: The Reader's Digest Association, 1986.

Shaudys, Phyllis. *The Pleasure of Herbs*. Pownal, Vt.: Storey Communications, 1986.

——. *Herbal Treasures.* Pownal, Vt.: Storey Communications, 1990.

Squire, David, with Jane Newdick. *The Scented Garden.* Emmaus, Pa.: Rodale Press, 1989.

Waterkeyn, Sarah. *The Creative Art of Dried Flowers.* Stamford, Conn.: Longmeadow Press, 1989.

Wiita, Betty Smith. *Dried Flowers for All Seasons.* New York: Van Nostrand Reinhold Co., 1982.

FLOWER ARRANGING

Ascher, Amalie Adler. *The Complete Flower Arranger.* New York: Simon and Schuster, 1974.

Dale, John, and Kevin Gunnell. *The Flower Arranger's Handbook.* New York: E. P. Dutton, 1986.

Fields, Nora. *Flower Arranging for Parties.* Cranbury, N.J.: A. S. Barnes and Co., 1975.

Guild, Tricia. *Designing with Flowers.* New York: Crown, 1986.

Hall, Jan. *The Creative Art of Flower Arranging.* Stamford, Conn.: Longmeadow Press, 1989.

Hall, Jan, and Sarah Waterkeyn. *Flower Arranging.* New York: Gallery Books, 1989.

Hillier, Malcolm. *The Book of Fresh Flowers.* New York: Simon and Schuster, 1988.

Lamancusa, Kathy. *Floral Fundamentals.* Canby, Ore.: Hot Off the Press, 1986.

Macqueen, Sheila. *The New Flower Arranging from Your Garden.* London: Macmillan London Limited, 1988.

Newdick, Jane. *The Five-Minute Centerpiece.* New York: Crown, 1991.

——. *The Five-Minute Flower Arranger.* New York: Crown, 1989.

Packer, Jane. *Celebrating with Flowers.* New York: Fawcett Columbine, 1987.

——. *Flowers for All Seasons: Fall.* New York: Fawcett Columbine, 1989.

——. *Flowers for All Seasons: Spring.* New York: Fawcett Columbine, 1989.

——. *Flowers for All Seasons: Summer.* New York: Fawcett Columbine, 1989.

——. *Flowers for All Seasons: Winter.* New York: Fawcett Columbine, 1989.

Stein, Deni W., ed. *Arranging Cut Flowers.* San Francisco: Ortho Books, 1985.

Tozer, Zibby. *The Art of Flower Arranging.* New York: Warner Books, 1981.

Verey, Rosemary. *The Flower Arranger's Garden.* Boston: Little, Brown & Co., 1989.

PRESSED FLOWERS

Bauzen, Peter and Susanne. *Flower Pressing.* New York: Sterling Publishing Co., 1983.

Black, Penny. *The Book of Pressed Flowers.* New York: Simon and Schuster, 1988.

Flesher, Irene. *The Pressed Flower Picture Book.* New York: Butterick Publishing, 1978.

Hannemann, Cellestine. *Glorious Pressed Flower Projects.* New York: Sterling Publishing Co., 1991.

Lawrence, Mary. *The Creative Art of Pressed Flowers.* Stamford, Conn.: Longmeadow Press, 1989.

Scott, Margaret Kennedy, and Mary Beazley. *Making Pressed Flower Pictures.* New York: Dover Publications, 1982.

FRAGRANT FLOWERS

Coon, Nelson. *Gardening for Fragrance.* New York: Hearthside Press, 1967.

Reddell, Rayford Clayton, and Robert Galyean. *Growing Fragrant Plants.* New York: Harper & Row, 1989.

Taylor, Norman. *Fragrance in the Garden.* New York: D. Van Nostrand Co., 1953.

Verey, Rosemary. *The Scented Garden.* New York: Van Nostrand Reinhold Co., 1981.

Wilder, Louise Beebe. *The Fragrant Garden.* New York: Dover Publications, 1974.

Wilson, Helen Van Pelt, and Leonie Bell. *The Fragrant Year.* New York: Crown, 1967.

Index

NOTE: Page references in *italic* indicate tables.
Boldface references indicate illustrations or photographs.